CLASSICAL SEATTLE

Melinda Bargreen

CLASSICAL SEATTLE

MAESTROS,
IMPRESARIOS,
VIRTUOSI,
and OTHER
MUSIC MAKERS

A McLellan Book

UNIVERSITY OF WASHINGTON PRESS
Seattle and London

This book is published with the assistance of a grant from the McLellan Endowed Series Fund, established through the generosity of Martha McCleary McLellan and Mary McLellan Williams.

4 CULTURE
KING COUNTY LODGING TAX

This publication also was supported by a grant from the 4Culture Heritage Special Projects program.

UNIVERSITY OF WASHINGTON PRESS
www.washington.edu/uwpress

LIBRARY OF CONGRESS CATALOGING-IN-PUBLICATION DATA
Bargreen, Melinda, 1947–
    Classical Seattle : maestros, impresarios, virtuosi, and other music makers / Melinda Bargreen.
        p.   cm.
    Includes bibliographical references and index.
    ISBN 978-0-295-99512-0 (hardcover : alk. paper)
    1. Musicians—Washington (State)—Seattle—Biography.
    2. Composers—Washington (State)—Seattle—Biography.
    3. Conductors (Music)—Washington (State)—Seattle—Biography.
    4. Impresarios—Washington (State)—Seattle—Biography.
    5. Music patrons—Washington (State)—Seattle—Biography.   I. Title.
    ML385.B297   2016
    780.9797'772—dc23   2015016658

CONTENTS

CLASSICAL
SEATTLE

INTRODUCTION

I T was a time that transformed Seattle's arts world. The half century that followed the Seattle World's Fair of 1962 saw a tremendous arts boom that gave the city not only several internationally recognized classical music institutions but also the great halls to showcase their work and that of visiting artists.

The history of this period in Seattle's music history is perhaps best told not as a series of dates or timeline events but as a succession of great people who made the music possible. Brilliant, quirky, inventive, idealistic, and sometimes egomaniacal, these are the people whose artistry, imagination, vision, and hard work made possible Seattle's world of symphonic, operatic, and chamber music. Thanks to them, Seattle has an opera company and a symphony orchestra, both of international prominence; thriving summer and winter music festivals; a richly varied early-music scene; venturesome new-music groups, and—despite some deep budget cuts—several commendable music education programs. The orchestral music is admirably showcased in Benaroya Hall, a palace of a symphony hall that draws envious kudos from visiting orchestras from as far afield as London and Saint Petersburg. In addition, Seattle has McCaw Hall, the innovative and colorful showcase for opera and ballet, and Meany Theater at the University of Washington, which visiting artists have extolled as their "favorite venue for a recital." What has made all this music possible? Or, more precisely, who has?

The answer: six interrelated categories of individuals whose colorful stories combined tell Seattle's classical musical history.

THE MAESTROS: The conductors who have determined the direction and the artistic development of not only the "majors"—the Seattle Symphony and Seattle Opera—but also the University of Washington's music program, the Seattle Youth Symphony, and the many dozens of community orchestras and choruses in the region.

THE IMPRESARIOS: The visionaries who have originated and directed the paths of musical organizations, created festivals, and founded orchestras.

THE VIRTUOSI: The soloists and players, most of them teachers, who have thrilled audiences and developed future generations of talent. Every noteworthy musician can point to a great artist or teacher who was the inspiration and the prod for his or her own attainment of excellence. Some stellar teachers in Seattle's educational institutions, as well as in its performing organizations, have made that kind of a difference in the lives of others.

THE COMPOSERS: The musicians who have written the songs, symphonies, and concertos that have enriched audiences and expanded their musical horizons, and in many cases also guided the younger generations who went on to emulate them.

THE POWER BROKERS AND PATRONS: The executives of the arts world whose nuts-and-bolts savvy made the music possible—arts activists, executive directors, and all the virtuosi of the boardroom. Many of these people have devoted untold hours of volunteer time, and they ensure the organizations' survival by providing the funding that makes up the 50 percent gap between ticket income and the total cost of presenting concerts and operas. Their intelligence and experience have been vital elements in planning new directions for the arts.

I've been writing about Seattle's classical music and opera since 1974, and one of the great advantages of a long life span in journalism is that I have had the chance to interview (sometimes frequently) and become well acquainted with the work of the prime movers in the Seattle music community. My memories and extensive interview notes, as well as my resultant articles in the *Seattle Times* and other publications, have been a great help in formulating the profiles I include in this book.

This book is not a biographical dictionary or a comprehensive who's who, and it's not a footnote-heavy research tome. It is, rather, a personal memoir of Seattle's classical music scene, and in it I present a cross section of people who have proved unforgettable and symbolize something important about their field, or are emblematic in some way. A book listing every remarkable figure in the past half century of Seattle's music history would be a vast, almost unpublishable undertaking, one that I have not even attempted. And yet it hasn't been easy to narrow the focus; I had many sleepless nights considering, "How can I leave out this person, or that one?" No doubt there will be disappointment among some readers who do not find their favorite notables on these pages. For this, I'm unhappy right along with you. But what a privilege it has been to know, and write about, the people you *will* meet here!

It All Started at Century 21

The contributions of the people profiled in this book unfolded against the backdrop of broader late twentieth-century history and Northwest social and economic trends, for which the 1962 World's Fair, known as Century 21, served as a symbolic overture. Century 21 was considerably more than the Space Needle, Belgian waffles, and ten million eager visitors. It was a major landmark in the city's cultural history—and not just because of the long and impressive lineup of musical entertainment, from Elvis (Presley) to Igor (Stravinsky), that dazzled visitors and Seattleites alike over the six-month duration of the exhibition.

Century 21 was the world's fair that transformed a neglected site just north of Seattle's downtown into the handsomely landscaped and much visited seventy-four-acre Seattle Center campus, stuffed with new performance venues that became the homes of the city's resident arts institutions. Most significant of these for the music community, of course, was the new opera house, created from the skeleton of the old, dumpy Seattle Civic Auditorium. (The highly regarded *New York Times* music critic Harold C. Schonberg called it the "flat-floored, unpleasant Civic Auditorium, which held about everything except bullfights.") But there were other facilities: the remodeled Civic Arena (later the Mercer Arena); the rebuilt Washington State Pavilion (which became the Coliseum, and then KeyArena, home to sports events and large-scale concerts); and the Plaza of the States (revamped as the Flag Pavilion and Plaza, and later the Fisher Pavilion and Plaza). The Playhouse hosted not only the nascent Seattle Repertory Theatre but also classical chamber concerts and recitals. The Food Circus became the Center House, which for several years housed the offices of such major nonprofits as the Seattle Symphony and the Seattle Opera, as well as many restaurants and community events.

Century 21 was an enormous boost to Seattle's cultural organizations. Was it perhaps too much of a boost? David Brewster, an arts watcher and pundit who was a founder of the *Seattle Weekly*, the Crosscut.com news site, and Town Hall Seattle, thought so, telling the *Puget Sound Business Journal*, "Seattle got too big too fast. Cultural institutions had to appeal broadly. Over-large audiences can be a problem—finicky, unadventuresome. That produced the kind of safe commercial programming that we have." International fans of Seattle Opera's imaginative *Der Ring des Nibelungen* productions, Seattle Symphony's groundbreaking recordings of previously obscure Americana, and the consistently inventive Seattle theater and ballet presentations might disagree.

When the last notes of Century 21 had died away, what did Seattle's classical music world look like? The big game in town, of course, was the Seattle Symphony Orchestra (SSO), flush with success (though certainly not with cash) from its World's Fair production of *Aida* and concert with Igor Stravinsky, and ensconced now in its newly remodeled home at the Seattle Opera House. (The opera house wasn't all glitz and chandeliers, though. Few Seattleites realized that the thirty-six horses of the Royal Canadian Mounted Police were stabled in the basement during their tenure at Century 21.)

The Seattle Symphony's music director was the very popular Milton Katims; only a few years later, Katims's profile would adorn the cover of the Seattle telephone directory. He increased the size of the orchestra, the length of the season, and the variety of the presentations, fighting budgetary constraints all the way. The rather venturesome menu for the orchestra's 1962–63 season included the premiere of the Seattle composer and University of Washington professor Gerald Kechley's oratorio *Daedalus and the Minotaur*, with the soloists Donald Gramm, Dorothy Cole, and Nancy Cronburg. The orchestra was also kept busy with eleven school concerts under the baton of the concertmaster Henry Siegl, as well as evenings featuring the pianists Van Cliburn and Arthur Rubinstein, and also Lockrem Johnson, the director of the music program at what is now the Cornish College of the Arts. The Seattle Symphony performed with the likes of Henryk Szeryng, Leon Fleisher, Gina Bachauer, Claudio Arrau, and the conductor-composers Leon Kirchner and Carlos Chávez. Among the season's galas were evenings with the Royal Ballet and the prima ballerina Margot Fonteyn. The symphony also presented Verdi's *La Traviata* with the diva Mary Costa (and staging by Glynn Ross, who soon after became the founding general director of Seattle Opera).

Reviewers were enthusiastic about many of the Seattle Symphony programs in that 1962–63 season. The future best-selling novelist Tom Robbins, then a critic for the *Seattle Times*, wrote of one 1963 concert, "It was a night of passion, pleasure and paradox; a stunning kaleidoscopic pattern that, after this evening, may never be duplicated." All symphony events were financed partly by gala parties, such as the long-running Symphoneve fall fund-raising party, and by the new mainstay of Seattle's arts groups, the mighty PONCHO (Patrons of Northwest Civic, Cultural, and Charitable Organizations), which was founded in 1962 by Paul Friedlander, Kayla Skinner, and Ruth Blethen Clayburgh. The 1963 PONCHO auction must have witnessed some frenzied bidding for a framed letter written by President James Madison, a live burro and cart, a hydroplane, a house in Somerset, England, and a trip for two to Samoa. (Both the Symphoneve and PONCHO galas are now defunct: times, tastes, and enthusiasms change over the decades.) By spring 1963, despite the season's many highlights and successes—and initiating a pattern that would unhappily repeat many times to come—the Seattle Symphony management and musicians, who had been negotiating since the previous November, were sufficiently deadlocked over salary issues that only a last-minute accord averted cancellation of the 1963–64 season.

At the conclusion of the 1962 World's Fair, there was as yet no Seattle Opera, nor was there a resident chamber orchestra or chamber music festival. There was, however, the venerable Ladies Musical Club, founded on March 24, 1891, by a group of twenty-two professional musicians. Before 1962, the LMC was responsible for an international concert series that had already brought to Seattle such luminaries as Rachmaninoff, Kreisler, Schnabel, Schumann-Heink, de Larrocha, Paderewski, Casals, and Heifetz, as well as the orchestras of New York and Chicago. (The club is still in existence at this writing, though its focus has changed to a more local one, presenting many concerts by its members and bringing music education to underserved Seattle elementary schools.)

Classical concerts were also in the mix presented by Northwest Releasing, a leading booker of theatrical shows, musical performances, and closed-circuit broadcasts of athletic events. The agency, founded by the entertainment promoter Zollie Volchok (1916–2012), who was later president and general manager of the Seattle Supersonics basketball team, brought to Seattle road productions of *My Fair Lady* and concerts by Harry Belafonte, Lena Horne, Elvis Presley, and the Beatles—but also recitals by such artists as Segovia, Menuhin, and the Vienna Boys' Choir.

One of the major sources of concert activity in those first post-Fair years was the University of Washington School of Music, whose faculty and students produced and performed a vast repertoire. On one end of the repertoire could be found the devotees of historically informed performances of early music (many of them in the Collegium Musicum ensemble), whose efforts spurred a growing movement that had started with the Seattle Recorder Society (still extant, with some one hundred members) and came to fruition with the founding of Seattle's Early Music Guild in 1977. On the other end were the bastions of the avant-garde, chiefly the UW's Contemporary Group and some venturesome faculty composers at UW and Cornish College of the Arts, who were certainly "avant" of anything Seattle had heard or seen. Positioned in the middle was a coterie of devoted and experienced professors, who worked to prepare their students for a mainstream musical life in symphony orchestras, opera companies, concert halls, churches, and schools as the performers and teachers of the next generations.

Socioeconomic Changes in the Region

At the culmination of the World's Fair, Seattle's population hovered around the half million mark, a figure that has held fairly stable at this writing, though the suburban communities have experienced explosive growth. Despite the optimism engendered by Century 21, the city soon after struggled during the global energy crisis and the Boeing Company slump of the 1970s. In 1971, two real-estate agents put up a famous billboard notice near Sea-Tac International Airport, "Will the last person leaving SEATTLE—Turn out the lights."

Even during the recession, though, the city undertook such projects as the renewal of the historic Pioneer Square district and gave new life to the iconic Pike Place Market. Thanks to the political clout of longtime Senators Henry M. Jackson and Warren G. Magnuson, the University of Washington experienced great growth as a research institution, and along with that the campus became a center for social change: the rise not only of new and ethnic musics but also of the counterculture of the 1960s, the nascent environmentalist movement, and growing demand for equal rights for women and ethnic minorities.

By the late 1970s, when Microsoft arrived in the suburb of Redmond, a new technology culture was under way, ushered in by an influx of millionaires—early Microsoft employees and backers—

and an atmosphere conducive to the founding of other startups. Seattle changed as these new companies took hold, and some tech leaders, including the Microsoft cofounder Paul Allen, took the lead in promoting civic projects such as a new football stadium and the venturesome Experience Music Project, which was originally conceived as a Jimi Hendrix museum. The 1970s also saw the rise of Seattle-based Starbucks, Tully's, and a constellation of smaller coffee companies that made the rainy city the caffeine capital of the country.

Commercial growth also changed Seattle's arts climate, though tech companies and their leaders have tended to favor social and sports causes above symphonies and opera houses for their philanthropy. A notable exception is the McCaw family, four cellular-phone pioneers who in 2003 honored their opera-loving mother, Marion Oliver McCaw, with a naming gift of Seattle's rebuilt opera house, now McCaw Hall.

Changing Roles for Women

All it took was a screen—and some chutzpah. By the 1970s, the Seattle Symphony had adopted a new nationwide policy of "blind" orchestra auditions, in which players auditioned behind a screen that allowed the evaluators to hear, but not see, the applicant. (In Seattle, even the flooring was changed so that the telltale tapping of women's high-heeled shoes could not be heard.) Nationwide, including in Seattle, the proportion of women hired in orchestras increased between 30 and 55 percent. In 2014, the percentage of women players in major US orchestras hovered around 44 percent. At this writing, the Seattle Symphony players' membership is approximately 40 percent female. When the Seattle Symphony went on tour of three European countries in 1980, almost every concert review commented wonderingly on the number of women in the orchestra; one critic wrote that "even the double bass is bowed by the tender hand."

"Tender hands" had also gripped a Seattle baton or two by then. Already in April 1921, the conductor Mary Davenport-Engberg had founded the Seattle Civic Symphony, at a time when the Seattle Symphony was flagging; its 1921–22 season was cancelled in October 1921. Davenport-Engberg's concerts received enthusiastic notices, lauded for demonstrating "a surprisingly high level of excellence," and she remained on the podium through 1924, when the orchestra folded. Davenport-Engberg is sometimes listed in the chronology of Seattle Symphony conductors, but this is inaccurate, though her sixty-two-member players' roster for 1924 did include twenty-one ex-SSO players. The Seattle Symphony was not revived until 1926.

Over time, many other women have conducted in Seattle, as elsewhere, but commentators continue to be mystified about the small number of "chicks with sticks." Change will probably remain slow in coming as long as opinion is determined by such commentators as the venerable Russian maestro Yuri Temirkanov, who declared as recently as 2013, "The essence of the conductor's profession is strength. The essence of a woman is weakness." In Seattle, women instrumentalists weren't allowed to audition for the University of Washington marching band until 1974.

But women were making a mark in other areas of Seattle's cultural scene. One of the most powerful of Seattle's philanthropists was Dorothy Priscilla Bullitt ("Patsy") Collins, a lover of the arts and a strong advocate of conservation and arts education. Collins had experienced tragedy when her young fiancé, Larry Norman, died in World War II; in his memory—though she did not publicize the reason—she funded Benaroya Hall's Garden of Remembrance in 1998 to honor Washington State's war dead. Collins was not only the granddaughter of the timber baron and Klondike Gold Rush millionaire Charles D. Stimson but also the daughter of the formidable Seattle legend Dorothy Bullitt, the founder of KING Broadcasting, which sold in 1991 for about three hundred million dollars. Classical KING FM is among the longest-running classical radio stations in the United States, and it is consistently ranked as one of the top five American classical radio stations. Patsy Collins and her sister, Harriet, took an active interest in Seattle's arts and music organizations, particularly the Seattle Symphony, Seattle Opera, and the Corporate Council for the Arts (later called Arts-Fund), and Patsy contributed largely to Seattle Symphony's education programs and the city's libraries to ensure classical music opportunities for the region's youth. Collins preferred to stay out of the spotlight while using her inheritance for often unheralded philanthropy, but during her last decade she gave away about one hundred million dollars to a wide variety of arts, environmental, and educational causes.

When Patsy Collins died in 2003, Seattle Opera's general director, Speight Jenkins, said, "She did more good in her life to more people than anyone I have ever known." Among the many posthumous tributes this farsighted and generous activist received was Seattle Opera's dedication of its inaugural season (2003–4) in the new Marion Oliver McCaw Hall to her memory.

Women composers gained increasing recognition during the period following the World's Fair. The New York composer Joan Franks Williams arrived in Seattle in 1962, after the Boeing Company hired her husband, and she decided to see if her idea for a contemporary music group might fly in this new environment. Starting in 1963, her New Dimensions in Music concerts, which mixed electronic and recorded sounds with live instruments, did indeed draw curious and enthusiastic crowds. The 1974 opening night of the Northwest Chamber Orchestra concert premiered Williams's *Frogs*, an atonal work that included croaking frogs, sung haikus, and traditional instruments.

Another prominent woman composer, Janice Giteck, who was born in New York and studied with Darius Milhaud and Olivier Messiaen, began teaching at Cornish College of the Arts in 1979. Since then she has produced a substantial body of inventive work, variously influenced by the music and culture of Native Americans and her studies of world music, including the Indonesian gamelan. Among Giteck's works are scores for several films and the award-winning compositions "Breathing Songs from a Turning Sky" and "Thunder, Like a White Bear Dancing." In 2004, a particularly successful collaboration with the Seattle Chamber Players resulted in the evocative multimedia work *Ishi*, based on the life of the last Yahi Indian.

Other Seattle-based composers—among them Diane Thome and Giselle Wyers, both at the University of Washington; Karen P.

Thomas, also director of Seattle Pro Musica; and Carol Sams, a Darius Milhaud protégée whose opera *The Pied Piper of Hamelin* was premiered at Tacoma Opera—have also made substantial contributions to Northwest music in nearly all genres, including chamber, orchestral, choral, and solo. Keeping a weather eye on all this activity for several decades was another remarkable woman, the critic and editor Maxine Cushing Gray (1909–1987), whose fortnightly journal *Northwest Arts* skewered the humdrum and applauded the revolutionary on the dance and music scene. Popularly known as the "Tweed Hornet," Maxine was famous for her pointed observations and watchdog attention to arts grants and expenditures. Fans of the avant-garde could count on seeing her in the audience at every premiere.

Transformation at the University of Washington

It would be hard to overstate the University of Washington's importance in Seattle's classical milieu. Its artist faculty members enrich the region's concert activity, enticing students (many of them from Asia) to the campus, where the 1,200-seat Meany Theater shines as one of the region's finest music venues. UW provides training for the musicians who go on to play (and sing) in orchestras, choruses, churches, schools, and chamber ensembles and in their turn become teachers.

In the months after the World's Fair, the University of Washington stirred to new artistic life, in large part because of the UW School of Music's ambitious new director, the composer and innovator William Bergsma (1921–1994). Bergsma was determined to make the school the vanguard of new music in the region, and if his oft-quoted aim to turn the UW School of Music into "the Juilliard of the West" was not fully realized, that certainly was no fault of his. He arrived in Seattle in 1963 and secured a Rockefeller grant that allowed him to add to the faculty the Soni Ventorum Wind Quintet, the composer-clarinetist William O. Smith, the trombonist Stuart Dempster, and the composer Robert Suderburg. These new hires joined the composers George Frederick McKay (who taught John Cage and was soon to retire), John Verrall, Gerald Kechley, James Beale, and Paul Tufts. For one year, 1965–66, William Bolcom, a future Pulitzer Prize–winning student of both McKay and Verrall, briefly joined the UW faculty to teach composition, before heading off first to New York and then to the University of Michigan.

A particularly prominent faculty member was Bergsma's immediate predecessor as director, Dr. Stanley Chapple, an enthusiastic and messianic conductor who espoused new music but particularly loved opera. Some admirers thought Chapple's highly entertaining UW lectures, long on anecdotes and personal musical memories and delivered in a posh British accent, outpaced his conducting abilities. He was a regular figure on the Seattle Symphony podium, too, during an interregnum period in the early 1950s, but as Hans Lehmann recounts in his memoir, *Out of the Cultural Dustbin*, Chapple didn't get the nod as symphony music director because of his UW responsibilities—and because the musicians didn't like the "distracting grimaces of his face" during concerts. Later, when age forced his retirement from the UW, the indefatigable Chapple founded an orchestra, Musicians Emeritus, for senior players.

On the piano faculty when Bergsma arrived in Seattle were the distinguished Hungarian-born concert artist Béla Siki, John T. (Terry) Moore, Else Geissmar, Berthe Poncy Jacobson, and Randolph Hokanson (who in 2011, at the age of ninety-seven, wrote a highly readable memoir, *With Head to the Music Bent*). Walter Welke, who taught many of the region's leading young brass players, conducted the marching band and the concert band. A respected pedagogue in the voice department was the venerable August Werner, a Norwegian-born singer and choral director who also appeared in UW opera productions. In 1964, the eminent basso Leon Lishner, who portrayed deities and devils on major opera stages for more than sixty years, came to the faculty; in 1969, he was joined by the former Metropolitan Opera regular Mary Curtis Verna. Still later, the department was augmented by such stars as the baritone Frank Guarrera, the tenor Augusto Paglialunga, and the great Julian Patrick, who could apparently do everything from Broadway shows, new operas, period operas, and the pivotal Wagnerian *Ring* role of

Alberich to groundbreaking music theater pieces such as Jake Heggie's *For a Look or a Touch.*

Three string players of international eminence—Eva Heinitz (cello and viola da gamba), Vilem Sokol (viola and conducting), and Emanuel Zetlin (violin)—predated Bergsma's arrival and presided over the string program in the 1960s and beyond. Then, in 1987, Steven Staryk came to Seattle to head UW's string division. Dubbed the "King of Concertmasters," Staryk had been concertmaster of four of the world's major orchestras—the Royal Philharmonic of London, the Amsterdam Concertgebouw, the Chicago Symphony, and the Toronto Symphony. Staryk eventually won UW's 1995 Distinguished Teaching Award. One doctoral student said of Staryk: "I have not come across a more competent, challenging and thought-provoking mentor in all my years of study, neither in any other subject nor at any other institution."

A tireless innovator, Bergsma lured the Philadelphia String Quartet (PSQ)—initially composed of the four Philadelphia Orchestra members Veda Reynolds, Irwin Eisenberg, Alan Iglitzin, and Charles Brennand—to Seattle in 1966. Starved for first-rate chamber music, Seattle music lovers and students queued for tickets, which were invariably difficult to obtain. The PSQ launched more than two decades of glory years of sold-out Seattle concerts, Beethoven quartet cycles, tours, recordings, and other adornments to the region's music scene, before the budgetary axe fell and their UW residency ended. There was a happy coda, however, because the Olympic Music Festival, which the PSQ's violist Alan Iglitzin founded in 1984 as a summer home for the quartet, became a highly successful new chamber music venue for Northwest audiences.

In the mid- and late 1960s, and with the help of a few key grants (primarily from the Rockefeller Foundation, but also from state and federal funding sources), Bergsma put his new faculty hires—dubbed the Contemporary Group—to work in concerts that made the campus a beehive of creativity. The visionary trombonist-composer Dempster expanded the universe of recorded sound with groundbreaking recordings in the Cistern Chapel (an echo chamber in an underground cistern at Fort Casey, Washington) and the abbey of Pope Clement VI in France (where Dempster performed in the sonorous acoustics with trombone, didgeridoo, and plastic sewer pipes). Joining Dempster was the highly inventive clarinetist-composer William O. Smith, whose stylistic range extended from improvisational jazz to composed works whose scores scrolled by the players on computer screens; Smith's system for his *Illuminated Manuscripts* worked in much the way that twenty-first-century musicians, more than twenty-five years later, now use iPads in concerts.

Bergsma was also responsible for the move to the UW of the woodwind quintet Soni Ventorum. This group, which had earlier antecedents as a student quintet at the Curtis Institute of Music, the American Wind Ensemble of Vienna, and the US Seventh Army Symphony Woodwind Quintet, officially formed in 1962 in Puerto Rico, where the success of the Casals Festival had led to the formation of a conservatory. The clarinetist William McColl, who had come to teach and perform in Puerto Rico, persuaded friends who had taken up teaching positions at the conservatory to join him in what they called the Soni Ventorum Wind Quintet. Initially, the group consisted of Robert Bonnevie (French horn player, and later the longtime principal horn of the Seattle Symphony), Arthur Grossman (bassoon), Felix Skowronek (flute), and James Caldwell (oboe). In the summer of 1965, Laila Storch—the first woman oboist to graduate from the Curtis Institute and later the biographer of the oboe legend Marcel Tabuteau—became the quintet's oboist.

In 1968, hearing that the UW was looking for a faculty woodwind quintet, Skowronek, a Seattle native who had been principal flute in the Seattle Symphony for two seasons, approached Bergsma about considering the Soni Ventorum. By this time, the quintet had replaced Robert Bonnevie with Christopher Leuba, the distinguished principal horn of the Chicago Symphony under Fritz Reiner, 1960–62. Skowronek's suggestion came with a letter of recommendation from the flutist Samuel Baron, whose quintet had premiered a Bergsma work, which may have paved the way for Bergsma's approval. Soni Ventorum became not only a noted Seattle performance group but also the core of UW's woodwind faculty. The group's thirty-three-year Seattle residency of teaching, performances, touring, and recording lasted until 2001.

The composition of Soni Ventorum changed a few more times, most famously in 1979, when Leuba left the UW, to be replaced by David Kappy. In what became an immortal parting shot, Leuba said, "I gave my resignation. I got a 45-rpm of the song, 'Take This Job and Shove it,' recorded by Johnny Paycheck. It's a famous country-and-western standard. Except Johnny doesn't quit the job. I did. I've never heard the end of it. . . . The word got around about how I did it. There is no such thing as humor in academia."

Once Bergsma had succeeded in luring the Philadelphia String Quartet, Soni Ventorum, and the Contemporary Group into the School of Music lineup, he turned to a further goal: a first-rate concert hall. His vision became Meany Hall. In this new building, built in 1974, the acoustically excellent 1,200-seat Meany Theater has pride of place, but there is also the 238-seat "black box" Studio Theater for smaller and experimental productions, as well as an array of classrooms. The hall has also been the university's gift to the region, for it hosts not only faculty and student events but also an acclaimed President's Piano Series, visiting chamber music ensembles, and a series with world music, dance, and theater presentations.

Bergsma stepped down as director of the School of Music in 1971 but remained on the faculty until 1986. In 1994, at his memorial concert in the hall he had worked so hard for, Soni Ventorum performed Bergsma's Concerto for Wind Quintet as an expression of their respect and gratitude.

Global Voices

The past half century has enriched Seattle's cultural scene with waves of immigration, particularly from Asia and Russia, bringing new musical traditions and cross-fertilization of musical ideas. Asian influences have permeated the work of many composers, from John Cage to Alan Hovhaness (who loved the sound of the Korean *ah-ak* instruments and incorporated it into his music). Over the years, Seattle's position as a West Coast port city has given the city an intriguing cultural mix. The proximity to Asia has brought an influx of East–West collaborations, particularly from Japanese and Chinese teachers, composers, and performers. Nowhere is this clearer than at the Seattle Symphony, where nearly every section of the orchestra includes Asian players. Many gifted young Chinese music students, including a high percentage of pianists, have come to the University of Washington to study. Especially when we consider that Western music was suppressed during China's Cultural Revolution (approximately 1966–76), the country's more recent outpouring of spectacular musical talent is nothing less than astonishing.

A strong contingent of Asian American music lovers, often led by Yoshi and Naomi Minegishi, who are affiliated with the Japan-America Society of the State of Washington, has helped to organize annual Celebrate Asia concerts at the Seattle Symphony. These concerts sponsor a composition competition and usually feature the orchestra with Asian soloists such as the Van Cliburn International Competition winner Nobuyuki Tsujii. Another rich source of musical cross-fertilization comes from the region's growing South Asian community (a major force in the tech industry), which has added the rich traditions of Indian classical music to the multicultural mix available to Seattleites. Much of this music has been presented under the auspices of the performance organization Ragamala, which hosted some of the world's great sitar and tabla virtuosi from 1981 to 2015.

Seattle's music scene has also been powerfully influenced by the wave of musical immigration from the former Soviet Union, following the sweeping political changes of the late twentieth century. By the 1990s, the influx of gifted Russian musicians that had begun in the late 1970s turned into a crescendo, with Seattle's orchestras and ensembles the beneficiary of loosening emigration laws in the former USSR. Newly arrived Russians have found important places in all the major musical organizations, including the Seattle Symphony, Pacific Northwest Ballet, Northwest Sinfonietta, and Music of Remembrance. They have conducted local community symphonies and become sought-after teachers, and they have cofounded new chamber groups such as the Seattle Chamber Players, the Odeonquartet, the Bridge Ensemble, and the Seattle Violin Virtuosi.

It is their training that sets many of the Russian musicians—especially the string players—apart. Instruction in the best conservatories and music schools of the former USSR was uniformly rigorous and instilled a tremendous work ethic. Second, Russian string players produce what is sometimes called a "typical Russian" sound, with a lot of passion and vibrato; the sound can tend to be so soloistic that incoming players sometimes have a steep learning curve to adjust to playing in an orchestra.

"I think that we [Russians] are very passionate about what we do, and feel we can always do more," the violinist Gennady Filimonov said in 2002. "The public is always enriched with the experiences of a truly cosmopolitan environment." Filimonov, who arrived in the United States in the 1970s and became a Fulbright Scholar before joining the Seattle Symphony, is also, together with his symphony colleague, the Latvian-born violinist Artur Girsky, a member of the internationally touring Odeonquartet.

Other Russian-born musicians in Seattle include the cellist David Tonkonogui, who joined the Seattle Symphony in 1990 and became one of the region's most celebrated players and teachers before his untimely death at the age of forty-five. (His widow, Mara Finkelstein, also a cellist, plays in the Northwest Sinfonietta and is an active teacher.) Mikhail Shmidt, Tonkonogui's close friend and a member of the Seattle Symphony's first violin section, is among the region's most active chamber musicians, performing in the Music of Remembrance series, often alongside his symphony colleague Leonid Keylin. Shmidt is also a key figure in the venturesome Seattle Chamber Players. Victoria Bogdashevskaya, now retired from her position as Seattle Symphony pianist, continues to be active as a teacher in a studio that has produced several young prizewinners. In 1991, the conductor-composer Alexei Girsh came to the Northwest from Russia, where he had been principal conductor of the Radio-Television Symphony of Vladivostok, music director of the Saint Petersburg Youth Symphony, and a professor at the Institute of the Arts in Saint Petersburg. Girsh's Seattle-area credits extend from youth ensembles to ballet orchestra, wind ensembles, and concert opera. Upon his arrival in Seattle, the violinist Yuriy Mikhlin, who had served for nearly two decades as associate concertmaster of the Kiev State Opera and Ballet, joined the now defunct Northwest Chamber Orchestra and also became concertmaster of the Federal Way Symphony Orchestra.

The Saint Petersburg–born violinist Alexander Velinzon, who immigrated to the United States in 1990 and later became the assistant concertmaster of the Boston Symphony Orchestra, was one of the more recent and stellar of the Russian arrivals in Seattle. Velinzon, who studied with the eminent Dorothy DeLay at the Juilliard School, joined the Seattle Symphony as concertmaster in 2012 (through 2015).

Two Russian-born pianists of particular note are Oksana Ezhokina, the pianist of both the Icicle Creek Trio and the Volta Trio, as well as the artistic director of the Icicle Creek Chamber Players; and Natalya Ageyeva, who heads the Russian Chamber Music Foundation. Ezhokina, who came to the United States in 1993, chairs the piano department at Pacific Lutheran University and holds a doctorate from the State University of New York at Stony Brook. In 2012, Ezhokina visited her homeland to play in the Beethoven Triple Concerto with the Saint Petersburg Philharmonic. Ageyeva, who began piano studies in Moscow at the age of thirteen, completed her doctoral degree at the University of Washington with the pianists Béla Siki and Robin McCabe. She went on to found the Russian Chamber Music Foundation of Seattle, which hosts a wide spectrum of performances, as well as an annual festival and competition for pianists and chamber musicians of all ages.

The Russian transplant Olga Sukhover is helping to keep Russian folk traditions alive. Trained in Moscow's highly regarded Gnessin Musical College as a pianist and choral conductor in folk music, she came to Seattle in the early 1990s. Now she leads the Russian folk group and choir Khorovod, which has performed several times at the Northwest Folklife Festival and at schools, fairs, churches, and the Russian consulate. The group takes all aspects of Russian culture seriously; you'll even find a recipe for blinis on their website.

Not all the incoming Russians have been performers or conductors. Elena Dubinets, who earned a doctorate from the Moscow State Tchaikovsky Conservatory and came to the United States in 1996, has published books and articles on music and presented music festivals in several countries. She is vice president of artistic planning for the Seattle Symphony and has chaired the City of Seattle Music Commission, as well as serving on the advisory board of the University of Washington's School of Music.

Few of the Russian-born musicians wear as many hats as Michael Miropolsky does. He is the assistant principal second violinist of the Seattle Symphony as well as the music director of several community orchestras, including the Cascade Symphony, the Thalia Symphony, and the Lake Washington Symphony Orchestra (the former Bellevue Philharmonic). Miropolsky attributes the successful influx of Russian musicians in Seattle primarily to Gerard Schwarz, who was music director of the Seattle Symphony 1985–2011 and respected Russian string players for the quality of their sound. Nineteen ninety-one was the "lucky year" for Miropolsky and his late wife, Larisa (also a violinist and teacher), who were "refuseniks" in their homeland and for twelve years denied permission to leave. When the doors to the West finally began to edge open, the Miropolskys were allowed to take only one violin between them. They had to leave behind in Kyrgyzstan all their family, friends, instruments, books, and personal possessions. Once they arrived in San Francisco, they had to share that one violin to practice.

Friends in San Francisco told Miropolsky about a vacancy in the Seattle Symphony assistant principal second violin chair, and he won the audition. Because Seattle Symphony musicians also play for Seattle Opera's productions, Miropolsky's first job with the symphony was in Seattle Opera's production of Wagner's *Ring*, which he describes as "millions of notes, terribly taxing, but so thrilling!" But he soon found the energy not only for playing in the symphony and opera but also for founding two new groups he modeled on ensemble forms that are popular in his homeland: the Seattle Violin Virtuosi and the Violin Virtuosi Chamber Orchestra. He also took on the Jewish Community Center Chamber Orchestra and educational groups such as the Northwest School Orchestra and the Seattle Conservatory of Music Chamber Orchestra.

Miropolsky had always wanted to conduct, and one of his most important music directorships is the Edmonds-based Cascade

Symphony Orchestra, one of the region's longest-running and most successful community symphonies. The Cascade was founded in 1962 by the conductor-violinist Robert Anderson, who spent thirty years patiently building the orchestra. Miropolsky took on the Cascade in 2002, after a rocky interim period following Anderson's retirement. Amity and enthusiasm have returned to the Cascade since Miropolsky's arrival.

In 2009, Miropolsky also became the music director of the Bellevue Philharmonic (founded in 1967 by R. Joseph Scott), whose long history had almost ended after a period of dissent and financial disarray; the orchestra has since been reorganized as the Lake Washington Symphony Orchestra. Four years later, Miropolsky took on the Thalia Symphony, another community orchestra with a lengthy history; it was founded in 1949 by Mikael Scheremetiew.

In 2013, Miropolsky and the Edmonds-based travel guru Rick Steves, a major donor to the orchestra, created the innovative program *Europe: A Symphonic Journey*, which was seen and heard in an hour-long presentation on PBS and released on both CD and DVD. In the soundtrack, the Cascade Symphony plays symphonic works that relate to the European sites that Steves explores.

Miropolsky likens concerts to cookbooks: what you get depends on the quality of the ingredients you use. He lives for the energy of live performance, where the audience and the musicians become part of that mysterious and invisible force field that extends from the conductor through the musicians to the listeners.

The Early-Music Scene

The decades after the World's Fair saw not only the burgeoning new-music scene but also an important development in the opposite chronological direction. For years, the Northwest had been losing artists who were drawn to authentic period performances of works of the baroque and pre-classical era but unable to find an outlet in Seattle. They were part of an international groundswell of fascination for music played the way it had been performed in earlier centuries, before the push for bigger and more vibrato-laden sounds familiar to nineteenth- and twentieth-century ears. Historically minded keyboardists were attracted by the subtler harpsichord and the fortepiano, string players and winds by the baroque-era versions of their instruments, played in a more intimate style.

There weren't enough performance opportunities to keep talented practitioners of early music in Seattle. Musicians such as the innovative baroque violinist Stanley Ritchie and his harpsichordist wife, Elisabeth Wright (who performed together as Duo Geminiani) and the lutenist Stephen Stubbs moved away to develop their careers elsewhere. Only with the gradual arrival in Seattle of such significant figures as the late Margriet Tindemans (formerly of the internationally renowned medieval ensemble Sequentia, and founder of the Medieval Women's Choir), the keyboardist Byron Schenkman and violinist Ingrid Matthews (cofounders of Seattle Baroque Orchestra), the lutenist August Denhard, the harpsichordist Jillon Stoppels Dupree, and the early-harp specialist Maxine Eilander, that the early-music scene in Seattle, already inhabited by such artists as the singer Nancy Zylstra, the flutist Jeff Cohan, and the harpsichordist Randall Jay McCarty, began to blossom.

A key figure in the development of early-music practices was the late composer-director Peter Hallock, longtime canon precentor at Saint Mark's Cathedral, who revolutionized the musical presentations there; the leadership of Peter Seibert (also a composer) at the long-running Seattle Recorder Society was also a boon to this development.

The significance of Seattle's Early Music Guild, founded in 1977, was profound. The group not only presents concerts by the finest international practitioners of historically informed music but also has served as the "mother ship" nurturing a wide span of groups such as the Seattle Baroque Orchestra and the Gallery Concerts. The arrival of Stephen Stubbs's Pacific MusicWorks confirmed Seattle as home to an array of ensembles, organizations, and venues specializing in early music.

Concert Halls and Arts Activists

Concert halls were an important part of the "great leap forward" for music in Seattle. Bergsma's Meany Hall proved to be only the first of the new and remodeled venues that arose in the years following the 1962 Seattle World's Fair. Even the most optimistic Seattleites couldn't have guessed the scope and magnitude of the "arts boom" that was to follow in Seattle as well as throughout the Pacific Northwest. New performance facilities and museums infused life and breathing space to the performers and supporters of ballet, theater, and the visual arts in Seattle and the outlying communities. Several of these new facilities were remodels of buildings created for Century 21. One could consider the Seattle World's Fair "the gift that keeps on giving" for Seattle's thriving arts community.

A key element in the changes to Seattle's art scene was the emergence of facilities that were built for specific art forms: Benaroya Hall, not an all-purpose opera house but a symphonic hall designed to showcase a particular orchestra; a specially adapted Marion Oliver McCaw Hall to serve the backstage and orchestra-pit requirements of opera and ballet, and provide the excellent acoustics needed for those genres; a greatly expanded Seattle Art Museum; a new repertory theater and four additional theaters; and the remarkable Rem Koolhaas Public Library. Even the most optimistic arts fan couldn't have predicted such a wealth of new facilities back in 1962.

Of course the road was not easy, and there were major snags along the way. A financial chill set in following the attacks of September 11, 2001, after which project funding for arts facilities from public and private sources was slower to materialize. At every step, however, there was the backing of the Kreielsheimer Foundation, whose two cotrustees made important grants to nearly every capital project in the arts. And along with all the new facilities came an essential administrative and networking entity in the Corporate Council for the Arts (CCA), revitalized and restructured as ArtsFund by its president, Peter Donnelly. The CCA had begun its life as an unexciting united fund for corporate support of the arts, but under the visionary Donnelly the new ArtsFund assumed additional roles: as a workplace giving program (similar to the United Way) and, perhaps more crucially, as a clearinghouse and vital network of communications throughout the entire arts community. The significance of Donnelly's smart, charismatic, and even messianic presence on Seattle's arts scene cannot be overstated.

When I asked Donnelly in 2004 whether it was "something in the water" that led to Seattle's remarkable post-Fair arts renaissance, he laughed and pointed upward at the drizzling rain: "No, it was something in the sky!" Maybe Seattle's celebrated wet climate did indeed help to drive residents indoors in search of culture.

◆ ◆ ◆

In 1962, the Seattle World's Fair set the stage for a remarkable five-decade-long transformation of the city's classical music world. What now follows is a panorama of some of the people who created that transformed world: the virtuosi and composers who made the music and trained the talent, the impresarios and administrators who founded and ran the organizations, and the patrons whose vision and generosity made both the performances and the venues possible.

THE MAESTROS

IN most cities that boast a major symphony orchestra, the music director usually is not only the figurehead of the organization but also the most influential musician in town. That is certainly true of Seattle, where the arrivals, achievements, and departures of its maestros have had a substantial influence on the arts community. It is the Seattle Symphony music director—a term that goes beyond the activities of a "conductor" to include the artistic oversight of all that the orchestra does—to whom the community looks when there is a musical component to an important civic event, whether it is the opening of a new sports arena, a visit of the Dalai Lama, or a somber commemoration of the 9/11 terrorist attacks. Usually the Seattle Symphony's music director also has a hand in educational issues, filling posts (often largely honorary) at the University of Washington and regularly encouraging rising young soloists and composers by providing performance opportunities. The maestros commission new works, decide on touring opportunities for the orchestra, and hire composers in residence to teach local youngsters, create youth-oriented and educational concerts, and make crucial and often controversial decisions about the orchestra's artistic programming and personnel. Music directors are loved by the musicians they favor and loathed by those who have been fired or overlooked, but they are far from omnipotent: they serve at the pleasure of the board of directors, who can extend or end a maestro's contract. Yet the influence of a music director on the city's musical scene is enormous.

That is why the greater share of attention in this chapter is devoted to the four music directors who have shaped the Seattle Symphony Orchestra (SSO) since the 1962 World's Fair: Milton Katims, Rainer Miedel, Gerard Schwarz, and Ludovic Morlot. The Seattle Symphony music directors, however, are far from the only important maestros in Seattle. A constellation of professional, semiprofessional, collegiate, and youth conductors of orchestras, choruses, and other ensembles contributes immeasurably to the region's musical scene. They, too, will come in for their share of attention.

Milton Katims

THE TOSCANINI PROTÉGÉ

Musicians are notorious perfectionists, and few of them recall their performances with completely unalloyed pleasure. But for Milton Katims, the evening of April 21, 1962, was one of those rare nights bathed in a golden glow of achievement and success. Katims, using a baton given to him by his legendary conducting mentor, Arturo Toscanini, stood on the brand-new podium of the brand-new Seattle Opera House and conducted the much-improved Seattle Symphony Orchestra in a concert that heralded the grand opening of Century 21, Seattle International World's Fair. Joining him on the program were two twentieth-century legends: the pianist Van Cliburn, at the height of his fame, and the composer Igor Stravinsky. Cliburn, the first gold-medal winner of the prestigious first Tchaikovsky International Competition in 1958, played one of the great warhorses of the Russian repertoire, Rachmaninoff's Piano Concerto No. 3. The eighty-year-old Stravinsky led the orchestra in one of his most famous works, the *Firebird Suite*, and Stravinsky's artistic collaborator, Robert Craft, conducted Stravinsky's Symphony in Three Movements.

The ecstatic audience was standing and shouting before Katims even ascended the podium with his customary little hop. The standing ovation was inspired not just by anticipation of the World's Fair. Many in the audience knew how hard Katims had personally lobbied for a new opera house, which had now arisen miraculously inside the exoskeleton of that acoustical barn, the old Civic Auditorium. (More than four decades later, the Seattle Opera House would be rebuilt again, with considerably greater acoustical success than this first renovation, as Marion Oliver McCaw Hall.)

That glittering opening night was the first in an impressive series of artistic World's Fair highlights, which were capped by a gala production in June of Verdi's grandest opera, *Aida*. The opera production was an expensive and risky venture, presented by the Seattle Symphony and involving everyone in the organization down to the volunteers who made the costumes, jewelry, and wigs. A *Los Angeles Times* reviewer called the production "an Oriental fantasy out of the Arabian Nights," and Katims won widespread praise for his artistic vision.

What a triumph! Katims, who had arrived in Seattle with his wife and two children eight years earlier to take the job as music director, must have felt on top of the world as he basked in the adulation of the exhibition crowds and his Seattle audiences. He could not have imagined that less than a decade later, while he was still in his sixties—in a profession in which conductors are often active well into their seventies and beyond—and even as *Musical America* magazine called him Seattle's "Culture Hero No. 1," a bitter struggle began to oust him from his directorship.

But so it goes, in Seattle as elsewhere. The changeover from one symphony orchestra music director to the next is often a process that more closely resembles a coup d'état than a succession. Rare indeed is the example of the Los Angeles Philharmonic's 2009 transition from Esa-Pekka Salonen's music directorship to that of Gustavo Dudamel, which began to be engineered behind the scenes two years earlier after Salonen quietly expressed his desire to leave the directorship and Dudamel had already proved to be a popular guest conductor. No public acrimony; no lengthy search for a successor; just a passing of the baton in a manner that apparently pleased just about everybody.

That doesn't often happen. The Seattle Symphony has seen a long succession of music directors over the more than one hundred years since its formation in 1903, with some of the conductors well liked and artistically successful, some of them unpopular, and some of them operating in the uneasy periods of hiatus between staff music directors. Among the Seattle Symphony's many transitions from one music director to the next, only a few have been peaceful and orderly.

Katims was chosen as Seattle's new music director following the abrupt exit of his predecessor, the distinguished French conductor Manuel Rosenthal, in 1951. Rosenthal had been deported from Ellis Island upon his return to the United States from France with Claudine Verneuil, whom he had earlier introduced to Seattle as his wife. Someone had tipped off the State Department that there was a legitimate Mrs. Rosenthal (Lucie Traoussier) back in France. "Rosenthal's Wife in Paris Claims Never Divorced from Conductor," trumpeted the *Seattle Post-Intelligencer*. Today, it's hard to imagine the deportation of an internationally known conductor from Ellis Island on the grounds of "moral turpitude," but Rosenthal was barred from returning to the United States, and his Seattle Symphony contract was cancelled. (Years later, in 1986, when he was in his eighties, Rosenthal made an astonishing return to Seattle to conduct Seattle Opera's marathon production of Wagner's *Der Ring des Nibelungen*. The production was a great success. Most impressive of all: it was Rosenthal's first *Ring*.)

After Rosenthal's 1951 departure, the English-born Dr. Stanley Chapple, who led the orchestra and opera at the University of Washington, filled the void, along with a number of other distinguished guest conductors, including Leopold Stokowski and Arthur Fiedler, who stood in while the orchestra conducted its search for a new permanent director. But the Seattle Symphony had no ongoing artistic leadership from the fall of 1951 until 1954. In fact, the players had seceded from the administrative Symphony Society and were running their own orchestra as a cooperative with a succession of guest conductors but no single artistic leader.

Into this vacancy stepped Milton Katims—first, in 1953, as a guest conductor, and then under contract for the entire 1954–55 season, with an option for the two seasons beyond that. The late Dr. J. Hans Lehmann of Seattle was responsible for luring Katims from New York and bringing him to the Left Coast, but that is a subject for a later chapter.

Katims had long been famous in musical circles. He was born in Brooklyn in 1909, into a music-loving Jewish immigrant family of Austro-Hungarian and Russian extraction. His father, Harry Katims, had come to America with his family as a six-year-old from Russia (the surname, originally Katimsky, had been shortened by a helpful Ellis Island official). Milton Katims's mother, Caroline Spiegel, had immigrated to America as a six-month-old with her family from what was then Austria-Hungary. Caroline, a lyric soprano and a great music lover, sang with the Schola Cantorum and performed often under the baton of Arturo Toscanini, who later became her son's mentor. She took her youngsters to hear the great cellist Pablo Casals perform the Bach Cello Suites. Little did anyone imagine then that one day her son Milton would perform with Casals and edit the Bach Suites for the viola.

As he wrote in a memoir authored jointly with his wife, Virginia, *The Pleasure Was Ours*, Katims formulated his belief system early, soon after completing the milestone of his bar mitzvah: "I decided that the Golden Rule, the foundation of all religions, was to be the guiding beacon in my life." Music, too, could be said to have been Milton Katims's religion. After starting out on the piano, Milton soon gravitated toward the violin, and he proved to be one of those rare kids who never need to be reminded to practice. But it was only after he graduated from Columbia University (with a major in psychology and a music minor) and began graduate studies there that he discovered the viola. Immersing himself in Leon Barzin's conducting course, Katims realized that he needed to learn the viola's C clef to be able to read the notes of transposing instruments in the orchestral score, so Barzin lent him a beautiful Gaspar da Salo viola, and Katims fell in love with the sound. The viola section wasn't a bad place for a fledgling conductor to sit: right in front of the maestro, where he could absorb every gesture.

Milton's future wife, Virginia Peterson, played a major role in his first big break. A beautiful blond cellist who was studying with Alfred Wallenstein, Virginia was one of the first to hear that her teacher had been appointed music director at WOR, then the flagship radio station of the Mutual Broadcasting System, and that he was looking for an assistant conductor and solo violist. Virginia immediately recommended her boyfriend—and Katims, playing string quartets in Woodstock, rushed to New York City. He got the job. The couple married two months later, and the eight years Katims spent at WOR proved his making as a conductor.

There is no Milton Katims story without Virginia Katims, a more vital partner than his viola bow or his conducting baton. Enthusiastic, flamboyant, indefatigable, and full of ideas, Virginia was a force to be reckoned with and a huge asset to her husband's career. She was also mercurial, just as Katims's mother had been. The couple were each other's best friends, a mutual admiration society, and, occasionally, sparring partners. Both Milton and Virginia had fiery tempers and strong egos and were never shy about airing their views, as local critics frequently experienced.

Katims's temper got him into serious trouble with his musicians during his career at the Seattle Symphony. But what else could have been expected, given that Katims's role model and adored mentor was Arturo Toscanini? The fabled conductor was known for berating and insulting his musicians and indulging in spectacular temper tantrums that sometimes resulted in a broken baton, ripped-up scores, and once his own smashed wristwatch; a few of his tantrums are still immortalized in audio form on YouTube. Toscanini belonged to an era in which the conductor was the ultimate autocrat, one whose word was law and who could hire and fire at will. His protégé operated in a different era, however, in which abusive behavior was poorly received and union contracts protected players from being fired without due process.

Katims's reverence for Toscanini is evident in his memoir, where he states, "Arturo Toscanini, the most wonderful maestro of them all, had a tremendous influence on me as a musician and as a conductor. For me, the title of Maestro is synonymous with his name and belongs to him alone, so profound was his impact on music—and on me." No superlative was too great: when it came to "tremendous personal magnetism," Katims likened Toscanini to Jesus, Moses, Napoleon, and Alexander the Great.

Katims's adulation of Toscanini started early. As a young man, in the late 1920s and early 1930s, he climbed to the top balcony of Carnegie Hall to hear the maestro in concert, and later he sneaked into the hall to hear rehearsals from a vantage point on his stomach in a box just to the left of the stage. It wasn't until Katims joined the NBC Symphony that he actually met "the Old Man," as Toscanini was often called. Katims was called in to apply for a first-desk chair when the legendary violist William Primrose left to further his solo career. Katims didn't even need to audition, as Toscanini was familiar with his playing from his recitals on WOR Radio.

Thus began Katims's eleven years with the Old Man and his own rise as a conductor. Toscanini's example taught Katims valuable lessons about interpreting music and bending an orchestra to one's will. Unfortunately, his example also taught the younger conductor to explode and hurl invectives at musicians in the service of great art. Temper tantrums on the podium by an acknowledged genius might have been pardonable a generation earlier; by the time Katims arrived in Seattle, conductors did not enjoy that same godlike status. Besides, Toscanini could get away with behavior that others could not: He was so Italian! Such a legend!

Toscanini's legendary ability to conduct almost everything without a score inspired Katims to emulation, but not always to Toscanini-like results. The older maestro had three excellent reasons for eschewing a score: he had a near-photographic memory, and he was both terribly nearsighted and too vain for spectacles. Katims had neither the blessing of a flawless memory nor the curse of myopia. Scoreless conducting looks mightily impressive to an audience, but it also carries terrible risks, and it works only if the conductor is so well prepared that the score is not necessary to the performance. Katims sometimes conducted works he had not fully memorized. That was apparent to his Seattle players and eventually lost him crucial support.

Milton was not the only Katims to have fallen under Toscanini's spell. Virginia, a glamorous and (like the older maestro) accomplished cellist, was mesmerized by the charisma and the force field of strong Italian cologne that always surrounded Toscanini, whom she "worshipped as a conductor and adored as a man," as she wrote in *The Pleasure Was Ours*. United in their adoration of Toscanini, Milton and Virginia were invited for visits to the maestro's palatial home in New York, as well as to his villa on an island in Italy's Lago Maggiore. Toscanini even served as godfather to the Katims's second child, their daughter Pamela Artura, who was serendipitously born on Toscanini's eightieth birthday, March 25, 1947.

During his tenure as a first-desk violist in the NBC Symphony under Toscanini's direction, Katims enjoyed a wealth of firsthand observations of his idol's podium technique, and as Toscanini's assistant he gained great experience conducting the orchestra in more than fifty coast-to-coast radio broadcasts. Now it was time for him to have his own orchestra: Toscanini had announced his retirement, and word had gotten out that the storied NBC Symphony was to be dismantled.

Katims started getting feelers and conducting offers from several directions: Indianapolis, Rochester, New York, reportedly even Detroit and Dallas. Seattle had an edge on all of them because of the tireless advocacy of J. Hans Lehmann, a member of the Seattle Symphony Orchestra board's search committee for a new music director. Lehmann's friend Alexander ("Sasha") Schneider had strongly recommended young Milton Katims as a hot prospect, after which Lehmann began campaigning vigorously to get Katims to Seattle.

When the offer from Seattle arrived, Katims did a lot of soul-searching. He was accustomed to the comparative luxury of a radio orchestra, where, as he wrote in a *Musical America* article in May 1989, "there was no need to be concerned about box office and the effect that programming might have on ticket sales." He was also used to the lively and cosmopolitan music scene in New York, including the pool of outstanding students he had been teaching at the Juilliard School of Music for eleven years. Virginia, furthermore, was engaged in a touring career of her own, with Columbia Artists Community Concerts.

Virginia, however, was feeling conflicted about so often leaving her children, Peter and Pamela, then eleven and seven, while she pursued a concert career as a chamber musician that was not always glamorous or fun. She tended to get great reviews—critics praised the zest and temperamental élan of her playing—but as Virginia later wrote in the couple's memoir, she felt "caught in the trap set for herself by the modern professional woman who wants both a career and a family, and can never really make a choice."

On balance, however, the Katimses were ready for Seattle—and Seattle was certainly ready for them. Once settled with their children in the first of several rented houses in the city's upscale neighborhood of Laurelhurst, Milton and Virginia embarked on a veritable whirlwind of novelties. The new maestro took the Seattle Symphony into neighborhoods and nearby communities where many listeners got their first experience of hearing a live symphony orchestra. School concerts inspired generations of children to learn music. Katims initiated a chamber series called Candlelight Musicales, which brought visiting guest soloists together with Milton and Virginia in trios, duos, and sonata performances such as had seldom been heard in the City of Boeing. An offshoot of the orchestra, a chamber-size Little Orchestra, provided performances of classics from the eighteenth through the twentieth centuries. Best of all the innovations was a Stars of the Future series that brought brilliant but at that point still unknown young musicians to play with the symphony, among them the cellist Yo-Yo Ma, the pianist Murray Perahia, the violinist Kyung-Wha Chung, and the pianist Horacio Gutiérrez.

That wasn't all. Milton and Virginia—both charmers with lots of star power—were adroit and tireless campaigners on behalf of the orchestra. They wooed potential donors with neighborhood get-togethers called "Coffee with Katims," caffeinating the city to a degree that wouldn't be equaled until the advent of Starbucks. On a larger scale, Katims lobbied hard for the passage of a 1956 bond issue to improve and enlarge Seattle's Civic Center, one of the key steps that later made possible not only the emergence of the Seattle Opera House but also that monument to civic pride, the 1962 World's Fair.

Throughout his Seattle tenure, Katims spent many years making civic presentations and speeches at clubs, community centers, and business events. His talks were variations on the theme of the civic responsibility to provide cultural facilities for arts organizations that already had an audience but not a proper home. To one potential donor, who said he wouldn't give money because he didn't attend concerts, Katims riposted, "Your tax dollars support the jail—how much time have you spent there?"

Financial success was not achieved overnight. Capital campaigns for cultural facilities are like huge ocean liners. They're very expensive; they're slow to maneuver, and there's always the possibility of a large iceberg in their way. Luckily, Katims's ocean liner struck relatively few such obstacles, in large part because of his immense popularity as the city's "Mr. Music."

As the Katimses made their innovative way through the 1950s and 1960s, they made an overwhelming impression on the collective consciousness of Seattle. By 1969, the year in which Milton's photograph adorned the cover of the Seattle telephone directory, it was the rare Seattleite who didn't recognize his name.

Despite the public perception of a harmonious partnership, both Milton and Virginia had strong wills and strong egos, which was not always a recipe for domestic felicity. Their daughter, Pamela, described her father as "the brains of this partnership, and mother was the brawn. She had a very good ear, and a lot of strong opinions. It was difficult for Dad to live with his toughest critic. She focused on being his PR manager."

Indeed she did. Over the years, right up to Virginia's last decade when her handwriting grew shaky, members of the local press could be certain that every professional and personal milestone would be commemorated by a missive from Virginia, typed on her favored purple notepaper and signed with a personal note about what "my Maestro" had just done: the reissue of an old recording, a favorable mention in a book about Toscanini, an eightieth or eighty-fifth or ninetieth birthday. Earlier on, when Milton was guest conducting abroad, Virginia, a highly colorful writer, always sent accounts of their travels to the *Seattle Times,* and her accounts were invariably assured a prominent spot in the paper.

Both by nature and by necessity, Milton and Virginia Katims were inevitably focused on their professional activities rather than family issues. "Our parents' life was all about music," remembers Pamela, "not about kids. They talked to each other, not to us. Music was always more important than family. I learned to serve hors d'oeuvres at cocktail parties, and how to dress up and look appropriate. We had to be independent and take care of ourselves. On the other hand, other kids didn't get to play Ping-Pong with Leon Fleisher." Nor did other kids get to meet the legendary Toscanini, as his goddaughter Pamela did when she was a three-year-old whose piano repertoire included "Twinkle, Twinkle Little Star." When she was asked to perform for Toscanini and he joined her at the keyboard to play an impromptu duet, she indignantly announced: "I play alone!"

If Pamela was the family's good girl, her brother, Peter, was unquestionably the free spirit. Peter left Seattle in 1968, as she remembers, and traveled widely, finally ending up in Australia. Pamela, meanwhile, earned a doctorate in educational psychology and went on to work in Northwest banking, broadcasting, education, communications, and conflict resolution.

Perhaps it isn't surprising that Milton and Virginia Katims devoted more energy to the orchestra than to the family. Since the orchestra had been operating as a cooperative prior to Katims's arrival, the musicians had grown accustomed to artistic prerogatives. After six months as the new music director, Katims found it impossible to carry out his responsibilities "when the orchestra was making decisions I should be making." In 1955, Katims called a meeting of the players and presented them with a blueprint for revamping and improving the orchestra, with the proviso that he take over the artistic decision making. Otherwise, he and his family would return to New York.

Katims's blueprint ultimately came true, after much hard work from everyone involved with the orchestra and achieving a longer season, improved artistic quality, and a new concert hall that would also accommodate opera and ballet (adding to the musicians' revenue, since they would be the "pit orchestra" for those two enterprises). At the time Katims presented his plan to the players, the Seattle Symphony's annual budget was less than two hundred thousand dollars; the orchestra, made up of what Katims termed "experienced professionals, schoolteachers, and housewives," presented only eight subscription programs and a handful of other concerts annually. Imagining Katims's vision for the future must have been quite a stretch, but after much discussion and argument the majority of the musicians voted to dissolve the collective and return artistic power to the music director. In his memoir, Katims noted that "a group was anti-Katims, but as long as they could play I wasn't going to fire them."

And he didn't. During his long tenure in Seattle (twenty-two years as music director, and, after his dethronement, an additional three years with the nominal courtesy title of music advisor), Katims grew famous for not firing even those players who clearly couldn't keep up with the orchestra's march toward greater professionalism. Instead, he hired new stronger players to conceal the inadequacies of the weaker ones. But this policy could not continue indefinitely if the orchestra were to improve. The role of "bad guy," the one who eventually had to do the firing, fell to Katims's successor on the podium, Rainer Miedel.

What was it like to be part of the orchestra during those early days? One of the longest-tenured musicians, the cellist Bruce Bailey, who first played in the orchestra in the fall of 1962 and was officially contracted in September 1963, remembers that most members had other jobs or side activities to supplement their orchestra wages; his own title was senior programmer at the Boeing Company, where he and another musician split their work hours between technology and Tchaikovsky. (Bailey, who is married to Mariel Bailey, a member of the Seattle Symphony's first violin section, left Boeing in 2002.) Orchestra rehearsals were held mainly on weekends and evenings.

"We knew Katims was a world-class violist," Bailey told me when I interviewed him. "And he could stand on a box and wave a stick, though he didn't have the best stick technique. He was not Big Five material, but Milton was well suited here. He had quite a temper, but I respected him. He was a man of many characters; he could be the most charming person on the face of the earth, and the next day, impossible to work with."

During Katims's tenure, the orchestra personnel were quite different from the players today. Bailey calls the SSO of the 1960s "a decent regional orchestra, far more characters—and character—than today's group, and far nicer. Visiting conductors would routinely say, 'You are the nicest orchestra.'"

Bailey remembers Katims's arrival somewhat differently from Katims's own account: "He arrived in Seattle when the orchestra essentially went communist and decided to manage themselves. The money people withheld the money and hired Katims to come out and form a new orchestra. He did that. He offered the musicians their jobs; most of them came back with varying degrees of acceptance. Maybe a half dozen never accepted the new way, though." Although some internal dissent continued after Katims's blueprint was accepted, an unparalleled flowering of the Seattle Symphony followed under Katims, who quickly became a popular community figure both on and off the podium. "I found him to be marvelously innovative," Bruce Bailey remembers. "He was the best programmer I've played under. Britten's *War Requiem* was premiered in 1963: we did it the next year."

Katims's programs included George Crumb's avant-garde performance piece *Echoes of Time and the River,* and in one performance of Bruckner's Seventh Symphony two visual artists, Bert Garner and William Mair, painted their responses to the music on canvases at both side stages as the orchestra played. Katims invited ballet dancers to share the stage with the orchestra, and in semistaged concerts he displayed Schoenberg's original paintings in a performance of *Erwartung,* an elaborate tableau in Honegger's *Joan of Arc at the Stake,* and the Broadway star Marni Nixon in a seductive costume in Poulenc's *La voix humaine.* "It seemed like every three months there was some blockbuster like that," Bailey recalled. "Milton also had wonderful outreach programs. He'd spoil it every now and then, after inviting little kids to sit at his feet on the gym floor. They'd be noisy and he'd blow up. This was the not-so-nice side of Milton."

One who decidedly remembers the nicer side is the well-known harpist Heidi Lehwalder, who calls Katims "my fairy godfather." She first played for him at the age of eight, when she was promptly

invited to solo with the Seattle Symphony, "and I answered, 'Okay.'"
(Her mother, Polly Lehwalder, had joined the orchestra's cello section in 1941 at the age of nineteen, during the brief conducting era
of Sir Thomas Beecham; Heidi's sister, Julie, was later also a Seattle
Symphony member.) Heidi Lehwalder went on to solo with the
orchestra and Katims in fifty-six performances, and she adored the
man she always called "Mr. Katims"—even when she was an adult
and he urged her to "call me Milton."

In 1977, after Lehwalder had grown up (and won the first Avery
Fisher Prize, followed by a Grammy-nominated recording), she
returned to Seattle to solo with the orchestra in Michael Colgrass's
Harp Concerto, *Auras*. This was after Katims's ouster as music
director, during his three-year stint as music advisor, when his
relationship with the orchestra was rocky. "Things were really bad,"
Lehwalder remembers. "At one point, Mr. Katims walked off the
stage in rehearsal. My mother said she could see that things had
to change. But we were both very fond of him as a person. There
were so many good times, so many concerts and dinners. He was
incredibly good to me."

Two longtime SSO members, now retired—the principal per-
cussionist Randy Baunton and his wife, the principal second violinist Janet Fisher Baunton—remember Katims as a tremendous
crowd-pleaser: "He had a very flamboyant stage personality that
attracted the public. He was very popular with the board and the
press and did a lot of entertaining." Janet notes that the community
benefited greatly from Katims's connections with great performers
he had known in New York, whom he brought in regularly as soloists and chamber players. "He also did editions of viola music—the
Bach Suites—which are very wonderful to have," she added. "Milton was very tough on the viola section, and they were cowed. As
for the rest of us, he definitely expected us to correct ourselves, and
I thought we played rather sloppily under him. He'd say, 'Play like
a string quartet!' Well, what does that mean? You can't holler out
from the section and say, 'Let's do this!' That is the conductor's job,
to indicate what he wants."

The violin section didn't get much leadership from Katims's
chosen concertmaster, either. Both Bauntons remember Henry

Siegl as "a gifted violinist who never prepared." Janet, who had a clear view of him from her principal second chair (and who also played chamber music with him), observed, "He was very lazy. Henry didn't do the bowings in advance; he thought it was enough if he just showed up and played, but the results weren't good. He was very able to do whatever he wanted on the violin, but he didn't care that much about the orchestra stuff." Both Bauntons concur, nonetheless, that Katims greatly improved the orchestra and its standing in the community. "For the twenty-plus years he was here, Milton really did a tremendous amount."

During the 1960s, the honors and awards poured in: Seattle's First Citizen in 1966, the phone-book cover in 1969, and respectful treatment in the national press (from the *New York Times* to *Musical America* magazine). The Seattle press covered every move the Katimses made, and they made a lot of them, from lunch at the Washington Athletic Club and guest conducting engagements in Paris and Israel and New York to hobnobbing with Marc Chagall and Princess Grace at the Menton Festival in France. Virginia gave speeches and concerts—unless she was on safari in East Africa, or shopping in Japan for a blue brocade fabric for a gown, or writing another account of the couple's many travels for the *Seattle Times*. They met the shah of Iran, Benny Goodman, Emilio Pucci, and Hubert de Givenchy (whom Virginia inveigled into starring at a Seattle Symphony fund-raising gala). Milton was honored by the Lions and Kiwanis and Elks and Moose and other fraternal organizations with antlers. The Katimses were Seattle's cultural all-stars.

But a rumble of discontent gradually rose in the early 1970s. Some of it came from the players who had resented Katims since he took away their autonomy upon his arrival; these players were out to get him from day one. Playing in an orchestra, Bailey reminded me, is "a dead-end job: you win an audition and get a seat, and fifty years later you're in the same seat. Some people can get extremely bitter: the guy on the podium tells you what to do, and maybe he doesn't know as much as you do about this particular point. I don't think [the players' discontent] grew faster under Milton than it would [have] under anyone else. But he did give reason, growling things like 'You play like a bunch of Seattle housewives!' A group of players went around sounding their fellow musicians out. It just grew." Pamela Katims acknowledges that her father had "quite a temper, though he quickly got over it. He went for the jugular pretty quickly."

One catalyst for anti-Katims sentiment, Bailey remembers, was the performance of Gunther Schuller's *Seven Studies on Themes of Paul Klee*, which includes prominent, challenging oboe and flute solos. The concert didn't go well. At intermission, Katims exploded, in what Bailey described as a memorable tantrum. "Before that, there were backstage factions. After that, there was only one faction. There was a general push to ease him out. The respect wasn't there." The players went to "every board member in sight" with their views, and the tide of dissent gradually rose. Katims later apologized and asked the players' committee for their support at a luncheon he hosted, but it was too late.

"He did wonders here," summarized Bailey. "He raised the level of the orchestra tremendously. Relatively speaking, he was a great musician, though he didn't have the best technique; he certainly had problems interacting with people and a sense of self-importance, but none of these things are unusual. I think he was well placed here."

Well placed or not, it was clear by the early 1970s that the tide had conclusively turned against Katims. The Bauntons recall that a five-member orchestra committee was formed to approach the maestro about changes the orchestra wanted. Randy Baunton told me, "I loved Milton—he brought the money in!—but we wanted more leadership from him, including a clear downbeat." However, at that time the orchestra committee's suggestions were ignored, as were, for a long time, their complaints to the board.

The orchestra players were not the only ones to complain of Katims. The pianist Randolph Hokanson, who soloed twelve times with Katims and the SSO, says that the conductor was "naturally very musical, but he did not always learn his scores. On at least two occasions that we played together, I was aware that he had lost his place. He could easily have been superb if he had worked. It takes a long time, and a lot of study, to become a conductor. The overall effect of a lot of his concerts, however, was very good."

Finally, a rebellious faction in the board prevailed. In 1973, Hans Lehmann, the board member who had recruited the maestro and, with his wife, Thelma, become among the closest friends of Milton and Virginia, was deputized, as Lehmann later wrote, to "persuade Milton to accept the inevitable downgrading of his position gracefully after twenty-two years of memorable service."

It didn't happen. Despite Lehmann's earnest persuasions, Milton's response was, "I am going to fight." What followed was highly damaging to the Seattle Symphony and its community support. The community, the board, and, to a lesser degree, the orchestra divided into pro- and anti-Katims camps. Nobody looked good: the pro-Katims camp appeared as fuddy-duddies who couldn't lead the orchestra toward greater artistic progress. The anti-Katims camp appeared as cruel backstabbers who refused to recognize the contributions of a man who had given them twenty-two hardworking years. Donors zipped up their wallets; patrons recognized the unhappy atmosphere and didn't want to be a part of it. It was a miserable time for all.

Thus it was that, in July 1974, the symphony announced the end of the Katims era: for the remainder of Katims's five-year contract, through spring 1976, he would retain the title of music director, after which he would serve for three years as "music advisor" and conduct four subscription programs annually. This plan, undoubtedly conceived as a face-saving and conciliatory measure to ease the maestro out gradually, backfired in two respects. First, Katims publicly declared that the "music advisor" title was an empty gesture, as his advice would not be sought. (In that respect he was certainly correct.) Second, his regular returns and departures from the podium, during which his favored concertmaster, Henry Siegl, first resumed and then relinquished his position, prolonged the ill feelings by reigniting the pro- and anti-Katims factions. The three years of Katims's "music advisorship" were uneasy years.

Virginia Katims, in her joint memoir with Milton, remembers her husband's ouster rather differently. In her telling, Milton, though wooed by the orchestras of Houston, Rochester, Indianapolis, Detroit, and Baltimore, decided to remain in Seattle. Virginia recounts that she urged him not to outstay his welcome: "For me, the bottom line on conductors' careers is very simple: After ten years, move on!!"

Why didn't they?

"Of course, if your name is Milton Katims, you never want to change. You feel comfortable, you like your home, you fall in love with your view of Mount Rainier, and you enjoy your audiences. . . . We finally realized that even with the charisma of a Cary Grant or a Jimmy Stewart as a conductor, audiences want change. How could we have been so unaware?" wrote Virginia.

They were not the only ones who were caught unaware. Many of the couple's fans were bewildered by the maestro's fall from favor. Pamela Katims remembers, "I never felt like I understood what really happened. They never explained it to me. I think it's true that after twenty-two years, it was time for new blood and new energy. But the way it was done was so upsetting. There must have been a better way to allow my parents to disengage with more dignity."

When an offer came in 1976 from the University of Houston, where two longtime friends of Katims invited him to become artistic director of the School of Music, Milton and Virginia considered, accepted, and took off for Texas, he in his yellow Corvette and she in her old Buick. They spent the next eight years in what by all accounts was a highly convivial setting, in which both were lionized. Initially, Milton felt "like an airplane pilot who had been grounded" in his academic office; later, he was able to make a number of improvements in the school, not the least of which was raising substantial sums for scholarships. Virginia was, as always, the remarkable hostess, wooing the community with both her parties and her cello performances. Pamela, when she visited her parents in Houston, was impressed with their social milieu. "They really liked my parents as people—not just as an important conductor and his wife, but with authentic friendship."

When, however, it was time for the Katimses to retire, they headed back to Seattle; they felt the pull of family (their daughter and two young grandchildren had settled there) and longtime friends. And in April 1992, at the age of eighty-two and thirteen years after Milton's last Seattle Symphony concert, he was finally invited back to the orchestra's podium to conduct a celebration of the thirtieth anniversary of the Seattle World's Fair. Much to the enjoyment of the audience, he made his traditional flying hop onto the podium for the opening number, Alberto Ginastera's *Estancia*, and picked up the viola to play Mozart's sublime Sinfonia Concertante with the highly regarded violinist Dmitry Sitkovetsky. Need I add that there were several standing ovations?

After their return to Seattle, Milton and Virginia became regular concertgoers, and Milton returned to the Seattle Tennis Club, where he became a beloved fixture. He was given the Lifetime Accomplishment in the Arts Award from Seattle's ArtsFund. The arrival of each of his big-number birthdays—eighty-fifth, ninetieth, ninety-fifth— was marked by newspaper photos by the *Seattle Times* photographer Greg Gilbert, whom the Katimses loved, and by press accounts of the maestro's secrets for good health and longevity.

And here, for those who hope to emulate the maestro, is a list of those secrets, divulged on Katims's ninetieth birthday:

1. Be a conductor. Actuarial tables for insurance companies confirm that conductors have longer life spans than average, although nobody is quite sure why. Here's Katims's opinion: "Conductors don't get ulcers. We give them. And then there's the vascular point of view; all that waving of your arms keeps the blood flowing to the heart. If conductors have hearts, that is."

2. Marry a woman young enough to keep up with you, and stay married.

3. Take lots of vitamins. Milton and Virginia took a veritable alphabet of vitamins, in addition to beta-carotene, lecithin, gingko biloba, ginseng and One-a-Day multivitamins (just in case they've left anything out).

4. It's OK if you start small. The maestro himself weighed two pounds, two ounces, at his premature birth. It also doesn't hurt to pick your parents well. Katims's Hungarian mother lived to the ripe old age of ninety-three.

5. Keep a positive attitude. "I see no reason to look at the dark side," Milton explained.

6. Don't play golf. Play tennis. Golf is for old people.
7. Keep on the move. "Travel and constant change are good for you," says Katims.
8. Keep off the sauce. "We never have a cocktail before dinner," Katims says. "At parties, I'm a one-drink man, usually a gin and tonic or a scotch and soda."
9. Eat radishes and drink ginger ale. Katims also loved sour cream with cottage cheese, as well as fresh fruit, chicken, and fish.
10. Get plenty of sleep. Typically the maestro turned in around 11:30 p.m. and got up at 8:30 a.m.—sometimes even 9 or 9:30.
11. Forget smoking.
12. Write your memoirs.

Over the years, no one heard much about Virginia's birthdays, big-number or other. As it turns out, there was good reason for this reticence. Unbeknownst to almost everybody except family, Virginia had subtracted an entire decade from her age when the Katimses moved to Seattle. It wasn't until her death, when I was trying to make sense of the dates provided for Virginia's obituary, that the truth came out. What chutzpah! And what glamour!

Milton's conducting career overshadowed by far his career as violist, an instrument he took up only occasionally during his Seattle years and thereafter. Yet when you ask the opinion of knowledgeable music lovers, they'll say, "Not a great conductor, but definitely a great violist." Over the years, he played chamber music with many of the finest musicians; edited works for the viola; made recordings (including his transcription of Bach's Cello Suites); and occasionally taught. He came to the rescue of the University of Washington when their faculty violist left before a replacement had been found. He did not finally give up the instrument until the age of ninety-one, saying that he no longer liked the sounds he was producing.

"I learned the most about my father when I listened to him play his viola," Pamela Katims remembers. "His music brought me to tears. He was more communicative with the viola than with words. Meaningful conversations were hard for him. He would make a lot of jokes, turning aside the topic. But I loved sitting in the living room three feet away from him, listening to him talk and breathe and make love through that instrument. He truly loved music."

His puckish sense of humor—and his love of competition—stayed with Milton Katims to the end. About a month before his death at the age of ninety-six, when it was clear that he was failing, he revisited the past in a conversation with his daughter.

"Would you do anything different?" she asked.

"Yes," he said quietly.

"Would you be a conductor?"

"Yes."

"Would you play tennis?"

"Yes—only better!"

Rainer Miedel and Cordelia Wikarski Miedel

THE MAESTRO AND THE MAESTRA

At first, nobody knew who he was. Tall, blond, good-looking, and full of Continental charm, Rainer Miedel was thirty-seven, and a complete unknown in Seattle, when his appointment to the music directorship of the Seattle Symphony was announced in 1975. He was Milton Katims's successor in that role, and the two maestros could not have been more different. Katims, who was sixty-eight when he left the position, was gregarious, voluble, hot-tempered, and fully at ease with all the entertaining and schmoozing required of a hometown maestro in Seattle. Miedel, young enough to be Katims's son, was private, intellectual, reserved, and on foreign turf (in all respects) when it came to the socializing aspect of his new job. But he was by no means inexperienced at the podium, having already guest conducted several top orchestras, including the Berlin Philharmonic, and held a music directorship in Sweden. He had also served as assistant to two excellent conductors, Antal Dorati and Sergiu Comissiona.

How did Miedel get from Regensburg, Germany, his birthplace, to Sweden, Baltimore, and then Seattle? His was an interesting career path, with many challenges, beginning with the circumstances of his birth in 1937, just two years before the start of World War II. Unlike most internationally successful conductors, Miedel was born into a nonmusical family; his father, Karl, was a lawyer and an authoritarian intellectual who would have preferred his son to follow him into the legal profession—as Rainer Miedel's son, Florian, would later do.

The advantages accrued from a childhood steeped in music are tremendous, giving a musician a great head start in learning how music works and acquainting the child with great scores at a time when the brain is particularly receptive to soaking up music. Miedel got a later start, but he made up for that with the breadth of his education in psychology, literature, philosophy, and drama.

The future Seattle Symphony music director was fourteen when he got his first experience as a conductor. "The church choir wanted me to be its conductor, and some people even came to my house to try to persuade my parents. They thought the idea was ridiculous," Miedel told me in a *Seattle Times* interview. "My father said I could conduct if I got better marks in Greek and Latin. I did conduct the choir . . . but I don't remember getting any better at Greek and Latin!"

The fledgling maestro also studied the cello, concentrating on that instrument during university studies in Detmold and Berlin. He worked with Franco Ferrara in Siena and Andre Navarra in Paris under a Fulbright grant (1962–63), and he pursued conducting studies with Istvan Kertesz and Carl Mellesz. In 1965, Miedel joined the cello section of the Stockholm Philharmonic and became its assistant principal cellist after a year; then, in 1968, he was promoted to the orchestra's principal cello position under the famed conductor Antal Dorati, who became an important advocate for him. At the same time, he worked hard on his conducting career, flying every two weeks from Stockholm to Copenhagen to study. In 1965, his first prize in the Swedish Broadcasting Corporation's Young Conductors' Competition started him on the path to his podium debut with the Stockholm Philharmonic in 1967.

Why Stockholm? Miedel said, "I went to Stockholm because I was not feeling very friendly toward Germany at that time, in common with many others who grew up in the postwar era." He further distanced himself from Germany by adding an *e* to his surname (originally Miedl) to make it look less Teutonic; years later, he added an accent over the *e* because Americans frequently mispronounced the name as "Middle." (Of course, in Seattle, with its proximity to Mount Rainier, getting people to pronounce his first name correctly was a lost cause: inevitably, he was called "Rainier" instead of "Rainer.")

But he also retained important ties to Germany, not only with his immediate family but also through his connection with the young cellist Cordelia Wikarski, whom he met in 1961 after she had graduated with a master's degree from Berlin's Hochschule für Musik, where she played the Dvorak concerto with the university's orchestra. Cordelia had a prodigious talent and was the more accomplished cellist of the two—a fact Rainer, proud of Cordelia's successes, always readily acknowledged. Three years before the couple met, Cordelia and her sister, the pianist Eleonore Wikarski, had already achieved fame by winning the 1958 Munich Duo Competition, launching a concert career that took them from Finland and Russia to Iraq and India. Cordelia had been studying the cello for a mere six years at the time of the Munich Competition.

Only Romeo and Juliet, however, could have had a more star-crossed relationship than Rainer and Cordelia. In their case it was not the feuding families of the Montagues and the Capulets but the Berlin Wall that made life together complicated and initially impossible. "The Wall was built in 1961, the same year we met," Cordelia remembers. "My family and I lived in what became East Germany. The Berlin Wall went up overnight; we had been in a friend's house the night before, and we went home, and the next day immediately the Wall was there—the soldiers built it so quickly. Suddenly, we were cut off from a lifestyle my friends, less than a mile away, enjoyed and took for granted. Many people were fleeing East Berlin—and many were shot. And all of a sudden we were in prison: we couldn't go anywhere. Rainer and I were separated. He was a West German, I was an East German. We continued our relationship, but when Rainer went to Stockholm, I could not go with him. He could visit me, but I couldn't visit him."

Nor could she get to her job, performing 1961–71 in a contemporary ensemble at East Berlin's Maxim Gorky Theater, without having to take an elaborate detour that took two and a half hours each way because of the way the Wall had bisected the city. In 1962, Cordelia was able to leave East Germany for a few days at a time, to take lessons for two semesters with the noted cellist and teacher Maurice Gendron. Later, she studied with another great cellist, August Eichhorn, in Leipzig (where he had been principal cellist of the fabled Gewandhaus Orchestra in the 1940s). In 1963, during her studies with Eichhorn, she won a diploma at the International Pablo Casals Competition in Budapest.

For Cordelia and Rainer, what followed the rise of the Berlin Wall on August 13, 1961, was fifteen years of the kind of life described so poignantly in the Oscar-winning 2006 German film *The Lives of Others*, which depicts how agents of the Stasi (the East German secret police) monitored East Berlin's cultural scene. Cordelia and Rainer knew that their letters were steamed open and their phone calls overheard. "Marriage was impossible," Cordelia remembers, "between a West German and an East German."

Cordelia and her family lived only about a half mile from the border to West Berlin; occasionally, at night, they heard border guards shooting a would-be escapee. It must have been a harrowing reprise of the violence the family had witnessed in the final days of the war, when Cordelia's father, Romuald Wikarski, a respected composer, pianist, and teacher at Berlin's Hochschule für Musik, was shot and killed by two Russian officers in front of his six children (the youngest of whom was two months old). No one knew why; perhaps it was a reprisal for an act someone else had committed against the Russian army, which had invaded Berlin from the south in the last days of the war. The date was April 29, 1945, a sunny and peaceful Sunday afternoon, and the family had been sitting around the table in the living room, with the doors wide open and the sun pouring in. Two Russian officers entered the house. Romuald Wikarski asked if they would like him to play the piano for them. The two officers grabbed Mr. Wikarski by his suit collar, dragged him outside to the garden, and shot him about ten seconds later.

Romuald Wikarski was one of six local fathers in their fifties who were shot by Russian officers during that time. The family buried him in the garden, and the neighbors came to pay their respects. "The flowers were all blooming," Cordelia remembers. "My mother played one of her husband's compositions on the piano in his honor, while the neighbors took the coffin out to the garden."

Cordelia was six at the time; her thirty-seven-year-old mother, now a widow with six children to care for and feed, sold everything in the house, from furniture to carpets, for food. The Wikarski family was well known and respected in the Berlin music community, and they received help from friends—among them the family of the famous singer Dietrich Fischer-Dieskau—and from such organizations as CARE, the Quakers, and the Red Cross. "And we received help from God," Cordelia adds.

Once, she walked for three miles to bring home a single can of milk. Another time, passing an American military base, someone gave her a cup of coffee, which she carefully carried home to her mother. "I dreamed that the pine trees around the house were made of chocolate," she remembers.

The five years following her father's death were years of privation and struggle for the family, but they rallied. The older children studied music, mostly with their mother. Little Friedemann, the two-month-old, who later became an actor, was already on the stage at the age of five, as the little son in Schiller's *William Tell*, whose father shoots an apple from his head. Like Rainer, Cordelia began music studies comparatively late, as a thirteen-year-old, but she was soon performing cello and piano duets with her talented sister, Eleonore, who was three years older.

Further south, in Regensburg, Rainer had begun his cello studies at the age of twelve; at first his mother took lessons alongside him. The Miedls were a highly intellectual family, who discussed the poems of Rilke over the dinner table. Rainer's father, Karl, was the head of the local Musikverein, or music society, which presented concerts. When the young cellist was sixteen, his mother died, and his father remarried a year later. Karl was a strict parent, but he was also proud of Rainer's success and supported his education by paying his undergraduate tuition.

After his move to Stockholm, Rainer's early wins in conducting competitions helped him acquire an agent in Berlin, which led to engagements with the Berlin Philharmonic and other major orchestras. His work caught the attention of the conductor Sergiu Comissiona, who invited him to the Baltimore Symphony Orchestra as his assistant, a position Rainer held concurrently with the directorship of the Gavleborgs Orchestra in Sweden.

While Rainer's podium career was on the ascent, Cordelia was touring the world's concert halls with Eleonore. "We toured as the Duo Wikarski from about 1958 to 1975," Cordelia says, "more so after our success in 1966 at the Tchaikovsky International Competition."

During all these years, we performed in concerts all over Europe, the Middle East, the Soviet Union, and Asia, and in solo engagements with orchestras. After 1961, when the Berlin Wall was built, someone from the government was with us all the time. We kept to a schedule of rehearsing, concerts, and parties afterward. Almost all the money we earned had to be changed into East German marks, which were of very low value outside of East Germany—about one-fifth of a West German mark. In Stockholm, they [the concert presenters] gave us a per diem. So in Sweden I bought a leather coat, but I had to throw my old coat away; I could not leave with one coat and return with two.

It wasn't easy to get permission to leave East Berlin, even for a few days. My brother-in-law, who played poker with the police chief, told him, "My sister-in-law would like to attend the master classes of Maurice Gendron." The police chief called to get me a visa for three or four days. I went there, bringing along my hundred West German marks so that I could buy something in the West.

Where should I hide it? If the money were found, it would be confiscated immediately, and I might be arrested. Everything was searched at the border—luggage, purses, even shoes. I decided to place the marks in my cello case, underneath the cello and between the pages of music. The guard came onto the train at the border and began searching everything, while I became more and more worried. Finally he looked at the cello case, and asked what was in there. My cello, of course!—but what else?

So I opened the case, and began showing him everything I could in order to stall him: "Here is the rosin, you use this on the horsehair of the bow, and these are the strings," etc. Finally he asked, "And would you please lift out your cello so I can see what is underneath."

Would she be caught, the money confiscated, and herself branded a dissident? Dissidents were frequently known to disappear. With shaking hands, she began to lift up the cello. But just then another officer came in, exclaiming, "Hurry up, we have to leave." Cordelia put the cello back into the case, locked it up, and took a deep breath. That was life behind the Iron Curtain.

For Cordelia and Rainer, 1966 was a watershed year. Cordelia became the only German player to make it into the third and final round of the prestigious Tchaikovsky International Competition and was named a laureate. What few people knew was that she also was in her fourth month of pregnancy. "I remember I couldn't eat anything," Cordelia says. Racked by nausea and exhaustion, she nonetheless found the competition exhilarating. In the third round, starting at 10:45 p.m. on the evening of a hot and humid day, she played the Dvorak concerto with the Moscow Radio Orchestra, conducted by Gennady Rozhdestvensky, and then, immediately afterward, Tchaikovsky's *Rococo Variations*. Seated in the jury at the Great Hall of the Moscow Conservatory were a veritable parade of cello legends, including Mstislav Rostropovich, Gregor Piatagorsky, Pierre Fournier, and Gaspar Cassadó.

"It was a major commitment and a major effort to develop such a deep connection with these great works and to play them before people who can really recognize what you are achieving," Cordelia explains. "It takes discipline, hard work, and the willingness to learn, but all this hard work gives you a tremendous focus as a musician. I knew I was playing my best, and I enjoyed it."

So did her sister Eleonore. "Eleonore and I played full sonata programs in the first two rounds, and the performance I especially remember was Beethoven's D-Major Sonata," she recalls. "I looked out at the judges afterward, and Rostropovich had folded his hands. I really think it was that performance that got me into the third round. The Beethoven has been a lucky piece for me!" And also for Eleonore, who received a special award for the best accompaniment of the competition. That same year, after being named Tchaikovsky Competition laureate, Cordelia was granted the Felix Mendelssohn Award of East Germany. Meanwhile, doors were starting to open for the ambitious young maestro, too. Following his successes in Sweden, Rainer found crucial opportunities in America with the help of two important mentors, Comissiona and Antal Dorati, who were impressed with his talent and ready to expand his career.

In Europe, Miedel's reputation spread quickly, and by 1975, when he came to Seattle, he had conducted the Berlin Philharmonic, Leningrad (now Saint Petersburg) Philharmonic, Berlin Radio Symphony, Bucharest Enescu Philharmonic, Stockholm Royal Opera, Montreux Festival Orchestra, Bamberg Symphony, and Hamburg Radio Symphony. And in the United States, he had guest conducted the Washington National Symphony and the orchestras of Baltimore and Atlanta. Signing with the prestigious Harold Shaw management in New York was both a crucial milestone and the stepping-stone to his Seattle Symphony post. He was hired in Seattle after conducting only one hastily arranged short rehearsal. "The musicians' Orchestra Committee was asked to come to a board meeting," remembers Randy Baunton, "to give their opinion of Rainer Miedel as a future music director. The consensus was that we couldn't give any thoughtful commentary, because he had only conducted about half a rehearsal with us. Come to find out, he had been hired already."

During the years Miedel was building his conducting career, Cordelia, still in East Berlin, found some of the restrictions on travel easing—especially after the birth of Florian. As long as she left her little son behind in East Berlin, there was no danger that she would defect. In 1970, when Florian was three, she was invited to Sweden to play Schumann's Cello Concerto with Miedel in two performances with the Gavleborgs Orchestra.

"Rainer was a very fine musician, and a rising star in Sweden. It was a wonderful experience to perform the Schumann with him." She remembers him as an adroit accompanist, who had no trouble following her in the complicated concerto. "In 1975, he got the contract in Seattle. I had no idea what it would be like. I thought Seattle would be somehow more exotic. I would never have been able to leave my mother behind, but she died in 1975, and then Rainer said, 'We will get you out.' We had a famous lawyer, Dr. Vogel, who did all these exchanges between spies of America and the Soviet Union. And so it took about a year and a half. There was a good reason for me to leave, because it was to reunite a family; it was very clear that Florian was Rainer's son." Rainer's father helped too, drawing on his legal skills to write a persuasive and articulate letter to the authorities on the young couple's behalf.

One fallout of Cordelia's application for permission to leave East Germany was the immediate loss of her teaching position at the highly regarded Hochschule für Musik Hanns Eisler in East Berlin. The concert tours of the Duo Wikarski also stopped. "I was considered a traitor to the Communists," she recalls.

In Seattle, no one had an inkling of Miedel's personal situation. Miedel didn't want to talk about it, because he didn't know when or if Cordelia and Florian would be allowed to leave. Later, he said of this period, "It was more than tough." Cordelia explained,

> If he talked too much about our plan to get out, maybe the East German government would stop it. So we had to be very quiet that we had applied to leave. I took some English lessons, but nothing prepares you for this change. I thought I would never learn English! I was thirty-eight.
>
> But I could not get married with an East German passport. When I got out, I got a West German passport and we could get married in Regensburg, with Rainer's family. Then I flew to Berlin with Florian and we could finally hear a concert of the Berlin Philharmonic with Karajan conducting. Then I needed an American visa, and that took awhile too. We came here on the 8th of February, 1977.

And what a bombshell that was! The Seattle Symphony administration, musicians, supporters, and subscribers had had no inkling that a wife and child were arriving to join their maestro. By a lucky coincidence, I spoke some German and was able to score the first interview with the mysterious former East German wife with the colorful past. But it wasn't until November 20, 1977, that the Northwest music community realized that she was not merely a wife but also an astonishingly good artist in her own right.

With the pianist Randolph Hokanson, of the University of Washington faculty, the cellist now known as Cordelia Wikarski-Miedel played Shostakovich's D-Minor Sonata, op. 40, Martinu's Variations on a Theme of Rossini, Boccherini's Sonata in A Major, and Brahms's mighty F-Major Sonata in the Great Hall of Tacoma's Annie Wright School, under the auspices of the Tacoma Philharmonic. The recital was a revelation. Listeners were bowled over by Cordelia's technical finesse, interpretive depth, and deeply personal musicality. Even Rainer Miedel, who knew her playing, was amazed; he later commented that she was a daring artist who "took so many chances" and that he never would have been able to play like that.

"People didn't expect that I played so well," Cordelia admits. The recital couldn't have been a better introduction to the Seattle Symphony family and the community at large. Both Miedels were now well launched in Seattle, but it was far from clear sailing for them nonetheless. Rainer was still learning that there was a big difference between being a guest maestro who sweeps into town with a single concert program and serving as a resident music director who conducts the bulk of the orchestra's season. He was all but overwhelmed by the social, administrative, and organizational demands of a music directorship, which required his doing much more than merely conducting concerts. Board meetings, for example, were crucial for staying aware of what was going on. Parties and receptions were essential for building relationships with donors and concertgoers. Sometimes he needed to stay up until 3 a.m. to study because there were enormous chunks of symphonic repertoire to learn for the big lineup of concerts he planned to conduct.

That was not all. At the time of Miedel's arrival, the Seattle Symphony still had many players who had joined the orchestra decades earlier, when it was a part-time job in which excellent professionals played alongside teachers, housewives, and other musicians whose "day job" provided the real income. Milton Katims had solved ensemble problems by hiring new players to cover up the inadequate ones, not by firing those who couldn't keep up with the orchestra's rising standards. That job of axe-wielder fell to Miedel, as was made clear to him by the board of directors.

Needless to say, this was not a popular development among the many orchestra players, especially the twenty-three who were dismissed. "Some of them probably should have gone," concedes Janet Fisher Baunton, "but I'd still cry over every single one." Mariel Bailey, who had joined the orchestra's first violin section in 1978, believed that Miedel thought there were "too many women in the orchestra. On tour, I noticed that he put all the men on the outside [closest to the audience] so they could be seen." In that era, women players were still scarce in European orchestras; almost all the reviews of the Seattle Symphony's 1980 European tour commented wonderingly on the high percentage of women in the orchestra.

Looking back on his early Seattle years in a 1981 *Seattle Times* interview, Miedel observed, "I came out of nowhere—a big gamble for the SSO. I stepped into the footsteps of a public figure and orchestra builder. He [Katims] did a lot for the community and the orchestra, but he left too late. If he had left voluntarily, I would have had a hard task to follow a hero. My ideas are popular among the musicians—except the ones who fear losing their jobs. But now we have 150 players applying for jobs in the orchestra when there is a vacancy, not seven. The reputation of the SSO has gone up. The musicians also know I have fought hard for a pension plan for them. I am on their side."

Miedel's arrival wasn't made easier by his relatively low salary, which was set at $27,000 for his first season. The board explained that this was necessitated by the salary Katims was still earning in his three-year post as music advisor. The Seattle Symphony community included those pro-Katims supporters who resented both the new maestro and his new concertmaster, the excellent Swedish violinist Karl-Ove Mannberg, who displaced Katims's concertmaster, Henry Siegl. (Needless to say, Siegl was displeased; Cordelia remembers that Siegl, who was Jewish, called her German husband a Nazi, until Rainer told him that further use of that term would result in a lawsuit.)

As Miedel worked through conflicts in the orchestra, he and his wife also found time to focus on their family. "Rainer had told me, 'It would be so good if we would have another child,'" Cordelia remembers. In 1980, a second son, Lukas, was born.

Life grew increasingly busy for the couple. Rainer guest conducted in Chicago, Detroit, and Japan, as well as taking a short-term post with the Florida Philharmonic. Starting in 1979, Cordelia had begun teaching half-time at the University of Puget Sound in Tacoma, where she later became artist in residence (1983–2010). Both Miedels came together onstage in January 1981 to perform William Schuman's *Song of Orpheus* for cello and orchestra at Meany Theater on the University of Washington campus, where Rainer had launched an ambitious "Miedel at Meany" play-and-talk series.

The artistic capstone of the Rainer Miedel years came in 1980, when he took the Seattle Symphony on a three-week tour of cities in Germany, Austria, and Switzerland; the brilliant Brazilian-born pianist Nelson Freire was the soloist in both Beethoven's and Rachmaninoff's third piano concertos. The tour, which was arranged through Miedel's connections in Europe, was opposed by some board members, and the general manager, Lanham Deal, was unenthusiastic. Consequently, the necessary fund-raising for the tour didn't take place, and the orchestra came home with a pile of favorable reviews—and a mountain of debts.

But they had developed a new level of ensemble on the road, and the concert programs were becoming better and more refined all the time. The orchestra had played in the Großer Musikvereinssaal in Vienna, one of the finest halls in Europe. For Miedel, personally, it was a coup to return in triumph with his own American orchestra to his home city of Regensburg. On this occasion the festivities included speeches, a Weißwurst (sausage) dinner for the orchestra and its entourage, the presence of Miedel's proud father, and a little jazz violin performance afterward by the concertmaster Karl-Ove Mannberg.

Only two years later, Miedel began suffering from persistent stomach troubles. This was nothing new: a dozen years earlier, he had developed stomach ulcers, and since then he was always on some new health regimen or new European eating plan. The conductor thought these new stomach problems were a recurrence of the ulcers. Miedel underwent extensive medical tests. On November 19, 1982, he learned that he had pancreatic cancer, one of the fastest and deadliest of all cancers. The news was devastating. Miedel was given a round of chemotherapy that slowed the growth of the cancer, and he continued to conduct as long as his strength held out. The last concert he conducted, on January 13, 1983, featured the legendary diva Leontyne Price as soloist.

Miedel went to the Seattle Opera House one last time to attend, as a member of the audience, the Seattle Symphony concert of March 7, 1983. It was a significant evening: Miedel's last visit to the hall where he had been music director, and the first visit of the man who would become his long-running successor, the evening's guest conductor, Gerard Schwarz. The program included the swan song of the orchestra's principal clarinetist, Ronald Phillips, in Mozart's Clarinet Concerto, marking the end of a great career. Miedel, looking gaunt and frail, sat with his family sequestered in a side box where he would not be the cynosure of all eyes. Always private, he had asked the orchestra management to delay the announcement of his illness until a couple of weeks before his death on March 26, 1983.

"When Rainer was so sick, he said that when little Lukas gave him a hug, the pain of the day would disappear," Cordelia remembers. "Rainer wrote me many letters and notes, even though we were together in Seattle. We talked for hours about music and our experiences, about people and the way things should be. Our communication was so great. He thanked me in so many ways for providing a home he had never had."

A distraught Sergiu Comissiona returned to Seattle for a last unhappy task: to conduct the Seattle Symphony in a memorial concert for his young protégé and colleague, for whom he had had such hopes. That evening the orchestra and its guest maestro rose to new expressive heights in one of Miedel's most beloved scores, Strauss's *Death and Transfiguration*. During this time, the Seattle Symphony family rallied around Cordelia and her sons, helping them move into a new house and make repairs.

Cordelia's job at the University of Puget Sound (UPS), always an important musical outlet, became increasingly essential to her in her widowhood. "At UPS, I taught and also played quite a lot of recitals around the state with fourteen or fifteen different pianists, including Victoria Bogdashevskaya and George Shangrow. After three years, my appointment was extended and I was contracted as full-time artist in residence and head of the chamber music department."

She found teaching deeply satisfying and is still in touch with many of her former students. "As an artist, you are destined to teach that which you have learned—to give it away to nurture another generation. Every student is a challenge to motivate and to give them the feeling that they are making progress. In chamber music, they must learn the wonderful interaction between players. When you teach in a small liberal arts university instead of a big conservatory, you may not always work with the very greatest talents, but it is inspiring to get them to master the great pieces—Mozart and Britten, Beethoven and Borodin. I was there for thirty-one years, which is a very deep involvement. And I tried to get them involved in music for their whole lives. We combined the strictness of the conservatory with the other subjects for an all-around education."

In 1988, Cordelia began the annual Bach Cello Marathon, a tradition that continues to thrive at this writing. "Bach is the composer who is closest to me. In college, you learn a couple of the six suites, and then perhaps you never play them again. So I thought it was good to divide these great works among many cellists, with each taking a movement or two. I knew who the good players and exceptional performers were, and the excellent teachers who recommended students."

Every year it takes Cordelia several weeks of telephoning to coordinate the various players' availability and which movements they will play. Her colleague, the Seattle Symphony cellist Roberta

Hansen Downey, rents the venue, does the programs, and handles the donations. Since 1988, the Cello Marathon has featured more than three hundred different cellists, ranging from kindergarteners to senior citizens. The atmosphere is friendly and relaxed, but the players are serious and focused. Cordelia notes, "The cellists are always very happy to play there. There are so many players, so many interpretations! Everybody brings what they have learned from their teacher and their background. This event is a real community project with no sense of competition, just cooperation. The Bach Cello Marathon is a wonderful reward for a lifetime spent in music."

Thirty years after Rainer's death, his observations in the 1981 *Seattle Times* interview still ring true: "An orchestra is not a business. It is a losing business, a nonprofit one, designed for enrichment. There's always going to be something more important than music for sustaining life. But if you compare orchestras to hospitals, if you have to choose one or the other, you'll never have any culture. Libraries and music and galleries are a necessary part of life. We need to build on what we have here. Does the quality of the orchestra go up, or just across, in the next several years? Will we make more effort, or are we happy with what we are doing? Complacency is the worst thing for artists: We are not there yet."

Gerard Schwarz

THE CONSUMMATE MUSIC DIRECTOR

On the night of March 7, 1983, music lovers who filed into the Seattle Opera House to hear the hometown orchestra's subscription concert could not have guessed that they were present at a major milestone in Seattle music history. In a private side box in the house sat Rainer Miedel, the music director, who was to have conducted the evening's program but was mortally ill with the cancer that would kill him only nineteen days later. In the spotlight onstage was the venerable Ronald Phillips, who was soloing in Mozart's Clarinet Concerto as a public farewell to his fifty-three years in the orchestra. And on the podium was a newcomer: Gerard Schwarz, the bright young New Yorker who was already music director of so many orchestras and institutions that one wondered how he would find time for a guest conducting stint.

Probably not even Schwarz imagined that he would become Seattle's preeminent Man of Music for a longer span than any of his predecessors in that city had done. In 1983, he was extraordinarily busy elsewhere: heading New York's Mostly Mozart Festival, founding the New York Chamber Symphony (originally the Y Chamber Symphony), and conducting the Music Today series, as well as directing New Jersey's Waterloo Festival and, over on the "Left Coast," running the Los Angeles Chamber Orchestra. "He'll never stay," said the pundits and the naysayers. "We won't be able to keep him in Seattle."

Taking on the Seattle Symphony might have seemed a risky venture for any conductor, even one with time on his hands. The orchestra's finances were sufficiently perilous to draw civic action in 1986, the year when Schwarz was named music director, in the form of a mayoral panel that included several leading citizens, among them Mary Gates, the mother of the future Microsoft founder Bill Gates. "The Gateses drove out to New Jersey, where I was conducting at the Waterloo Festival, to talk about the panel and the issues facing the Seattle Symphony," Schwarz remembers. "There was a Chinese restaurant off Route 80 that stayed open late, and the four of us went there and had a long talk." The mayoral panel eventually outlined critical steps for the orchestra's economic recovery and stabilization, which ended up not only saving the orchestra's finances but also demonstrating its importance to community leaders.

Furthermore, to most culturally minded New Yorkers, Seattle was a distant frontier outpost, and its orchestra was all but unknown. There had been no East Coast tours, no nationally acclaimed recordings, and nothing to distinguish the Seattle Symphony from the average hometown orchestras that were mere dots on the map to those who frequented Carnegie Hall and Lincoln Center.

All that was about to change. What Schwarz ended up accomplishing—along with his players, his donors, a new musicians' union created in Seattle, and an increasingly involved community—amounted to a complete reinvention of the Seattle Symphony as a powerhouse recording orchestra dedicated to heretofore neglected Americana and the commissioning of major new works. This transformation happened at the same time that concerts continued to present the traditional repertoire beloved of Seattle subscribers: mainstream symphonic works and solo appearances of famous (or soon-to-be famous) guest performers. The excitement of the Seattle Symphony's transformation came both from Schwarz's blending the new and the time tested and from the orchestra's steady improvement.

"He cleaned up the sound and improved the ensemble," explained Janet Fisher Baunton. "He loved a good tone on any instrument, and he excelled at the complex rhythms of contemporary music. He was great at raising money. Everyone liked him; all the players came up to him at rehearsal to talk." Her husband, Randy Baunton, added: "He brought us up to record at a national level, and we were more interesting to auditioners. People were hearing us now."

When the Seattle Symphony moved into the brand-new Benaroya Hall in 1998, the concert calendar exploded in all directions. In addition to all the usual mainstays of orchestral classics and pops concerts—the latter conducted by the pops meister Marvin Hamlisch—there were now visiting orchestras, educational concerts, programs for tiny tots, experimental music, themed minifestivals, and, after the completion of the Watjen concert organ in 2000, organ recitals.

Despite the dire predictions, Schwarz did indeed stay in Seattle, where his career went from being guest conductor and then music advisor to twenty-six years as music director and a subsequent post as conductor laureate. His association with the Seattle Symphony, including his post-directorship conducting contract, extended over a thirty-one-year span, 1983–2014. During his tenure, the orchestra has risen in every measurable way: the number and excellence of the players and their financial compensation, the number of performances, the size of the budget, the national profile, and the more than 140 recordings, fourteen of which were nominated for Grammy Awards. Over the years, Schwarz has also served on the National Council on the Arts and accumulated a remarkable array of awards from such national organizations as ASCAP, the National Academy of Recording Arts and Sciences, and Musical America, which chose him as their first American "Conductor of the Year." Concurrently, he has been active on other continents as well, holding a music directorship of the Royal Liverpool Philharmonic Orchestra in England and an artistic advisorship to the Tokyo Philharmonic and Orchard Hall, as well as a long-running directorship of the Eastern Music Festival in North Carolina. At home in Seattle, he received the 2009 Seattle's First Citizen Award, and, in 2011, the city named one block of the street outside Benaroya Hall after him, honoring Schwarz's central role in the conception and completion of one of this country's finest symphonic halls.

Schwarz's most visible Seattle legacy remains Benaroya Hall. Would the hall have been built without Gerard Schwarz?

Possibly—but possibly not. The Seattle Symphony had been looking for a new home during the entire tenure of Schwarz's predecessor; Rainer Miedel investigated several existing halls for their potential suitability, most closely the Paramount Theatre, located less than a mile northeast of the eventual Benaroya location downtown. Schwarz, too, looked carefully at the existing theaters, particularly the 5th Avenue Theatre, which had acoustical possibilities but was too small. All of the halls under consideration had, in fact, had insurmountable limitations of space and design. But it had gradually become clear that the Seattle Opera House—home to the Seattle Symphony Orchestra, the Seattle Opera, and the Pacific Northwest Ballet—was overbooked and seriously cramping the opportunities of the three resident groups. By the early 1990s, the Opera House was booking 360 dates annually, and schedules for the orchestra (which also played for the opera and, until 1989, the ballet) had to be juggled with the daring of the Flying Karamazov Brothers.

After many years of studies and the Kreielsheimer Foundation's offer of a site across the street from the existing opera house (the foundation was then led by two successive trustees, Charles Osborn and Don Johnson), the new concert hall project began to take shape when the Seattle philanthropists Jack and Becky Bena-roya—close friends of Gerard Schwarz and his wife, Jody—gave a $15.8 million gift, at that time the largest of its kind in the region. (The gift, first discussed in a lunch between Schwarz and Benaroya in Seattle's posh Rainier Club, stipulated that $15 million be spent for the hall, but that an additional $800,000 should help secure the orchestra's financial survival.)

City leaders favored shifting the location of the project from the Seattle Center area to a downtown site about two miles away that was badly in need of revitalization. "Most great cities have a cul-tural heart that defines the city," Schwarz observed. "We all love the Seattle Center, but it is a little out of downtown and overly crowded. We couldn't have had ancillary issues like the recital hall. And the parking and traffic issues were difficult." With the assent of the Benaroyas, Schwarz, and Johnson, Benaroya Hall was built on a quasi-derelict downtown site at 200 University Street. The hall, which includes the 540-seat Illsley Ball Nordstrom Recital Hall, in addition to the 2,500-seat main stage, opened in 1998 to a nationwide chorus of approval.

Schwarz now sees the success of Benaroya Hall as the culmi-nation of a growing-up process that evolved over several decades. "The last fifty years in Seattle's classical music have been extraordi-nary," Schwarz reflected in a January 2, 2012, interview at the his-toric Queen Anne–district home he sold a few months later. "We had three components. First, there was a history and a foundation that we could build on; then, there was a period of tremendous artistic ascent. And then there was civic leadership—people like [the mayors] Norm Rice and Greg Nickels, and [the longtime sym-phony board activist] Robert Denny Watt, who not only got behind the orchestra but also realized that building a new concert hall downtown would revitalize the city with a vibrant cultural core. It is never easy raising the money for a new concert hall. But if you wait for the perfect time, nothing is ever going to happen. And we were absolutely determined to succeed."

Determination has been a part of Schwarz's life since early childhood. The son of two Viennese-born doctors who had relo-cated from Europe to Weehawken, New Jersey, he grew up with his two sisters in a family environment that prized learning so much that the parents piped foreign-language instruction into the children's bedrooms at night. In a 1986 interview for a *Seattle Times Pacific Magazine* feature, Dr. John Schwarz discussed what it was like to have a son like Gerard, who, at the age of eight, went to a music store, rented a trumpet, and began playing six or eight hours a day—"not always to my greatest joy," his father confessed. A few years later, the aspiring trumpeter announced to his parents his decision to quit Weehawken Junior High School and attend the New York High School of the Performing Arts, to be followed by New York's top-rated Juilliard School. "He didn't ask us what he should do; he told us what he was going to do," Dr. Schwarz said.

The young trumpeter was a man in a hurry; he was a wunderkind at Juilliard, then the New York Philharmonic's youngest-ever principal trumpet, whose recordings are still considered among the greatest. He perfected every detail of his playing, and he practiced by recording and then playing back every passage at half speed so that he could hear every nuance. When he resigned from the New York Philharmonic at the top of his game in 1977, it was because there were no more trumpet worlds to conquer.

This young man in a hurry also had two early marriages, the second of which gave him his two older children, Alysandra and Daniel. Then, in 1984, he married the flutist Jody Greitzer, daughter of the longtime New York Philharmonic principal violist Sol Greitzer. Gerard and Jody have two children, Gabriella and Julian.

After Schwarz left the New York Philharmonic and sold his trumpet collection, his conducting career took off like a Paganini cadenza, and the former chairman of New York's Lincoln Center, Martin Segal, predicted, "He is going to be one of the greatest conductors of this century." Soon Schwarz was profiled in magazines from *People* to *New York* and *Musical America*, adding conducting posts to his job résumé at a remarkable rate. He felt that he had found his métier at last: no longer confined to the minuscule repertoire of the trumpet, he had entered the vast precincts of the orchestral world—instead of "playing the Hummel Concerto for the rest of my life," as he once put it in an interview with me. The budding maestro found that he loved learning, rehearsing, and performing a new and more spacious world of music, and he found that he was highly adept at all the other responsibilities of a conductor—planning, socializing, immersing himself in the community, giving speeches, meeting the public (especially symphony audiences), courting donors, and even dealing with the press. Indeed, when it comes to the press, Schwarz is a virtuoso—a fluent, colorful interview subject; an honest, straightforward news source; and a keeper of promises. If he said he was going to return a call asking for a quote for a newspaper, he did so, even if it meant phoning from his seat on an airplane.

After he became the music director in Seattle, Schwarz brought in as concertmaster the Finnish-born violinist Ilkka Talvi, whose work he knew from the Los Angeles Chamber Orchestra. It was widely assumed that the new maestro had fired the previous concertmaster, Karl-Ove Mannberg, to make way for Talvi, as conductors often prefer to bring in their own "right hand" for the concertmaster role. But that's not the way it happened. "I offered Mannberg the job," Schwarz explained in 2012. "He was here about six weeks a year, but we needed him to spend the majority of his time in Seattle. His wife didn't like it here, and he wanted to return to Sweden, but I made it clear that we wanted him to stay on here."

Talvi's twenty-year tenure in the concertmaster's chair ended in a public fracas over the nonrenewal of his contract when it lapsed in 2004; he subsequently sued, and the issue went to arbitration. Talvi, who started a blog in which he excoriated Schwarz and the former associate concertmaster, Maria Larionoff (who had replaced him as concertmaster), soon faced legal action in his turn. It was a tumultuous time for the orchestra, and although Schwarz refrained from public comment about Talvi at the time, he has spoken up more recently, in our 2012 interview: "I loved Ilkka; he was a good friend of mine. At a point we all have to push the artistic envelope, though. I do always, and I expect everyone to do it, too. And sometimes that does not happen. It [Talvi's ouster] was a terrible change, and I was so sorry to have made the change, but artistically, it was the right thing to do for the orchestra."

Reflecting more broadly on the conductor's responsibility for making personnel decisions, Schwarz added, "I liked them all—all the players I have asked to leave over the years. They hate me. But I don't hate anyone, and I never will. I do what is best for the music; I always put the institution first. As an artist, you try to make a difference in the life of your community."

When Schwarz first arrived in Seattle, he wasn't thinking about how long he'd stay. "I had no idea I would have such a long tenure or make this kind of impact," he said in an interview on May 3, 2011. "I didn't really think about it. When you're young, you do what comes along, and I thought, 'Great, let's go to Seattle.' I never thought about what it meant to my career. I was not exactly into longevity. I was in the [New York] Philharmonic for four years, in the American Brass Quintet for over seven years, in Tokyo for a specific three-year appointment, in Los Angeles for seven years. And in Liverpool for five years; that was not the place of my greatest impact and significance. But I did not set out to stay in Seattle." And yet, he is very glad he did.

"What am I happiest about?" he pondered. "To be able to be here, and raise all four kids here; to lead a normal life—musicians rarely have that opportunity. To be able to make a home here with Jody. And to be able to make repertoire the way I do. I must have done fifty or sixty Beethoven Fifths, but every performance is meaningful."

No one can say that Schwarz made it easy on himself. Because he advocated twentieth- and twenty-first-century American music and was determined to give opportunities to today's composers, he conducted an extraordinary number of new and often unusual scores, a process that takes study and effort far beyond that required in reviving familiar masterpieces. In his final season as Seattle's music director (2010–11), Schwarz conducted thirty world premieres, eighteen of them in a record-breaking series of commissions to celebrate his tenure. Just looking at some of the scores— many of them thorny and orthographically unorthodox—makes it clear that it isn't easy to stretch into the unknown.

"Sure, a conductor could have a great time in a new city, spending five or six years just showing up and doing your repertoire, and then leaving," Schwarz observes. "But you can't make an artistic impact that way. Not in five years; not even in ten. The growth in the Seattle Symphony's audiences and the interaction with the community has flourished in the last five years. I always wanted to make a difference in the life of this community by inspiring the musicians and their listeners."

Schwarz has also inspired a resurgence of interest in Americana among many other orchestras who have rediscovered and recorded works by such twentieth-century symphonists as Walter Piston, Howard Hanson, David Diamond, William Schuman, and Alan Hovhaness. Happily for Diamond and Hovhaness, this recognition came while they were still alive to enjoy it. In the late 1980s, Diamond accompanied Schwarz to Moscow, where Schwarz conducted the composer's Symphony No. 4 to rapturous acclaim. The many Diamond recordings Schwarz made in Seattle also brought the composer new fans, much to his enjoyment. His ties to Seattle include his composition of the brief "Chimes" piece that summons concertgoers to their seats in Benaroya Hall. "I get so many letters, maybe ten to fifteen a month," Mr. Diamond said in a 2001 interview, "from people I've never heard of in all parts of the world—people who buy CDs of my music and want to tell me that it moved them. It fulfills my feeling of what I was put on Earth for."

In his twenty-six years as music director in Seattle, Schwarz amassed some imposing records: more than two thousand performances, rehearsals, and recording sessions; over 140 recordings, fourteen of which earned Grammy nominations; two Emmy Awards; multiple tours to Southern California and New York's Carnegie Hall; and well over a hundred world premieres. He also earned a network of devoted supporters among public figures, politicians, captains of industry, city fathers, and donors; many of them—Jack and Becky Benaroya, Sam and Gladys Rubinstein, and Sam and Althea Stroum, among others—became close personal friends. Not even the most cold-hearted cynic could see the Schwarzes with these supporters and imagine that the bonds connecting them were merely financial; clearly, they had become integral parts of one another's families.

Another fortunate connection of Schwarz's has been with the Seattleites Dale and Leslie Chihuly. Dale, a celebrated glass artist, designed spectacular glass sets for a 2007 Seattle Symphony production of Bartók's opera *Bluebeard's Castle*. In this performance, Bluebeard's wife "opens" a succession of forbidden doors, with the vista behind each door slowly revealed as the respective installation rotated to display huge multicolored glass elements depicting Bluebeard's riches, for example, or his armory. Audible gasps arose from the audience as each door was opened in turn. Leslie Chihuly went on to play an important role for the orchestra, serving as board chairman—no easy task, particularly in the wake of the 2008 recession. She has brought considerable savvy and energy to the orchestra and its board of directors.

Over time, there were complaints from musicians and community members who thought Schwarz had stayed too long on the Seattle podium. It is perhaps understandable that he was not eager to leave: no conductor in his right mind would want to step down from a position that offered the acoustical riches and performance possibilities of the brand-new Benaroya Hall. "I'm here to bring the orchestra to a level they wouldn't reach otherwise," Schwarz said ten months before Benaroya Hall's opening in 1998. "It doesn't matter if the players like me. Conducting can't be a popularity contest; you have to make tough decisions. I'll stay here as long as I continue to lead and inspire the orchestra, and as long as I'm making an artistic contribution. The moment that ceases, I will leave."

By 1998, some cracks in the cordiality between the musicians and the maestro had formed, some of these dating back to 1995, when Schwarz insisted on hiring John Cerminaro—one of this country's greatest French horn players—as principal horn over the wishes of the musicians' audition committee. "John's a good friend of mine; we've known each other since childhood," Schwarz said in a 2011 interview. "But I've never done anything in terms of friendship. Whatever I've done has been musically motivated. Yes, the appointment was controversial, but it was crucial to the growth of this institution."

The Cerminaro appointment came at a cost for Schwarz, however. When a committee of orchestra musicians deemed Cerminaro to be unqualified for the position of principal horn, in what one commentator deemed "an expression of rebellion" against him, Schwarz turned to the board of trustees. This was just before the opening of Benaroya Hall in 1998. The board thereupon made its ratification of a three-year musicians' contract contingent on Cerminaro's appointment as principal horn. Schwarz got the artistic outcome that he wanted, but there was resentment among some musicians over both the methods he used to get it and the result.

By 2003, Schwarz was facing criticism from a contingent of the players over his own five-year contract renewal. A new focal point of opposition was Schwarz's decision not to renew the contract of the concertmaster, Ilkka Talvi. In 2006, when the symphony board voted to extend the conductor's contract by three more years (to end in 2011, not 2008), further unpleasantness erupted in the orchestra, and there were press reports of orchestra players' having committed vandalism and other reprisals against Schwarz loyalists.

One of these reports, an overwhelmingly negative *New York Times* story by Daniel J. Wakin and James R. Oestreich, which focused primarily on players who had grievances against the conductor, ignited controversy on a national level. The writers devoted several paragraphs to a court case brought by a first-violin section member who claimed discrimination against him on the basis of his disability, a severe anxiety disorder. (The charges were dismissed shortly after the *New York Times* article appeared.)

Over time, all conductors amass grievances and complaints, particularly from musicians who have been demoted or fired, and the longer a conductor stays, the greater the number of potential opponents. When a conductor makes hard choices, musicians' egos are wounded. Further, a symphony orchestra is something of a captive workplace for all but the most gifted and ambitious players; they can audition elsewhere and move, as many in the orchestra's rank and file often cannot. A span of a quarter century under a maestro you don't like can be a very long stretch.

In retrospect, tensions in the orchestra might have been ameliorated if the management had decided to appoint a principal guest conductor to provide additional perspectives of both leadership and music making. In fact, the symphony's management later did just that, appointing the Danish conductor Thomas Dausgaard as principal guest conductor in 2013, two years after the arrival of Schwarz's successor, Ludovic Morlot. Meanwhile, during the period when SSO players' opposition to Schwarz's contract renewals was escalating, the conductor's career outside of Seattle was also suffering some reverses: his tenure of more than twenty years as music director (and later music advisor) of New York's Mostly Mozart Festival had come to an end in 2001, when the festival changed directions, and in 2004 Schwarz announced his decision to step down from his Royal Liverpool Philharmonic post at the end of that contract, in 2006.

According to the respected British critic and author Norman Lebrecht, Schwarz's Liverpool departure wasn't because of the conductor's inadequacies. "Schwarz recruited new section leaders, offending long-embedded incumbents. The concertmaster, Malcolm Stewart, who twin-jobs at the orchestra in Toulouse, quit in a huff. When Schwarz refreshed the programming, players grumbled at having to play strange new pieces." The Liverpool musicians were unused to playing repeat concerts, which is standard procedure in the United States, where it's rare for a subscription program to be performed only once. They therefore voted not to renew Schwarz's contract, according to an April 16, 2004, report in the Liverpool press. The same report also indicated that the orchestra had at one time voted against hiring Sir Simon Rattle, who went on to Birmingham and then to the podium of the Berlin Philharmonic Orchestra. Even as Schwarz was on the way out in Liverpool, however, the local press there credited him with having stabilized the orchestra's previously debt-ridden finances, and in early 2005 the reviewer Joe Riley rated Schwarz's concert "10—Electrifying" in the *Liverpool Echo*.

There were also several coups in Schwarz's career during this period of escalating opposition in Seattle: In January 2004, he was nominated by then-president George W. Bush to serve on the National Council on the Arts, the advisory body of the National Endowment for the Arts, and that same year Schwarz led the Seattle Symphony on a tour of the northeastern United States in celebration of the orchestra's centennial. The tour included the orchestra's debut in Carnegie Hall, where the reviews ranged from respectful to enthusiastic. The *New York Times* reviewed the Carnegie concert only in its online edition—which many considered to be a slap at Schwarz and the orchestra—but the review by Jeremy Eichler was generally favorable, referring to the orchestra's sound at Carnegie Hall as "full and rich," and stating that "the musicians play for Mr. Schwarz with palpable commitment. . . . The Strauss had generous volume and theatrical sweep, with these qualities only occasionally coming at the expense of balance and textural clarity. Everything clicked for the impressive encore, a movement of Busoni's Suite from *Turandot*." In the London *Financial Times*, the Pulitzer Prize winner Martin Bernheimer, who is known as a tough critic, called the Seattle Symphony a "splendid ensemble," referring to its "sonic brilliance" and playing that was "vital, virtuosic and almost taut."

Schwarz's decision to stay in Seattle attracted much critical attention over the years. After the heady era of the 1980s, when such critics as Harold C. Schonberg of the *New York Times* wrote the equivalent of "The sky's the limit for this young conductor," the tone in the New York press gradually changed when it became clear that Schwarz was doing most of his conducting in Seattle. In 1999, a thought-provoking article in the *New York Times* by Allan Kozinn suggested that Schwarz's career may have stalled "below the highest rung" because he was based in Seattle, that is, below the "Big Five" orchestras of New York, Philadelphia, Boston, Cleveland, and Chicago.

"You look at someone like me, and when Cleveland, say, is looking for a music director, I'm not there," Schwarz told Kozinn. "I've never conducted there. They've never seen me. And in New York, which is the most important city in the world for most people, most concertgoers have never seen me conduct a Brahms, Mahler, or Bruckner symphony. I do those things in Seattle. In New York, I conduct chamber orchestras, and the fact is, important conductors have always emerged from large orchestras, not from chamber orchestras."

As Kozinn observed of Schwarz, "Few conductors have devoted themselves to 20th-century American music with his methodical devotion, and those who have—among them, Michael Tilson Thomas, Leonard Slatkin, David Zinman and Dennis Russell Davies—also seem to have hit a glass ceiling that keeps them from

Big Five directorships." In conclusion, Kozinn quoted an observation on Schwarz's work in Seattle by the New York Chamber Symphony founder and longtime Schwarz watcher Omus Hirshbein: "He has taken that orchestra from one level to another. That's the success a music director should have in a community. Maybe the community should have been Boston. But it was Seattle. And so what?"

So what, indeed. If Schwarz has unfulfilled ambitions, it's not his style to bemoan them. He has spent his life looking forward, not backward. And the third phase of his musical career—after first his trumpet career and then the Seattle Symphony directorship—is one that he finds fulfilling. Chief among Schwarz's post-Seattle achievements has been the creation of the All-Star Orchestra, a specially assembled group of top American professionals that performs and records great pieces of the repertoire for a series of musical programs that are broadcast nationally on public television; the concerts are also available as downloads and in DVD and CD format, as well as being freely available to educational institutions. Built around eight programs annually, the All-Star project lined up a publishing house, a recording company, and several television stations (the first was WNET TV, New York City's channel 13). This kind of project appeals to corporations, research firms, media, and music lovers of all kinds. The TV series won the 2013 ASCAP Deems Taylor Television Broadcast Award, and the first episode won two 2014 Emmy Awards, for "special event coverage" and "Audio: Post Production."

"The first violin section is entirely composed of concertmasters from our country's major orchestras," Schwarz says of the All-Star. "I have to deal with some egos!" But not much daunts Schwarz when he is on the trail of a project that's important to him." Those who know me well see me as optimistic—I rarely take no for an answer or listen to people who tell me something is impossible," he told a *New Music Box* interviewer on May 31, 2011. "If I have a dream—like building a new concert hall or commissioning eighteen composers in one season, or founding an All-Star Orchestra to bring classical music to a broader audience—I simply keep at it until I make it happen."

The initial, euphoric success of the first All-Star Orchestra in 2012, with music making that Schwarz said "exceeded my wildest dreams," also heralded Schwarz's first favorable New York review in a long time. A respectful 2012 *New York Times* article by Daniel Wakin about the project and its first recording sessions was followed a few days later by a modest reassessment on the part of the *New York Times* critic Anthony Tommasini. Previously Tommasini had often slammed Schwarz's work at the Mostly Mozart Festival, as when in 2004 he described the conductor as "just wrong for the job"; Tommasini now wrote, "Mr. Schwarz brought good intentions and tireless energy to the [Mostly Mozart Festival] job. His work was solid, and he instituted more innovations than he is given credit for."

In addition to the expanding All-Star project, Schwarz has continued his commitment to education as music director of the summertime Eastern Music Festival in North Carolina, where both professional and student orchestras produce work and recordings of genuine excellence. He has found, however, that one of the greatest rewards of the third phase of his career has been the freedom to compose music. After concluding his Seattle music directorship, Schwarz took some time away from the podium. For thirty years, he had been "conducting almost every week and loving it, and never taking a break—until now." The post–Seattle Symphony years find him relocated to New York City, where he and his wife have an apartment and are near to their two youngest children. The process of setting down the baton and picking up the pencil has resulted in the composition of new works, as well as the freedom to go to concerts, operas, and museums and on outings with friends. "I get up in the morning and think, 'Gee, I'd like to listen to [Beethoven's] Opus 131,' and I do it, and then I write. It is great to have the freedom to do this."

What is the Schwarz legacy in Seattle?

"We're now the place where people want to be," says Mariel Bailey. "We have the concert hall that one visiting Boston Symphony musician said he'd like to 'take back to Boston.'" Her husband, Bruce Bailey, who has seen four Seattle Symphony maestros come—and three of them go—adds, "He got us noticed; he brought us into a new age. Because of him, the orchestra is now a finely tuned instrument. The initial reaction to virtually any new conductor will be euphoria. The euphoria will last until the next turn of the wheel. Things are greatly exaggerated in both directions."

The former principal flutist Scott Goff, whose Seattle Symphony tenure lasted from 1969 to 2011, calls Schwarz "one of the great conductors of the world, possibly of all time. Time will tell: Gerard Schwarz's tenure will be viewed as a golden age in the history of the arts in Seattle."

Ludovic Morlot

THE SYMPHONIC INNOVATOR

It's a lovely July morning in 2012, the day after Ludovic Morlot led the Seattle Symphony Orchestra in a spectacular multimedia performance of Holst's *The Planets*. Benaroya Hall is a beehive of activity, because auditions for two orchestral cello chairs—including that of assistant principal—are going on, and backstage is buzzing with nervous-looking cellists of all ages and nationalities.

Inside the music director's suite, Morlot looks relaxed, in spite of all the demands on his time. Blond, short, and personally engaging, with a smile that reaches his blue eyes, the conductor produces torrents of heavily accented but speedy English—honed in his early student days at London's Royal Academy of Music and Royal College of Music. The London years were followed by several more Anglophone years with the Boston Symphony Orchestra (2001–7), first as one of the Seiji Ozawa Fellows at the Tanglewood Music Center, and then as assistant conductor under the Boston music director James Levine.

In Seattle, Morlot was just finishing his first (2011–12) season as music director. The season had been filled with Morlot's musical and organizational innovations, despite his frequent absences from the city; among other places, Morlot was often in Brussels, where through 2014 he held a concurrent post as chief conductor of La Monnaie, and in California, where he took over from an ailing Levine during a Boston Symphony tour. In Seattle, the Lyon-born maestro has turned his considerable talents toward building new, younger audiences; he has inspired a Family Connections program, which allows up to two kids aged eight to eighteen to attend symphony concerts for free with the purchase of an adult ticket. With his wife, Ghizlane, a landscape designer and translator, Morlot also joined forces with a foundation to donate up to 150 tickets to each Discover Music family concert, which go to underserved children and families.

Morlot's history indicates why he understands so well the importance of early music education. "My grandparents were amateur musicians," Morlot explains, "and my grandfather, who was a prisoner during the war [World War II], picked up the violin during that time. As a kid, I spent a lot of time with my two grandfathers, on vacation or traveling around Europe, and they communicated their passion for music. I actually lived with one of my grandfathers from the age of twelve. He would take me to the opera, or play some music and make me guess who was the composer. This was where I started to comprehend that I should be practicing the violin more if I wanted to be serious about it."

Morlot describes his ability level then as "an okay violinist," but early on he realized that his technical limitations on that instrument were going to be a barrier to his hopes for a career in music. "Early on I realized I did not have the right journey from age six to eighteen to actually be happy with the instrument. I was always frustrated that I didn't have the right technique—even though I knew that I wanted my life to be in music. I still wanted to tell those stories!"

During his teens, Morlot left France to study violin in Montreal, and during this time he went to summer camp in Maine at the Pierre Monteux School. Because he loved chamber music, he thought that "orchestra or chamber music might be my way" into a musical career. He went to further his knowledge of orchestral repertoire.

Then Morlot was asked a fateful question: Why don't you try conducting? "I gave it a shot. I conducted Bartók's *Hungarian Sketches*, a piece that has become very dear to me. I did what I could do. Very quickly you realize that beating 1–2–3–4 is completely useless. Conducting is not about 1–2–3–4. It is about psychology and feeling completely lonely and becoming the enemy of the people. I wasn't too keen at first. But then the Hungarian conductor Charles Bruck [1911–1995], who had been an assistant of Monteux, was teaching there, and he pushed me a little bit. 'Why don't you come back next year as a conducting student?' I owe him a lot. Before he died, I visited him in his house. He told me that he felt really guilty because he really pushed me into that direction."

"It is not about glamour, being friends with the whole world; it is the opposite of that," Bruck told Morlot. "People will hate you for telling them what to do and for killing their creative side." Morlot adds, "Bruck made me aware of what the job was really about."

Undaunted by Bruck's frankness, Morlot went on to London to study conducting, and there he met Seiji Ozawa, who invited him to Tanglewood, where he became cover conductor for the Boston Symphony. At Tanglewood, Morlot also met another important mentor, David Robertson, who saw him conduct as a student. Coincidentally, Robertson was also music director in Morlot's home city of Lyon, France. "So that's how I started a wonderful relationship there," says Morlot of Robertson, who subsequently invited the younger conductor to become resident conductor of the Orchestre Nationale de Lyon. "I had three great years in Lyon; that's where my first daughter [Nora] was born." (The Morlots' second daughter, Iman, was born after his return to Boston, so they have "a little American in the family," as he puts it.)

Robertson also introduced the young conductor to Pierre Boulez ("and to the whole world, really," as Morlot puts it), and this meeting led to Morlot's debut with the elite Ensemble Intercontemporain and his acquaintance with a great deal of contemporary repertoire. It was Robertson, too, who gave Morlot advice he has never forgotten. As a guest conductor, Robertson explained, it's easy to get frustrated when an orchestra is not giving you what you want. "Long ago," Robertson told him, "I decided never to get frustrated, but to take what I have before me and take it to the next level, rather than complaining about the level where it is. How do we bring it from A to B?" Morlot has always remembered that advice and the kind of positive energy that it can generate from the podium. It is, he says, "a motto that I use a lot."

The results have certainly borne out the wisdom of this approach. Wherever Morlot has appeared as a guest conductor, the reviews have been almost universally favorable. The *Guardian* said of his 2009 debut at the BBC Philharmonic, "Every so often in the musical world, a comparatively unknown quantity comes along and takes everyone's breath away." Possibly the closest Morlot has come to a lukewarm review was the *Chicago Tribune*'s critic John von Rhein's May 7, 2010, summary of his four seasons as guest conductor at the Chicago Symphony: "not great, but admirable."

Morlot, however, does not expect uniform praise. "I don't like the critic who says it's all beautiful," he declares. "Ultimately we know that's not true, that things can always improve. A constructive review is what we all want as human beings, to make that next step possible." Despite the occasional frustrations, Morlot believes that one of the positive aspects of the guest conductor role is that it's easy to be loved. You don't have to work on the orchestra's long-term problems; you can concentrate on the program at hand, make it as good as possible, and then wave good-bye. Fixing the long-term problems is the challenge facing the music director.

And at this writing, Morlot now has had two such directorships. Any unease in Seattle at his appointment as chief conductor of Brussels' La Monnaie/De Munt Opera House (before he had even conducted his first opening night in his American post) has been largely laid to rest because he has made Seattle his family's home and considers it his major post. The bio on Morlot's website, www.ludovicmorlot.com, introduces him as "Music Director of the Seattle Symphony"; only the former second paragraph added "Ludovic Morlot is also the Chief Conductor of La Monnaie." (Morlot resigned the Brussels post in December 2014, citing differences with the orchestra.)

Morlot originally saw those dual roles in Seattle and Brussels as "a great balance." The Brussels job occupied him for about fifteen weeks a year, and his family came along. Family is very important to Morlot, who married Ghizlane about ten years before his arrival on the Seattle podium. The couple's early years involved a lot of travel and acclimating to different cities, even different countries, a process that Morlot believes can greatly strengthen a relationship.

His student years in London are a time he remembers with particular warmth because of the city's cultural riches: "Along with Berlin and Munich, it is the most musical city in Europe. I always felt like Paris was more a visual city, one that loves opera, of course, and cinema and theater and photography, but not as much of a great passion for music as London has. All those orchestras!"

Compared to London, Lyon, Boston, and other cities where Morlot has spent a great deal of time, Seattle must at first have seemed like a frontier outpost. What drew him to the Pacific Northwest? "The fact that it is out of the way made it more appealing," Morlot explains. "When you are at this time of your journey as a musician, you want to explore and take risks, and play in the way that makes your next experiment stronger and more valuable. Seattle has an amazing appeal geographically—not that you want to fail anywhere, but this is a city that is screaming for experimenting and taking risks and being bold. This was more attractive to me than landing at a Big Five orchestra." Morlot was also drawn to Seattle, which he called "tremendously under-acknowledged," because it played both symphonic and opera repertoire. The orchestra's home, Benaroya Hall, Morlot found "mind-blowing," a place where the orchestra has room to grow and change.

Given that the first thing Morlot wants to change is access and attraction to new audiences, particularly the young, the programming he feels will be most successful in drawing new audiences is exactly the programming that conventional wisdom deems "surefire audience repellent": contemporary music. "For the younger generations that have had no chance to have a musical education or instruction, they might be able to relate to contemporary music better than any other," Morlot explains. "The memories of music are connected to movie industry, or television, or advertising—things that have nothing to do with the music itself. So if you decide that advertising for chocolate or coffee should have the music of Pierre Boulez as a sound track, I can bet you that in ten years people will find that music completely comfortable. When you hear the last movement of Bartók's Concerto for Orchestra, you hear car horns and traffic noises he heard from the hospital on the thirtieth floor in New York."

Younger audiences, Morlot believes, enjoy the freedom of "getting out of the harmonic tradition. We love Beethoven so much today because we have been given a chance to hear it for two hundred years and we have a tremendous memory about it; it has become bread and butter. A lot of today's music will be bread and butter in two hundred years."

Does he really think young audiences will be drawn to, for example, serialist scores? Serialism, Morlot believes, is "just an interlude, in the way that major and minor triads have been. We use a combination of all those things to find what is a voice now. [Henri] Dutilleux uses all that and creates something beautiful out of it. I think you enjoy the food you like best when you experiment a little outside of it."

Morlot is irritated when he hears that people don't go to a concert because they don't know the music. He asks rhetorically, "Would you go to only three restaurants in your life? We want to serve that food they love because we love it too, but we also want something new and different." Because it is essential to educate audiences to bring them into the concert hall, Morlot's motto in Seattle—"Listen Boldly"—is meant to embolden potential listeners to take a chance on the unfamiliar. "My message is saying: We don't really mind that you think you don't like Beethoven and Schumann and Mozart, but why shouldn't you experience the emotion of a live concert? Hear your first Mozart with an orchestra!" The annual Day of Music, which at the start of each season invites the public into Benaroya Hall for free music of almost every variety, brought in about twenty kids to hear hip-hop music in the hall's lobby during Morlot's first September in Seattle.

"They stayed for the classical music, too, and came backstage afterward and said, 'Maybe we won't write the same music anymore.' I think it's true of everything in life. If you only read the book you know you will like, what kind of a challenge is that? I like to be spontaneous. I think there is a place for everything, including experimenting with concert dress for the orchestra. I don't want to kill the tux thing, because I myself enjoy the tux once in a while. But that's not the only way. I'm not arguing that another way is terrible, I'm just saying there's not just one way. History has taught us that." Morlot's innovative Symphony Untuxed series features shorter, intermission-less concerts with the orchestra in dark but informal attire. His Untitled series lets audiences experience contemporary repertoire like Schoenberg's famously thorny *Pierrot lunaire* in the hall's lobby, with the freedom to walk around the ensemble, sit on the floor or on a chair, "or hide somewhere," as Morlot adds with a grin. The orchestra's Sonic Evolution series raised eyebrows around the world and drew millions of YouTube viewers in 2014, when the rapper Sir Mix-a-Lot joined the musicians for a reprise of his 1992 hit "Baby Got Back."

Another of Morlot's nontraditional views is his acceptance of audience applause between movements of symphonic works. "I don't mind it," he explains. "What I really mind is the talking and the coughing during the music. I am a guy who also loves theater, and when you are in the opera of course the applause happens during the performance, so why not in the theater. I don't want to kill applause if it is spontaneous. If I hear applause between movements of a symphony, I think there are people who are new to music in the house, which is good. Tradition has some beauty, but it also can be dangerous."

Not surprisingly, Morlot doesn't want to stagnate in Seattle. Ask him how long he's planning to stay in a town where conductors have had long relationships (consider his predecessor, Gerard Schwarz), and he doesn't have a fixed answer. "I think too short a tenure is ridiculous," he explains. "To make an impact on an organization as a leader, you at least need those six, eight, ten years to happen. Beyond ten years it can become a very special relationship, like the one Zubin [Mehta] has in Israel when he becomes conductor for life. Every situation has its own dynamic. It can't be counted in years. It takes incredible humility and guts for any person in the world to become objective about when you are not the best leader for the organization anymore. If you are able to question all those things, you should be able to question your own journey, your own path and ability. I hope I will be able to feel when it's time for me . . . when I'm no longer serving the organization the best. It's not the number of years. Every case is different. You're not being a leader to be popular. If you do that, you're not going to change a thing. The minute you want to change things, you become unpopular with many people."

Morlot's first seasons in Seattle made it clear that he was far from unpopular. He and Ghizlane have ramped up the chic factor outside Benaroya Hall, too, with fund-raising social events like the June 2012 Club Ludo event at the Chihuly Boathouse in Seattle, the workshop of the glass wizard Dale Chihuly, whose wife Leslie was chairman of the board of the Seattle Symphony. There they partied with Mike McCready (Pearl Jam), the singer-songwriter Brandi Carlisle, and the alt-country performer Star Anna, raising a hundred thousand dollars for the orchestra's education and community programs. Earlier that season, the Morlots bought a $1.4 million historic eight-bedroom house in an elegant Capitol Hill neighborhood between the Seattle Asian Art Museum in Volunteer Park and the Washington Park Arboretum. In every way, they were settling in.

But Morlot wanted his audiences to know him better—specifically, to understand his reactions to the music and his reasons for programming certain pieces. With that in mind, he took to the microphone several times during his inaugural season in Seattle, breaking with the tradition that the maestro does not offer his thoughts on a formal subscription program. Doing so also represented a break with Morlot's own earlier thinking.

I grew up thinking that talking onstage is totally unnecessary, and sometimes was something many people don't want to happen onstage. But I also came to experience a concert when a few thoughts were expressed from the stage in a very spontaneous way. Now, when you are going to tell a story musically, sometimes you want to "write a preface" that changes the mind-set of the story. I think that's what those little talks should be about.

I remember saying before the Varèse *Amériques* [performed at the start of the 2011–12 Seattle Symphony season] that I wanted to make the connection with that work and Stravinsky's *Le sacre du printemps*, but I also wanted to say: if you don't like the next thirty minutes of music, it's OK—but please don't tell me it did nothing to you! At least, if you don't like it, hate it with passion!

Then it puts the audience in the frame of mind to really just give the piece a chance, because it's OK if I don't like it. As long as it is not condescending, I think there's nothing wrong to share those few words from the stage. There's not one single piece of music I'm going to conduct here that I don't believe in 200 percent. Never would I apologize for it. I'm going to tell [the audience] a story that I believe in. Maybe I have some tools so you understand why I like it so much. Some music requires no introduction whatsoever.

For Morlot, it is important to be spontaneous and open to change, not only in deciding when or if to talk to the audience but even in occasionally feeling free to change the order of pieces on the program. And because he is French, after all, Morlot likens this process to the creation of a dinner menu—putting a sorbet between courses or changing their order so that what comes next can be appreciated in a new way.

Morlot is also interested in composing and orchestrating, but he can't devote much time to that at this point in his career. "Composing is full time, something you cannot do lightly. At the moment in my schedule it's out of the question. I think it's great to compose in the later stage of your life, you can really embrace the whole scope of the music you have heard."

Always open to new works, Morlot scored a coup with the commission of John Luther Adams's *Become Ocean*, a lengthy neominimalist work that went on to win a Pulitzer Prize and was the centerpiece of a widely praised Seattle Symphony visit to Carnegie Hall in 2014. Reviews in the New York press of the performance (and the subsequent Grammy-winning recording) ranged from admiring to rapturous.

Many European conductors are dismayed when they take on directorships at American orchestras and find themselves expected to embrace a huge schedule of extramusical duties, most of them aimed at fund-raising. Morlot finds these tasks "difficult, but at the same time exciting. In Europe you can count on that state subsidy every year, but you know you're never going to exceed it. The beauty of the system here is you can not only exceed it, you can double it, you can triple it.

"The conductor is more the face of the organization here. Yes, it is challenging because it is time consuming, and our greatest focus always should be studying and resting. Your work is interrupted by the off-podium duties, but these duties also give you the chance to do the projects you dream of, which might be impossible in Europe. As an artist I find fund-raising difficult, but when you are successful it opens many possibilities, and you also meet tremendous people, which is so rewarding on a personal level. The fund-raising can also build incredible friendships."

Morlot feels he is still at the beginning of "a tremendous journey that I can accomplish for myself in terms of growth with the Seattle Symphony." He isn't thinking about the span of his directorship in Seattle, nor is he ambitious for career advancement with bigger-profile orchestras.

Wouldn't he be tempted by an offer from, say, one of America's Big Five orchestras? They include the symphonies of Philadelphia, Boston, Cleveland, Chicago, and New York, followed fairly closely these days by Los Angeles and San Francisco. "Of course you have the aspiration to have the best instrument in front of you," he says of his career. "But I don't think about the Big Five orchestras. I have the good fortune to work with them now [as guest conductor]. If in twenty years an orchestra that I adore is approaching me, of course I will be thinking about what I can do with them. But my focus is tonight's performance. And next week is already a different chapter in my life."

Peter Erős

THE OLD-SCHOOL MAESTRO

Seattle audiences are accustomed to thinking of the conductors of the two "majors," the Seattle Symphony Orchestra and the Seattle Opera, as the city's most important orchestral figures. But for twenty-two years, over at the University of Washington, a conductor with credentials as fine as any of the downtown maestros led a future generation of musicians by giving them the benefit of his experience at the Royal Concertgebouw Orchestra, the Berlin

Radio Symphony Orchestra, the Bayreuth and Salzburg Festivals, and orchestras from Australia and South Africa to Denmark and San Diego.

Peter Erős, the Hungarian-born maestro in question, turned down an invitation to preside over Yale University's conducting programs during the third of his twenty-two years as conducting professor at the University of Washington (1989–2011). Blunt, outspoken, frequently outrageous, and usually hilarious, Erős was the kind of professor students did not soon forget, and the kind of conductor who made orchestra players pull up their tuxedo socks and play their best.

The diminutive maestro with the piercing blue eyes always kept a photo of two of his most admired political figures—Dame Margaret Thatcher and Ronald Reagan, walking side by side—on his refrigerator; that gives you an idea of his ideological leanings. On the piano was a battered score of Mussorgsky's *Boris Godunov*, to which Erős had returned for further study. "After fifty-six years of conducting, I have learned to make my own sound with an orchestra, but I can't tell you exactly how I do this!" said the master raconteur in an interview in his north Seattle home, two years before his death in 2014. "I don't 'play the maestro,' and I don't do anything artificial; it's not in me. I just concentrate on the music, on the orchestras that are playing it, and [on] the students who are learning it. I've gotten every job I ever wanted, and turned down the ones I didn't want. And really, I have been incredibly lucky."

That Erős could say this, after his early experiences, is testament to his great resilience. Born in Budapest in 1932, he was raised as a Protestant by Jewish-born parents who had changed their religion in 1925. "I had a pretty comfortable life from zero to twelve," says the conductor, whose mother had been a child prodigy violinist. Agnes Rozgonyi owned a Stradivarius, was a pupil of the legendary Leopold Auer, and had toured the world before the age of twelve. At twenty-four, she married Peter Erős's father, an architect and viola player, and temporarily retired from the concert world.

Young Peter inherited her talent, learning to play the piano by ear until he was given lessons at the age of five. By ten, he was studying in a conservatory with other gifted young kids. "Then the Germans came. I suddenly went from being a young Calvinist Protestant boy to being a Jewish kid. I had no idea about my Jewish background; I didn't even know what it meant to be Jewish. But I was in for the biggest shock of my young life."

When the Nazis unearthed their origins, the Erős family hid in a cellar, where there was no water, no food, no heat. Peter likens their life in hiding to that of Anne Frank, but he is matter of fact about these privations: "We suffered. So did hundreds of thousands of others." Erős's father went out of the cellar one day, to smoke a cigarette, and never came back. The family never found out what happened to him. "There was nothing unusual about people disappearing," explains Erős. "Sometimes you would recognize people lying on the pavement, frozen and dead, in the winter months. More than six hundred thousand Hungarian Jews were transported to Auschwitz. That was what our world was like. From the age of eleven to thirteen, there was nothing else but the war and the cellar and the hunger and the cold."

Erős survived; so did his mother and sister. Then the Russians came to Hungary. For the Erős family, who were labeled as Jews, the Russians were liberators; for the nation as a whole, it was the opposite—"the collapse," as Erős puts it. Another difficult period followed, when the war was over but there was still nothing to eat. "It took about a year to come back to a normal childhood," he explains. "There were no windows, no doors; everything was broken, and people were basically going around to find food wherever they could."

These experiences had another outcome for Erős: after 1946 he never again entered a place of worship, unless he had to conduct a concert there. Once he told his countryman Janos Starker, the famous cellist, that he was the only person ever to sneak down to the cellar of the hallowed Mormon Tabernacle—he was there to conduct Mendelssohn's oratorio *Elijah*—to smoke a cigarette. Starker, an inveterate smoker whose wartime experiences as a young Hungarian Jew were similar to Erős's, said, "Uh-uh. The second!" He had done the same.

By the time he was about fourteen or fifteen, young Erős resumed his musical education at the Franz Liszt Academy of

Music, studying at first composition and piano, then adding the conducting class with László Somogyi and studying for four years with the famous composer and teacher Zoltán Kodály. "He made an incredible mark on me," Erős says of Kodály. "His teaching was nothing! He was cross-eyed, bearded, with a tiny little voice, and he was a bad teacher. But I felt an incredible atmosphere around him. He had a big red pencil, and he would take your composition and draw a big circle on it. 'What's wrong?' I would ask. And he would say, 'If you don't know, you don't belong here!'"

Finally, a nervous Erős turned in his last composition, his greatest effort, and handed it to Kodály. The young student stood— "Nobody ever sat down in his presence!"—while the master looked it over, holding his red pencil. At last, Kodály handed the composition back to his pupil, muttering, "I have written this already."

In 1956, the Russians came again to Hungary. Erős, in common with many young people, decided it was time to leave. "I was not communist, and not anti-communist. I was a conductor. But there was a fever in my generation: everyone was going. I was twenty-three, and my girlfriend, Györgyi [later his wife], was nineteen; I told her, 'We should leave.' I said good-bye to my mother, and we left for the Austrian border, some of the time crawling on our stomachs because we knew there would be guards with their flashlights to stop those who were escaping. More than once, Russians would ask us where we were going. Finally we saw one last guard with a flashlight, but he was smiling—I couldn't believe it. He said, 'Willkommen in Österreich' (welcome to Austria). We were there."

But the couple's problems were only beginning. They were two of about two hundred thousand Hungarian escapees who poured into Austria. After hitchhiking to Vienna, Erős sent a telegram to his sister, who had moved to Sydney: "Please send money." And she did, enough to allow the couple to buy a few necessities.

They hoped to immigrate to America, but after waiting for days in the long line that surrounded the American consulate in Vienna, they were told that they would have to stand in line for two more days. They went to the Dutch consulate instead, because only a few people were waiting. There they encountered a tough question: Was there anyone in the Netherlands who could guarantee that they wouldn't be a burden on the state?

As it happened, there was. Peter's aunt Lily, the sister of his father, had moved to Holland during World War I, before Peter was born. He had never met her. She was "very Dutch," as Peter remembers. To his astonishment, she exclaimed, "Little Peter! I saw you when you were a year old. What is your profession?"

"I'm a conductor," he responded.

"Oh God," groaned Auntie Lily. "A waiter would have been better." Nonetheless, she vouched for her nephew and his girlfriend, provided the latter promptly became his wife—which she did. Despite her despair over his profession, Auntie Lily provided a crucial connection that helped launch Erős's musical career in Holland. She was acquainted with a priest who held a post with a radio station, and he interviewed the young conductor.

"How is your piano playing?" he asked Erős.

"It's absolutely great," was the response.

To test Erős's accompanying skills, the priest called in a soprano, one Mme. Perugia, and put three Fauré songs on the piano. Luckily, Erős was a good sight reader. He now had a job as an accompanist. He and his wife were living with a family with thirteen young children—"We were the fourteenth and fifteenth," he says—and Erős gave the family whatever money he earned.

An opportunity arose: a chance to be an assistant to a conductor up north in Groningen. "He was a real schnook," says Erős of that maestro, "but he took me on as his assistant. I got to bring him his coffee. Then one day he got sick, and they couldn't find a real conductor to replace him." The program included Schubert's lovely "Der Hirt auf den Felsen" (The Shepherd on the Rock) and the mighty Brahms Second Symphony, neither of which, of course, Erős had ever conducted. "So now I was a success in a city nobody knew about," he says. "But I started getting small jobs."

Then came his opportunity: Erős was invited to Berlin to work with the noted Hungarian conductor Ferenc Fricsay, who needed a Hungarian-speaking assistant. Erős tells a remarkable story of how that association developed. "Fricsay said, 'Be on the stairs of a certain church at a certain time; I will be in a white Mercedes with red seats.' The Mercedes arrived. Fricsay announced, 'Now I need to see you conduct. Do you know the Bartók Third Piano Concerto? Good! Geza Anda [a well-known and much-recorded pianist] will now play the Bartók Third. And do you know the Bartók Second?— Not as well? Geza Anda will now play the Bartók Second.'"

"You are undoubtedly very talented," Fricsay finally concluded.

"I know," Erős responded.

Then Fricsay asked him to conduct the Tchaikovsky Sixth Symphony. Erős did his best, reveling in the sound of the orchestra. "There was a little telephone [at the podium]," Erős remembers, "and in one point the phone rang and Fricsay demanded: 'Machen Sie das ein bißchen schneller' (Take it a little faster). But I told him: 'I can't get out of my own skin.' I knew this was life or death for me as a conductor, but I just could not do something I knew was unmusical." There was a pause. Then Fricsay said: "Sie sind angestellt." (You are hired.)

Later, Fricsay told Erős, "I never met a young person with as much chutzpah as you." Maybe it took chutzpah, but Erős's career was now in the ascendant. He was only twenty-seven when he was named associate conductor of Amsterdam's Royal Concertgebouw Orchestra, a post he held for five years. He assisted Otto Klemperer in opera productions for the Holland Festival; served as a coach and assisted Hans Knappertsbusch at the Bayreuth Festival; and, in 1961, rejoined Fricsay as assistant conductor for the Salzburg Festival production of Mozart's *Idomeneo*. He continued to assist Fricsay both in Salzburg and in Berlin with the RIAS Symphony Orchestra and Deutsche Grammophon through 1964. The following year, when Erős was twenty-eight, brought his US debut, at the invitation of George Szell of the Cleveland Orchestra, with whom he worked as a Kulas Foundation Fellow.

Over the years, Erős made several recordings, some of them at the request of Richard Wagner's granddaughter Friedelind, who asked him to conduct the Aalborg Symphony Orchestra in two discs of symphonic works by Siegfried Wagner, the son of Richard Wagner and father of Friedelind. Another disc, made with the San Diego Symphony, was the first recording of the Gabriel Wayditch opera *Jesus Before Herod*.

You could say that Erős got around. He was music director and conductor of the Malmö Symphony Orchestra in Sweden 1966–69; the Australian Broadcasting Commission Orchestras in Sydney and Melbourne 1967–69 and in Perth 1975–79; the San Diego Symphony and La Jolla Chamber Orchestra 1971–80; and the Aalborg Symphony Orchestra 1982–89. Some of the appointments came by sheerest chance. When Erős was guest conducting in Mexico City, a friend told him that there was an opening for a music directorship in Santiago. Turns out the friend had misheard: it was not Santiago, but San Diego, and since Erős had a week to kill before his prepaid air ticket back to Europe, he drove to San Diego and met with the San Diego Symphony board ("They were sitting around asking me the most stupid questions!"). His interest in the position heightened when he was told about the salary ("I almost died, it was so much!") and looked around the beautiful seacoast and environs of San Diego. Then came a guest engagement there with Van Cliburn. "We played the Grieg Concerto," Erős remembers, "and afterward he told the board I was the greatest genius in the world and they should hire me immediately. I later asked him how come he said that, and he said, 'Well, you didn't lose me. Everyone else loses me.'"

Erős's sense of humor in rehearsals was such a hit with the San Diego musicians that they published a pamphlet of his witty and colorful remarks from the podium in his inimitable accent. (One of this writer's favorites: unhappy with the percussion section during a rehearsal of Ives's *Decoration Day*, Erős inquired: "Can anyone hear the bells? I can't! I think I am getting the No Bell Prize.") On another occasion, disgusted with tentative playing, he exclaimed, "That sounds like Alberich's widow! I vant SIEGFRIED!"

In addition to Erős's music directorships, he had guest conducting engagements on five continents, with the Chicago Symphony Orchestra, Cleveland Orchestra, National Symphony Orchestra, Seattle Symphony Orchestra, San Francisco Symphony, Israel Philharmonic Orchestra, Royal Philharmonic Orchestra, Hamburg Philharmonic Orchestra, Stockholm Philharmonic Orchestra, Royal Swedish Opera in Stockholm, Hamburg State Opera, Hague Residentie Orchestra, and Scottish National Orchestra.

Not surprisingly, Erős finally began to tire of life on the road, despite all the musical rewards. He decided he had "had it with sitting in an airplane, looking out the window." At the University of Washington, he was happy. He treated his orchestral and conducting students with respect. "I refuse to see young people differently or treat them differently," he told the *Seattle Times* in 1998. "I call them 'ladies and gentlemen.'" (When Erős said it, it sounded more like "lazen genlmen.") In many respects, Erős found students to be more appreciative than more jaded professionals, and more rewarding to conduct: "I believe we musicians are artists, and not military generals. I always make a few jokes to loosen them up a little. They've worked so hard to master the music, and now in the performance they should forget all their troubles and their earthly miseries. Now is the time to become part of the music and enjoy it. This is their opportunity to shine."

Almost everyone wants to be liked, but for Erős, it was not necessary to have the adulation of fans. "I have an incredibly thick skin," he confessed. "Somewhere along the line I developed a total lack of interest in what the people in the [professional] orchestras thought of me. I never took it personally. I always said exactly what I think. I still do! Szell once came to see me at the Concertgebouw in 1960 and asked, 'How is your situation here?' And I told him, 'The orchestra likes me.' He responded, 'What do you need that for? Doesn't your wife like you? The orchestra doesn't have to like you!'"

But somehow they always did, whether it was Europe's top players or a group of earnest university musicians. Even when Erős was at his bluntest and most politically incorrect, musicians responded to his authenticity, authority, and crazy sense of humor. "His classes were wonderful," remembers his student Jonathan Pasternack, who succeeded Erős at the University of Washington post.

> He is hyper-smart, hyper-brilliant. I learned how to be a musician from him. His classes were electrifying. Peter was a conductor in the vein of musicians like Janos Starker and Arthur Rubinstein: pure intelligence and musicality, with a minimum of physical effort and a maximum of expression.

At the UW, he stripped away all the pretenses to get to the core of the music with real, practical, technical instruction—cajoling, demonstrating, joking, yelling. He taught us the character of the music, the rhythm, and the line, the way he had learned it from the conducting of the great masters: Ferenc Fricsay, Pierre Monteux, Otto Klemperer. In his conducting classes, you could feel the electricity around him when he was conducting, because of his great concentration. Peter got to the core of the individual student conductors' weaknesses and the clichés we had picked up. He was incredibly generous with his time. What a fantastic musician, and a great man!

Vilem Sokol

THE PATRON SAINT OF THE PODIUM

If Seattle can be said to have a patron saint of music, that role would surely fall to the late Vilem Sokol. And as I write this sentence, I can almost imagine Sokol reading it over my shoulder, shaking his head, and exclaiming, "Bargreenova!" (He was occasionally fond of rendering names as if they were in Russian.) "You're exaggerating!"

But it's no exaggeration. Larger than life, riveting to watch, and inspiring to hear, this great-hearted man of faith—in God, and in Mahler and Beethoven, too—introduced many thousands of young players and listeners to the joys of the symphony orchestra. Vilem ("Bill") Sokol wore many hats: concert violist, orchestra conductor, teacher, University of Washington professor (1948–85), popularizer of great music, and, above all, role model for the youngsters who wanted to make him proud of them. And they did, too: students who swarmed to his Seattle Youth Symphony Orchestra (SYSO) and Marrowstone Music Festival (originally Pacific Northwest Music Camp), which he conducted as music director from 1960 to 1988, ended up playing in major orchestras in cities all over the world, from Seattle to Paris, Berlin, Milan, Cleveland, Vancouver, Hong Kong, Boston, San Francisco, and Los Angeles.

Sokol's University of Washington colleague Robin McCabe called him "a true pied piper of music," as indeed he was, drawing youngsters of all ages from throughout the region to experience great music firsthand. It would be hard to imagine a better role model than this devout father of ten, who practiced his viola, swam, and did calisthenics almost every day and went to church every Sunday. Thursdays were his day to pick up bread, fruit, and vegetables at local supermarkets to deliver to the needy. He was never too busy to counsel the many youngsters who dropped by the Sokols' big nine-bedroom house in Seattle's Capitol Hill neighborhood, in quest of advice or some family fellowship—or one of Agatha Sokol's home-cooked dinners.

How revered was Vilem Sokol? In 1997, when he returned to the Seattle Youth Symphony podium for the first time since his departure in 1988, his former orchestra players came from as far afield as New York and Hawaii to reunite for a massed fund-raising concert under his baton. And his friends and admirers packed Seattle's Saint James Cathedral for his 2011 funeral mass, which included orchestras, choirs, soloists—and even a cameo "appearance" by Sokol himself: at the end of the service, mourners were startled to hear the maestro's voice, recorded earlier by the sound engineer Al Swanson, a former student and close friend, greeting the attendees and inviting them to listen to his swan song. It was a performance of "Danny Boy," recorded at a 2003 reunion concert of Sokol's former students and admirers. There were very few dry eyes in the cathedral when that recording drew to its close.

Over the years, Sokol received a gratifying and never-ending stream of letters, photos, cards, cartoons, wedding and birth announcements, and concert notices. His students never forgot him. Even in the last few years before his death in 2011 at the age of ninety-six, he still looked so much like the "Mr. Sokol" of the old days—thick, wavy hair, craggy profile, penetrating blue eyes—that he couldn't go anywhere in the Seattle area without having someone come forward with some delighted query like "Mr. Sokol! Do you remember me? Second violin section, 1966 and 1967?"

Amazingly, he really did remember them. Fabled for his memory during the Youth Symphony days, when he always learned the name of every player in a huge orchestra that changed every year, Sokol retained a remarkable recall of names and faces. He even remembered where they went on to college and whom they married (and several of them wed other members of the Youth Symphony).

His formidable memory may have been the result of good genes, but Sokol built on his natural abilities by the continued exercise of his mind, even into his nineties. He reread the plays of Shakespeare, studied musical scores, and read the latest biographies of great composers like Brahms and Liszt. He listened with pleasure to new recordings, went to concerts, and typed lengthy letters to his correspondents. No cobwebs were allowed to form in that busy brain.

Sokol's energetic approach to life was rooted in the earliest days of his boyhood in western Pennsylvania, where his parents emigrated from Moravia (which became the eastern part of the Czech Republic in the 1993 breakup of Czechoslovakia). He worked alongside his father, a bricklayer turned contractor, and helped haul building materials from the railroad boxcar to the 1926 Model T that he learned to drive as an eleven-year-old. By that point, however, young Sokol already knew that he wanted to be a violinist when he grew up. A Fritz Kreisler recital in Pittsburgh, when Sokol was ten, inspired him to ask for his own violin, which was purchased from a door-to-door salesman.

A major turning point in the youngster's life came on the day his parents happened to read in a Bohemian newspaper that the noted violinist and teacher Otakar Ševčík was coming to this country to teach in Boston. "It was in the height of the Depression. Dad had been building homes, and his business was decimated. He said to me, 'Bill, this is the most important decision you will ever make. Do you want to make music your career? It will be a sacrifice for the family if Ševčík accepts you. It will mean you have committed yourself to be a musician.'"

The younger Sokol said yes. In Ševčík, who proved a demanding teacher, he found an important role model. His teacher commanded him to learn music from the inside out, and he set the high standard that Sokol later followed with his own students: "I'm very tough on them, but they know why. I tell my students, 'Do you know why I want you to play so well? Because I love you.'"

After winning a statewide competition for Pennsylvania high school violinists as a senior, Sokol advanced to the Oberlin Conservatory, where his horizons expanded: he learned to play the viola, which he was later to prefer to the violin, and he had his first experiences as a conductor. Sokol was awarded a fellowship grant at the Juilliard School of Music. In 1938, he won a fellowship to earn a master's degree at the Prague State Conservatory of Music. This was an enticing prospect, since Prague was not far from the Sokol family's origins in nearby Moravia, and the young musician already spoke Czech.

But the Nazis were already on the march. Sokol was there when German troops overran Czechoslovakia, while people wept in the streets. "It was March of 1939," Sokol remembered in 1995. "The Czech police were pleading with people to stay back, away from the tanks, telling them it was no use. They wanted to attack the tanks with their bare hands." Later, Sokol discovered that two of his Czech uncles were killed by the Nazis for helping Jews escape the country.

Back in the United States, Sokol was listening to a radio broadcast of the New York Philharmonic when the music was interrupted by a somber announcement: Pearl Harbor had been bombed. Not long thereafter, Sokol joined the Army Air Forces. In Biloxi, Mississippi, he met another recruit, a pretty violinist named Agatha Hoeschele, who was playing next to him in the jazz band as they performed "Dance of the Spanish Onion." Sokol joked, "It was love at first downbeat."

The two were married in 1945. After teaching in Georgia, Kentucky, and Missouri, Vilem Sokol came to the University of Washington in 1948, and the couple made their home in Seattle. Busy years ensued, particularly when the children started to arrive. Each played at least one instrument: Mark (violin), Damian (cello and piano), Anne (violin, viola, and piano), Paula (violin), Angela (cello), Rebecca (violin), Claire (cello), Mary (violin), Jenny (violin), and John (piano). Somehow Sokol also found time to play principal viola in the Seattle Symphony from 1959 to 1963 (including solo performances in Berlioz's *Harold in Italy*). At the university, he taught and coached instrumental performance and conducting, and his classes for nonmajors on the significance and beauty of great music were regularly cited as inspiring.

And no wonder: even in his eighties, Sokol confessed that he still got "a chill up and down my spine" whenever he heard the Brahms Fourth Symphony, and that he found Mahler's music "an unbelievable thrill." Mahler was the center of some of Sokol's peak experiences with the Seattle Youth Symphony, especially Mahler's great, unfinished Tenth Symphony. In London, Sokol met Deryck Cooke, the English scholar who created a performing version of Mahler's Tenth. At his untimely death at the age of fifty, Mahler had left behind seventy-two pages of the full score, fifty pages of a continuous "short score" draft (two pages of which are missing), and forty-four additional pages of preliminary drafts, sketches, and inserts. Over the years, several composers had attempted to complete or expand the unfinished work, some producing partial two- or three-movement versions that were ultimately unsuccessful. But Cooke persevered, and with the help of other composers, and after gaining access to the full set of Mahler's previously unpublished manuscript sketches in 1964, he produced a successful performing version of the Tenth. Sokol, who particularly loved Mahler's symphonies, met with Cooke in London 1972 and 1975, and the two quickly became friends.

Few in the music community could believe that a mere youth orchestra could undertake the challenge of performing the Tenth, which makes tremendous demands on all forces, particularly the brass section and the wind soloists. And yet, Sokol and his SYSO did the Mahler Tenth thrice: first in 1972, then in 1975, and finally in 1983, to great acclaim and with many of the orchestra players—and also their conductor—moved to tears by the end of the performances. Just as Sokol was to go onstage to conduct the 1975 performance, the New York recording engineer Jerry Bruck handed Sokol a baton that Mahler had used—a great honor, and also a dilemma, because the baton was dark colored, and the young musicians were accustomed to Sokol's white baton. What to do? In anguish, Sokol turned down the offered baton, thinking that the baton would not show up enough against the background of the darkened hall behind the podium. "I politely refused, but now that I think back on it, I wish I had taken the baton," he wrote in a February 22, 1975, letter to Cooke. "I was torn. It was such a beautiful gesture on his part. But just to have held Mahler's baton made me tremble."

When Cooke heard a recording of the 1972 performance, he wrote to Sokol, "The performance was such a magnificent one—no one could tell that it wasn't a professional orchestra playing, and the sense of commitment and enthusiasm had to be heard to be believed. And all this without the chance of a re-take—just a straight performance! . . . I must confess that when you first wrote to me, and offered to send me a recording, I expected more enthusiasm than skill, but in the event, I was absolutely overwhelmed by the presence of both in full measure. Heartiest congratulations on a wonderful performance."

Others concurred. The eminent composer George Rochberg, who also heard a recording of the 1972 Tenth, expressed his enthusiasm in a December 22, 1973, letter to Sokol: "To say that your orchestra is incredible is the understatement of the decade (at least!!)! I could hardly believe my ears. I had to keep reminding myself that these were young people, not older than 21 . . . I must say you have achieved something fantastic. The whole experience was rich, exciting, deeply musical. You must be a magician!" Rochberg later composed his Symphony No. 4 for Sokol and the Seattle Youth Symphony.

The recordings continued to resonate throughout the music world. In 1978, the Gustav Mahler Society's Mahlerthon featured Sokol's recording of the Tenth as the finale to performances of the other nine symphonies by Rafael Kubelik and the Bavarian Radio Symphony; Claudio Abbado and the Chicago Symphony; Leonard Bernstein and the New York Philharmonic; Maurice Abravanel and the Utah Symphony; Bernard Haitink and the Royal Concertgebouw Orchestra; George Szell and the Cleveland Orchestra; Georg Solti and the Chicago Symphony; and Carlo Maria Giulini and the Chicago Symphony. Herbert von Karajan and the Berlin Philharmonic performed *Das Lied von der Erde*. Not bad company for a youth orchestra.

William Malloch, then the director of the Gustav Mahler Society, offered a detailed critique of Sokol's conducting in the Tenth:

"Everywhere there was evidence of your own free and independent thinking yet nothing was capricious. It was a very viscerally exciting performance, full of subjective appeal, yet everything was utterly musically intelligent and well proportioned. There is nothing really more exciting than coming across an intelligence naturally placed."

Sokol's intelligence was supplemented by a sense of humor that just never quit. Despite his sense of strict and rigorous discipline, Sokol never could resist a joke, and he told them frequently at rehearsals and when with friends. Most of the jokes, of course, had a musical turn, such as one that was posted in a church bulletin: "Tonight's Sermon: 'What is Hell?' Come early and listen to our choir practice." Sokol also couldn't resist telling stories about famous conductors and funny musical gaffes. And he rewarded his players' rare moments of inattention or insufficiency with pronouncements of agony: "Do you know where I am right now? I am suffering!—in purgatory!"

The maestro was also a noted innovator. He was one of the earliest American proponents of the Suzuki method of violin instruction in the United States, as he proudly explained in his privately published memoirs. During a 1965 visit to Seattle, Shinichi Suzuki had dinner with the Sokol family at their Capitol Hill home. Sokol later remembered that "the plates had barely been cleared when Dr. Suzuki announced it was time for music lessons." Sokol, an enthusiastic photographer, shot photo after photo while Dr. Suzuki demonstrated his innovative instruction techniques with Sokol's daughters. The Sokols had the highest admiration for Suzuki's methods, which achieve remarkable results with even very young players.

Similarly innovative was Sokol's approach to programming: his Youth Symphony players mastered adventurous new scores, in addition to famous classics. Over the years, the SYSO received national awards for its performances of contemporary music. Sokol was particularly devoted to bringing to light works by the Seattle-based composers Alan Hovhaness, William Bergsma, John Verrall, and George Fredrick McKay, and he was an enthusiastic proponent of the African American composer William Grant Still.

The years following Sokol's departure from the SYSO in 1988, following a difference of opinion with the board of directors, had their share of difficulties. He didn't like the way the organization was run under his first successor, but he maintained a dignified silence out of concern for the well-being of the students and the organization—always his foremost priority. He was disappointed when the organization moved its summer camp, the Marrowstone Music Festival, away from the secluded historic site at Fort Flagler State Park on Marrowstone Island to Fort Worden (in 1990) and eventually to Western Washington University (in 2001). But he remained positive about the young musicians and their potential, a subject that delighted him.

In later life, both Sokol and his wife, Agatha, were given loving, attentive, and tactful care by their daughter Jenny, a violinist and writer. Jenny was at Sokol's side when he dictated, in his last days, letters of appreciation to cherished friends whom he no longer had the strength to receive or phone. How typical of Bill that even in the last days of his life his thoughts were directed toward others in gratitude for their friendship.

Stephen Stubbs

THE EARLY-MUSIC INNOVATOR

Do I go, or do I stay?

This is the question that often presents itself when a young person of exceptional musical talent considers the future. Do you leave the area where you grew up, where you are already known and connected, and seek to expand your horizons in music by studying and working with experts in major cultural centers elsewhere? Or do you stay in your own niche, seeking to expand it and capitalize on your successes at home?

Two very talented Seattle youths of about the same age, Stephen Stubbs and George Shangrow, confronted those questions in different ways during their formative years. Both were confident, gregarious, highly articulate, and gifted in similar ways: as excellent keyboard players, experimental composers, and impassioned advocates of great historical works; they were also both good at creating their own musical organizations and highly adept at conducting.

Growing up in Seattle with similar skill sets, Stubbs and Shangrow became friends—and jockeyed for supremacy—during their student years in music. As Stubbs puts it today, "We were the best of rivals." But though their friendship remained, their paths diverged; it was Shangrow who later urged Stubbs to leave his flourishing career on the Continent and return to Seattle in 2003.

Gifted in a multitude of musical directions, Stephen Stubbs has been an important figure in Seattle both in the early and late phases of his career, with a thirty-year hiatus in between. Few would have been able to predict that the talented young lute player who left Seattle in the mid-1970s would return three decades later to conduct the Seattle Symphony and stage critically acclaimed baroque opera productions with his own company, Pacific MusicWorks.

Stubbs's decision to leave Seattle didn't stem from any belief that his hometown was a backwater, as he explained in a 2012 interview. After early studies on piano and guitar, he had started at the University of Washington in 1969, where he found "some formidable piano teachers, Béla Siki, and my teacher Randolph Hokanson, and Ken Benshoof. Ken was really my mentor, for both composition and piano; I had started studying with him before I came to the university. But I immediately saw the possibility of learning more about early music with [the harpsichordist] Silvia Kind. George [Shangrow] and I plunged into Silvia's world of the harpsichord." Stubbs was already singing with Shangrow's group, the Seattle Chamber Singers, when he and Shangrow and another gifted friend, Roupen Shakarian, entered the UW and discovered faculty members such as the cellist Eva Heinitz and the composers Bill Smith and Gerald Kechley, as well as what Stubbs calls "the incredible brew going on downstairs at the ethnomusicology department."

"We young and thirsty students had fallen into a really interesting place," Stubbs remembers. "I never thought, 'Too bad I didn't get to go to Juilliard,' because things were so great here. Seattle tends to think of itself as second tier, but there were a lot of first-rate people there, and a lot of exciting things happening. Silvia organized her two- and three- and four-harpsichord events, and we all played in those."

Stubbs was immersed in a happy musical milieu that included everything from studying obscure sixteenth-century works to writing tunes for his rock-and-roll band, Dancing Bare. The band included Stubbs on guitar and bass, Allen Sanders on keyboard, and Steve Adamek on drums, and among their high points was a 1972 Ashland, Oregon, gig in which they opened for, and backed up, the legendary Chuck Berry. "Allen was the one who had the large background of jazz, blues, and pop music and was my educator on that front," Stubbs remembers. He learned a lot about Bach and Handel from Shangrow, who had been steeped in those masters from an early age. Another important influence was the harpsichordist Randall Jay McCarty, whose untimely death in 1989 is still lamented in Seattle musical circles. "Randy set some things in motion that are still very much in evidence here, such as the little virginal [an early keyboard instrument] that he put together, which is still at Cornish, and an important harpsichord at Pacific Lutheran University, where he initiated so much early music. He was really a visionary and would be playing a very active role in musical Seattle now if he were still with us."

When he entered the university, Stubbs considered himself primarily a keyboardist, but he gradually became more and more interested in the lute: "I had always had a romantic idea about the lute because I encountered the music of John Dowland and others at Nathan Hale High School, where we had a little madrigal group and sang Dowland madrigals. It seemed like a very short step for me to turn attention from guitar songs by McCartney to lute songs by Dowland." Stubbs was among many composers at the UW who were looking for a compositional way forward, past serialism (a compositional technique that builds a work out of a given series of notes, usually atonally), which seemed like a dead end. He found many new currents interesting, including minimalism, which was espoused by such composers as Philip Glass and Terry Riley, and the infiltration of pop techniques into classical music, at which Stubbs's mentor Ken Benshoof was highly adept. "I remember reading something by Pierre Boulez where he claimed that 'Anything being written today which is not completely based on serial techniques was irrelevant and useless. And I thought, 'No, *you're* irrelevant and useless.'"

Maybe it was in reaction to serialism that Stubbs and his peers turned toward the rich and tuneful repertoire of Bach and his sixteenth- and seventeenth-century predecessors. Early music was for both Stubbs and Shangrow "the most creative thing going." Another important development in Seattle's burgeoning early-music community came in 1974, when the violinist Stanley Ritchie and the harpsichordist Elisabeth Wright began performing together as Duo Geminiani. "When formidable artists of various kinds from the strictly modern point of view made the crossover and did fine work in the baroque repertoire," Stubbs observes, "it made a huge difference."

How did Stubbs's early keyboard training relate to his work as a lutenist? "To my mind, the keyboards and the lute are the same thing: the supplying of texture and harmony to a musical event. Whether I was in a rock band or a baroque band, I was the texture, rhythm, and structure giver, so I don't see a real dichotomy between playing the keyboard and playing the guitar or lute. It's like you grow up speaking several different languages but they don't compete with each other," he explains.

During his college years, Stubbs took some time off from the University of Washington to go to Holland and England for lute studies, returning to Seattle to graduate in 1976. There he joined his like-minded friends John Gibbs, Jerry Kohl, and McCarty to found the Early Music Guild (EMG). Stubbs was EMG's second president. The new EMG had two foci: the importation of top international artists like the keyboardist Gustav Leonhardt and the Kuijkens, a famous Dutch family of early-music specialists, and the presentation of local artists performing period repertoire. That mission continues today; the EMG has an impressive roster of local and imported concert activity, and it nurtures a number of important individual and ensemble performers.

Despite the establishment of the EMG, however, it was clear to Stubbs that he needed to return to Europe for more performance opportunities; there simply wasn't enough work for him in Seattle.

So back he went, establishing a career that took him in many new directions. Right from the start, serendipity accompanied Stubbs on his quest. On his first trip to England, he struck up a conversation with a woman on a train, who told him, "You should meet the family I work for." The family turned out to include Hephzibah Menuhin, the famous violin virtuoso's sister, who sized up Stubbs by inquiring, "Well, young man, what are you here for? What do you want?"

Stubbs wanted an introduction to Julian Bream, at the time the most famous of all the lute players. Menuhin didn't know Bream, but she did know the eminent harpsichordist George Malcolm, and she promptly phoned him: "George, I have this young man here from America, and he plays the harpsichord and the lute, and what do you want to do with him?" And George Malcolm replied, "Well, I'll have him along to the Athenaeum Club for tea."

So within weeks of landing in London, Stubbs was sitting in the posh Athenaeum Club having his first French cigarette and his first Italian espresso, and then accompanying Malcolm to several record stores to buy records of Malcolm and Bream playing the Bach trio sonatas. Malcolm also set Stubbs up for his first lute lesson with Robert Spencer, who became his lute teacher. "It was just serendipity," Stubbs marvels now. "But when you are young and have a burning passion for something, things do happen."

He was still in his early twenties, and he cobbled together an income any way he could. After touring at London schools with a small group of players, he was hired by a Montessori school as a music teacher. From there, he moved on to Amsterdam for further lute studies with Toyohiko Satoh, and soon he became a mainstay of the burgeoning early-music movement there. He then worked on Italian opera in Italy with Alan Curtis and French opera in France with William Christie, after which he collaborated with the Hilliard Ensemble in England. "Everybody's going to have a little bit of the truth, and I went panning for gold with everybody," says Stubbs of his mentors. "If I had it to do over again, I would do basically the same thing."

For Stubbs, 1987 was a big year, marking not only his first outing as an opera director (presenting Stefano Landi's *La morte d'Orfeo* at the Bruges Festival) but also the founding of his highly regarded and much recorded ensemble Tragicomedia. In 1997, he began as artistic codirector (with fellow lutenist Paul O'Dette) of the biannual Boston Early Music Festival Opera; his recordings with the BEMF have earned three Grammy nominations and a Grammy Award for conducting in 2015. Stubbs's conducting and solo lute discography now extends to more than a hundred recordings.

And yet . . . there was the lure of home. When Stubbs came back to Seattle with the baroque harpist Maxine Eilander on his arm for their 2003 wedding, he was mulling over his options. "I talked to George [Shangrow] and asked him, should I come back? Can I find a way to make a living in Seattle?" Shangrow immediately answered: "Just do it! Just come!"

Because Stubbs could take a three-year hiatus from his post in Bremen, Germany, where he was professor at the University of the Arts, he decided to move back to Seattle and soon discovered that "I was in here for the long haul. I had jumped into the wild blue yonder to come back here—but it was the blue yonder that I knew." He returned to Seattle to found first a summer early-music workshop, the Accademia d'Amore, and then his production company, Pacific MusicWorks, which was to be devoted primarily to the presentation of vocal music and chamber operas of the seventeenth and eighteenth centuries. The arrival in Seattle of the early-dance specialist and choreographer Anna Mansbridge has been a boon to the company; Stubbs says he is "always on the lookout for people who might want to move here and be part of the landscape. You need critical mass—in talent, support, opportunities, infrastructure—and donors."

An early and important connection upon Stubbs's return to Seattle was made with Nancy Zylstra, an internationally known specialist in historically informed vocal instruction and techniques, who invited Stubbs to dinner with James Savage, the director of music at Seattle's Saint James Cathedral, one of the city's major presenters of music. Stubbs came to the cathedral to hear Savage conduct the Mozart Requiem: "I was blown away by the architectural amplification there, and I immediately thought how wonderful Monteverdi's Vespers would sound in that space!"

In addition to his ongoing commitments to Seattle's University of Washington and Cornish College of the Arts, Pacific Music-Works, and the Boston Early Music Festival, Stubbs continues to guest conduct productions in Spain and at the Netherlands Opera in Amsterdam. Stubbs's successful guest conducting collaborations with the Seattle Symphony began in 2011 and have led to remarkable productions, including a landmark 2014 *Saint John Passion*. In 2013 Stubbs was appointed senior artist in residence at his old alma mater, the University of Washington, to lead a groundbreaking 2014 coproduction with the UW and Stubbs's company Pacific MusicWorks of Handel's opera *Semele*.

"I think we need to rethink some of what we are doing in higher education, where we have established a parallel between how you study to become a nuclear physicist and how you study music," Stubbs says. "An academic degree is not an apprenticeship; it is a research function. It's a tragic dead end for many people to get into a doctoral singing program." At the University of Washington, he brings in Pacific MusicWorks professionals to infiltrate the orchestra with some of the best Seattle-area players, sitting side by side with students, to create an instantly professionalized orchestra and provide a great teaching experience. The only way to have young professionals emerge from a college program, Stubbs believes, is to have them work next to professionals in a true mentoring situation. "I want to do professional opera at the UW, and the UW brings to the table an infrastructure for doing opera and a great performance space," says Stubbs of the university's 1,200-seat Meany Theater.

Thomas Wolfe's famous title *You Can't Go Home Again* is clearly not true in Stubbs's case: he has come full circle, with a hometown return that capitalizes on all the strengths of his boyhood and the fruits of three decades of experience in Europe. "I feel that all my experience has combined to lead me to this point," he says. "And it's a point where I'm really glad to be."

George Shangrow

In the photo, the seventeen-year-old pianist is seated at his instrument, one hand on the keys, gazing out at the newspaper readers with a sweet smile. It's George Shangrow, then a high school senior and already an experienced performer, composer, and conductor.

In the *Seattle Times* article that includes this photo, Don Duncan describes the young George Shangrow as a genius who "you'd swear must be at least 50. The speech patterns, the maturity, the wry wit just don't fit a teenager," Duncan notes, and he predicts a future that might include a doctorate in conducting or composition and a future in church choir directing and composition. Much of that transpired over the course of Shangrow's too short life, which ended in 2010 in a tragic accident when he was fifty-nine.

But the 1969 interviewer's final comment was particularly prescient: "We will be hearing more about George Shangrow in the years ahead." And indeed we did. This gifted musician, already at the age of seventeen rooted in several musical disciplines, made the crucial decision early on to grow where he was planted. During the early 1970s, he debated whether to go to Los Angeles and study with the distinguished British conductor Neville Marriner, founder of the much-recorded Academy of Saint Martin in the Fields and at that time the music director of the Los Angeles Chamber Orchestra. In the end, George decided against and chose instead to forge his way on his own.

Was it the right decision? Did Shangrow, who founded several important musical ensembles here and was for years a beloved fixture at KING FM, bypass a chance at fame and fortune as a nationally prominent conductor? His friend Stephen Stubbs, who did leave Seattle to work in Europe and earned an international reputation as a lutenist and conductor, took a look backward at their earlier thoughts on this issue: "I miss George very much. Right from the beginning, we really spurred each other on; we were best friends and best rivals. Our trajectories were very different. George and I definitely challenged each other in every way, over music, over girls, everything. The competition ran high. I remember very clearly George and I issued each other a real challenge, because we both felt we were the 'young lions' in Seattle: 'Go out there and see if you amount to much in the real world, or stay here and be a big fish in a small pond.' We made a solemn pact that whoever stayed here should be heartily laughed at by the one who went out into the real world. But though I did go out in the real world, I didn't feel at all like laughing or denigrating George's life because he had done a wonderful thing. I believe that George was an inspired musician. I believe that from start to finish."

One of Shangrow's closest lifelong friends, Dennis Van Zandt, first met him in the seventh grade, when George—always a prankster—voted for Clem Kadiddlehopper as the homeroom's student council representative. The two bonded over Mozart's famous C-Major Piano Sonata K. 454 and spent most of their youth exploring music together. Van Zandt also feels that Shangrow made the right choice to stay in Seattle. "To be frank, I was never quite sure that George had the 'format' for a bigger career," Van Zandt explains. "He did things his own way. He didn't finish his degree at the UW, despite many super experiences with important mentors like Silvia Kind and Gerald Kechley. He was impatient to get on with it. But I think he might have been skeptical of having to prove himself worthy in a more conventional setting with the big pros. And the role of apprentice or underling just doesn't seem to fit George. He appreciated that part of his success in Seattle, such as it was, was based on the fact that people knew him and knew what to expect from his groups. Also, a lot of his popularity was due to his job at KING, which is also a unique feature of Seattle. I can't say whether he would have been successful in the wider world, but I do believe staying in Seattle was the right decision for George."

George's daughter Daisy concurs. "I imagine him as a little fish in a big pond," she said, "and I don't think he'd like that at all. He really loved being a big fish. He inspired people, and the people he ended up performing with in Seattle are all incredible people. He really was happy doing what he did." As George put it himself, in a 1997 interview with this writer: "I'm the longest-term music director in Seattle now. This is the age of jet-setting conductors who don't stay home to tend their own garden. Well, I'm tending my own garden, and the harvest makes it all worthwhile."

Both Stubbs and Van Zandt point to one of George Shangrow's defining characteristics: his abiding joy in music, whether it was the thrill of discovery or the fun of sharing it with others. Whether he was on the air or in the rehearsal room, this delight in music never left him, and it was infectious. Members of his Seattle Chamber Singers (founded in 1969, when he was a senior at Roosevelt High School) and Orchestra Seattle (founded in 1979) sang and played their hearts out for him; listeners and audiences for his long-running "Live, by George" series during his sixteen years at Classical KING FM were swept up in his enthusiasm for great performers and exciting new works. George was devastated, as were many listeners, when the station didn't renew his contract in 2004.

He was tremendously loyal to the local composers he championed, whose music he saw as superior to most of the premieres that went on "downtown": Carol Sams, Robert Kechley, Murl Allen Sanders, Huntley Beyer, and Roupen Shakarian chief among them. From his high school days on through the early years of the Seattle Chamber Singers, Shangrow gathered around him a coterie of gifted musicians who went on to make an important mark in Seattle and elsewhere. In addition to the composers and performers already mentioned, his circle included Van Zandt's wife, the mezzo-soprano Margaret Russell (the couple moved to Germany when she was given a contract by the Essen Opera in 1979); Elizabeth Gaskill, who is still an active musician in Amsterdam; Bonnie Blanchard, a successful Seattle flute teacher and author of two books; Deede Evans Cook, a violinist who now teaches and performs in New York; Vernon Nicodemus, a singer and trumpeter who subbed with the Seattle Symphony; the sisters Shirley and Marlene Kraft, who played flute and bassoon, respectively, and also sang; the late Peter Kechley, Robert Kechley's brother and a fine singer; and the late Randall Jay McCarty, brilliant harpsichordist, professor, and one of the leading lights of Seattle's early-music community.

For George, music was meant to be exciting—never dutiful or routine or merely scholarly. He and his longtime duo partner, the flutist Jeff Cohan, launched Bach sonatas as if they were rocket grenades, full of splash and dash and drama. As a conductor, if he had to choose between period-performance standards for a work like Handel's *Messiah*, which he conducted countless times, or a performance that extracts the maximum juice from the music, the latter option always won. Even after conducting years of multiple performances of the *Messiah*, he loved to preside over the annual *Messiah* sing-and-play-along at the University Unitarian Church, where he was for many years the music director. Yet for all his love of irreverent jokes, George could be a real stickler about details he considered important. "It's not THE *Messiah*," he would say; "Handel never put an article in the title. It's *Messiah*."

A huge Bach enthusiast, Shangrow honored Bach's three-hundredth birthday in 1985 by performing thirty-six Bach cantatas and all of the major orchestral and choral works with the Seattle Chamber Singers and Orchestra Seattle. His organizations far outstripped any other Seattle presenters' musical offerings in celebration of the Bach tricentennial.

Were the concerts always as good as he thought they were? Maybe not always. But as Van Zandt explains, perfect and error-free performances were not George's primary goal. "Being 'out there,' performing frequently, presenting interesting, rarely heard music, promoting local composers, and just trying to make other people get excited about music may have been more important to him than the idea of excellence," Van Zandt says. "Élan, spontaneity, beauty, fun are also worthy of consideration."

And then there were the pranks. Rehearsals were frequently hilarious, with serious business interrupted by jokes and terrible puns. In the concert hall, George occasionally indulged his penchant for the outrageous. Conducting the colorful "He spoke the word" from the Handel oratorio *Israel in Egypt*, he was not above whipping out a flyswatter instead of a baton (for the "all manner of flies" stipulated in the libretto and echoed in the music), or pulling a baton out of his belt as if drawing a sword for a particularly martial aria. He was an expert sight reader, an inveterate punster, an enthusiastic Boy Scout (he and Van Zandt "dueled" with quarterstaves at camp), and an impressive water-skier. He was also adept at taking chances. Van Zandt recalls the time when the young George saved the house for his widowed mother by playing the stock market after his grand-mother had died and the other heirs wanted to liquidate the house so that they would all get equal shares of the inheritance.

Over the years, George became deeply entrenched in Seattle's musical community—as a radio presence, conductor of live music, and teacher at Seattle Conservatory of Music, Seattle Community College, and Seattle University. Discovery was always a thrill for him. I sang with his Seattle Chamber Singers in the 1970s before becoming a music critic, and he was always dragging me off to listen to a newly discovered recording; I remember him chortling as he played the comical bass aria "O ruddier than the cherry" from Handel's obscure but lovely *Acis and Galatea*. "I think it was his enthusiasm for all things fascinating, 'cool,' beautiful, wonderful, etc.—not only, but especially, in music—which drew people in," Van Zandt remembers. "He would turn to you with a huge smile and say, 'Can't you just see how cool that is?' And he'd be right, of course: you just had to get with the program."

His many enthusiasms made George a quick convert, and soon an ardent missionary, for music he discovered. Nor was he afraid to change his mind: He pooh-poohed Wagner's *Ring* until I invited him to use my second set of tickets to Seattle Opera's *Ring* one summer. Transformed by the experience, he immediately began reading everything he could find on the subject. He became a passionate advocate and eventually an inspiring lecturer on these operas. Of course, he couldn't resist puncturing the ultra-serious atmosphere surrounding Wagner by renaming the Valkyries' famous utterances "Toyota-to-ho."

And then there was travel, which he adored: George toured with his musical groups several times in Europe, and he lectured and performed on cruise ships to such destinations as the Panama Canal and Antarctica. He was an accomplished cook and a wine connoisseur, and consequently a connoisseur of weight-loss programs as well. He lived his private life with the same gusto: there were many girlfriends, two wives, one daughter, and two stepsons.

As a soloist, George performed on both piano and harpsichord with a wide variety of ensembles, including the Orcas Island Chamber Music Festival. A popular and well-known lecturer, he loved to talk about music and was a mesmerizing speaker, a genuine missionary for music. He gave talks for many local civic and musical groups, and was on his way to lecture at the Methow Music Festival in Eastern Washington when he was killed in a head-on collision near Winthrop, Washington.

Eight months after his death, his family appeared in a courtroom in Wenatchee, the nearest major town to the accident site, to tell the sixteen-year-old boy who had been driving the other car that they forgave him. They told him that the best way to honor Shangrow's memory was to do good things with his life, and to cherish every moment of it. "It is my hope that you give yourself permission to smile, and have joy," fifteen-year-old Daisy Shangrow told the boy at the sentencing hearing in Okanogan County Juvenile Court. She told him that none of them could change the past, and that she hoped he didn't see her as the enemy or the victim. "I want all of us to be able to go on in our lives."

George Shangrow left a big legacy in Seattle: new works commissioned, obscure works unearthed, composers and performers discovered, audiences and radio listeners entertained and informed. But his personal legacy—his love for music and the magnanimity of his family—will also be long remembered. In 2013, Daisy observed, "He was doing exactly what he wanted to do, and that is what he wanted for all of us. He always told me, 'If you do what you love, you will never *work* a day in your life.' And that was how he lived."

Resident Conductors

THE VITAL LINKS IN THE MUSIC COMMUNITY

In the vast, complicated ecosystem of Seattle's classical musical scene, the big groups at the top of the food chain get the lion's share of attention and funding. The Seattle Symphony and Seattle Opera are, by and large, the two giants of Seattle music: the internationally famous markers of Seattle's musical excellence, drawing audiences from all around for major productions and world premieres. When one or both get into trouble, with financial difficulties that force artistic retrenchment or labor difficulties that threaten to shut them down, the world sits up and takes notice. Their music directors are so important and powerful in the community that anyone with even slight cultural leanings knows who they are and what they do.

Yet there's a lot more to the musical ecosystem than those two large icebergs of symphony and opera floating in increasingly dangerous seas. As we work our way through the early decades of the twenty-first century, it seems increasingly clear that those classical icebergs are encountering a global warming of the arts, in which rising temperatures (or, more accurately, the increasing dominance of populist entertainments that don't require the rigorous training and unique talents of the symphonic and operatic worlds) are making classical music an increasingly endangered art form.

Big orchestras and opera companies do not operate all on their own. They are accompanied and supported by hundreds of organizations ranging from fully professional ensembles to community performing groups that are open to all comers. The extensive network of music festivals, early-instrument ensembles, chamber music societies, chorales, community and regional opera companies, youth orchestras, gay and lesbian choruses, ethnic-music groups, educational ensembles, soloists, and teachers help support and give grassroots life to the "majors" and extend the reach of great music throughout the region. It is in the extensive network of ensembles that students learn, teachers expand their performance opportunities, communities learn lessons in diversity and tolerance, concert audiences for groups large and small grow, and the joy of music is indulged in what may be its purest form.

Much of the most visible, and audible, professional activity is underlain by this vast and vital network of community ensembles and organizations. Seattle has a rich trove of semiprofessional and community performance groups, both choral and instrumental. The choruses in particular serve an additional function: the promulgation of various cultures, ethnic and otherwise, in song. If you find the right chorus, you can sing in Welsh or Norwegian or Chinese or Swedish; you also can specialize in early music, Gregorian chant, or esoteric contemporary repertoire. If you're the right age, you can sing in a high-level touring boys' or girls' choir. It's hard, in fact, to think of a niche that isn't served by one musical organization or another. The Seattle Men's Chorus, which with its sister organization, the Seattle Women's Chorus, is the largest community chorus in America, annually sells out more performances for its spectacular holiday show in Benaroya Hall, home of the Seattle Symphony, than any of the symphony's offerings. The mission statement of both the men's and women's choruses "recognizes the value of gay and straight people and their relationships."

Several of Seattle's choruses, both youth and adult, have received national and even international acclaim for their excellence, as have their founders and directors. The longest-running and prominent Seattle Symphony Chorale, which was founded in 1953 by Leonard Moore, was later directed by the crème de la crème of Northwest choral conductors, including Robert Scandrett, Richard Sparks, Abraham Kaplan, George Fiore, and Joseph Crnko.

Other choral directors also have made a tremendous difference in Seattle's music scene: Robert Bode of Choral Arts; Seattle Pro Musica founder Richard Sparks, who also founded Choral Arts, and his longtime Pro Musica successor, Karen P. Thomas; Eric Banks of the Esoterics; Doug Fullington of the Tudor Choir; Dennis Coleman of Seattle Men's Chorus and Seattle Women's Chorus; Loren Pontén of Opus 7 Vocal Ensemble; Freddie Coleman and his Seattle Choral Company; Margriet Tindemans and her Medieval Women's Choir; Fredrick Lokken and his Bellevue Chamber Chorus; and the directors of the Northwest Chamber Chorus: Peter Seibert, Joan Catoni Conlon, Ken DeJong, Steven Demorest, and Mark Kloepper. These conductors have given thousands of regional singers the chance to perform; they have given the best of local vocal talent a valuable boost by providing solo opportunities in their *Messiah*s, requiems, holiday presentations, and other major productions. The best choruses, among them Choral Arts and Seattle Pro Musica, have earned first-place national awards for excellence and can stand with the finest choral groups in the country.

What Dennis Coleman has done since 1979 with his Seattle Men's Chorus (SMC), the world's largest gay men's chorus, and, since 2002, the Seattle Women's Chorus—which together number more than five hundred singers and are larger than the Mormon Tabernacle Choir—is nothing short of miraculous. Working with nonprofessional singers from every walk of life, Coleman has crafted precision ensembles whose blend and pitch acuity are excellent, and whose programming skirts a fine line between the sublime and the rambunctious.

Seattle-area singers have many more options than that of choosing a chorus. In some cases, singers and directors like the Metropolitan Opera baritone Erich Parce, who made an excellent career elsewhere but wanted to return to the Northwest, have found opportunities with new opera companies, which offer their communities affordable opera presentations and their singers valuable performance experience—and everyone has fun in the process. Small opera companies have sprung up around Seattle: to the east in Bellevue, to the west on Vashon Island, and to the north in Skagit Valley, in addition to the larger and longer-established Tacoma Opera to the south. Productions sometimes feature such graduates of Seattle Opera's Young Artists program as Vashon Opera's Jennifer Hines, who has sung several roles on the Seattle Opera main stage.

Opera conductors, too, have enriched the musical scene of the greater Seattle area, none more prominently than Henry Holt (1934–1997). Holt was Seattle Opera's music director from the time he was hired by Glynn Ross in 1966 until 1984, and he was Seattle Opera's first *Ring* master, conducting Wagner's four-opera epic for ten seasons in Seattle Opera, before following Ross to Arizona Opera for more *Ring* performances. A passionate advocate for his beloved *Ring*, Holt was also a born educator, whose lifelong involvement in student programs influenced young people across the country. Holt was an activist in many of the region's performing-arts organizations, helping devise a joint contract for musicians of the Seattle Symphony, Seattle Opera, and Pacific Northwest Ballet, of which he was the first musical director. He was a strong proponent for all the arts and represented local arts interests in boards and panels of the National Endowment for the Arts, the National Opera Institute, and the Ford and Rockefeller Foundations. Holt was a connoisseur of the voice in both professional and personal arenas: over the course of his life, Holt married four singers.

There could be no greater enthusiast for opera than the visionary conductor and producer Hans Wolf (1912–2005). The German-born Wolf, who held a PhD from the University of Vienna, was a conductor with experience at the Vienna Symphony, the Mozarteum Orchestra, and the orchestras of Augsburg, Graz, Mannheim, and Wiesbaden. Charming and dapper, with an ascot invariably topping his dress shirt, he always punctuated his conversation with excited pronouncements of the latest discovery of a wonderful young soprano or baritone—someone who was "the real thing." His eye was always on the next production, which was going to be "the best one of all."

A cofounder of Tacoma Opera, Wolf staged operas in many outlying communities, devoting extra attention to his beloved operettas in a series called Neglected Masterpieces of Operetta. Seattle Opera made him the company's chorus master and associate conductor in 1969, and he conducted many of the company's productions of opera in English, concluding with Mozart's *The Abduction from the Seraglio* in 1982. As the company's director of community outreach, he led cooperative community productions of opera with such organizations as Pacific Lutheran University's Summer Opera in Tacoma, Seattle Junior Programs at the Center Playhouse, and Renton Community Opera.

Wolf's long history at Seattle Opera was matched by the conductor George Fiore, longtime chorus master at the Seattle Opera and also choral director at the Seattle Symphony. The indispensable Fiore, also a gifted pianist and organist, led the Northwest Boychoir during a crucial transitional period and additionally held posts at several churches with big music programs: Saint James Cathedral, Seattle First United Methodist Church, Seattle First Presbyterian Church, and Prince of Peace Lutheran Church. His talents were clearly passed on to his son, John Fiore, an internationally successful orchestra and opera conductor whose posts have included music directorships in Düsseldorf and Oslo.

An important contributor to Seattle Opera, the conductor Dean Williamson, has now gone on to a wider career after twelve years as principal coach and pianist for the company, followed by the directorship of Seattle Opera's Young Artists Program, for which he conducted all productions from 1999 to 2007. He has conducted several main stage operas for the company as well and has more lately branched out to conduct at such companies as the Opera Theatre of Saint Louis, Wolf Trap Opera, Boston Lyric Opera, Minnesota Opera, Nashville Opera, and Opera Colorado.

The Israeli-born conductor Asher Fisch, highly popular with the Seattle Opera orchestra and audience alike, joined the company in 2007 as resident conductor, following a string of successes that began with a *Parsifal* production still discussed with reverence. A concert pianist of considerable ability—he recorded Liszt's challenging Wagner paraphrases—Fisch has an instinctive understanding of Wagner, which has made him a natural at Seattle Opera. He can adapt quickly to a series of inexperienced singers performing different arias, as in Seattle Opera's Wagner Competitions, and he can also see the big picture of a masterwork like Wagner's *Ring*, which he conducted brilliantly for Seattle Opera in 2013. Fisch's musicality has brought him acclaim and lots of work in cities from Vienna and Paris to London, Munich, Chicago, New York, and Philadelphia. Seattle fans hope he will return to the Emerald City regularly, despite a new post in Perth, Australia, as principal conductor and artistic advisor of the West Australian Symphony Orchestra.

The conductor and recording producer Adam Stern has made a considerable mark at the Seattle Symphony, where he was assistant conductor from 1992 to 1996 and associate conductor from 1996 to 2001, and at the now defunct Northwest Chamber Orchestra, where he served as music director from 1993 to 2000. The Hollywood-born former prodigy is also a noted pianist, composer, and winner of a 1990 Grammy Award as "Classical Producer of the Year." Stern's list of music directorships includes the Seattle Philharmonic Orchestra and the Port Angeles Symphony Orchestra, as well as teaching responsibilities at Cornish College of the Arts. Highly regarded as an engaging and articulate musical raconteur, Stern is also in demand as a speaker and preconcert lecturer for concerts and music festivals, and as a guest conductor at the Seattle Symphony.

The British-born conductor Stewart Kershaw led the Pacific Northwest Ballet (PNB) Orchestra through nearly six hundred *Nutcrackers* during his long and stellar twenty-five-year tenure as PNB's music director and, starting in 1983, principal conductor. In 2009, at the age of sixty-eight, he decided to resign his PNB post but is continuing with the Auburn Symphony Orchestra he had founded in 1997 to broaden his and his players' musical experiences beyond the ballet repertoire. The Auburn is considered one of the region's best symphonies.

Originally a schoolboy chorister at England's Chichester Cathedral, Kershaw—who has never lost that urbane British accent—has conducted about seventy-five orchestras in twenty different countries and continents, including Australia, Canada, Japan, South Africa, and South America. His major posts have included positions at the opera houses of Paris and Lyon in France, and Munich and Stuttgart in Germany; he was also music director of Japan's Kyoto Symphony and has guest conducted the Japan Philharmonic in a series of concerts. Prior to coming to Seattle, where he has been a major factor of the success of PNB in the theater, on tour, and on their *Nutcracker* recording, Kershaw was the conductor and music director of the Evansville Philharmonic Orchestra. In 1989, Kershaw was made a Fellow of London's Royal Academy of Music in recognition of his conducting throughout the world.

One of Seattle's groundbreakers is Frances Walton, a remarkable woman who was second seed on the 1948 US Women's Olympic swim team and won a piano scholarship to Tanglewood. There, she met Leonard Bernstein, who encouraged her as a conductor. Later, she studied the cello in Seattle with Eva Heinitz and—despite initial opposition from the influential University of Washington maestro Stanley Chapple (he later relented)—earned a master's degree in conducting. Walton went on to found and cofound several organizations, including the Olympic Youth Symphony, Olympic Music Camp, and Philharmonia Northwest, and she established the Debut Tour for winners of Seattle's Ladies Musical Club auditions. Walton has inspired musicians of every age and nearly every instrument, particularly young women, for whom she has been an important role model.

The allied ensembles of Orchestra Seattle and the Seattle Chamber Singers, reeling after the premature death of their founder and lifetime conductor George Shangrow in 2010, took a long time to consider their options and audition potential successors before choosing Clinton Smith as music director in 2013. Smith, who bested a field of six finalists, has had several symphony and opera posts in Michigan, and he is on the music staff of Santa Fe Opera.

In the Northwest, most of the community orchestras exist because of the vision and dedication of their founding conductors. That was the case with the Bellevue Philharmonic, founded in 1967 in Bellevue, just across Lake Washington from Seattle, by R. Joseph Scott, a florist by trade and an oboist with some experience as an assistant conductor. When Scott decided to start his own orchestra, he placed a newspaper ad inviting musicians to a rehearsal on September 14, 1967. They came—a couple of dozen of them—and others followed; sixty-five musicians performed in the first concert three months later in the gymnasium at Bellevue High School. The orchestra grew, gathering subscribers and sponsors, though the venue—first in Westminster Chapel, later in the theater at the new Meydenbauer Center—has always been a problem for being too small and stuffy. Scott took the orchestra on tour, playing outreach concerts on the decks of Washington State ferries, and he established education programs in Bellevue schools.

In 1997, Scott left the Bellevue Philharmonic, which was ready for a change. He was not long without a podium: In the following year, 1998, he took on the seventy-five-member Sammamish Symphony Orchestra in a community near Bellevue, building on a small core group that was originally named the Providence Point Players. The Sammamish Symphony has performed several times in downtown Seattle's Benaroya Hall, frequently in collaboration with local choral societies.

After Scott's departure from the Bellevue Philharmonic, the orchestra went forward under the music directorship of Fusao Kajima, who was in turn succeeded by Michael Miropolsky, a Seattle Symphony violinist who also is a busy orchestra conductor. The Bellevue Phil organization disbanded in 2011 because of insufficient donor support and a shrinking subscriber base. But

Miropolsky rescued and redeveloped the orchestra as the Lake Washington Symphony Orchestra, which is now collaboratively run by Miropolsky, the players, and community volunteers.

One of the most highly regarded of the community symphonies, the Cascade Symphony Orchestra, which is based in Edmonds, to the north of Seattle, also came into existence because of the vision of its founding music director, Robert Anderson, a respected violinist and beloved teacher who had begun his career on a violin his father bought for five dollars in a beer parlor in Nome, Alaska, where the future conductor was born. Anderson played in the Seattle Symphony before going to work at the Edmonds School District in 1946; during his tenure there, he expanded the district's music program by more than tenfold before his retirement in 1974.

In a ninetieth-birthday interview with me in 2007, he explained, "I always told students to learn to diversify. And this means teachers, too: people would often tell me, 'I'm a music educator,' but were they really also musicians? Any idiot can get a degree. Professional players bring to the classroom or the band something that far transcends education—a world of experience playing shows, Dixieland, and classical music. Some who teach have never played professionally and battled the problems. I always told students, 'Get several twigs in your bow.'" After Anderson got a grant from the Rockefeller Foundation to attend the American Orchestra League's summer conducting sessions, he tried out his skills on a struggling community symphony in Bremerton. In 1962, he was inspired to found an orchestra in his own community in Edmonds, and the resulting Cascade Symphony was a rousing success.

When Anderson retired from the Cascade in 1991, his replacement was the experienced Seattle-based conductor-composer Roupen Shakarian, but in 1995 Shakarian decided to focus on other projects, including the chamber orchestra Philharmonia Northwest, which he led from 1986 to 2010. The Cascade musicians thereupon appointed Gregory Sullivan Isaacs as music director, but his plans for a professional orchestra were sufficiently at odds with the players and the financial realities of the time that the majority of the Cascade musicians seceded from the orchestra and started another orchestra, which they named the Classic Cascade.

Their retired original founder was proud of them. "I don't know any other orchestra in the country," Anderson said in an October 2002 interview, printed in the *Seattle Times*, "whose people got up, walked out, and said, 'We won't play for you.' But that's what the Cascade players did." After six months during which two rival orchestras inhabited the same town, Isaacs's Cascade Symphony folded and the Classic Cascade, taking its original name back, began the search for a permanent music director. They found one in Miropolsky, who has become one of the region's busiest music professionals.

The Seattle Youth Symphony Orchestra, since 1942 one of the Northwest's most cherished institutions, followed the long tenure of its music director Vilem Sokol (1960–88) with a succession of music directors: Ruben Gurevich (1988–93), Jonathan Shames (1994–2001), Huw Edwards (2002–5), Christian Knapp (an interim conductor, 2005–6, following Edwards's resignation), and Stephen Rogers Radcliffe, who arrived in 2006. Radcliffe, who had studied with Leonard Bernstein, has imposing credentials, including directorships and posts at the University of Massachusetts, Boston Lyric Opera, New York Chamber Ensemble, Cape May Music Festival, and the Hungarian Virtuosi. He has led youth orchestra programs throughout the United States, Europe, Latin America, and Asia, and he has earned admiration for his innovations in Seattle, which include collaborations with Seattle Opera in educational presentations.

The important field of church music has also attracted some of Seattle's most remarkable musical leaders. The career trajectory of the conductor James Savage has culminated in the region's most impressive church music programs at Seattle's Saint James Cathedral, where he arrived in 1981 after undergraduate studies at the University of Oregon and a Fulbright grant. Savage completed his doctorate at the University of Washington, taught at Cornish College of the Arts and the University of Washington, and transformed Saint James into the city's third-biggest employer of musicians, directly behind the combined Seattle Symphony and Seattle Opera and the 5th Avenue Theatre.

When Savage arrived at Saint James, no money had been spent on organ repair since the Great Depression, and several members of the scrawny choir informed him, "We don't rehearse." But Savage was inspired by the visionary Seattle composer and conductor at Saint Mark's Cathedral, Peter Hallock, who had hired him to sing there in 1974: "Peter made my job [at Saint James] possible. I knew what a cathedral could be." An inspiring leader, composer, and presenter of liturgical music, Hallock created a beloved Seattle institution in the long-running compline service at Saint Mark's on Sunday evenings, which provides weekly inspiration to listeners live, on Classical KING FM and on the Internet (www.king.org).

With the support of Father Gallagher and, later, Father Ryan, and "beautification" money from a bequest by the Seattle couturier John Doyle Bishop (who famously specified that the new carpets be ordered in his favorite color, "John Doyle Bishop green"), Savage plunged ahead at Saint James and hired a quartet of singers. He also bought a small portative organ and a grand piano so that the church would have at least a couple of working instruments.

The neighborhood around the cathedral was dangerous, and crime always spiked at New Year's Eve. Instead of closing and cowering, however, the cathedral threw open its doors to everyone on New Year's Eve, performing Bach's cantatas for the end and the beginning of the year, and ringing the cathedral's bells at midnight. This tradition has inspired many other churches to present their own New Year's Eve programs. The populist approach at Saint James is reflected in its policy of "pay as able" for all concerts. "No one is ever turned away because they can't afford a ticket," Savage explains.

Over the years, the beefed-up choir—whose members now do indeed rehearse—was joined by the chant-based Women of Saint James Schola, the men's Cathedral Chant Choir, the professional (and virtuoso) Cathedral Cantorei mixed choir, the Schola Cantorum children's choir, two other children's choirs (the Saint Cecilia Choir and the Saint Gregory Singers), and Cathedral Soloists, a six-member group that includes some of Seattle's finest oratorio singers. There's also the Cathedral Brass, composed of players from the Seattle Symphony and Pacific Northwest Ballet Orchestras, and the Cathedral Chamber Orchestra, whose ranks are drawn from the Pacific Northwest Ballet and Auburn Symphony Orchestras and have included such players as Ilkka and Marjorie Kransberg-Talvi, both prominent Seattle-based violinists and longtime orchestra concertmasters. A cathedral guitarist performs unamplified every Friday evening for a half hour, and a cathedral piper and pipe band are on call several times a year for special events and memorials. It takes 260 musicians to present the massive Easter services. There are also resident ensembles at Saint James, top-ranked local choruses who apply for twelve-month residencies and present wide-ranging concert programs extending from Rachmaninoff's *All-Night Vigil* to the North American premiere performance of Shigeaki Saegusa's *Requiem*.

Savage, who retired from his post at the end of 2014, continues to conduct choral festivals from Orange County to Atlanta, as well as writing for journals about music and books, and addressing groups such as the Conference of Roman Catholic Cathedral Musicians. But he was perhaps most at home on Sunday mornings in front of his biggest choir: the congregation at Saint James, which at the Sunday ten o'clock mass "really sings, just like a choir," according to Savage in our 2013 interview. "It brings joy, wholeness, and rapport when people sing together like this."

Milton Katims with his mentor, Arturo Toscanini, in an undated photo courtesy of the Katims family.

Rainer Miedel, music director of the Seattle Symphony from 1976 to 1983. Photo by Greg Gilbert.

Cordelia Miedel in 1968, during her years as a touring cellist. Photo by Friedemann Wikarski.

Gerard Schwarz conducts the All-Star Orchestra. Photo courtesy of All-Star Orchestra.

Ludovic Morlot, under whose leadership the Seattle Symphony won its first Grammy Award in 2015. Photo by Brandon Patoc.

Peter Erős brought to his University of Washington conducting students his experience conducting major European orchestras. Photo by Mary Levin, University of Washington Photography.

Vilem Sokol inspired generations of young Seattle-area musicians whose later careers extended from Germany to Hong Kong. Photo courtesy of Seattle Youth Symphony Orchestra.

The Grammy-winning lutenist and conductor Stephen Stubbs has brought his international experience to Seattle performers, students, and audiences. Miranda Loud Photography.

Conductor George Shangrow concludes
a concert with a farewell salute. Photo
by John Cornicello.

THE IMPRESARIOS

WHAT exactly *is* an impresario? In the field of music, the
best definition of this term is probably "producer": the
person who creates musical institutions and presents
major events (usually, though not always, grand opera). An impresario is a manager, a director, an artistic visionary—the person who
makes the music possible. In Seattle, this category includes two
remarkable, unforgettable men who created the internationally
respected Seattle Opera and brought it into the twenty-first century; a farsighted woman performer and educator whose practical
dreams and hard work launched the Seattle Chamber Music Society and its festivals; and the cellist-turned-dreamer who founded
a chamber orchestra that ranked in the "major league" category on
Seattle's arts scene for more than three decades.

Successful impresarios are ideas people, but they also must
know how to function in the real world of practicalities. They aren't
deterred by all the doubters who say their enterprise couldn't be
done—but they aren't so grandiose in their vision that they outstrip
what is actually possible, though they stretch that boundary as far
as they can. They are the first to acknowledge their own mistakes,
and the first to find a solution that nobody else quite imagined.

Imagination and energy are certainly key aspects of Seattle's impresarios: the ability to imagine a groundbreaking artistic outcome, and the energy to push past all obstacles to achieve their vision. In so doing, they changed the landscape of classical music in Seattle.

Glynn Ross

THE BANTAM OF THE OPERA

In July 1997, when Seattle Opera's founding general director, Glynn Ross, announced his retirement from his subsequent post at Arizona Opera, he sent me a letter that was unique in my thirty-one-year journalism career at the *Seattle Times*. Then eighty-two, Ross—as always—had his eye firmly on posterity. The letter, which included two attachments, reads as follows:

> *Dear Melinda,*
>
> *I've always felt that a person of high-profile has more than one "obituary." The first, when that person steps down from their prominent position. The second, when that person leaves the field of activity; and three, when he or she goes to "that undiscovered country from whose bourn no traveler returns."*
>
> *The first two are herewith. You write the third. (Unless, I outlive you!)*
>
> *Faithfully and devotedly,*
> *Glynn*

How like Glynn Ross!

The octogenarian still had eight years to live. But he was planning for two contingencies: his own death, and the possibility that a music critic thirty-three years his junior might not outlive him. I did write that third obituary, in 2005. I hope it was a good one, because I'm pretty sure he read it, in whichever undiscovered country he resides.

At the time of his death, Ross was still working on his enormous autobiography, 560 pages crammed with colorful narrative and incredible detail: what he wore, what he ate, how his Norwegian ice-skating grandpa could outrace a running horse, and the fact that he allowed his high school girlfriend to wear his glee club sweater.

What a visionary Glynn Ross was: tough, determined, imaginative, and always 100 percent in love with the great art form he championed. He was always a fighter, too; in his youth the diminutive 135-pound future opera director had a brief career as a Golden Gloves boxer, which led to the sobriquet that lasted a lifetime, "the Bantam of the Opera."

What Glynn Ross may have lacked in size, he more than made up for in imagination, vision, and chutzpah. As the founding general director of Seattle Opera, Ross moved mountains when he started up a venturesome and stable company that always balanced its budget, whether putting on *La Traviata* or the rock opera *Tommy*. For all thirty-four years of his directorships, first in Seattle and later at Arizona Opera, Ross posted a balanced budget in a performance genre that is the world's most expensive. He defied the cautious and the cynical by successfully staging the ultimate opera challenge, Wagner's four-opera *Der Ring des Nibelungen*, and then he made the *Ring* into an annual international tourist attraction for Seattle. Then, when it was time for him to move on, at a point when Ross was well past retirement age, darned if he didn't do it all over again at Arizona Opera, where he astonished the opera world by giving the Arizonans two *Ring*s of their own.

Ross was an incredibly hard worker, even as an octogenarian. He had learned toughness during his youth, growing up during the Depression on a ten-acre Nebraska farm for which he had to shoulder the responsibility while his Norwegian-born father was dying of cancer. (The family name was originally Åase, and then phonetically anglicized to Aus; Glynn changed it to "Ross" in February 1941, when he was night news editor on the radio station WESX in Salem, Massachusetts.)

After the death of his father, Ross got the family out of debt by dint of sheer diligence—getting up at 3 or 4 a.m. and holding down several jobs—and by using his imagination. He rounded up classmates and got them to work on the farm for very little pay, though swarms of locusts and dust storms ultimately made farming almost impossible. His high school drama teacher recommended him to the Leland Powers School of Radio and Theatre (now Leland Powers School of Radio, Theatre, and Television), and Ross set off eastward in the caboose of a freight train with seven dollars in his pocket. In Boston, he had his first experience of opera—as a supernumerary in *Lohengrin*—and more culture awaited him in two Shakespeare-drenched budget trips to England, the second of which took place just as World War II began in Europe. On his way back to the United States, Ross became friends with such ship-mates as the singer Paul Robeson, the pianist Arthur Rubinstein, and the ballerina Alicia Markova.

The next few years were a relentless and only partly successful quest to establish a career. On the coattails of the celebrated con-ductor Albert Coates, Ross headed for Los Angeles, where he heard all the young singers auditioning for Coates and stored up knowl-edge about the concert and opera worlds. During the 1939–40 sea-son, he became assistant director for what was then the Southern California Opera. Then, back in Boston as the opera department's stage director at the New England Conservatory, Ross staged a new Aaron Copland opera, *The Second Hurricane*, with a young Leon-ard Bernstein on the podium. By that time, the United States had entered the war and Ross had just married Ruth Owens, one of his students in a fledgling organization he called American Youth Opera. Ross enlisted in the army six months later, on his twenty-eighth birthday, December 15, 1942.

He was shipped off to North Africa, where he was put to work digging ditches for latrines and unloading truckloads of bombs— and got a "Dear John" letter from his wife, who had decided to file for divorce. During a 1944 night air raid, while Ross was on a Lib-erty Ship, he was hit by a shell that wounded his leg. A helpful colonel sent him to Washington, DC, as a volunteer to test a new drug, penicillin.

After rejoining his outfit, now in Naples, Italy, Ross was ordered to the island of Ischia—where the other residents included Mus-solini's daughter and the British composer Sir William Walton— to oversee a "rest and recreation" (R&R) hotel. There he met the elegant artist Angelamaria (Gio) Solimene, who, after a two-year courtship, became Ross's wife. The Ischia R&R hotel was so successful that Ross was sent to Naples to take over seven similar hotels, and there he jumped at the chance to stage *Boris Godunov* at the venerable Teatro San Carlo. He had finally found his métier as a man of the theater, putting on three shows a day of such operas as *L'amico Fritz* and *L'elisir d'amore* with stars like Beniamino Gigli, Giuseppe di Stefano, and Tito Gobbi. "They called me Maestro, and I called them Maestro," Ross told Winthrop Sargeant in a 1978 *New Yorker* profile, "but there was no doubt about who was doing the learning."

In 1947, Ross and his new wife returned to the United States. In San Francisco, he was hired to be a stage director at the San Francisco Opera by the company's director, Gaetano Merola; other bookings soon followed in Los Angeles, Fort Worth, and, in 1953–54, Seattle, where the short-lived and underfunded Northwest Grand Opera booked him for several productions. Meanwhile, Ross had been spending his summers at the Bayreuth Festival, the Wagnerian holy of holies, where, at his first *Parsifal* rehearsal, he had an experience that he recounted in his autobiography: "I was exalted. I was pole-axed. I had never been so affected, so spiritually lifted out of this world in my thirteen years of theater. I walked out of the theater into the misty rain to go home and walked a half-mile in the wrong direction. I was a different person. I had experienced an epiphany beyond my understanding or reach. It was like the ephemeral consideration of afterlife."

Back in California, one of Glynn's major employers, Cosmopolitan Opera of San Francisco, went under. He and his family, which now included four children, moved to Naples for three years (1961 through 1963), where the kids were enrolled in a convent school and Ross directed opera at two theaters. But job offers continued to come in from America, including, in 1963, from both Seattle and Laguna Beach, California; Seattle was then still struggling to mount a stable and successful opera company. To herald the 1962 Century 21 World's Fair, Seattle's cultural community had united under the leadership of the Seattle Symphony to produce a suitably grand production of *Aida* for Seattle's new opera house; the production featured singers from the New York Metropolitan Opera, and it left the symphony with a deficit of $35,000, disastrously large in those days. Thanks to the leadership of the jeweler and civic leader Paul Friedlander, who with several others had created PONCHO (Patrons of Northwest Cultural and Historical Organizations) and used the organization's huge corps of volunteers for a spectacularly successful fund-raising auction, the deficit was replaced by a modest surplus.

Meanwhile, however, a brief battle for supremacy emerged between two rival opera producers, the Seattle Symphony (which had produced the 1962 *Aida* under the baton of Milton Katims), and the independent Western Opera Company, whose "inadequate scenery and shabby costumes bore witness to the anemia of the pocketbooks of the sponsors," according to the late arts patron and author J. Hans Lehmann. Fortunately, representatives of the two companies sat down to talk, and a merger was drawn up, resulting in the brand-new Seattle Opera Association. Western Opera Company's general manager, the longtime arts activist and patron Helen Jensen, wasted no time repining over the demise of her company (in her 2002 memoir she called the merger "great news"), and eighty-five-year-old Cecilia Schultz (1878–1971), a pioneer promoter of the arts in Seattle, suggested Ross as general director for the new company.

The stage was now set for Ross's arrival in Seattle in December 1963, and it was the start of two transformative decades that had worldwide repercussions. For the first time, Ross had the opportunity to direct not just onstage but everywhere, including opera administration, education, repertoire selection, and publicity. He threw himself into all these roles with a zest that amazed the community.

However, as Ross notes in his autobiography, there were some snags along the way. Gio Ross wanted to return to California; the two Seattle Opera secretaries, Mildred Proctor and Virginia McClure, wanted to stage a coup d'état and run the company themselves; Milton Katims had upstaged him by hiring the soprano Roberta Peters for the September opera; Maria Callas had cancelled her agreement to open the 1964 season in *La Traviata*. The list of trials and tribulations was downright—well, operatic.

Ross prevailed anyhow, largely through his efforts to prove that opera wasn't just for the haughty and well-heeled elite.

He staged each opera in two versions—English as well as the original language—and made sure that Seattle audiences realized that opera wasn't "a lot of fat people standing around and singing in an incomprehensible language," as he later told the *New Yorker*. Trumpeting his favorite slogan, "Nothing succeeds like excess," he went to work on the publicity, and soon all over Seattle bumper stickers proclaimed, "Opera Lives!" and "WITCO" ("What is this thing called opera?"). Cement trucks appeared bearing the slogan "Get Mixed Up with Opera"; skywriting planes flaunted banners saying, "Bravo Opera!" No pun was beneath Ross, not even "Get Ahead with Salome." Later, when he realized his dream of producing Wagner's *Ring* in Seattle, he was photographed arm in arm with two costumed Wagnerian characters—a giant, Noel Mangin, and a Valkyrie, Jeanne Cook—in images that ran in *People* magazine and newspapers around the world.

In those early years, production and theatrical values ranked far behind star power in the leading roles, and subsidiary singers were cast mainly on the basis of reliability and availability (with the notable exception of the elderly legend Giovanni Martinelli, who took the small role of the Emperor in *Turandot* during Ross's third season). Seattle audiences were thrilled to hear such major stars as Beverly Sills, Joan Sutherland, and Franco Corelli, all of them in their prime and drawing national exposure to Seattle Opera.

Busy as Ross was, his fertile mind kept concocting new ideas, among them the use of projected, computer-designed sets, which he first tried out in a reprise production of *Turandot* with the superstar Birgit Nilsson in the title role. And, of course, he had to deal with the steady string of crises endemic to the world of opera: would Corelli come to Seattle, refusing the enticements of San Francisco, a larger house that was also wooing him? Would audiences come to hear the stellar Don Giovanni of Sherrill Milnes, even during a 1979 orchestra musicians' strike that meant the show would go on with only two pianos accompanying the opera? (Yes, and yes.)

Ross wasn't content with just business as usual. He decided to stage the world premiere of the American composer Carlisle

Floyd's *Of Mice and Men*, despite its rejection by two other companies, and he invited the general directors of twenty-five North American opera companies to assemble for what became the first meeting of OPERA America ("Opera Producers Enterprise for Related Activity"). When the mighty Rudolf Bing, who then headed the Metropolitan Opera, didn't attend, Ross sent Bing a telegram saying, "Remember, in three thousand years nobody has named a son Goliath." (Bing didn't show up at the next meeting, either, but he sent his assistant manager.) OPERA America became a lasting success, an invaluable network for the member companies.

Ross never lost sight of the beacon of Wagner, whose works had "pole-axed" and "transported" him back in Bayreuth. When the philanthropist and opera lover J. W. "Bill" Fisher (1914–1990) created a personal foundation, the Gramma Fisher Foundation, to honor his mother and benefit the arts, Ross was invited to a meeting in Chicago to choose a production that the foundation might underwrite. In his memoir, Ross recalled that Walter Herbert of the San Diego Opera "leaned back in his chair and suggested that someone should take on the *Ring*! I would never have attempted to propose the *Ring* without specific funding such as this! Finally I mumbled that it might not be a bad idea and hoped my eagerness was not obvious. Without any discussion, it was decided and as I was third in line [two other companies had already gotten productions], Seattle would do the financed proposal."

Exhilarated and nervous, Ross told himself, "After all, it is just four operas." And then he was off and running, lining up the stage director George London, the set designer John Naccarato, and the Seattle Opera house conductor Henry Holt. Finally, he got the approval of the Seattle Opera board in 1970, and with that the plans were under way to present the four *Ring* operas one at a time during the regular opera seasons, and then all together in the complete *Ring* of 1975. Little did Ross then imagine that the *Ring* would be the beating heart of Seattle Opera for decades to come.

There were trepidations. The Seattle Opera board president, Sheffield Phelps, told the *New Yorker* that the idea of doing the *Ring* frightened him; one board member predicted that Ross would have "a wonderful time sitting in the audience all by himself." But Ross went into PR overdrive, putting out "The Ring's the Thing" lapel buttons, posters declaring "Siegfried for President!" and even a "Free Wagner Orgy Kit." "I may pull some cheap tricks," he told *People* magazine in 1978, "but I'd do anything to shock the public into coming to opera."

During Ross's tenure, the Seattle Opera presented the *Ring* operas in both the original German and the English translation of Andrew Porter, with most of the supporting cast members singing performances in both languages—a feat fraught with difficulties and occasional disasters, as when some performers slipped in and out of German during the English-language cycle that followed. Ross had a gimlet eye for casting, and some of the singers—among them Ute Vinzing, Herbert Becker, Rita Hunter, Alberto Remedios, Johanna Meier, Geraldine Decker, Paul Crook, Malcolm Rivers, Dennis Bailey, Marvelee Cariaga, William Wildermann—gave utterly unforgettable performances during Ross's *Ring* era.

Audiences loved the inaugural *Ring*. Fans, producers, musicologists, and critics came from all over the world, including Sri Lanka, South Africa, Japan, and Russia, because Seattle was the only place in the world (except Bayreuth) where they could hear the complete *Ring* each summer. At the end of each *Götterdämmerung*, a football-stadium roar went up, as the audience stood and applauded and shrieked and carried on. The production was officially blessed in the *New York Times* ("Wagner's *Ring* as he conceived it"). The company was on a Wagner-size roll, and Ross became an international cultural hero. He was knighted by both Germany and Italy. "I 'took the current when it served' and it became the flood that Brutus speaks of, 'which taken at the flood leads on to fortune.' It sure did! And Seattle would now no sooner consider not presenting the *Ring* than not presenting opera!" Ross exulted in his memoir.

Building on the success of the *Ring*, Ross formulated an even grander concept a few years later: to create a dedicated site for a special Pacific Northwest Festival in the Forest, of which the *Ring* would be only a part. He secured backing from the Weyerhaeuser Company, which pledged thirty acres of forestland (surrounded by 110 additional acres to guarantee privacy) about halfway between Seattle and Tacoma and twenty-five minutes from Seattle by car.

In the 1978 *New Yorker* article, Ross radiated the enthusiasm of a born prophet and salesman. "He argues that Seattle, as the nearest port to the Orient in the contiguous 48 states, is bound to become the center of the cultural world," Sargeant wrote, going on to quote Ross in full visionary mode:

The Orient is not the Far East anymore. It's the Near West. The Festival in the Forest will develop into a year-round activity. It will include a larger Wagner series, a World's Fair of the Arts, an international conference on the humanities, and presentations of other performing arts, such as symphony and theatre. We are not only a cosmopolitan place—we are the cultural capital of the Pacific Rim countries. . . . There's a big momentum toward the Festival. There will be Wagner. There will be millions of dollars in tourist revenue. This all comes down to a theory I have: the commodity market has largely been satisfied, and now people are going to go in for the experience market. They are not going to leave their money in the bank; they are going to travel and see things. Free time is not enough. People are not going to sit around. A lot of older people are going to say, "What am I saving my money for?" I expect the world to respond. It will be more than a world's fair—it will be a continuing world's fair of the arts. And the idea is already taking shape. As far as I am concerned, provincialism is dead. Long live regionalism!

This time, however, there was a crucial difference in realizing Ross's dream: Seattle arts supporters were not willing to follow Ross down the path to the forest. As Lehmann, long one of Ross's backers, later wrote, "At this juncture, I and others displayed our skepticism. The site of the festival was too far from urban centers. (Who wants to travel 20 miles to return to Seattle on a dark and rainy winter night?) Glynn's fierce brainstorm not only was a financial nightmare but it sapped too much of his energy away from his main *raison d'être* which was to put on good operas. It seemed to many of us that, except for the yearly *Ring* splash, the remainder of the season had become listless. Whatever the truth of this matter was, the whole episode became the scenario in which opposition to Glynn would coalesce, and in 1983 Glynn's 20-year association with the Seattle Opera company came to an end."

There were no undignified squabbles, public laments, or recriminations from Glynn and Gio. In his farewell speech at the annual meeting of the Seattle Opera Association, held on June 21, 1983, in the august precincts of the Rainier Club, Ross calmly recapped the successes of his tenure, observing that because he was still under contract with Seattle Opera for another two years, his projected balanced budget for the coming season had "not taken into account that the Opera will have two, not one, director's salaries to pay." Following the end of his contract, there would be a general manager's retirement fund to provide "a modest income for Gio and me for life."

But there would be no retirement.

Not yet seventy, Ross was certainly not ready to hang up his opera cape. Ahead of him lay fifteen years as general director of Arizona Opera, and, as Emil Franzi wrote in the October 1991 issue of *Phoenix* magazine, "Ross arrived in Tucson, took over a teetering operation, and made it into one of our proudest and most stable artistic institutions." When Lehmann went down to Arizona in 1992 to check on the opera for himself, he wrote to me, describing Ross's vow: "As soon as I can find financial backing, I will do for Arizona what I did for the State of Washington, I will give it a RING and put it on the world's operatic map."

Ross himself recounted that on his plane trip to Arizona, when the pilot announced they were passing over the Grand Canyon, "an idea fell into my lap. Of course! A *Ring* at the Grand Canyon. A great setting by God and the most colossal creation of music and theater by man!" It wasn't long before Ross was in full huckster mode. One of his Arizona backers reported driving by a bus transit bench with a big "Don't Lose Your Seat!—at the Opera!" slogan, while simultaneously a bus passed by with a *Madama Butterfly* poster on it and his car radio was blaring "The Arizona Opera! It'll blow you away!"

By 1990, the once all-but-bankrupt Arizona Opera, having purchased a former supermarket as the new production and administrative headquarters, had a balanced budget and no deficit, and Ross could give serious thought to a production of the *Ring.* He had already hired his former Seattle comrade, the conductor Henry Holt, as artistic director. Ross also mined the cast lists of the old Seattle *Ring* for singers who were only too eager to work with him again, including Karen Bureau as Brünnhilde, Edward Sooter as Siegmund, Malcolm Rivers and Paul Crook as Alberich and Mime, and Noel Mangin as Hunding. Influenced by the famous Bayreuth stage *Scheibe* (disc) of the 1950s Wagner productions, Ross came up with an elevated trapezoid for the stage and projections from a Hollywood lighting company. Then, year by year, just as in Seattle, the Arizona *Ring* took shape, starting in 1992–93 with *Die Walküre,* and progressing to the complete *Ring* in 1996 and again in 1998.

Capping his thirty-four years of opera administration without a deficit, Ross became general director emeritus in Arizona and retired with Gio to the Yarrow Point, Bellevue, summer home where they had lived full time during the Seattle years.

In 1976, during Ross's Seattle heyday, Mahmoud Salem published a management study of Seattle Opera's financial and organizational structures, in which he characterized Ross's leadership style as "that of a charismatic benevolent autocrat." This means he has "the ability to command a following by force of personality and an imagination that is beyond the traditional and routine. He is benevolent in his civic-mindedness and interesting the arts, the community, and the moral role of his organization, but he is autocratic in that he appears to have unrestricted power by virtue of his expertise and personality."

No one has unrestricted power in any sphere for long. If Ross left Seattle before he wanted to, however, he rallied—even when well into retirement age—by starting over again in Arizona at a point when most executives would be looking for an easy chair. Like the characters in the *Ring* that he so loved, Ross had the ability to forge gold in support and realization of his beloved art form, and the American opera world is forever the richer because of him.

Speight Jenkins

It is a rare impresario who falls in love with Wagner's *Ring* at the age of six. But that's exactly what happened to Speight Jenkins, the Dallas-born opera genius whose thirty years at the helm of Seattle Opera transformed the company and the arts community as a whole. Jenkins's uncanny identification of talent (singers, directors, educators) and his creative vision have earned him international respect, and he also left a visible landmark: his relentless energy helped transform the aging and inadequate Seattle Opera House into Marion Oliver McCaw Hall, home to both the Seattle Opera and Pacific Northwest Ballet.

Inevitably, there has also been controversy: the *Don Giovanni* with all those chairs on the stage; the *Aida* whose triumphal scene army was represented by little gold statues; the *Walküre* in which the zaftig Brünnhilde was lowered out of a tower on a jerky harness. All caused major eruptions among the opera's attendees and the company's donor base. But Jenkins's track record has eclipsed the occasional controversy with work that is so spectacular and important that *Opera News* named him one of the "25 most powerful" figures in all of opera, and in 2011 the National Endowment for the Arts (NEA) gave him the nation's highest opera award, the NEA Opera Honors. At the award ceremony, the celebrated director Stephen Wadsworth, a longtime Seattle Opera collaborator, called Jenkins "a cross between the best professor you ever had, and a revivalist preacher. He is completely serious, completely engaging, and completely fun."

One of Seattle's most recognizable arts leaders, Jenkins—tall, slim, round-faced, and endlessly energetic in his seventies—is often imitated for his Texas twang overlain by rapid-fire New York delivery, and also for his evangelical intensity. Anyone sitting next to him on an airplane won't escape without promising to "at least attend a rehearsal" of the next Seattle Opera show. Jenkins's fans are famous for charging up to him with tears in their eyes to tell them how life changing they found a production they had just seen.

No one probably foresaw this glorious future when Jenkins's second-grade music teacher mentioned the word "opera" to him in 1943. At dinner that night, he asked his parents, "What's opera?" As he told me, he still remembers his mother's response: "It's like a play, but they sing. They have crazy stories. There's one story about a woman who is put to sleep on a rock, surrounded by fire, and her sisters fly through the air on flying horses, and they sing 'Ho-yo-to-ho.'" The excited youngster got up and ran around the table, imagining the scenario. Jenkins's practical father (also named Speight Jenkins) advised him to sit down, and he did, inquiring, "If they're stories, can I read about them?" Jenkins's mother said, "Probably so."

Jenkins's parents were not opera fanatics, but they were cultured people who were familiar with the art form. They had attended opera in New York, where they had heard such legendary singers as Enrico Caruso and Luisa Tetrazzini. Jenkins's mother, Sara Bishop Baird Jenkins, found a book of opera stories by Helen Dike, and there was the story of *Die Walküre*. The young operaphile read it, and then he read the other three *Ring* stories, and then the whole book. "But then, my teacher said, 'You know, you can listen to the Saturday afternoon opera broadcasts on the radio.' The first time I heard *Die Walküre*, I was just rapt: I can't explain it, but I was totally suckered in, absolutely dumbfounded. It was a wonderful cast, Melchior and Traubel."

When Jenkins was seven, the touring San Carlo Opera came to Dallas, presenting six or seven operas twice. He went to *Aida* and *Faust*, sitting next to a teacher, Miss Beck; when the curtain went up for *Aida* and Ramfis started singing, Jenkins leaned over to her and whispered, "What language is this?"; she said, "Spanish."

"I loved *Aida*," Jenkins remembers with a reminiscent smile. "And in *Faust*, when the devil invoked the flowers, Christmas lights went on. The next year they came back and I saw *Carmen* and *Trovatore*. Three months later, the New York Metropolitan Opera came back to Dallas, in 1946. The first opera I saw was *Rosenkavalier* with Risë Stevens, and it was beyond me at that age; I didn't get it. But the next one was critical: it was *Rigoletto*, with Leonard Warren and Jan Peerce and a soprano who wasn't so great. And when I came home, I remember I was sent outside to water the plants with a hose, and I clearly remember standing there with the hose and thinking, 'The opera is my life.' There was never any question."

Jenkins's parents were initially pleased and proud to have such a precocious opera buff in the family. Every year, they went to all the Met's touring operas, which Jenkins remembers as "my Christmas, my New Year's, my Easter, Thanksgiving, everything. I was in paradise." In those days, when the Met went on tour, even famous singers came along, so the young operaphile got to hear the "A Team" during a golden era of great singing.

"My first *Bohème*," Jenkins recalls, "was with [Bidu] Sayão and [Ferruccio] Tagliavini, and I saw [Ezio] Pinza three or four times. The big thing was *Lohengrin*—it was the first Wagner I saw, and I was completely enamored of this music. Helen Traubel, a wonderful but well-upholstered soprano, was the Elsa. We were sitting fairly far down in front; she came out on the balcony and, being Helen Traubel, the balcony wobbled a little. And my parents giggled. I was totally scandalized! I was already a Wagnerian. This was Wagner, and you don't laugh!" He heard Bjoerling, di Stefano, all the Met's top stars at the time, and these experiences built a huge memory bank of great voices and how they sounded in great operatic roles.

The senior Jenkinses initially thought that their son's opera obsession was sweet, but when young Speight continued to be opera mad into his teens, their enthusiasm waned. "When I was twelve or thirteen, my father, who knew me very well, realized there was trouble, and the battle began—and it lasted for the next twenty-five years," Jenkins says now. "Opera was not going to be my life; I was not going to be an idiot and give away my life." Jenkins's father, a successful ophthalmologist, knew he had a bright, high-energy son. He asked him, "What are you going to do with your life?—sit in an orchestra seat all your life and watch opera?"

In all fairness, as Jenkins looks back, he doesn't blame his father. "I didn't want to sing, conduct, or direct. What I wanted to do is what I do now, but I had no way of knowing about that," he says. So he went on with school, graduating Phi Beta Kappa from the University of Texas in 1957. Since he had no particular passion for any available career, Jenkins enrolled in medical school at Cornell—because of its proximity to the Met. He had no vocation for medicine and a huge enthusiasm for going to the opera; he flunked out. Trying Plan B, Jenkins enrolled in Columbia University Law School, but this time he stayed in school; he found that law required a more congenial skill set than medicine.

After law school, "blessedly, I was drafted," Jenkins remembers (and that's a phrase that may be unique in the biographical annals of opera professionals). "The army was great to me. I had a wonderful time in the army. I was thrown in with every kind of person from every class in society. It was an enormous challenge; I had never worked outside and was not athletic." As a member of the Judge Advocate General's Corps, he became a legal clerk, after which he was sent to Iran. Eventually he took a commission in the Judge Advocate General's Corps, becoming a first lieutenant and then a captain. He augmented his responsibilities by teaching English to groups of between eighteen and fifty people for twenty hours a week and producing a radio show that broadcast twenty-three of the Met's operas (from his own tapes) on the army's radio station. ("It was very much listened to in Iran.")

Iran was also where Jenkins met his future wife, Linda Sands, who was teaching French in the American School; they met in the summer of 1962.

In the army, Jenkins polished the skills that were to serve him so well later in his opera career, above all writing (all those opera broadcasts required a lot of copy) and public speaking (at twenty-four, he was required to lecture the enlisted men on military justice and how it applied to them). He learned how to ensnare and enthrall an audience, and how to get people to listen. "I was speaking to two or three hundred people," he says of those lectures, "and I can promise you they were not asleep. I had them awake, and I really told them their rights. For me, it was fantastic, because I learned how to speak to large groups and understand what it is to 'catch' an audience, to work until you get 'em. So much of my life was shaped in those four and a half years. It was as a speaker that I first came to Seattle Opera."

Columbia Law School also, of course, provided some excellent training for the skill set Jenkins later needed as an opera general director, particularly with regard to contracts. "I had great teachers there, even though I didn't always pay too much attention to what they did. How I got through tax law to this minute I do not know. Probably it was my ability to memorize."

When his army service ended in 1966, Jenkins made a beeline for the Met, deciding that one way to make sure he was in the middle of the opera world was to write about it. He became an editor and writer for *Opera News* and the *New York Post*; he lectured on opera for the Metropolitan Opera Guild; and he gained wide prominence as the host of Texaco's *Live from the Met* telecasts and as a speaker on the Met's radio broadcasts.

Jenkins's fame and his enthusiasm for Wagner made him a natural choice when Seattle Opera administrators were looking for guest lecturers for the 1981 *Ring*. His Seattle lecture on the second of the four *Ring* operas, *Die Walküre*, was so riveting and authoritative that Seattle Opera's longtime board trustee Beverly Brazeau asked him to speak to the search committee about opera and the role of the general director. The board was looking for a successor to Seattle Opera's founding director, Glynn Ross, who had accomplished wonders and balanced every budget but also presided over a gradual decline in ticket sales for the regular season (caused in part, many observers felt, by the company's annual focus on the *Ring*).

Jenkins's expertise and enthusiasm swept his Seattle listeners away. "I was flabbergasted," he later said of the board's suggestion that he apply for the directorship. "I told the board members I had not mounted a production in my life. But I was fascinated." Jenkins soon grew excited about the possibilities, and he consulted family, friends, and such opera experts as the conductor James Levine, then the artistic director of the Met.

When the Seattle Opera company announced that Jenkins would be the new impresario, the opera world was stunned. A critic as general director? Some of the responses were rude: the *Los Angeles Times* called him the "Dallas-born opera dilettante." The biweekly Arts Reporting Service predicted, "Either Jenkins will have to learn very fast while the ship sinks slowly in the harbor, or he will need a lot of kindness. In either case, Seattle Opera will lose momentum for a while."

The ship didn't sink slowly in the harbor, though Jenkins had to plug a lot of leaks. He was very lucky in his executive directors, first Kathy Magiera and then (after her tragically early death in 2002) another gifted manager, Kelly Tweeddale. But Jenkins made some beginner's mistakes in underestimating the staggering cost of mounting new productions, as opposed to that of renting existing sets and costumes from other companies. He raised Wagnerians' eyebrows by deciding first to abandon the English-language *Ring* (which he had never found convincing), and then in 1988 cancelling the summer *Ring* altogether, changing this tradition from the annual event it had been since 1975 to a less frequent special event for which extra funds were raised. But his gambles began to pay off, as operagoers learned to trust that Jenkins meant what he said in his trademark radio-ad line "It's going to be a great show—don't miss it!" One turning point was a 1988 *Orpheus and Eurydice*, an eighteenth-century opera by Gluck that received a spectacularly modern treatment with Vinson Cole as Orpheus and choreography by Mark Morris. The performances sold out to almost universal raves.

The early criticism of his ascension to general director was "daunting," Jenkins remembers. So were a few of the early unpreventable snafus, like the Wotan who went out to sing his first *Das Rheingold* in the 1984 *Ring* and completely lost his voice. Jenkins miraculously pulled off a save for the rest of the *Ring* when he discovered in his pocket the phone number for the veteran Wotan Thomas Stewart, who affably agreed to fly right up to Seattle that day and take over for the subsequent *Ring* operas. Jenkins learned from that experience to "cover" every role in the *Ring*, right down to the bear that makes a brief appearance in the third opera, *Siegfried*.

Jenkins's daring, postmodern production of the *Ring*, unveiled in 1985–86, outraged some Wagnerian purists so much that many audience members booed lustily (a Seattle *Ring* first), and some threw tomatoes at the director, François Rochaix. (Some also threw flowers.) Among Jenkins's hate mail were letters denouncing him as the Antichrist.

And then there were the dragons created for the various *Siegfried* productions, beasts that Jenkins calls "my bête noire." The most infamous of these was a dragon so huge that all the audience could see of it were its dangling legs, which looked like the appendages of a crab. Instead of stabbing the dragon to the heart, poor Siegfried could only poke it in the fetlock. After the resulting jibes about "crab legs," Jenkins refused for years to eat crab.

Jenkins was never afraid to dream big. He'd always wanted to see the Valkyries actually flying through the air on horseback, and that finally transpired, through the aerial horses created by the design and direction efforts of Robert Israel and François Rochaix joined with the wizardry of Seattle Opera's tech team. Jenkins's dreams also extended to programming. After his appointment, Jenkins said that he wanted to produce all ten of the standard canon of Wagner's works at Seattle Opera, beginning in his first season with *Tannhäuser*. And that's exactly what he did in the twenty-five years that followed, including two complete *Ring*s and, in August 2003, a memorable new production of Wagner's last opera, *Parsifal*.

With Jenkins every step of the way was his mother, Sara, affectionately called the "grande dame of the Seattle Opera." She was a gracious, warm presence at every Seattle Opera performance, a de facto mom to the casts and crew, and the object of devotion for her son, who prepared dinner for her every evening, no matter what else was happening. At the age of eighty-eight, she made her opera debut as a supernumerary in *The Dialogues of the Carmelites*, as the chapter's oldest nun in a vintage wheelchair.

The list of national and local honors that Speight Jenkins accrued over the years is impressive. He received an honorary doctorate of humanities from Seattle University, an honorary doctorate of music from the University of Puget Sound in Tacoma, and an honorary doctorate from the New England Conservatory. He also served on the National Council on the Arts from 1996 to 2000. In Seattle, he was honored for his "immeasurable contributions to the city's cultural arts and civic life" by a mayoral proclamation naming April 25, 2009, as Speight Jenkins Day; he also received a Mayor's Arts Award in September 2009. The *Seattle Times* named Jenkins one of the 150 most influential people who have shaped the character of Seattle and King County; ArtsFund, Seattle's united fund of corporate donors to the arts, presented him with its Out-standing Achievement in the Arts Award, and, as already noted, *Opera News* cited Jenkins as one of the twenty-five "most powerful" names in opera in America. And in 2015, he was decorated by the French government as "Chevalier des Arts et des Lettres."

A big baseball fan, Jenkins even threw out the ceremonial first pitch for a Seattle Mariners' game. But, of course, he's an even greater Wagner fan, and in recognition of the centrality of Wagner to Seattle Opera's mission, the company's offices are closed every May 22 in observance of Der Meister's birthday.

In the last few years of Jenkins's directorship, the monetary woes of a major recession dealt the company blow after major blow. Three planned reprises of Wagnerian productions, for which new and enticing casting arrangements had been made (*Tannhäuser, Die Meistersinger*, and *Parsifal*) had to be replaced by less expensive shows, much to the chagrin of the company and fans alike. In 2012, Seattle Opera announced that an unprecedented million-dollar deficit would necessitate one fewer production for 2013–14 (Jenkins's last season as general director) and 2014–15, as well as the temporary suspension of its successful Young Artists program, to be replaced in 2014 with a return of the International Wagner Competition for young singers.

Galling though these changes must have been for Jenkins, he is philosophical about the need to retrench in keeping with the times. He prefers to focus on the company's achievements. Ask him what he's proudest of and, after citing each of his family members, he'll mention a dedication that he has stuck to throughout his opera career: "I am proud of being one of the people committed to casting and fostering black male singers," he says. "The first article I wrote for the *New York Times* in 1972 was on that subject. I have always felt, as an American, and as a Southerner, that this was important. Our audiences have learned that great talent is not a matter of race. The first time we put Vinson [the tenor Vinson Cole, who became a Seattle Opera mainstay] in bed with a white girl, no one said a word."

The most famous of the African American singers whom Jenkins has championed is Lawrence Brownlee, who now performs and records on the world's leading opera stages. In 2006, Brownlee won both the Marian Anderson and the Richard Tucker Awards, a feat never before achieved by any artist in the same year. "I look at my career and I am thankful for so many who have helped me along the way," Brownlee said during a 2013 engagement in Vienna, "but none have had the indelible personal and professional impact on my career as Speight Jenkins. Speight holds a very special place in my heart. From the very beginning of my career during my days as a Young Artist at Seattle Opera, Speight has been the biggest supporter, advisor, mentor, and friend. I am eternally grateful to him for having believed in my gift and giving me my professional start." Jenkins, too, is proud of Seattle Opera's success, but he terms this an ensemble and not a solo effort. "Everybody together has made Seattle Opera as significant a theater as it is. This is not a personal accomplishment. Together we have created a great opera company to which everyone contributes: It is not 'the Speight show.'"

Well, maybe. There are some who would disagree, considering Jenkins's tremendous and wholehearted involvement in every aspect of producing opera. As the director Stephen Wadsworth pointed out at the NEA Honors ceremony, Jenkins "visits his lead singers before, during, and after every single show and meets the audience in postshow talkbacks. He has vast knowledge, gleeful intelligence, charm, frankness, warmth, utter fearlessness, and unparalleled enthusiasm for the art he serves." On the same occasion, the stellar mezzo-soprano Stephanie Blythe observed: "Speight sits in the room with you from the first rehearsal to the last. He has as an encyclopedic knowledge of opera. He makes the experience feel very safe."

In his interview with NPR's Nina Totenberg at the NEA Honors ceremony, Jenkins explained his philosophy: "My job is to welcome singers, conductors, and directors to Seattle and to make them understand how important it is what they're doing. In 1968, Birgit Nilsson gave an interview in which she said, 'Songbirds sing when they're happy. I'm not happy.' Our job is to make the singers happy. If they are difficult to the wigmaker or the people they work with, I won't bring them back. You'd be surprised how many so-called difficult people have walked through Seattle without any trouble."

He also explained the reason he sits in on all the rehearsals: "In any rehearsal there are two bosses: a director and a conductor. There are times when they have absolutely different ideas. I would prefer to deal with those ideas right there, to negotiate between them. My job is to stand behind what I present to the public. If the director does something with which I violently disagree, I would rather be there to talk it out. I don't understand going to the opera at the piano dress [rehearsal] and saying, 'That won't work.'" He also takes very seriously his role as an ambassador and popularizer of opera. "If an opera director isn't a proselytizer, what *is* he?" he asked Totenberg rhetorically. "We're not a baseball team. We have to constantly bring people to opera." Even when controversy about the company's 1986 Rochaix-Israel *Ring* was at its height, Jenkins never shirked what he saw as his responsibility to the public. He answered all three hundred letters—split about half and half between the cheers and the jeers—that impassioned *Ring* fans sent him after the final scene in the 1986 *Götterdämmerung*, in which performance artists bearing red cloth represented the immolation.

Jenkins is famous across the country for being a hands-on general director. As Santa Fe Opera's general director Charles McKay put it, "Speight may be unique in the world of opera in observing and participating in this [rehearsal] process. A general director needs to be there particularly if a scene isn't working or if there is a problem with the creative team. The rehearsals are where those problems get fixed; it's much harder to fix them later, on the stage." As Evans Mirageas, the artistic director of Cincinnati Opera, has observed, "You can't complain about the food if you haven't been in the kitchen." Mirageas admires Jenkins's total involvement in the whole production process, calling him "one of the finest opera impresarios on the planet, and a real mentor. He has an appetite for work and for total involvement that is just astonishing. He's my hero."

It is the discovery of great voices that thrills Jenkins the most. He does all the company's casting, and after having heard almost all of the great voices since the 1940s, he knows how to identify that inexpressible quality that will entrance the ear. Thus it was in 1994, when an unknown English soprano made her American debut in Seattle as Norma, as the last-minute replacement when Carol Vaness had to cancel. After hearing Jane Eaglen sing, Jenkins immediately took her out to lunch and asked whether she would like to sing Isolde and Brünnhilde in Seattle. "I am not hesitant about deciding what voices can do," Jenkins explains. "When I heard Christiane Libor in Berlin, Patrick Summers [music director of Houston Grand Opera] came with me, and she offered to sing the 'Abscheulicher!' [Leonore's challenging big aria in Beethoven's *Fidelio*]. We looked at each other in amazement. This was a voice worth doing a *Fidelio* for!" That is exactly what Jenkins did, in October 2012.

But it is Wagnerian opera that most occupies Jenkins's attention. He calls the *Ring* "absolutely central to us, for one big reason: not many companies have a niche of their own, but the *Ring* is our niche. La Scala has Verdi; the Met has the world's best singers. But Seattle Opera does the *Ring*. That's what has made us famous, and it's one reason we are among the largest opera companies in the United States despite the fact that fast-growing Seattle is *still* way down on the list of the country's largest cities [number 21, according to the US Census Bureau in 2013]."

Jenkins has taken some criticism over the years for certain lacunae in his programming. He doesn't program much baroque music "because it doesn't mean a lot to me." Jenkins's strong likes and dislikes also mean that operas he isn't wild about, like Stravinsky's *The Rake's Progress*, weren't a part of his administration. Operettas, by and large, don't translate well to contemporary opera stages, he believes ("I saw the Met die with *Gypsy Baron* in the 1960s"), though he exempts such operatic operettas as *Die Fledermaus* and *Merry Widow*.

And no musicals, please, not for this opera company. "I like Rodgers and Hammerstein," he says, "and I love *West Side Story*. But I don't have a company of Jets and Sharks, so doing that doesn't make sense to me."

Perhaps things will be different in Seattle Opera's next era under his successor, Aidan Lang. Jenkins hopes that the company's core values will, however, remain intact, including the emphasis on Wagner, which is in Seattle Opera's mission statement. It's not an easy job: "Running an opera company properly requires total involvement: it's an all-day, all-night, every-day-of-the-year job. There will be cancellations; singers drop out, they get sick. But you're paid to keep the curtain up, and also to find great singers and bring them to Seattle," Jenkins observes.

Jenkins advocates finding new operas that haven't been performed in Seattle (eighty-seven operas were done during his tenure) and a mix of familiar and new singers to create balanced casts. An incurable optimist, he believes that the recession that caused the 2012 cuts in programming will be reversed, and that before the end of four years or so, America will experience "a huge burst of energy." "I haven't given thirty years of my life to this company to leave it in bad shape," he declares. "That's not the way I am. We are working hard on that eternal war with the budget."

Not surprisingly, this super-organized director has three plans for his retirement years. First, he would like to return to his roots as a writer, to complete the book he has long postponed, *Opera through the Eyes of Singers*, which is based on interviews with many of the great singers he knew in their prime. The interviews have been done and transcribed. "Now all I have to do is fill in the last thirty years," he quips. "But you know what [Renata] Tebaldi said: 'There are no singers now.'" In addition to lecturing on opera for Stanford University's continuing education program, Jenkins also plans to do some consulting for opera companies, not on the business side of the organization, but as a talent prospector who finds and assesses voices and works with singers. Finally, he's also planning to write his memoirs— "to be published after I'm dead," Jenkins says firmly.

And he would like to travel, this time for pleasure rather than for the endless scouting and auditions of the past decades. He and his wife, Linda, a sensory motor therapist who treats posttrauma patients, "travel well" together, as he puts it. You can bet, however, that they'll still be making stops at the world's great opera houses.

"So much of my life has been work," Jenkins notes of his career in opera. Indeed it has been. And Seattle has been the beneficiary of this hardworking general director who has been the artistic leader, the architect of the directorial teams, the messiah of opera to the masses, the schmoozer of donors and soother of divas, and the visionary who pulled Seattle Opera into the twenty-first century. Any way you look at it, the grand opera of Speight Jenkins's thirty-year run will be a tough act to follow.

Toby Saks

THE IMPRESARIA

It was such a modest idea at first, back in 1981. Toby Saks, the University of Washington cellist and displaced New Yorker, just wanted "something small and cozy, with a few musicians," to make chamber music together. She was fairly new in Seattle, having arrived at UW in 1976 as a young mother with two children and a six-year history in the New York Philharmonic's cello section. "I wanted so much to have a project of my own," she remembers, "and I was just a ball of energy then. When Paul Rosenthal invited me to the Sitka Festival, I sounded him out and asked, How do you start a festival? He said you have to find some people who are interested, and a site, and some musicians—it's easy!"

Well, the term "easy" is perhaps relative. Saks knew music, and she certainly knew the cello, but she had almost no administrative or entrepreneurial experience. Born into a working-class immigrant family in 1942, she had begun music lessons at the age of five and gone on to study at the Juilliard School with the great cellist Leonard Rose. Among her achievements were prize-winning performances at both the Tchaikovsky Competition in Moscow and Casals Competition in Israel, Fulbright and Rockefeller grants, and studies with Andre Navarra at the Conservatoire de Musique in Paris. She made her Town Hall debut at the age of eighteen, after winning the New York Young Concert Artists auditions, and this was followed by many more engagements as a soloist. In 1970, Saks became the third woman member of the New York Philharmonic.

"I was not someone who had been a go-getter," Saks reflected. "As a soloist, I had a manager who said, you can play here and here and here. In the [New York] Philharmonic, I had a schedule, and here in Seattle, I had a teaching job with an assignment. But I was actually very shy." Spurred by her desire to follow in Rosenthal's footsteps and create her own festival, Saks got up the nerve to phone Maxine Cushing Gray, a noted and acerbic Seattle writer and critic who published her own biweekly journal, *Northwest Arts*, for advice. "Calling Maxine was a big deal—calling up a stranger who wrote for her own arts journal!" says Saks. "That was the first time in my life I'd ever done anything like that, and I was exhilarated beyond belief."

Gray came up with the idea of a destination festival at the Pilchuck Glass Institute, which had a hall and dormitories. It was pretty far from Seattle—about an hour's drive to the north, near the town of Stanwood—but Saks and Gray both liked the idea of a scenic spot where music lovers might spend several days in residence.

During a talk with the Seattle tax attorney and arts activist Meade Emory, whom Saks called "a doer and a real Renaissance man," Saks brought up her dream of starting a small chamber music festival that wouldn't compete with the then-annual residency of the Santa Fe Chamber Music Festival each August. Emory asked Saks to clarify her thoughts by posing specific questions: How long a duration for the festival? How many concerts, how many musicians, and how much would you have to pay them? And where would it be held? Saks was interested in the Pilchuck site, but it was far off and, more significant, it lacked a real concert hall. Emory drew up a proposal based on their conversation, and Saks had a real document with a real plan, as succinct and organized as a legal document.

By chance, Saks was at this same time looking for a good private school for her daughter, Claire, and she attended a prospective parents' introduction at the Lakeside School in north Seattle. And there it was: the handsome little 425-seat Saint Nicholas Hall, located next to the expansive green lawns and leafy trees that would in time shelter many preconcert picnickers. "I looked at the campus, and I realized: this was it," Saks remembers.

A few days later, the arts supporters Hans and Thelma Lehmann were holding a fund-raising dinner party of about thirty people for the Santa Fe Chamber Music Festival, and they invited Saks. On Saks's left at the dinner was the businessman and arts fan George Wade. Hearing about her idea, Wade was immediately enthusiastic and asked to see Emory's proposal. "I was thinking, 'This cannot be happening!'" Saks marvels.

Saks, Wade, and Wade's wife, Arlene, stayed after the dinner ended to discuss the idea with their hosts. Hans and Thelma Lehmann had "lightbulbs in their eyes," says Saks of their immediate enthusiasm for her idea. All of them loved the Santa Fe Festival, whose highly popular summer visits repeatedly sold out the 1,200-seat Meany Theater on the University of Washington campus. But they also saw the value of something indigenous and homegrown, a festival that would be Seattle's alone and not a "run-out" from a different state.

The enthusiasm of this group buoyed Saks up as they went about recruiting more board members and patrons, including Arlene Wade's friend Jeanne Ehrlichman Bluechel, who was a dynamo of an arts advocate. Emboldened by Bluechel, Saks called Sam and Gladys Rubinstein, who were among the region's leading arts philanthropists, and Sam invited her to choose at which of his many clubs she would like to meet. In offering a challenge grant (one in which the release of specified funds is contingent upon matching funds achieved from other sources), the Rubinsteins also gave the fledgling festival a solid legitimacy that helped attract further support. They also later subsidized the much needed air-conditioning in Saint Nicholas Hall, where the concerts were held.

Emory called a meeting of the conspirators at 7 a.m., timing that floored Saks: musicians are not usually active in the early hours, and, as she put it, "Never in my life had I attended a 7 a.m. meeting." At that meeting, they decided to expand the board and hire a business manager—that was to be Cindy Streltzov—to print tickets, arrange contracts, and rent a hall. "This was all happening in October and November," Saks remembers, "for a festival that was going to open in June! It was very mom and pop. We asked so many people to give and to help, and . . . somehow everybody said yes."

With only about eight months before the festival was to launch its first concert, the board figured that about twenty thousand dollars would be needed. (The real budget, of course, ended up twice that size.) By December, Saks was calling up musicians, hustling to make up programs in time for printing, and trying to lay out photos and copy for the brochures. George Wade donated office space, and UW donated rehearsal space. The Lakeside School made its performance facilities available at a very reasonable rent. The *Seattle Weekly* publisher, David Brewster, provided important sponsorship, and Arlene Wade and Jeanne Bluechel took care of the artistic issues, right down to the color of the ink on the stationery. "I invited artists I knew and respected," Saks recalls, "people like Paul Rosenthal, Stephen Kates, Edward Auer, Stephanie Brown, Ik-Hwan Bae. We got a lot of community support, and a lot of great press, and we actually oversold tickets that year. It was like a fairy tale."

The first year was the model for the subsequent festivals. Board members and other supporters housed the musicians and made them feel thoroughly at home, providing cars for them to drive. Saks even asked her neighbors, on both sides of her house, to put up musicians. Saks's own house became command central, with everyone given a key so that they could hang out and eat and relax there. People picked up pizza, beer, salad, and paper plates for impromptu dinners, which later became considerably more elaborate. Saks later hired a resident chef, Tom Bennett, and the food is now so popular that musicians joke they're only there for the dinners.

Saks's two young children, Claire and Mischa Berlinski (now both successful novelists), were a part of it all and loved hanging out with the musicians, who were unfailingly kind and receptive. The cellist Ron Thomas taught Mischa how to bat a baseball. Both kids got to watch rehearsals.

Not surprisingly, the hugely successful six-concert debut year was followed by an expansion to three weeks. By the third year, 1984, the festival had expanded to four weeks, which has been the standard ever since. In celebration of Bach's three hundredth birthday in 1985, free preconcert recitals were added, and these were kept on for subsequent seasons.

Personnel issues weren't a major problem for Saks, who recognized that chamber music is a skill that not all excellent players possess. Some musicians are incredible soloists, but they don't have either the experience or the ability to listen to others. Along the way, there were people like that, who found difficulty fitting in with fellow musicians, and they weren't real chamber players who could pick up the nonverbal cues or respond to ideas thrown out by others. Sometimes there were personality issues, or people who could be inflexible. They weren't invited back. "My responsibility always was for the quality and happiness of the group. I wanted to be first on the list of where they wanted to play in the summer. The board was full of high-powered and distinguished people, and I was responsible for the artistic side. Connie Cooper [who came aboard as executive director in 1996] really professionalized the board and staff, and because she was a musician, too, she understands both sides—administrative and artistic—so well." Saks learned tact, and she learned how to get consensus among the various sides of the organization. She learned to say, "Let's explore this further" and "That's worth thinking about" instead of "No."

"I did get some pressure from the board to play less, and that was a good thing, because I was exhausted," Saks said. "I played a lot at first, because I wanted to save the festival money. Finally Marty [the gastroenterologist and bibliophile Martin L. Greene, whom Saks married in 1987] said, 'You cannot continue at this pace as you get older.' I was ready to stop feeling like I was a performer and more like I wanted to be out in the audience at intermission raising money and talking to people. This came about at the time when we were also talking about longevity and securing the festival's future. Some board members said, 'There's not going to be a festival after Toby.' But we wanted the security of knowing that there would be a successor when the time came. And that process took five years. The goal was to pass the succession on to someone who could carry it forward in a brilliant way into the twenty-first century. After all, I belong to the twentieth century."

The violinist and current artistic director James Ehnes started performing with the festival in 1995, when he was just a teenager and too young even to rent his own car. Saks knew him to be an extraordinary artist, much more mature than his years. "I saw him organize things for his own career, assembling an orchestra for a concerto recording and finding an apartment in another city. I saw him handle musicians in rehearsals with great dignity, tact, and authority. I saw him beloved by all the other musicians for his kind nature and his artistry. I saw that he was the perfect successor."

Saks took exhaustive notes on her computer during the development of each festival, so if anything happened to her, all the details would be available to her successor. She noted every conversation with every musician. "I was religious about that, because if something did happen, I wanted someone else to know exactly what was going on with the festival."

Around 2007, Saks and the board scheduled a retreat to discuss her succession. She had sounded Ehnes out privately beforehand, asking him if he would eventually like to take over the festival, and his reply had been an enthusiastic "YES!" But Ehnes had concert bookings for many years in advance and would need five years of notice to block out the time in his calendar and secure the dates with his managers. "I knew I would be very fine with stopping as artistic director at the age of seventy," Saks recalled. Ehnes talked with the board's executive committee about all the details. He asked Saks, "How do you handle this, and when do you start doing that?" and she advised him. Saks also asked his opinion about which pianists, violinists, and composers he would like to invite.

Then came the issue of what to call Saks, after Ehnes took over in 2012. How about "founding director" or "director emeritus"? "It sounds like I'm dead," Saks quipped. "Since I'm still involved and go to all the board meetings to relay things to Jimmy, and I'm helping with the fund-raising, why not call me associate director? Then I feel like I'm alive, and when Jimmy can't be in residence I have a title that makes it bona fide. I'm not just hanging around like a groupie. I can be helpful to the extent that anyone wants help."

The title was a sort of security blanket for organizers and audiences, to reassure them that Saks would be around in case of need. She in turn was less pressured and harried because her responsibilities were fewer. She left all the key decisions to Ehnes, who has introduced new music and new artists and is shaping the festival in his own creative ways. Because he is a stellar violinist, colleagues are eager to perform with him and quick to trust his judgment. And the public has confidence in the festival's future.

That confidence is important. Saks confessed that the festival organizers were nervous when in 2010 they had to move the festival venue, after the Lakeside School decided it needed the use of its campus in the summer and could no longer host the concerts. But audiences followed the festival to its new downtown home in Benaroya Hall's 540-seat Nordstrom Recital Hall. They also followed the festival across Lake Washington from Seattle to concerts on the Eastside, when additional programs were offered there 2005–11, though that expansion was ultimately cancelled because the smaller venue was not profitable.

One innovation that has worked particularly well is the organization's Winter Festival, which began in 1999 as a weekend of concerts in January at the Nordstrom Recital Hall and has since expanded; the 2015 version included everything from some seldom-heard Turina to Schubert's beloved "Arpeggione" Sonata. Another important innovation, the Commissioning Club, brought together festival supporters in 2007 in a group that annually underwrote new works for the festival.

Innovation was also a central principle in Saks's career path:

> I've changed my life many times over the years. I was a soloist
> and sent on tour, but I never liked traveling, and those years on
> the road were sad. Then I had children, and I loved being in the
> [New York] Philharmonic—I loved the sound of the orchestra
> and the repertoire. But I saw what happened with a lifetime in
> the orchestra, staying there until age seventy and sitting in the
> same seat. I knew I wanted to live in the Northwest, so I told
> my teacher, Leonard Rose, and he was contacted by Eva Hein-
> itz, who was retiring from the cello position at the University
> of Washington. I respected her very much and she scared the
> hell out of me. She was fascinating, and I learned a lot from her
> musically, because we had discussions about many pieces. She
> was so European, so German. I never could say a personal thing
> to her, like if I was feeling sad about something. She did all the
> talking, but she was an amazing woman, a pioneer who was
> denied certain positions she should have gotten just because
> she was a female.

And Vilem Sokol influenced me so much. I loved him and Agatha and his love of music and students and teaching, and how kind he was to me. He was our best man when Marty and I got married. This man and his wife were my surrogate parents in Seattle. If I ever had a problem, they said, "Come on out." They would invite me for Christmas Eve. His goodness was an inspiration to me. Near the end of his life, he told Marty that he was dying, and that he was ready to die. Marty told him: "You are a great conductor of life." Bill's last note to me was dictated to his daughter Jenny, and in it he said, "You know, if you forget about me, I'll come after you!"

Over the years, Saks grew more and more interested in chamber music, constantly listening to music and scavenging CDs, which later formed the backbone of her festival programming. "Nobody knew the Elgar quintet before we started playing it," she remembers, "and we introduced our festival audiences to so many great pieces. I was naïve and shy, and I never imagined starting a festival like this one. It changed my life in so many ways. I met so many wonderful people I never would have known about otherwise. Now I'm a mentor and a teacher, and a patron of the arts, and an assistant in any way I can be for the festival. For some reason, teaching has grown to be such a love of mine. I can't tell you how much I enjoy my teaching and my students. I enjoy every second of it. It's the mentor stage of life, when you suddenly realize how inspiring it is to be able to impart what you know to young people. As Marty calls me, I'm a grande dame—old enough now to command respect. When you're seventy, you're an icon in some ways. Not that I'm boasting—but it's a very luxurious feeling."

Saks had all too short an interval to enjoy that new stage of her life. On August 1, 2013, she died, only a few months after her pancreatic cancer diagnosis, mourned by musicians and music lovers all over the world. Many of them gathered in Seattle's Benaroya Hall to perform a memorial concert on October 14, 2013, that will be long remembered. Her legacy continues on in the festival and in the lives of her colleagues and students.

Louis Richmond

The black brochure folds up like a map, printed on luxurious stock that still feels new after more than three decades. An arty photo of two formally dressed mimes—one with a violin—is captioned, "Music Rendezvous . . . Come With Us." Inside there's a tantalizing list of world-famous chamber orchestras, all of which will appear that season in the Seattle Opera House and Meany Theater. The lineup is certainly unequalled by anything presented in Seattle three decades later: the Academy of Saint Martin in the Fields Octet, Toronto's Tafelmusik, the Chamber Orchestra of Versailles, the Swiss Chamber Orchestra, the Bohemian Virtuosi of Prague.

And who presented all these chamber orchestras? Here's the surprise: the city of Seattle. Specifically, it was the Seattle Department of Parks and Recreation, whose Music Advisory Committee was then headed by the conductor, cellist, and impresario Louis Richmond.

Imagine that Seattle's commitment to the musical arts included funding and presenting not only this stellar series but also many other concert or recital presentations in parks, theaters, and small venues all over the region. It was certainly a different era, both in the world of politics and in Seattle's music scene. Richmond was just the man to know which groups to hire and how to promote them. It's no accident that the decades that followed his concert-presenting and conducting career saw the development of his successful public relations firm, Richmond Public Relations.

The decade or so that followed the 1962 World's Fair brought a number of significant musical innovations, but among the most important of these was Richmond's arrival in Seattle to found the Northwest Chamber Orchestra (NWCO), especially as at the time there were no visiting or resident chamber music festivals and very few performances of the rich centuries-wide repertoire for chamber orchestra.

Not every successful musical enterprise goes on in perpetuity: one thinks of the Seattle International Chamber Music Festival, which originated in 1977 as the highly popular annual Seattle residency of the Santa Fe Chamber Music Festival in the 1,200-seat Meany Theater (where the festival sold out *two* nightly performances to enthusiastic crowds). The new International, as it was nicknamed, was created by the Seattle board that had presented those Santa Fe residencies for fifteen years. But despite the organizers' efforts to sign stellar artists like Dmitry Sitkovetsky and Truls Mørk and to find a new niche, the festival—which twice changed name, venue, format, and almost every other aspect of the previously winning formula—failed to catch on with audiences and donors. That big, devoted audience of chamber music fans went elsewhere.

Louis Richmond's tenure as music director of the Northwest Chamber Orchestra lasted only seven years, and the NWCO filed for bankruptcy in 2006, thirty-three years after Richmond founded it in 1973. During those thirty-three years, however, the NWCO was a major force on Seattle's classical scene, and it almost certainly would never have existed in the first place but for Richmond.

So who is this imaginative promoter and conductor?

Richmond, who has just edged into septuagenarian status at this writing, bounds to the door with the energy of a guy who has run fifty marathons and is still active in the PR firm he founded. He and his wife, Betty Ann, have a poodle the size of a calf, a nice house surrounded by trees, and a penchant for travel. He has a warm welcome even for a music critic who did not always review him as favorably as he might have wished. Upon request, Richmond provides a condensed version of how it all started in an interview over coffee at his home. "I came to the Northwest to teach cello at the University of Puget Sound and conduct its chamber orchestra, in 1970, from the University of Nevada where I was teaching and conducting, and where I also founded a chamber orchestra."

Richmond had studied with Orlando Cole, the cellist of the Curtis String Quartet, and then with Lorne Monroe, the principal cellist of the Philadelphia Orchestra. "Lorne took me on as his student," Richmond explains. "He was very important to me: I named our son after him." After graduation, in 1964, he played in the National Symphony for two years ("I think I was the youngest person in the symphony—I was twenty-one"). He then returned to Philadelphia to pursue a master's degree and spent his summers playing concerts of Bach Suites, the Brandenburgs, and cantatas with the noted harpsichordist Seymour Lipkin at Tanglewood.

Richmond's first major teaching job was at the University of Nevada at Reno. "I was asked to play in the clubs, and I started a chamber orchestra of the club musicians, who were superb," he remembers. "I played shows with four cellos, featuring Glen Campbell, Bill Cosby, Bobbie Gentry, Chet Atkins—and Liberace—for several weeks. He asked me to go on tour." Richmond and his colleagues also performed with two elephants, Bertha and Tina. Bertha, as he recalls, had painted toenails. This was not a high point in his musical career. "I hated Reno," Richmond confesses. "It was culturally all wrong for us: we were East Coast hippies. There were only a couple of copies of the Sunday *New York Times* in town, and no daily *Times*. We wanted to leave the East Coast and try the West, but I knew as soon as I got there I had made a mistake. We considered moving to six cities that were on the water and had culture, from Montreal and Boston to Portland and Vancouver. When we came to Seattle, it was a beautiful day, and we thought, 'Great!' Then we moved here and didn't see the mountains for almost two months."

Richmond was hired at the University of Puget Sound to teach cello and conduct the chamber orchestra, but he left because "I didn't get along with the dean." He moved to Seattle's Montlake district, but his new job in the Highline school district didn't prove a better fit. So Richmond decided to start a chamber orchestra. "I put up flyers in the neighborhood for the Montlake Chamber Orchestra, and people actually came to the rehearsal. One of them was [bass player] Nancy Griffin, from the Seattle Symphony. She and other people said, 'Why don't you start a real orchestra?'"

Out of the Montlake Chamber Players grew the Northwest Chamber Orchestra. It was a different time, as the orchestra evolved in the years 1972 and 1973. Those were the days when performers could tap into the Music Performance Trust Fund (funds for live music provided by a share of royalties from the recording industry). Richmond put together about a dozen musicians and was able to get a thousand dollars for two rehearsals and a free concert at the Poncho Theatre at Woodland Park Zoo. The program included music by Alan Hovhaness, who, Richmond knew, lived in Seattle, as well as such hits as the Albinoni Adagio and the Pachelbel Canon.

City councilman John Miller (later a congressman) came to the concert and wrote Richmond to tell him that he loved the concert—and how could he help him? Richmond told him that his goal was to start a chamber orchestra. "And lo and behold, there was a chamber orchestra, playing four concerts in Occidental Square and applying for Seattle Arts Commission grants. That's how it started," Richmond recalls.

Two factors were in his favor: the eagerness of music lovers to discover and hear the chamber orchestra repertoire, and his own eagerness to promote it. As he puts it, "I went around to people and asked for money; I got grants. People loaned us money and later converted nearly all the loans to contributions. We had musicians who wanted to play, and we had an audience."

The fledgling Northwest Chamber Orchestra presented a six-concert series in 1973, performing each concert twice, with support from the Seattle and King County Arts Commissions and Allied Arts. The NWCO was the first Northwest music organization to organize a fund-raising auction; Richmond's neighbor, John Collins [the later founder of Fifth Avenue Records], donated twelve Mark Tobey drawings. "No one was doing stuff like this at the time," Richmond says.

The connection with Hovhaness was great for the brand-new NWCO. Hovhaness, a colorful, listener-friendly Seattle composer with an international profile, was delighted by the young orchestra, and audiences were delighted by him. Hovhaness began writing music for the NWCO, and he also wrote a birthday piece for Richmond.

The orchestra created a traffic jam at the city's Bumbershoot Festival when the NWCO did two capacity-audience concerts for First Chamber Dance with Charles Bennett and *The Moor's Pavane*, José Limón's dance meditation on *Othello*. The NWCO presented Stravinsky's *L'histoire du soldat* at the old ACT Theatre (which was later converted to On the Boards), where the orchestra regularly performed, and they did kids' concerts and music by local composers with student soloists. The orchestra later moved to the Intiman Theatre at Seattle Center, and then to the now defunct Seattle Concert Theatre next to the *Seattle Times*. The Philadelphia String Quartet and the violinist Stanley Ritchie performed with the NWCO, as did the soprano Elly Ameling, the pianist Lorin Hollander, the bassist Gary Karr, and the conductor Jean-Philippe Paillard.

"All of a sudden I was a conductor!" Richmond recalls.

The NWCO came to life in a period just before the huge early-music revival of the 1970s brought historically informed performances to the fore in this region. There already was a long history of early-music activity in Seattle, but the Early Music Guild, today's major presenter of period music in the Northwest, wasn't launched until 1977. "We didn't have any concerns about stylistic stuff back then," says Richmond of the 1973 NWCO. "I knew about the early-music movement, but I wasn't interested in it. It was like driving a Model T today: I knew about them, but I didn't want to drive one. I was interested in doing what I liked, and what the audience liked. We just played and had fun. We did the Brandenburgs and the *Art of the Fugue*. We didn't have the greatest critical support, but the audience loved it."

So did the players, from the concertmaster, Jim Shallenberger (formerly of the Kronos Quartet), to the cellist Terri Benshoof (later of the Seattle Symphony), the violinist Corinne Odegaard (now retired from the SSO), the violist Eileen Swanson (Pacific Northwest Ballet Orchestra), and such performer-teachers as the violist Greg Savage and the harpsichordist Virginia Moore.

"We were a ragtag bunch of young musicians back in the 1970s—passionate, committed to our art, and, at times, insufferably full of ourselves," remembers the violinist Dorothea "Deede" Cook (formerly Evans). "We had to learn the hard way how a professional orchestra works; we didn't have a group of wise elders in the group guiding us. So we stumbled around and stepped on each other's toes while we figured out orchestral etiquette and protocol. In addition to learning how to play together, we had to learn our role as union musicians—how to negotiate agreements with the management and board. We made lots of mistakes. But when it came to playing music, we played with spirit and fervor. What we lacked in refinement we made up with enthusiasm. Many of us who were in the orchestra under Louie's direction are still leading active lives as professional musicians. We owe him a lot—and Seattle owes him a lot."

Though funding grew to be more of a problem as government entities tightened their budgets, Richmond "hustled and wrote grants" to pay for the hundred services the orchestra was playing annually by 1979.

And that was the year in which, as Richmond puts it, "I lost the board." In a move announced on July 10, 1979, in the *Seattle Times*, Richmond was divested of his artistic leadership position and most of his conducting duties for the 1979–80 season because of a "reorganization of leadership," which the board chairman Mike Rees announced as "a joint decision between Richmond and ourselves."

"At the end of seven years, bang! I'm out," Richmond recollects today. "And things changed pretty radically. In all fairness, things do change after a few years. People want something new. I was just Louie; I wasn't a star. I had no credentials. I was just a cello teacher. I didn't promote myself or build relationships. If I look back, I probably would have spent more time cultivating the board. I didn't do that. Why? I don't know. We had people on the board who were more interested in providing cheese and crackers at the reception than in raising money and maybe understanding music a little better."

Richmond contrasts the NWCO board then with that of the Saint Paul Chamber Orchestra, whose primary responsibility is seen as fiduciary. They raise money for the executive director, he notes; they "don't decide on repertoire, conductors, soloists, or which cheese to serve after the concert." Clearly, however, all boards of directors also have a say in hiring and firing the music director, as the NWCO board did. "Could I have done things differently? Of course I could have. But my life has turned out pretty cool. At the time when I lost my job, though, of course it was horrible. It was my baby. I had an agreement that I got paid for a year, and I didn't get paid very well—I never made twenty thousand dollars—and I couldn't say anything negative about the orchestra, of course."

When Richmond left the NWCO, he went to work for two Seattle hotels (the Alexis and the Sheraton) and the Seattle Department of Parks and Recreation as a programmer and presenter of concerts. He didn't look back, and he didn't do any conducting. Revisiting the NWCO, Richmond says, would have been "like returning to an ex-wife. My life had taken such a radical turn." Spurred by his PR successes, he started his own firm, Richmond Public Relations, in 1992, and he has done very well. "I could never have gone back to living hand to mouth," he muses. "I've driven a Jaguar for eleven years. I love my car. I like this house. We travel a lot. I've just run my fiftieth marathon, and we're going on a cruise of the Middle East. Things are pretty wonderful."

Richmond still plays the cello for fun, with the jazz pianist Overton Berry and also in a trio. He still misses the NWCO, and he misses conducting, but he muses that these days he would perform works of Arvo Pärt and Michael Nyman. Ultimately, Richmond feels, the orchestra should never have been allowed to fail. "I feel very bad about that. Something died that you created. I still think that even with all the Early Music Guild programs, and the Seattle Symphony doing their chamber concerts, there was a niche for the NWCO. It should still be around."

Ironically, one reason was the lack of the kind of PR that Richmond did in his successful public relations career. Richmond feels that the NWCO eventually suffered because many of its conductors weren't local. "I was out there hustling, writing grants, touring all over the state with Arts Commission money. We toured in two vans. An absentee conductor doesn't work with an orchestra like this. It's not about stars, or celebrities, or your European curriculum vitae. The conductor has to be part of the community, like Gerard Schwarz: everybody knew who he was. I was always part of the community, too; I became a conductor out of necessity because there was all this great music that wasn't being played."

Today, Richmond says he's a happy man. "You know, I had it great: I got to do the *Art of the Fugue*. I got to do *L'histoire* [*du soldat*]. We played for thousands of people. I'm very blessed that I had that opportunity for seven years. I don't look back."

A promotional genius as well as opera producer, Glynn Ross ignited audiences, performers, and the occasional sparkler. Courtesy of Melanie Ross.

Speight Jenkins on one of the Valkyrie flying horses from the second of his three *Ring* productions, 1985. Photo by Gary B. Smith.

Toby Saks, founder of the Seattle Chamber Music Society's Summer Festival, played the cello regularly in her festival. Photo by Harriett Burger.

Louis Richmond, a lifelong cellist, began his music career on that instrument before founding the Northwest Chamber Orchestra. Photo by Judith Gordon.

THE VIRTUOSI

I T is probably safe to say that in every American city, except possibly New York, the majority of the performing artists featured on concert and opera stages are not local residents. Touring artists—many of them based in New York, but others residents of cities throughout the world—make up the majority of the soloist rosters of Seattle Symphony, Seattle Opera, Seattle Chamber Music Society, Meany Theater's World Series, Early Music Guild's International Series, Pacific MusicWorks presentations, and other professional concert activity.

But a significant core group of local performing artists is active in teaching as well as on the concert stage and in the recording studio. All of these performers are well represented on disc and have notable reputations outside of Seattle; one of them, Robin McCabe, was the subject of both a major profile in the *New Yorker* and a subsequent book. In this group, we meet some of the region's most senior and respected musicians—two of them now well into their nineties—whose collective experience and wisdom span remarkable lifetimes in music. Some of Seattle's resident musicians played key roles in the transmission of their musical heritages in Germany and Switzerland to students and performers (and audiences) in Seattle. Two others spent decades in some of the most prominent and perilous "first chairs" in the Seattle Symphony, and they made a big impression on audiences (including the international audience for the All-Star Orchestra video series), as well as on young students. Many of them, not surprisingly, are affiliated with the University of Washington, the region's leading seat of higher learning and traditionally the home of many of Seattle's finest resident musicians.

Béla Siki

THE ELEGANT STYLIST

From the standpoint of posterity, it is probably a good thing that Béla Siki's mother didn't like jazz. Born in Budapest on February 21, 1923, young Béla was the last child in his father's second generation of children. His elder siblings—two brothers and a sister—were between ten and fifteen years his senior and children of a different mother; all played the piano, but they favored jazz.

"My mother hated jazz," remembers Siki, a quiet-spoken, courtly gentleman, whose Seattle living room still manages to look somehow European despite its views of Lake Washington and Pacific Northwest greenery. We were sitting near the pianist's well-used Steinway, sipping espressos prepared by Siki's elegant wife, Yolande, and revisiting what Béla Siki called "the ancient history" of his past.

Siki's mother, recognizing her son's early talent, took him at the age of eight to the Academy Franz Liszt in Budapest, where he was one of ten successful applicants in a field of three hundred aspirants. Then began four years of training in preparation for the academy, with four different teachers from the upper class: "Every year, there was another very nice person who took me," Siki recalled. "I appreciated especially the second one; she was so beautiful!" At the age of twelve, he could officially enter the academy, and there Siki spent three years with an old professor, four years with a younger teacher, and finally, in 1942, once he had ascended to the highest level, with the legendary pianist-composer Ernö Dohnányi (1877–

1960), who took very few students. "He had two, three, maximum five people," Siki remembers. "He took me. I was twenty years old, and it was in the last two years of the world war [World War II]."

Siki recalls the phenomenal keyboard skills, above all the beautiful touch, of Dohnányi, who also had an incredible memory. "One reading of any work was enough to imprint it indelibly in his memory," Siki wrote in 1981, "and he could play it years later with little or no practice." This ability made it hard on Dohnányi's students, because he expected them to have equivalent memorizing skills.

In 1943, Siki had an important concert as soloist in a Liszt program with the Budapest Symphony Orchestra. He was sick, with a high fever, and after the concert he went to the hospital in a taxi. As it turned out, he had diphtheria and was not released from the hospital for two months. By then, the Germans had invaded Hungary.

"Everything stopped. The academy stopped. Everything! Three months later, the Russians came. Those days were . . . very interesting," he recalled. "One day, one of the Russian generals passed by and heard me playing the piano, so he came in and invited me once to go and play for the Russian post. I played there, and it was very good, because I could put in my pocket something to eat for my parents. There was nothing to eat. Then I played my first recital in Budapest. Budapest was half demolished. I played in the Academy Franz Liszt, which was a very nice hall, except that there was a hole in the ceiling."

In 1946, when Siki ironically observes that he was "very old"—twenty-three—he became a professor in another school, where he earned a very welcome stipendium. After winning the Franz Liszt Society Piano Competition twice (in 1942 and 1943), he went to Geneva "more or less by chance," to visit the Liszt Museum there. The legendary Romanian pianist Dinu Lipatti lived in Geneva at the time. One day at the Liszt Museum with a friend, Siki noticed a small man going by, to whom the friend bowed respectfully. "Who is that?" Siki inquired. His friend identified Lipatti, and Siki asked, "Who is Lipatti?" The friend took Siki home and played Lipatti's recordings for him. It was a revelation. "I had never heard such perfection," he remembered in our interview.

After that, Siki wrote to the noted pianist Edwin Fischer, with whom he was to study next, and said, "Sorry, I'm not coming." Siki didn't speak any French; Lipatti spoke only French and his native Romanian. But they connected immediately over the keyboard. A thorough, conscientious, and serious teacher, Lipatti encouraged his students to learn all of a composer's output in other genres—chamber music, orchestral music, whatever was available—to fully know the composer's piano music. Siki had only a year studying with Lipatti, whose premature death from leukemia was one of the great tragedies of that time. But it is not hard to trace the silky elegance, taste and restraint, and quest for perfection that marked Lipatti's style in the playing of his pupil.

Siki's characteristic modesty colors his account of victory in the prestigious Geneva Competition. "There was a competition; I was lucky, and I won it." That victory led to the start of his concert career, a manager, and some engagements. He also began courting his future wife, a lovely young Swiss woman, and accelerated his study of French because Yolande spoke that language. He realized, as he later observed, that "it was never too late to learn a new language."

Siki's schedule got steadily busier, as he combined teaching at the Geneva Conservatory with lengthy international tours—forty-four concerts in Australia, ten in New Zealand, still more in Hong Kong and Singapore. When he was home, he regularly visited Lipatti. "He was a very sick man," remembers Siki, "and he stopped teaching after my year with him. I went often to visit and play for him. I took him for treatments in somebody else's car. He was only thirty-three when he died."

The touring engagements increased: Egypt, Europe, South America, South Africa, the Far East. Meanwhile, Siki's wife and two young children were left alone for months at a time. In the midst of this frenetic lifestyle, the phone rang. It was Terry Moore from the University of Washington, who was in England scouting for faculty talent. The university's School of Music director, the composer William Bergsma, wanted him to find a pianist who would attract international students. Ilona Kabos had recommended Siki, but she had warned, "He won't accept."

But he did. At first, though, Siki wasn't too sure about geographical issues. "I saw a plane that said 'Made in Seattle,' and I thought it was somewhere around New York." After a private recital with about two dozen Seattle and UW insiders, Siki was immediately offered a full professorship—and with that, the Sikis said good-bye to Geneva.

"The first year was not easy, with the students who were already there," says the perennially tactful Siki. "I felt very bad when I had to tell a young girl at the end of the year that she could not come back because it was hopeless. But after, many people came, many of them very good and gifted." Among those students was the young Robin McCabe, a Washington State native who picked the University of Washington expressly to study with Siki. "We had a hot class full of big talents," McCabe remembered in our 2012 interview of those years in the mid-1960s. "Everyone fought to get the last lesson of the day, because you would get a little extra time with Béla. It was a heady atmosphere. [After graduation] I was a little scared to go to New York, but Béla said, 'No, you have to go.' He was very wise."

Siki found his students and the UW atmosphere congenial. He was encouraged to continue touring and concertizing, and during longer tours he sometimes took off an entire academic quarter. The pianist also had a handy secret weapon when it came to evading the inevitable service on faculty committees: he would look apologetic, thicken his Hungarian accent, and respond, "My English is not very good."

He liked his piano colleagues Else Geissmar, Neal O'Doan, and Randolph Hokanson, and he liked spending time with the conductor Milton Katims, who lived across the street from him in Seattle's leafy Laurelhurst neighborhood. The pianist and the conductor often collaborated on concerto programs with the Seattle Symphony. And because the Katimses were tremendous entertainers of visiting and resident musicians, there were many parties across the street. "If I could see a red carpet and candles," says Siki of the house across the way on party night, "we knew to dress up. We enjoyed many things [together]; I played tennis with Milton, and one winter when it was very snowy, a picture of the two of us on a sled appeared in the newspaper."

More foreign students than American ones were now crowding Siki's studio at the University of Washington, but he had begun to contemplate a move. Yolande resisted the idea, but her husband was being assiduously wooed by the College Conservatory of Music at the University of Cincinnati, a place that boasted "two wonderful orchestras" and sought Siki's participation in master classes. Finally, in 1980, the Sikis sold their Seattle house, pulled up stakes, and headed for Cincinnati, accompanied by thirteen of Béla's Seattle students, who followed him to the new school. The news of his departure from Seattle was considered so shocking and momentous that it made the front page of the *Seattle Times*.

The College Conservatory of Music was, in Siki's words, "a marvelous place to be." First-rate students came to his studio, including the renowned pianist Anton Nel. "My classmates and I were very much in awe of Béla during our student years," Nel told me.

My previous great mentor, Adolph Hallis in South Africa, had prepared me in a superb way as a young aspiring pianist. What Béla added was to make me an independent thinker. He helped me find my own voice as a pianist and showed me the way to become an artist versus just being a good student. My ears were opened anew; it was like being in the world's most sophisticated "finishing school" for pianists!

He was very exacting in what he wanted musically from every work we studied, but I never felt inhibited or constrained. He was never a man of many words, but when he spoke, we all listened— very carefully! He also occasionally would write a fingering or the odd instruction in my scores, and I treasure all of these markings very much.

I still remember the first piece I studied with him was the Ravel Concerto in G. I play this piece a lot and love finding his writing in my music each time I rework it—it makes me so happy! I studied a lot of repertoire with him in the two years we were together: standouts were my first forays into the Brahms D-minor Concerto, Schubert's Wanderer Fantasy (which has really become one of my signature pieces), the Liszt Dante Sonata, Haydn, and Mozart.

While teaching at the College Conservatory of Music, Siki also continued his concert performances, both in Cincinnati and in Victoria, BC, where he taught in the summers. Nel recalls Siki's concerts at the University of Cincinnati as "real events. I will always remember his performances of Liszt: the ultimate B-minor Piano Sonata, Paganini études, also beautiful Debussy, imaginative Bach. The work that drew me to work with him initially, by the way, was a fantastic LP record I heard of him playing the Dohnányi *Variations on a Nursery Song* [with the Seattle Symphony Orchestra, Katims conducting]."

As a teacher, Siki impressed Nel with his "almost transcendental calm and kind demeanor" and also the speed with which the lesson seemed to go by. "At the end of the hour so much had been accomplished, and it seemed like no time had passed at all. I know that I did some of my best playing ever in those lessons!"

Only five years after the move to Cincinnati, however, Béla and Yolande moved back to Seattle. What happened?

First, a new UW School of Music director had asked Siki to reconsider. Then family issues made a return sound irresistibly attractive. "Our son got married," Siki explains. "The family really wanted us home. We were getting a little older; maybe it would be wise to come to be near the children. It was hard to leave; the school [College Conservatory of Music] was incomparable. Money-wise the two schools were about the same. But we also had a lot of good friends in Seattle—and this time my students came with me from Cincinnati," Siki explained. They found a house in the neighborhood where they had previously lived. Siki remained at the University of Washington until his retirement in 1993; in his last year there, he taught twenty-nine students, who sat around him on the Meany Theater stage for his farewell recital in April on the President's Piano Series.

Over the years, Siki has played an enormous amount of repertoire. When you win a Liszt competition, you're expected to be something of a Liszt specialist, and that composer has always been represented in Siki's concert repertoire. (A favorite strategy in his programming has been the inclusion of a dazzling, finger-busting Liszt set at the end, followed by a delicate little Scarlatti sonata as a throwaway, lighter-than-air encore.) "I'm not really a specialist in one composer or another," Siki demurs. "Contemporary music . . . some I listen to and I know, but that's not me. Bartók, of course, is an exception! I've played Bartók's Concerto No. 3 the most; I especially remember a performance with Ernest Ansermet and the Orchestre de la Suisse Romande. And the classical period is very close to me."

Because of his desire to help students "to get to the results, from Bach to Bartók," Siki gave a favorable answer to the publisher G. Schirmer when they wrote to say that they would like to publish a book by him. "I called them on the phone so they could hear my English," says Siki with a humorous smile. "There was a big silence. Then they said, 'Yes, we knew that much.' They wanted the book anyway! From then on, I got up an hour earlier and headed down to the basement where my book [*Piano Repertoire: A Guide to Interpretation and Performance*] was waiting for me. I went very slowly, but one day it was finished. My editor read the manuscript in exchange for piano lessons. He helped me more than I could help him!"

Over the years, Siki has become a connoisseur at assessing young talent, so it is not surprising that he has often been sought as a judge or jury member for such major international piano competitions as the Gilmore, the Geneva, the Bolzano, and most of all the prestigious Leeds Competition, where he has served as a judge "at least five times." He has helped identify such international stars as Radu Lupu and Murray Perahia, as well as his UW colleague Craig Sheppard, who placed second in the 1972 Leeds. When Siki spots a winner, his reaction is usually almost immediate. "You listen to two minutes, and"—he makes a gesture that indicates—"and that's it." He continues, "With Murray Perahia, I heard him play two measures, and I just knew."

Knowing that the man with those sharp and perceptive ears is in the audience is still enough to raise the pulse of his former students when they return to Seattle to perform. They know he'll notice everything; he always does. One raised eyebrow or one slight smile from this courtly perfectionist speaks volumes.

John Cerminaro

THE MAN WITH THE GOLDEN HORN

The cameras and microphones were ready, and the pressure was on in New York City: this was the first recording session for the new All-Star Orchestra video series of an assortment of the world's greatest symphonic repertoire. There was no margin for error, as there were to be only two takes of each piece. The All-Star conductor, Gerard Schwarz, gave the cue for the crucial opening French horn solo of Stravinsky's *The Firebird,* and John Cerminaro began the pure, iconic descending solo line that opens the final movement.

The take was perfect, a noble sound that rang out softly and then blossomed. The surprise was that at sixty-five, an age when many top players have packed up their French horns and taken up less challenging pursuits, Cerminaro was still playing at this level of perfection. It was no surprise to Schwarz, however. Their long friendship notwithstanding, Schwarz knew that in Cerminaro he had a player he could count on to get it right the first time.

Cerminaro, who arrived at Schwarz's behest to take up the principal horn position at the Seattle Symphony in 1996, was for fifteen years one of the most visible and controversial instrumentalists in the city. Principal French horn players are not noted for their small egos; it takes a lot of nerve to walk that tightrope where the smallest flaw in the sound produced on a notoriously tricky instrument is painfully obvious. Cerminaro, with his firm sense of self-worth and the candor to share his views, was a catalyst for dissent in the orchestra among players who disliked the high-handed way he had been brought in, envied his formidable skills, and resented his high salary. Shortly after Schwarz's music directorship of the Seattle Symphony ended in 2011, Cerminaro, too, departed, under terms that he does not discuss. He continues to practice and stay in shape as a soloist on his concerto repertoire.

Cerminaro spent a significant portion of his career in the orchestra world. In addition to the Seattle Symphony post, he has also held principal horn positions with the New York Philharmonic, Los Angeles Philharmonic, and Aspen Festival Orchestra, and he has been a guest principal horn with the Dallas Symphony,

Milwaukee Symphony, and Houston Symphony, among others. In his post–Seattle Symphony years, however, the hornist has turned away orchestral opportunities to focus solely on solo repertoire.

Cerminaro is always making little modifications to his instrument, and it is not unusual to find several redesigned mouthpieces and other brass parts lying on the dining room table in his Seattle home. He picks up a tiny pipe that leads from the main instrument to the mouthpiece and holds it aloft. "It occurred to me that this pipe and the mouthpiece that fits into it could be one piece, so I had it made. There's a little bit more clarity in the sound, but I'm not so sure about how the sound is going to be for solos."

Solos are clearly of the greatest interest to Cerminaro, who has made his mark on the recorded repertoire of virtuoso pieces for his instrument. "In the horn world, there are certain people who have 'the title' to certain pieces that they have recorded. And I have quite a few titles that I'm defending! Certain repertoire of mine nobody records because nobody is willing to take me on, and I kind of like that. It's kind of a silly thing, but horn players are watching. The big stuff is where I have all my 'belts,' like the Hindemith Sonata, and the [Eugène] Bozza *En foret*. But now all I focus on is solo work. Several orchestras are testing the waters with me, but I don't even want to be tempted with orchestra offers. I'm not interested; I've been there, done that."

Cerminaro started being there and doing that as a youngster in Navasota, Texas (in Grimes County, northwest of Houston), where he grew up in a rich musical environment in which "band was even bigger than bowling." His father was a band director; his mother led a drum and bugle corps, and both were what Cerminaro calls "good solid musicians." Young John started horn studies at the age of ten with a "profoundly good teacher," Alfred Resch, a German immigrant who had been in the Boston Symphony Orchestra and immediately saw the potential in his student.

"He had glasses so thick they looked like shot glasses; he was bald; he was scary. He made horn playing so important," recalls Cerminaro of his teacher. "He believed in me as a soloist. I didn't sit down to play; I always stood and played before the mirror during lessons."

By the time he was sixteen, young John was soloing in Mozart's Fourth Horn Concerto with the Dallas Symphony, and a traveling jury from New York's Juilliard School had selected him for a full scholarship. It didn't take long for him to start making big waves. When the young hornist was invited to play for the conducting legend Leopold Stokowski in his penthouse suite, "Stokie," impressed, offered him principal spots in the American and Dallas Symphonies. But Cerminaro followed the advice of others: complete your education first.

"During my senior year at Juilliard, I landed the New York Philharmonic principal job, and my advisors said, 'Hmm, maybe you should take that one.'" He had clinched the job by playing Siegfried's Long Call (from Wagner's *Siegfried*, the third *Ring* opera) for the legendary podium tyrant George Szell, who was conducting the New York Philharmonic for a year. "I hit the high C and held on," Cerminaro remembers. "I knew I had the job. I saw it in his eyes."

Those were heady years. Leonard Bernstein was the New York Philharmonic's conductor laureate and a frequent figure on the podium. The orchestra went on a succession of exciting international tours and made several acclaimed recordings. Cerminaro's colleagues were remarkably interesting and gifted. Among them was a young trumpeter named Gerard Schwarz, who had recently become the orchestra's youngest-ever principal trumpet. No one realized then that his days in the brass section were numbered and that Schwarz would eventually sell all of his instruments in favor of the conductor's baton. "Jerry was the greatest," remembers Cerminaro. "He had a phenomenal embouchure [the position of the mouth when playing a wind instrument]. It was very symmetrical and gorgeous. But Jerry also was the one who always had a score in his hands. I knew the trumpet wouldn't be enough for him."

Nor was the New York Philharmonic enough for Cerminaro. By the end of his first decade there, music director Pierre Boulez had left and Zubin Mehta (whom Cerminaro tactfully calls "a different kind of conductor") was on his way in. Around the same time, Cerminaro was being courted by the famed and fearsome orchestra manager Ernest Fleischmann on behalf of the Los Angeles Philharmonic.

Fleischmann was displeased because the New York Philharmonic had stolen Mehta away from Los Angeles; according to Cerminaro, he decided to steal New York's principal horn in retaliation. "Ernest called Zubin and said, 'I've just signed John Cerminaro as our new principal horn [in Los Angeles]. Hope you can find somebody!' It was a terrible thing to do." Telling the story, Cerminaro laughs riotously.

He had accepted an offer from Los Angeles that paid a little more than New York had done but also, more important, gave him a position as coprincipal horn. That meant that he had every other week off—and could play in the Los Angeles commercial recording studios. "You've heard me more on TV and in the movies than in all these years in the concert hall," he says with a laugh. "I'm on the soundtrack of the Indiana Jones movies and the NBC Nightly News. It was a lot of fun."

He had "six glorious years" with the LA Phil and especially enjoyed working with music director Carlo Maria Giulini during his tenure with the orchestra. Ultimately, however, Cerminaro decided he wanted to be a soloist and try living another kind of life. Fleischmann was not best pleased when Cerminaro explained this to him. "A grim expression set on his face," Cerminaro recalls. "I was his first horn player, and I wanted to leave."

Thus began a decade-long solo career, which Cerminaro describes as "feast or famine." During this period he met his "third and last" wife, Charlotte, a gifted horn player who had been his student. They married in 1993 and now have two children.

During his solo career, Cerminaro also accepted an occasional guest principal horn spot—including in Houston, Milwaukee, and Dallas—if he liked the orchestra and the conductor. That was the situation when he first came to the Seattle Symphony as a guest. "I came to Seattle because they were building Benaroya Hall," Cerminaro reflects, "and they wanted stability and a great horn section. I came in as guest principal, but they asked me to stay. I would have said no, but this time it was different." Charlotte was expecting the couple's first child, and they reasoned that Seattle would be a good family place.

And so they stayed. "It just seemed natural" to remain in Seattle, Cerminaro explained. He stayed a lot longer in Seattle than he had expected to, almost twice as long as any of his other orchestral posts. "Seattle is a wonderful place for kids. It's also an amazing and demanding orchestra season, and so I let a lot of other things go—solo opportunities, and the summers at the Aspen Festival. It just gets to be too much."

Seattle proved a controversial post for Cerminaro, in part because of the manner of his appointment to the principal horn position. When Gerard Schwarz, Cerminaro's former New York Philharmonic colleague, chose him to fill an interim vacancy in the Seattle Symphony's principal horn chair, Cerminaro immediately began winning favorable reviews for his performances. In 1997, however, when Cerminaro played a preliminary audition for the permanent post before a committee of orchestra players, they judged him ineligible to compete in the regular auditions. Some saw this artistically controversial judgment as a slap at the powerful conductor. The vote may also have reflected professional jealousy of a player whose reputation and performances were both formidable.

"He came here with undoubtedly the most distinguished résumé of any member in the orchestra, someone sought after by two of the most eminent names in twentieth-century music, Leonard Bernstein and Carlo Maria Giulini, who invited him to join their orchestras in New York and Los Angeles," R. M. Campbell wrote at the time. "Cerminaro also has recorded, performed as a soloist and taught at prestigious institutions."

A few months prior to the 1998 opening of Benaroya Hall, Schwarz made Cerminaro's appointment as principal horn a contingency of the musicians' contract renewal. The musicians approved the contract variance, but there was said to be resentment in some quarters at how Schwarz had trumped their prerogative. Cerminaro took the high road, refraining from comment and continuing to play at a standard that earned highly favorable reviews from critics at home and elsewhere; his playing was regularly singled out for praise in national reviews of the orchestra's recordings.

Cerminaro has been in a good position to survey the orchestra world at the top, including what positions are available to excellent players and their chances for advancement. He sees shrinking options for instrumentalists, even excellent ones. The Cerminaros have not enrolled their two children in music lessons—despite a family history of exceptional musical ability. "Both Johnny and Rose have profound perfect pitch," Cerminaro says. "But I've managed with all my skill to keep them away from instruments. The pond is all fished out, don't you think? When no [orchestral] jobs are being filled, and there are so few opportunities, a career in music doesn't make a lot of sense."

There has been considerably more to Cerminaro's life, however, than music. At one time, he was a high-level chess player, but he eventually gave it up because it took too much time. He is an accomplished painter, particularly in tiny paintings whose details he completes with the aid of a magnifying glass. The Cerminaros also share a strong faith as messianic Jews, following John's conversion after a lifetime as an intellectual atheist.

"I'm lucky to have one thing that I did really well," he reflects on his horn-playing career. "I'm very blessed. My time in Seattle has been great in so many ways." Looking back on his time with the Seattle Symphony, Cerminaro reflects that the evolution of the orchestra made things more difficult for some players. When he first arrived in Seattle, he found the horn section in some disarray. Some older players, Cerminaro explains, had started in one kind of an orchestra and found themselves in another kind after Schwarz arrived with his expansion plans and drive to improve the Seattle Symphony. Schwarz was "seeing things further down the road" than Cerminaro and the rest of the musicians. As some players left and new ones arrived, the brass section grew in strength and became more competitive.

And then Cerminaro left, too. "The orchestra is in a new period now," he observes, "like a painter who moves from a blue period to a green. The orchestra has been brought to a certain level and is in other hands, and it is completely understandable that they would want to take it in another direction. I think everything points to a sunny future for the Seattle Symphony. Seattle is on the move, and it will be more important than LA before you know it. We're still here; we wouldn't think of giving up Seattle."

Cerminaro feels he has a good number of years left as a horn player. "I'm in terra incognita," he jokes.

> Most horn players are retired by my age. But I'm still playing
> really well. You do it until you can't. Right now I'm taking only
> concerto solos and the All-Star Orchestra. I'm painting, and
> writing a little, mainly things pertaining to the cutting edge of
> equipment experimentation. I help horn makers with improve-
> ments; if I have a good idea, they can have it. I'm giving back.
>
> I love playing; I'm always in condition and ready to go. The
> most difficult part of playing great concerts is knowing that you
> can, but while you're sitting back there waiting to go on, there's
> so much terror. A real part of my preparation, in addition to
> extreme technical control, is prayer: conceding your flaws and
> getting that peace that passes all understanding. It's very impor-
> tant to know what you are and what you can do—and what you
> can't do.

Randolph Hokanson

THE OLD MASTER

He hobnobbed with George Bernard Shaw, H. G. Wells, and Edith Wharton in London during his piano-student days "between the wars." He also once climbed icy thirty-five-foot poles in the Signal Corps, drove a twelve-ton Sherman tank, and survived the torpe-doing of his troop ship in the English Channel en route to wartime service as a translator in France.

No one could say that the concert pianist and University of Washington emeritus professor Randolph Hokanson hasn't had an eventful life. Among Hokanson's most remarkable aspects, in addi-tion to his musical prowess, is a creative and active longevity that must inspire awe. He published his insightful autobiography, *With Head to the Music Bent: A Musician's Story*, at the age of ninety-five and sat for my interview at nearly ninety-seven, with both his prodi-gious memory and his sense of humor intact. (At this writing, he is preparing to perform in his one hundredth birthday concert.)

When he opens the door to his Seattle apartment, you see his bright and perceptive blue eyes, the aureole of white hair, and above all the radiant smile of a man who truly loves his life in music. Past the grand piano that dominates the living room—the piano still gets a regular workout—there's a view of the Space Needle. While Hokanson provides coffee, he gives me a very condensed version of his life story.

Hokanson's love of music shines through everything he says. Discussing retired musicians who have stopped playing their instruments, he shakes his head and says, "I really feel that music is what keeps you going. If you're a truly musical person, you don't stop; you don't retire. You keep learning! And I feel I am certainly still learning. Some piano works are beyond me now, in terms of what I can accomplish with technique. But I am still probing the mysteries of the great composers, especially Bach and Beethoven."

The son of Swedish immigrants, Hokanson grew up in northwest Washington State and gravitated early to the piano to hear his older sister making what he called "mysterious and wonderful sounds." He tried to emulate her so enthusiastically that he, too, was given piano lessons: first by his sister, then by her teacher, and then by a respected Seattle teacher, Paul McNeely. His life changed when he came to the attention of Trixie Cameron, a married woman of means who was the local impresaria in Victoria, BC. She read Seattle reviews of Hokanson's concerts and decided to present him in recital at the Empress Hotel, the grand hotel of Victoria that is still famous for its "high tea."

"Aunt" Trixie (his courtesy title for her) brought young Randolph to the attention of her English friend, the noted pianist Harold Samuel, who taught at London's Royal College of Music but frequently came to Canada to adjudicate festivals there. Samuel was most famous for his highly praised seven-day series of Bach recitals at London's Wigmore Hall; when he heard young Hokanson play, he decided that the younger man might well become his successor.

Thus began the great formative period of Hokanson's young life. As a scholarship student, he accompanied Harold Samuel back to London, where he spent several years soaking up musical and cultural influences of all kinds in a wonderful arts milieu. He attended Shaw's *Saint Joan*, featuring the actress Wendy Hiller, and chatted with the formidable Shaw himself at a tea party afterward. Soirees and receptions brought him face-to-face with such great actresses as Helen Hayes and with minor European royalty; he stayed at the home of English composer Gerald Finzi.

Above all, Hokanson heard the great musical artists who performed in London. There was Dame Myra Hess, who became his teacher; there were performances by Bartók, Prokofiev, Richard Strauss, Toscanini, Horowitz, Rubinstein, and Rachmaninoff. In the theaters, Hokanson saw performances by Laurence Olivier, John Gielgud, Edith Evans, Peggy Ashcroft, Ralph Richardson, and Alec Guinness. Heady stuff, for the boy from Bellingham!

He haunted London's great art museums, where he learned to liken great pictures to musical scores. As Hokanson wrote in his autobiography, "How is the musical space (canvas) filled out? How do the musical periods (schools and groups) relate to the whole? How is the harmony (color) employed?"

All these experiences were combined with intensive piano studies with Harold Samuel and (after Samuel's early death) his colleague Howard Ferguson, and then the exacting and famous concert pianist Dame Myra Hess. (Hess told him, "Imagine strongly what you want before doing it," and "Think three times before you touch the keys.") At the same time, Hokanson was taking lessons in counterpoint and composition from Ferguson, who was also a noted composer.

But there was time for travel, as well, and he made trips to such destinations as Ireland, France, Germany, and Austria. The latter two countries, visited in 1938, were filled with the swastika banners and evidence of a Nazism that was "in full bloom everywhere," as Hokanson wrote in his autobiography. In Salzburg, Hokanson and his friends attended a performance of Wagner's *Die Meistersinger von Nürnberg*, with Hitler and his henchmen in a swastika-draped box directly above their seats.

Returning to England, Hokanson saw the increasing preparations for war: fortified gun emplacements (on London's Hampstead Heath), trenches, searchlights, and other disturbing indications of what was to come. It was clear that Hokanson needed to return to the United States, but he makes his bitter disappointment clear in his autobiography: "I was very much a student and, while gifted, far from being a finished artist. If I were to become one, it would take time and further experience. . . . Myra and Howard assured me that I had the 'right stuff,' but also that I had a long way to go."

Indeed he did. Returning to New York and living in a tiny apartment while he accompanied singers at Juilliard, Hokanson got a lucky boost from "Aunt Trixie," who wrote to her friend, the general music director of NBC radio. A twenty-minute concert on a national network led to an opportunity at Columbia Concerts Corporation, where he was so successful at accompanying vocal auditions that he was invited to audition on his own. After studies with the eminent teacher Carl Friedberg in New York, more opportunities followed. Hokanson was booked into a fifty-concert tour of the United States and Canada's Maritime Provinces, and he encountered some highly unusual instruments, venues, and critics. (One midwestern critic, Hokanson remembers, wrote that the audience was "electrocuted" by his performance of the toccata from Ravel's *Le tombeau de Couperin*. Fortunately, he says, he has never yet caused death among his listeners.)

After Hokanson had spent a couple of seasons touring, the United States entered World War II, and only six months later he was picking up cigarette butts from the grounds of Fort Lewis; soon after he was going on "foot-flogging marches" and peeling potatoes in Fort Knox, Kentucky. Fortunately, he ended up at Stanford University for language school, training for the Signal Corps and waiting for his overseas deployment. His troop ship zigzagged across the Atlantic to London, successfully evading Nazi torpedoes, and there Hokanson had joyous reunions with Dame Myra Hess and Howard Ferguson. The trip across the English Channel to France, however, was not so successful; when a torpedo hit their ship and caused heavy casualties, Hokanson and a buddy raced down to their bunks to retrieve their duffel bags (Hokanson's contained some of his compositions), and they were barely in time to board the French frigate that rescued them.

In France, Hokanson served with his language-translation unit in several locations between Lyon and Marseille; inevitably, he had chances to perform and entertain at the keyboard. At the war's end, Hokanson returned to New York (a safe voyage, this time, with no submarines) and thence to Seattle. There, his chance attendance at a party held by a University of Washington faculty member led to an invitation from Stanley Chapple, then the music department chair, to perform. His performance was so successful that Hokanson was invited to join the faculty. "What a wonderful break this was for me!" Hokanson writes in his memoir. "It was to become my musical life's greatest challenge and pleasure, partly because I could continue to pursue my playing career as time permitted."

What was the University of Washington music faculty like in 1949, when Hokanson arrived? First and foremost, the director was Chapple. In our interview, Hokanson called him "an amateur of genius." By this he means that Chapple, who was a pianist as well as a conductor, neither played nor conducted at the highest professional standard, but that his love, knowledge, and enthusiasm for music were tremendously infectious and spurred a corresponding enthusiasm in his students and all who performed with him. With his charming English accent, witty sense of humor, and limitless fund of anecdotes about great musicians and their works, Chapple was also a born raconteur, and his music-appreciation classes were highly popular.

"He also was a great fan of opera," Hokanson remembers. "He performed a lot of operas that had never been heard here before, including the early operas by Monteverdi and Purcell. The UW had a small venue downtown for chamber opera, and he did the first Seattle performance there of Britten's opera *The Rape of Lucretia.*"

Chapple also made adroit faculty hires, including that of the violinist Emanuel Zetlin (formerly the associate concertmaster of the Metropolitan Opera Orchestra in New York), who had studied with Leopold Auer and was the assistant to Carl Flesch at the opening of the Curtis Institute; the internationally noted cellist and viola da gamba specialist Eva Heinitz, whom Hokanson heard play in London during his student days there; and Vilem Sokol, an excellent violist whose later work as conductor of the Seattle Youth

Symphony was one of the most important developments in Seattle's music community. Chapple was also responsible for hiring the pianists Else Geissmar and Berthe Poncy Jacobson (nicknamed Clare); Hokanson remembers Jacobson as "a marvelous musician with a great capacity to pick out any detail in a performance that needed improvement." Among the composers Chapple hired to join the department's star, George Frederick McKay, were James Beale, Gerald Kechley, John Verrall, and Dorothy Cadzow—who later became Hokanson's wife.

"I have never counted the number of recitals and chamber music performances I gave there," Hokanson mused. "There must have been a couple hundred over the years. With Stanley, who often called on me to perform concertos with him, I did the first movement of Beethoven's Piano Concerto No. 3 on a Standard Hour broadcast." Of course, Chapple was only one of many conductors with whom Hokanson soloed in those years. One memorable collaboration was with Chapple's famous countryman Sir Thomas Beecham, who was music director of the Seattle Symphony for two seasons. As Hokanson said in our interview,

> Beecham was a great fan of Delius's music, and he tried on every occasion possible to include some Delius works. The Piano Concerto is not a great piece, but it's effective as a virtuoso piece, and very pianistically written.
>
> I remember meeting Sir Thomas in New York. His mistress, Betty Humby, was a lovely, beautiful woman and an excellent pianist, and I think he wanted her to be the soloist in this occasion, but people were critical of the immorality of the situation. So I think it was Ruth McCreery [then manager of the Seattle Symphony] who suggested that he have me as soloist instead. He knew nothing about me, but he may have known that Dame Myra Hess was my teacher; she had made her debut with him when she was only seventeen.
>
> It was in the 1941–42 season; I had just returned from England and had gotten a Columbia Concerts contract in New York, and I had begun to play around the country, there was a lot of publicity here about that. It was fun playing for Sir Thomas! I

met him at Steinway Hall in New York to go over the concerto. I wanted to play Mozart, but he preferred the Delius. I had never played the piece, but it was easy to learn quite quickly. We went over the score together, and he just sang along with me and suggested minor tempo changes here and there. In Seattle [the performance was on November 17, 1941], it went swimmingly—it was fun.

Beecham was ostensibly a very austere fellow, but underneath it all he was very funny. I recall he called somebody who had annoyed him a "footling pipsqueak of a functionary." Earlier, I had gone to all Sir Thomas's rehearsals in London; they were excellent, and I heard a lot of British music. I listened to his jokes, too; he was terribly funny and had the orchestra in stitches most of the time.

Hokanson also knew the other conductors of the Seattle Symphony during that era; he recalls a lunch with Manuel Rosenthal, in which Rosenthal was worrying about the orchestra's future, declaring that "wealthy people here spend money on yachts and island homes, not on music." Hokanson had a much longer association with Milton Katims, performing "at least twelve" concerti with him and the Seattle Symphony.

"Milton had a very big reputation as a first-class violist," Hokanson recalls. "He was very influential in bringing wonderful people to Seattle. I think he could have been superb as a conductor if he had worked harder on learning his scores. Certain things went very well, but I recall one performance of d'Indy's *Symphony on a French Mountain Air* [a work with a prominent piano solo part] in which he lost his place miserably. And the orchestra just went on."

These days, as Hokanson reflects on his life in music, he calls it "a lifelong study—and you never quite feel you are there. Rubinstein, for instance, recorded the [Chopin] mazurkas three different times. The first recording was very good . . . but the third one was better! As you age, you see music differently; I think you get a wider and more flexible view with age."

Certainly Hokanson's own viewpoint evolved over time. His experiences as an artist who had toured all over the United States and Canada made him aware that life on the road was not what he wanted. Never a "great practicer," as he notes, he knew that the amount of work required to keep and build repertoire, and to tour and perform it, would leave him no time for any other interests, whether playing chamber music or composing works of his own. "I saw teaching as being my main function," Hokanson observes, "though I also wanted to continue to perform. It wasn't easy. I had to work awfully hard, practicing three hours a night after teaching all day in order to present my series of Beethoven concerts."

Over the years, he has also found time to compose, primarily piano pieces and songs based on poems by Tennyson, Dickinson, and Robert Bridges. Hokanson is still working on developing compositional sketches from the years when he was teaching full time. His late wife, Dorie (Dorothy), gave him a lot of useful advice about composing. "I was able to help her, too, especially with her opera *Undine*. She would always play what she had written for me that day, when I got home from teaching. She had to give up her teaching position at the end of the term when we were married, because of the university's nepotism rule, but later she was thankful for the time because she could compose more," Hokanson recalls.

"We had a wonderful marriage—such a rapport! I had had two previous thoughts of marriage with two other girls, but neither of those worked out. The minute I met Dorie, I knew [she] was really 'the one.' She was taken ill a little before 2000 and died in 2001 just a few months before our fiftieth anniversary. During that time I really did very little with music because I just didn't have the heart for it. I still miss her terribly."

Now, in addition to his recitals and chamber music with the violinist Marjorie Kransberg-Talvi, Hokanson periodically offers Bach classes for aspiring students, sometimes at the home of his former student Judith Cohen. "What I do, I want to do well," Hokanson says. "It takes me more time these days! This is how I honor the great teachers and artists who have given me the gift of their wisdom over the years. I am so grateful to them."

Silvia Kind

She was an unmistakable figure on the University of Washington campus: tiny and fast-moving, her tousled mop of short blond hair slightly askew, and those bright blue eyes missing nothing. Silvia Kind, the Swiss-born harpsichord virtuoso and free spirit, had a transformative effect on many of her students and audiences during a relatively short time on the University of Washington music faculty (1967–78). She became an indispensable influence on Seattle's early-music scene, which when it took shape in the years following her retirement was full of her former students, many of whom went on to professional careers in music.

Silvia herself—and everybody, from her students to custodians, critics, and fellow beachcombers, immediately called her Silvia—commanded international adulation in her heyday as a performer in Europe. Press notices from the early 1960s ranged from laudatory to euphoric. The *Times* of London loved her "splendidly bold and free declamatory playing with a keen perception of the work's continuity and nobility of outline" in 1961, and, in 1962, her "vivacious musical personality and fluent finger technique." Also in 1961, Berlin critics raved in *Der Tag* about her "grace, brilliancy, and colored registration" and, in the *Berliner Morgenpost*, about her "sounds of never-imagined splendor." That same year in Geneva, they praised her "imperious intelligence and remarkable security of fingerwork" and her "beautiful interpretations," and Vienna's *Welt am Abend* cited her "spiritual profundity and breadth."

At the time of the Seattle World's Fair in 1962–63, Silvia was swanning about Switzerland and Italy, being lauded for her concerts displaying her "great musical sensitivity" and "passionate temperament and fascinating interpretation." Her 1964 US debut in Carnegie Recital Hall drew a capacity audience and a *New York Times* review that praised the "high caliber" and "free, rhapsodic style" of her performance.

Another concert tour in the New World brought her for the first time to Seattle and Vancouver, BC. In her German-language Internet memoir, titled *Monologe*, Silvia writes with evident gusto of that tour, for which she performed to "authentic cowboys and Indians" in Missoula, Montana, as well as playing a duo evening in Seattle with "the great gambist Eva Heinitz." Only a short time later, Kind joined Heinitz on the faculty of the University of Washington, first as a visiting professor (1967–68), then as a full-fledged faculty member (1969–78); she also conducted the Collegium Musicum ensemble.

Arriving in Seattle right after Silvia was Cordelia Wikarski, the German-born concert cellist and, later, wife of the Seattle Symphony music director Rainer Miedel. In an intriguing twist of fate, Cordelia Wikarski had studied with Silvia at Berlin's Hochschule für Musik. "I studied works of Rameau and Couperin with her," recalls Cordelia. "She was very independent minded and very musical. She invited us to her home—it was chaotic! I was surprised how many things there were on every surface, every table or window; things she just found somewhere and considered beautiful."

Silvia Kind's life journey began on August 15, 1907, in the Swiss town of Chur, and as a child she was drawn to the arts, especially music and sculpture. She studied piano, flute, counterpoint, composition, rhythmic gymnastics, and both choral and orchestra conducting during her years at the Zurich Conservatory; from there she went on to the Academy of Music (Hochschule für Musik) in Berlin and continued her conducting activities with the choir of the Freie Universität Berlin. She also studied with the renowned pianist Edwin Fischer and the composer Paul Hindemith. "I walked into a room where everyone was working busily away," she recalled in my 1978 interview with her, "and summoned up my courage and asked 'Is this the class of Professor Hindemith?' Someone declared 'Ja!' and a tiny little man stood up, right in the middle of the group. He looked at an immense double fugue I had written, and he said, 'Well, we do things a little differently here, but I think you will be just fine.' And I was."

In Berlin, Silvia became hooked on the harpsichord. Previously a piano student, she horrified her mentor, Edwin Fischer, when she defected from the piano to the earlier instrument, which had come to the fore in the baroque era and was the beloved "work tool" of J. S. Bach. Silvia studied with the harpsichordist-clavichordist Eta

Harich-Schneider (1897–1968) and the musicologist Curt Sachs (1881–1959), and she conducted almost obsessive research on her own into baroque keyboard practice.

Gradually she became an acknowledged expert on keyboard ornamentation, the interpretation and embellishment of music in which the player is expected to exercise imagination, virtuosity, good taste, and a thorough understanding of what was historically acceptable. She collected her research, augmented by a lifetime of concertizing, into a book on baroque keyboard ornamentation, which she supplemented with tapes that explain and demonstrate certain figures. Silvia also created a series of huge charts on scrolls, listing keyboard ornaments by century and composer. The book was considered for publication by two major publishers, but neither has yet published it.

During World War II, Silvia returned to Zurich, where she worked with the conductor Hermann Scherchen and continued conducting, concertizing, and contributing articles to magazines and newspapers. After the war, she returned to Berlin to teach harpsichord and chamber music classes at the Hochschule für Musik. According to her Swiss grandnephew, Ueli Dubs, Silvia's arrival in Seattle was probably the result of a constellation of factors, including her concert tour route, the presence of her colleague Heinitz, the highly favorable reaction of the University of Washington community to her Seattle performances, and Silvia's noted susceptibility to beautiful scenery. The snowy silhouette of Mount Rainier drew her like a beacon; so did the wild forests and coastlines of the Olympic Peninsula, which Silvia soon discovered and which became her home. She was delighted with such UW colleagues as the bassoonist Arthur Grossman, with whom she concertized and recorded and who became a congenial friend.

Another factor in Silvia's move to Seattle, according to one longtime friend in Europe, might have been that the strictures of the Berlin Hochschule were not a good fit for Silvia's very un-Germanic disregard for authority and rules. "What Silvia told me about the move from Berlin to Seattle," the friend recounted in an e-mail forwarded by her grandnephew, "was that they really wanted to have her, which was of course good for her ego. But from others I heard that Berlin wanted her to leave; that had to do with her irregular hours, her not sticking to the curricula, and other 'bureaucratic reasons.' But, as in Seattle, her Berlin students adored her and some kept in touch with her till the end."

The principal sources among Silvia's Berlin employers are long gone, but the comment about Silvia's students is on target. "Silvia is a tremendous life force," said her student Eileen Swanson in a 1978 interview with me shortly before Silvia's retirement. Swanson, who trained as both a harpsichordist and a violist, played the viola in both the now defunct Northwest Chamber Orchestra and the current Pacific Northwest Ballet Orchestra. "[Silvia] seems to have a mysterious connection with the baroque. In her studio she always brought that period to life, not only in keyboard ornamentation but also in her discussions of pictures, architecture, and history. She is interested in everything. In her studio, she inspires us to put life and music in our playing, as she does. She can make music come alive like no other. She can be strict when it's important, especially when you have a recital to get ready. She does have strong ideas of her own about articulation and phrasing. But she's usually very gentle; she doesn't force her ideas on you."

Another student at that time, the violinist Bryan Boughten, called Silvia "a wonderful inspiration as a human being, really like a grandmother to me. She inspires students in musicianship beyond the baroque period. She makes going to the University of Washington worthwhile. She has taught me more about music than anyone else in the school."

The late George Shangrow, who studied harpsichord with Silvia for four years and visited her in her post-Seattle locations (Tovo, Italy, and Port Angeles, Washington), said, "Silvia opened a Pandora's box of music to me. She opened one door after another, from a Rousseau landscape to a pack of endangered wolves that she was helping to support. At the harpsichord, she showed me the incredible things you could do with rhythm, accent, and interpretation, and she made it fun. 'My boy, you are very musical,' she would say to me, 'and you should bring it out.' She actually taught me the most about conducting and making music."

Stephen Stubbs, the lutenist and conductor of Seattle's Pacific

MusicWorks, Cornish College of the Arts, and the University of Washington (as senior artist in residence), recalls Silvia as "a firecracker. I remember the first time I saw her in concert; she was doing a Couperin piece illustrating various characters, which she announced herself in her famous accent: 'Und now come ze lions und ze tigers!!' George [Shangrow] and I immediately, and happily, plunged into Silvia's world."

Kind herself said, "I cannot teach just the fingers. I must teach the whole person." Clearly she did.

You never knew quite what Silvia was going to do. Upon receiving friends, she might do a headstand (her favorite way to start the day) or assume some other yoga position. She would almost certainly serve you tea (or champagne, depending on your age) and fortune cookies, but she might also whip out a camera if she liked the shape of your face or your eyes. You would be shown the latest of the acquisitions that studded every space, horizontal or vertical, in her apartment—posters, photos, unusual rocks, seashells, small bits of elegantly shaped driftwood, a decorated box, a letter from a friend. She was interested in everybody and fascinated by life stories.

Perhaps that is why Silvia had so many friends. Among them was the great pianist and Bach specialist Glenn Gould, who showed her around his hometown of Toronto and sought her advice on musical matters. They became friends quite by accident. Silvia was invited, along with a German composer and a few other guests, to listen to Gould's recording of Bach's *Goldberg Variations.* When the composer barked of Gould's unorthodox recording, "One cannot play Bach that way!" Kind lost her temper and yelled at him, "Do you perhaps have a patent on it?" The host of that gathering later brought Gould and his new fan together, and they struck up a friendship that lasted for the rest of Gould's short life. He was instrumental in urging her to move to the New World when the Seattle appointment was offered. They discussed specifics of keyboard performance and ornamentation, and they had a lot in common, even some nonmusical matters.

As Kind wrote in *Monologe,* "When I walked into his apartment, it literally took my breath away. God knows I'm a messy person, but in comparison to what is offered here, in my eyes, I was almost neat: it was a mess, but a terrific mess—never an empty seat, sheet music and books everywhere, on the chairs, on the floor, on tables and cabinets, on the piano. We stood and I hoped fervently that he would play. But then he had long since given up the public appearance and didn't play in front of anyone, not even in front of friends. He played his new recordings and showed me all around the balcony running along the magnificent view of the fantastic city of Toronto and the enormous water."

For Silvia, the world was populated by potential friends. When student dissidents announced plans to take over the UW music building during the era of student unrest in the early 1970s, Kind was told that she and the rest of the faculty had to evacuate the building. But she didn't. Instead, she greeted the angry protesters at the door of her harpsichord studio, invited them to "just talk about this," and ushered them in for tea and fortune cookies.

After her retirement in 1978, Silvia didn't rest on her laurels. Instead, she designed an octagonal house in a tiny town just uphill of the Italian Riviera—Tovo di Faraldi—which friends then built for her. "It is very beautiful there, very civilized. Music is a polite art, and you can't be a musician with bad manners," she told me in 1978. "Italy is very conducive to music. I found the property more or less by accident—never did I think I would own a house, because money does not like me very well. It never stays around me. But an industrialist friend financed my design, and then I added to it when I could. It has an open terrace, and a roofed terrace, and a high ceiling—look! Isn't it beautiful?"

Between 1979 and 1994, Silvia lived in Italy, with occasional trips back to the Pacific Northwest to spend summers above an ocean beach in her beloved truck camper Pablo (christened in honor of Picasso), which she had outfitted comfortably with a stove, bed, and small Egon K. Wappmann harpsichord. In 1994, she moved permanently back to Port Angeles, where she spent her days with friends and ex-students; occasionally she took trips farther afield, as when for her ninetieth birthday she traveled to Ulan Bator, Mongolia.

Silvia always continued her beloved yoga, the discipline she used to concentrate her energies prior to the recitals and concerts of her younger days. "Her headstands were famous," her grandnephew Ueli Dubs said in 2012. "At the tender age of about eighty-five, she introduced herself to her medical doctor with a headstand, which he prohibited at the even more tender age of ninety."

Silvia played her beloved harpsichord almost to the day of her death in 2002, at the age of ninety-four. "On her last day," said her old friend and UW colleague Arthur Grossman, "she called me around 6 p.m. She asked her nurse to play recordings we had made together." Then Silvia told Grossman, "This is the last time I will talk to you." Grossman demurred, but when Silvia hung up, she turned to her nurse and said, "I think I'd like to die now." And she did.

Eva Heinitz

THE GREATEST GAMBIST

It is an irresistible temptation to place Eva Heinitz's chapter together with that of her University of Washington colleague Silvia Kind. Two women of strong opinions, they often performed together, and it must have been illuminating, and perhaps a little intimidating, to be in the practice room when they were both airing their views on how the next musical phrase should go.

The gambist and the harpsichordist, both grande dames of their instruments who made indelible marks on their listeners and students, were born in the same year, 1907—Heinitz in Berlin, and Kind in the German sector of Switzerland. Heinitz was slightly the elder (February 2 to Kind's August 15), and she joined the University of Washington faculty considerably before Kind did (1948 to Kind's 1967). But Heinitz's earlier arrival had been accelerated by a situation no one could have predicted in 1907, the danger attached to being half Jewish and living in Berlin during the Nazi era.

Heinitz was a temperamental, brilliant wunderkind. Named for the heroine of Wagner's *Die Meistersinger*, she soared to the top as a cello soloist with Europe's great orchestras while she was still in her twenties. She played with such legendary conductors as Wilhelm Furtwängler, Bruno Walter, and Otto Klemperer. Around

1929 or 1930, according to a 1991 interview with me, she fell in love with the viola da gamba, an early relative of the cello that is quite different in many ways, and she taught herself how to play it.

"It was love at first sight," she said of the viola da gamba. She brought her instrument to the famous Dolmetsch family of musicians and instrument makers in Haslemere, England, to be restored and then, with some advice from the Dolmetsches, set about deciding how to play it. "I changed my whole [cello] technique: how to hold the bow, and how to make the instrument sound like the human voice, the way old treatises advised players to sound," she explained. "The sound must have life and spirit in it. Bowing is the arm of the soul of the musician; the bow shapes everything."

As a youngster, Heinitz said, she was "too stuffy, from a good but limited German background. We lived in a large and beautiful apartment with a German Steinway piano that I loved to play. I was the youngest of three sisters. My parents were very strict. I was not allowed to leave a morsel of food on my plate. When we had a dish of potato dumplings with stewed fruit, which I hated, I pretended to eat it and sneaked it to our little dachshund."

But it wasn't all dumplings and stewed fruit. Heinitz remembered having a "fantastic childhood," with a Jewish lawyer father and gentile mother who chose only the best schools for their girls. Little Eva's pure singing voice and obvious musical talent made her parents proud, and they encouraged her with music lessons. They had a cook, housemaids, a governess, a seamstress, and laundry maids. All that changed, however, with the death of Heinitz's father and the disastrous economic climate that hit Germany in the years during and following World War I. Left to cope somehow was her mother, whom Heinitz described as "a lovely, charming, gifted Victorian lady who did not know how to boil water. It was terrible for my mother when my father died." The young Eva and her sisters knitted socks for soldiers, and the family survived one entire winter on a diet of kohlrabi, which she termed a rather nasty variant of cabbage.

"I must have been a horrible child," she remembers. "I was very strong-minded." When she was seventeen, young Eva came home and announced to her astonished family that she had it all figured out: she wasn't going to school any longer but would instead enter the Academy of Music, for which she had prepared on both cello and piano (with the help of her favorite uncle, who had bought her a better cello). "I still remember the audition," Heinitz told me back in 1991. "The faculty were all sitting around in a half circle, all the professors, and the composer Franz Schreker, whose wild hair stood up in all directions. I played very well the piano, too." Coincidentally, one of the faculty members at the Academy of Music was Romuald Wikarski, the father of another cellist who eventually ended up in Seattle, Cordelia Wikarski Miedel.

At the Berlin Academy, Heinitz studied with the renowned teacher and editor Hugo Becker, but in many respects she found this experience an ordeal. Already a person of strong musical opinions, she balked at having to do things according to Becker's Teutonic way. Word spread about her talent, however, and Heinitz was swept into the milieu of top performers in Berlin. She played Mozart's B-flat-major Piano Trio with the famous physicist Albert Einstein on the violin, who, as she later said, played with "a very soft tone—perfectly correct, but totally uninteresting. But what a fantastic face! The face of the famous Albert Einstein is something I could never forget. It was like a landscape, not quite human, unforgettable, the face of one of the greatest minds in history."

Best of all, she came to the attention of the great Otto Klemperer, who called her "die beste Gambistin, die ich kenne" (the best gambist I know). Heinitz always remembered the performance of Bach's great *Saint John Passion* they did together. At the moment of Jesus's death in the score, the incredible tension dissolves in an eloquent solo for the gamba. Klemperer turned to her and quietly said, in German, "Heinitz, just go." And she put her bow to the strings and played the lines she called "the complaining sweet voice of the viola da gamba," while he watched and listened and set the rest of the orchestra into motion.

"The culture, the energy, the talent we had in Berlin when I was a very young girl, cannot be replaced," she mused. "Everybody in the arts in Berlin was Jewish. All the string players were Jewish. I defiantly still consider myself 51 percent Jewish and only 49 percent non-Jewish!"

Then came Hitler. Heinitz, like the multitudes of Jewish musicians who dominated the Berlin arts scene, found her life to be in jeopardy. "That we [Jews] could be in danger from a political movement never entered our minds," she said of that era. "We were the most loyal of all Germans, the backbone of society. Many, including several of my relatives, went to the concentration camps still unable to believe it could happen."

After the sudden death of her mother, Heinitz fled Germany in 1933, going first to Paris for a short time (where she studied with Pablo Casals's assistant, Diran Alexanian), and then to London, which was flooded with refugees. There she gave a viola da gamba recital with the excellent harpsichordist Thurston Dart ("We clicked like hell!" she happily said later). She wanted to stay in London, where she gave frequent concerts on the BBC, but couldn't get a labor permit to teach. It was impossible to live on the income from her concerts.

The pianist Arthur Schnabel, whom Heinitz knew from Berlin, advised her in 1939 to go to New York, and he helped her get started with a concert in the New Friends of Music series in New York's Town Hall. Heinitz came over by boat at a time when the seas were menaced by submarines and the passengers were filled with terror. She remained in New York for eight years.

Heinitz was married briefly to an older man, a lawyer and fellow German refugee with no musical background. "A musician should never marry somebody who has nothing whatsoever to do with music!" she said later. "He had these hobbies which I considered horrible, like hunting and sport. He never learned English, and surrounded himself with German-speaking friends, and finally he went back to Germany." Marriage and her musical career proved incompatible. "I wasn't that crazy about having children," she confessed. "For me, music came first. I was actually quite honest about it."

She joined the Pittsburgh Symphony under the renowned conductor Fritz Reiner as assistant principal cellist (because, she said, Reiner would never have allowed a woman to be principal cellist). Reiner, however, regularly invited her to play chamber music with such visiting violin soloists as Heifetz (whom in the interview she called "a dreadful chamber player"), Menuhin, Milstein, Szigeti, and Stern.

Meanwhile, in New York, Heinitz also met the violinist Emanuel Zetlin; she remembers the man who would become her University of Washington colleague as "a great teacher, but an impossible performer because he was so nervous. I am the reverse; I am usually better in performance than in rehearsal." In 1948, Zetlin called her to ask if she could recommend a good chamber cellist to form a string quartet at the UW, at the suggestion of Dr. Stanley Chapple, then the music department chair. Instead, she recommended herself—"I think I did that twice in my life, with excellent results." She briefly considered an offer in Texas but discovered "there was not even one tree on which to hang myself. And I knew how beautiful Seattle was from an earlier tour."

With $2.50 in her pocket, she went to Seattle and was immediately hired. She had to borrow money from the pianist Else Geissmar to tide her over before the first meager UW paycheck arrived. Chapple went to bat for Heinitz, however, after she gave her first recital and it was clear that she deserved not just a quartet spot but a professorship. She got one.

There were some tough times; Seattle did not match the cultural mecca that Berlin had been. "The Seattle Symphony was in terrible shape under the conductor then, Eugene Linden," she said with her usual candor. "It was unbelievably awful. I went to the *Messiah*, and at intermission I asked, 'Where is the bar?' I took two stiff drinks."

Things got better, however, with the arrival of the conductor Milton Katims, whose work Heinitz generally approved. At the university, relationships with her fellow faculty members—even the faculty string quartet, for which she had originally been hired—were occasionally rocky, but in general Heinitz had found a congenial niche. She also became a good friend of the renowned artist Mark Tobey. "She was a musician's musician," remembers her student Pamela Roberts. "It's not only that she was exacting, but her music was outside of this world. Her musical understanding took us into a realm that most of us never touch. The expression was sublime. The pathos of it could make you breathless."

Heinitz was a gifted, unorthodox, and (at times) terrifying teacher who said exactly what she thought and had no reservations about pointing out shortcomings. One of her students who went on to a career in the Seattle Symphony, the cellist Bruce Bailey, recounts his experiences in her studio when he was already good enough to sub for Heinitz in the faculty string quartet. "When I met Eva, I could play the cello, but my technique was unorthodox. She of course was a strict Teutonic traditionalist. I had exactly four lessons with her. At the start of the fourth, she announced that she would no longer accept me as a student, that she would give me an A for the course, that I did everything wrong and would have to be rebuilt from the ground up but was playing far too well for that. She could not help me. For years thereafter, whenever she heard me play she said, "Very good, Bruce, I don't know how you do it!"

The lutenist Stephen Stubbs, who braved her home studio for several coaching sessions on his instrument, recalls her acerbic comment when Heinitz observed one of her cats walking through a newly installed cat door in her house. "My cats are more intelligent than my students. I only had to show them the new door *once.*" On another occasion, a highly regarded Vancouver early-music ensemble (which Stubbs declines to name) came to Seattle to give a concert that Stubbs remembers as "very advanced and very boring." Heinitz drily observed, "We must remember that when these composers wrote this music, they were alive."

My own experience of Heinitz as a coach came when I accompanied Page Smith, who became principal cello of the Northwest Chamber Orchestra and Pacific Northwest Ballet Orchestra, as her pianist in a session at Heinitz's home. Heinitz made a number of penetrating and approving comments about style and technique, directed toward the cellist, who had been her student for five years. And then she shifted that brown-eyed gaze toward the piano bench. "You," she said. "You are too loud." She sighed. "Pianists are always too loud."

Heinitz did not shrink from giving her opinion on many subjects, from musical matters to journalism and world affairs. After I became the music critic of the *Seattle Times*, she regularly explained my shortcomings (as well as cases where she thought I had hit the mark), often in public and at top volume ("You were completely wrong about the Beethoven! How could you write that!"). She was always a highly colorful interview subject.

"Our world has changed," Heinitz reflected in 1991, "which is perfectly natural, if you read history. I frankly don't think that we are improving. Culturally speaking, I'm pretty horrified. I wonder sometimes whether people will play Schubert, Bach, and Beethoven in the next century. These days a saxophone player will perform the Arpeggione Sonata [which Schubert wrote for a now-defunct bowed instrument with some similarity to the viola da gamba]. There are no restrictions anymore."

Yet Heinitz broke with tradition herself, most prominently by putting an endpin in the end of her viola da gamba, an instrument traditionally held between the legs rather than resting on the floor, as the modern cello does. The gamba kept slipping on the fabric of her concert dress, however, and the composer Paul Hindemith suggested that she simply place an endpin in the instrument. She played the instrument that way ever after, shrugging when anyone had the temerity to question her. And she played it in a historically informed, highly musical style that made her a prime mover in the development of Seattle's early-music scene.

"I have my own musical tastes, and by the way, they do not include Vivaldi," she told me. "The prospect of an all-Vivaldi concert would make me hide underneath the harpsichord. I don't really have a favorite composer, but I would not want to live without Bach's music, and Mozart, and the late Beethoven quartets."

"I say what I think, and I don't lie," she added. "It makes life too difficult. I have a great respect for the truth." She never minced words; describing a performance of a Bach adagio by the famed Mstislav Rostropovich, Heinitz said, "I'll never forgive him. Disgusting. *Ritardandi* from here to Kirkland."

Eva inspired both respect and affection. "She was such an amazing role model for living your dream and doing what you're good at, never giving up, and that you can do what you want as a woman," remembers her grandniece Catherine Schatzel. "She taught me how to have an appreciation for good food, good wine, and music and nature, and to this day I think of her (and thank her) as I prune her fifty-plus-year-old roses that are a part of my garden."

At the age of eighty-four, Heinitz traveled to Indiana to receive a signal honor: the designation "Grande Dame du Violoncelle" (Great Lady of the Cello), while Janos Starker and several other international luminaries gathered to acclaim her for her "significant lifetime contributions to the art of both the playing and the teaching of the cello." She gave a master class there for more than a hundred students and cognoscenti.

Heinitz eventually returned the favor in 1994 by donating her 1700 Gofriller cello to Indiana University School of Music under the care of Starker, stipulating that a scholarship fund be established from the proceeds of the sale of the cello. Every year, the scholarship students write grateful thank-yous to her grandniece. "I am not that interested in money," Heinitz explained at the time. "In fact, I hate it. But I am interested in what money can do, and I want to help young cellists. I've had a full, rich life and achieved almost everything I wanted. Now it's time for this wonderful instrument to go on."

Heinitz's life went on, too, although she often raged against the strictures of old age. At ninety, she declared, "I am quite old and full of constant pains. My present life is a struggle, and what drives me crazy is the loss of memory. But I can't complain: I have had immense joy in my life. I have had success, and love, and ups and downs—but without the beauty of music I wouldn't have had a life. I believe in beauty. Without it, there is no point at all." Toward the end of her life, Heinitz liked to answer phone calls from friends saying, "I'm not dead yet! But I'm close!"

At her death in 2001, her admirers paid tribute to her memory. "She was one of the great artists of our time," said Starker. "She was an absolutely uncompromising musician." The cellist Cordelia Wikarski Miedel, herself an international prizewinner, called her "truly great." The pianist and UW colleague Randolph Hokanson described her as "one of the best musicians I've ever known." The Seattle composer and singer Peter Hallock, one of the key figures of the city's early-music scene and a longtime Heinitz devotee, called her "a treasure."

And the legendary conductor Otto Klemperer had called her the best viola da gamba player. In her last years, she spoke again and again of their collaboration, of those few moments in the *Saint John Passion* when her viola da gamba carried the emotional weight of the death of Christ and she made the music take flight. Hers was the satisfaction of a life lived in service to music, without compromise, in total honesty. Eva Heinitz was not always easy to be with, but the reward of her company, musical and personal, was always well worth the effort.

Robin McCabe

THE KEYBOARD DIPLOMAT

In the world of classical music, few things are as difficult for a gifted young artist as getting that crucial big break. Sometimes winning a major international competition will do it—though the annals of music are full of young Cliburn or Tchaikovsky Competition winners who promptly disappeared from sight, unable to capitalize on their success or develop a concert career. Sometimes a young artist gets one of those "a star is born" moments when the opportunity comes (as it did for the aspiring pianists André Watts and Lang Lang) to step into an important engagement at the last minute, create a sensation, and go on to superstar status.

Rare indeed is the career path of the pianist Robin McCabe, who achieved public notice not just on her journey from Puyallup to Juilliard and on to a successful New York concert debut but also by means of an enormous *New Yorker* magazine profile— which in 1979 was developed into the book *Pianist's Progress*—by Helen Drees Ruttencutter. Their meeting, a chance encounter at a friend's apartment in New York, was serendipitous for both: the journalist Ruttencutter was looking for a subject for a *New Yorker* feature that might boost her writing career, and the piano student McCabe, a pretty, bright youngster from remote Washington State was about to make her mark on the concert stage and proved to be just that subject. In the hard-charging atmosphere at Juilliard, where a hopeful pianist is far more likely to wash out than to succeed, McCabe's story turned out to be a success story well worth covering, through the drama and excitement of competitions, concerts, and reviews.

The meeting of two aspirants—pianist and chronicler—led to three years of intensive conversations, research, interviews, and the kind of publicity of which an aspiring artist can only dream. The book ends in 1979, by which point the young McCabe had realized her early ambitions: she had made her mark at Juilliard and in competitions, earned favorable reviews from New York critics for her concert debuts in Carnegie Hall and Alice Tully Hall, and entered the august roster of one of New York's prestigious artist managers, Herbert Barrett.

McCabe's path began with her early childhood as the oldest of three daughters born to the physician Edward McCabe and his wife, Lou, a registered nurse. Robin, a self-described "little show-off," was only five when it was discovered that she had perfect pitch and a strong musical aptitude; her piano studies started shortly thereafter. Practice, performance, and contests continued her ascent as a musician.

At the age of fifteen, Robin first encountered Béla Siki, the Northwest's leading pianist and teacher, at a competition. She immediately wanted to study with him, but he wasn't taking any high schoolers; he told her to wait. (McCabe notes, "To my vainglorious satisfaction, he has since told me he regretted that decision!")

The senior McCabes wanted all three of their daughters (Robin and her younger sisters Rachelle and Renée) to have the same advantages, including piano study with Siki. Robin and Rachelle "took"; Rachelle is now a professor of piano at Oregon State University. Renée chose a different path. "There's a great story about Renée at probably age ten, in a lesson, and Béla says, 'Renée, let's hear a little bit of the Bartók,' and Renée looks at her watch and responds, 'I think we're just about out of time.' This was to the great Siki!" Robin laughs at the memory.

When she finished high school with straight As, Robin was drawn to the University of Washington because of Siki's excellent reputation, but she auditioned elsewhere as well. "I got in to Indiana and some other schools, but in the end I decided on the UW," she remembers. "My parents were of course delighted that I could stay in the area. I was fairly tied to the strings of the family, too; I was not eager to go away."

She got a "big scholarship" to the UW that year, in 1967. McCabe certainly didn't imagine then that about twenty years later she would be sitting with the rest of the UW faculty, voting on the auditions of young aspirants. "From the moment I started with Béla, I knew I was really privileged," McCabe says. "We were a hot class of real talents. The atmosphere here was heady, with Robert Suderburg running around composing things, and the Soni Ventorum, all vivacious personalities, and the Philadelphia String Quartet playing, and people like [the pianist] Else Geissmar, who had worked with the legendary conductor Wilhelm Furtwängler. There was a master class every Friday afternoon. I no more would have thought of skipping that 4:30 class than—! And now today you try to get kids to come to a 4:30 class and it's not so easy!"

McCabe calls her student self "pretty much a workaholic." She wanted to get As in everything and go to the football games and the frat parties, but she remembers doing far more working than partying. The faculty were supportive and also inspiring; there was chamber music with the violist-conductor Vilem Sokol, sonata lessons with the violist Don McInnes and the violinist Dénes Zsigmondy—"all those larger-than-life characters like Peter Erős is now," McCabe said in 2012. (Erős passed away in 2014.) So congenial were the faculty members, in fact that McCabe wasn't in a hurry to leave: "I was afraid to go to New York, but to their credit, they pushed me out the door. I try to do the same thing now for my own students, for their own sake."

She was accepted to the Juilliard School's doctoral program and studied with four noted teachers: Rudolf Firkusny, Ilona Kabos, Ania Dorfmann, and Joseph Bloch. Bloch has called her "an ideal student . . . a natural pianist, a marvelous sight reader." In 1978, she joined the Juilliard faculty.

The New York years, chronicled in the highly readable *Pianist's Progress*, were a heady period of struggle and triumph as McCabe made her way in a milieu of two hundred other talented young Juilliard pianists. The rigors of competitions, concerts, recordings, international tours, and New York debuts at Carnegie Hall and Alice Tully Hall are all vividly described in the book, along with the ups and downs of success and despair. Reviewers weighed in, as when the *New York Times* declared that she was developing into a "major keyboard artist" with playing "so lovely that few pianists would be apt to equal it." At the book's conclusion, McCabe's career has taken flight, and her highly regarded New York manager Herbert Barrett has declared that she is "a repeater"—that is, an artist whom concert presenters enthusiastically reengage. After 1979, there were concerts and recitals in New York, Prague, St. Louis, and Tokyo, and tours in South America and Asia, where she proved particularly popular; over the years McCabe made several concert tours of Japan, where reviewers have dubbed her "a pianistic powerhouse."

So why after these successful years of career development did McCabe return to Seattle in 1987 to teach at her alma mater?

This clearly isn't a case of "failure to launch"—not with that résumé and those reviews. A lot of McCabe's decision making has more to do with what the pianist describes as "the life of the suitcase." She realized that life is more than a trek through airports, hotels, concert halls, and receptions. She also knew she wanted to teach, and she had a "yearning for permanence," in part because Juilliard then gave its teaching staff only one-year contracts. The uncertainty of a concert career, where "there's nothing as dead as yesterday's performance," also weighed with McCabe. "I yearned for security and seeing the path before me," she observes. "It's not that I'm exactly a homebody, but I was always hoping to find a nice fellow, too—and I still haven't given up. But I'm very guarded; it's my own fault."

When McCabe returned to Seattle from New York, the idea of a position at the UW also excited her parents. She continued to do some touring and concertizing, but the Barrett management ended after a while; they were "very gracious about it," as McCabe recalls.

"I think those of us who get a lot out of life decide we are going to optimize where we are. I missed New York in the first few years but I kept the apartment for a while. When you live in New York, you think, 'If I leave here, will I be a little less interesting, less alluring? Will I be dull?' There is something magical about being there and making a career.

"But I got here, and I loved the UW students, and loved the larger intellectual life—that life of the mind. To me, that's even more important than playing the piano. It is fulfilling and challenging. That's what is magical about moving back to Seattle. I was quite enchanted by the way my colleagues used the English language. I heard a musicologist talking about Fauré in a way that just amazed me. I could go to any lecture. A conservatory did not give me that. I get a lot back from my students, too. And I'm teaching more now.

"I also love the security of knowing that today I can just teach the piano; I don't have to prove something," she adds. "And as for the artist's life: I remember Ruth Laredo saying to me, 'At twenty-five, I would have gone anywhere to play the piano, and now I don't feel that way anymore.' You realize life is about more than how many encores do you get, and do you get reengaged by the Fort Lauderdale Symphony. As you get older and more mature, you see the ephemera of it all."

Playing is still deeply important to McCabe, as she found once when an overuse injury curtailed her playing for about a year. What surprised her was the discovery that she also liked administrative work when she was recommended to become assistant director of performance and public affairs and, eventually, to succeed UW's School of Music director Dan Neuman. At first, Siki, still an important mentor to her, disapproved of administrative developments for his keyboard protégée; then he changed his mind, telling McCabe: "You can make the school your orchestra."

Close relationships with the music faculty helped sustain McCabe during the difficult years in the early 2000s, when both her parents died after a harrowing series of health crises. "The faculty here is an odd little family," she observes, "and it is terribly dysfunctional by its own destiny: disparate and competing dynamics that create both real and imaginary separations between academics and performers. But most of the faculty do have a sense of humor, and you can usually get to them that way. This isn't the kind of a department where they do a lot of potlucks; there is a tendency to be jealous and contentious. But the faculty also is a group of such interesting and gifted people."

McCabe hopes that she will be successful in teaching her students what Béla Siki taught her, that "music is the art of suggestion." It's hard work, because many aspiring students who have a gift for the piano are not trained as well or as intensively as students ten or fifteen years ago were. Some of them have "tiger mothers" who expect their kids to master chess and dressage and French and a wide spectrum of other achievements that will look good on those crucial college entrance applications. The result is that the undergraduates are "overscripted and overstimulated," as McCabe puts it. "The patience with the process of musical development is not honed at the level it should be. The attention span is different. 'Give me the answer! I don't want to think critically, I'll just do a Google search.' They still think music is all about dexterity and speed. I ask them, 'Do you think that picture on the wall is about paint?'"

Because so many incoming piano students are from Asia—students in China are flocking to the keyboard by the millions—McCabe says that one of the challenges for UW's future will be to evolve degree programs like artist diplomas and professional doctorates that reflect the needs of these students. She is also working to expand the summer piano institute at the UW. A higher administrative post has no allure for McCabe, who was at one time courted for a deanship at the UW. "My passion is here," she says, gesturing to the two pianos in her studio. "I did play at divisional dean on a temporary basis, for six weeks, but I didn't like the job; it was policy wonking, large notional issues, and I was away from people." Clearly, for McCabe, it's working with people that lights her fire. She works hard to give students that aha! moment, "the moment when the tumblers in those locks are changing" and the young pianist sees the possibilities of the music in a new way.

"I think I still have some fire left," she jokes. "I want to do more teaching, more playing. I loved the directorship and was lucky to have it, but this is where I want to be now."

Ronald Phillips

THE CONSUMMATE CLARINETIST

Ronald Pickering Phillips was a one-man music history book who witnessed the development of the Seattle Symphony from 1927, when he played his first symphony concert, until his death at the age of ninety-eight in 2004. He oversaw much of that history from inside the orchestra, where he was the mainstay of Seattle's clarinet section for an amazing fifty-six years.

Dapper, aristocratic, and consummately professional, Phillips once played the famous opening clarinet solo in George Gershwin's *Rhapsody in Blue* with the composer conducting, in Seattle's old Civic Auditorium back in 1936. ("Boot it out," the composer advised the clarinetist. "It's a big place.")

Born on an Indian reservation in Lac du Flambeau, Wisconsin, Phillips, according to one of his greatest fans, the late arts enthusiast and activist Hans Lehmann, was "delivered by a hunchback doctor working by candlelight during a night of violent blizzards." Lehmann studied the clarinet with Phillips (not very successfully, by Lehmann's own account) and wrote an appreciation of him in his book *Out of the Cultural Dustbin.*

Young Ronald moved with his family from Wisconsin to Seattle at the age of three in 1909 and subsequently was enrolled in Ravenna Elementary School; already at the age of five he had a clarinet in his hands. His father, a violinist and cornet player, superintended Phillips's budding musicianship, and his two sisters accompanied him on the piano. Ronald later studied with Hilmer Ekstrand, who had played principal clarinet in the Seattle Symphony's inaugural concert in December 1903. He also studied in Paris with the distinguished French clarinetist Daniel Bonade (1894–1976), among others. But young Ronald was a natural; in his early years he was mostly self-taught.

Ronald entered Lincoln High School in 1920, but transferred to the newly opened Roosevelt High upon its completion; he won a composition contest to produce the first school song, "Roosevelt High, Here's to You." The song, in B-flat major and 2/4 time, concludes: "And the bright green and gold / Of our colors shall fly / In the sunshine of vict'ry / For ever Roosevelt High." (This song, and many other documents, including a small red pocket diary from 1920, survive in the Ronald P. Phillips Archives in the University of Washington Music Library.)

Three years after Ronald's 1924 graduation from Roosevelt (where he was an adept pole-vaulter as well as promising musician determined to become a conductor of the New York Philharmonic), he joined the Seattle Symphony Orchestra as second clarinet under the music director Karl Krueger. His appointment came about by word of mouth rather than formal audition, as he later told the Seattle historian Greg Dziekonski, because his abilities as a young virtuoso were already well known in musical circles. Ronald rose to principal clarinet of the orchestra in 1932, during the directorship of conductor Basil Cameron.

As a young clarinetist, he had been playing less formal gigs from the age of ten, when he began performing with the orchestra at Cowen Park Theater for a dollar a night. Then, in the fall of 1924, he became first clarinet in the Coliseum Theater's orchestra, playing for silent films. He simultaneously moonlighted with the Olympic Hotel Concert Orchestra and a smaller ensemble in the tearoom at the venerable Frederick and Nelson department store. The "extracurricular" work in ballrooms, theaters, and hotels all over town continued through the early decades of Phillips's Seattle Symphony career.

Prior to joining the Seattle Symphony, he also played in the Seattle Civic Symphony under the conductor Mary Davenport-Engberg; around 1923, when young Phillips was still in high school, he had earned the principal clarinet chair in that orchestra. In an interview by fellow clarinetist Mary Kantor for the *Clarinet* magazine in 2003, he explained that the former Seattle Civic Symphony principal clarinet, a Mr. Stone, found the third movement of Beethoven's Pastoral Symphony "too hard," and when Phillips played it correctly, Stone got up and left the orchestra.

Phillips later recalled an early unforgettable experience playing in the outdoor Seattle *Aida* of 1927, possibly the first uncut performance of the Verdi classic in the Pacific Northwest. "There were no mikes," remembered Mr. Phillips in my interview with him. "They [the performers] were all out in the open. The staging was quite beautiful. I recall that at the beginning of act 2, a full moon came up over Lake Washington."

Phillips married a pianist with the same surname, Gladys Bezeau Phillips (1892–1978), who played with the Seattle Symphony and had also performed in the 1936 *Rhapsody in Blue* concert with Gershwin. Lehmann's memoir remembers Gladys as a "fiery redhead" who was "nervous and irritable," but these characterizations (as Lehmann concedes) may have been due to his interruptions of her piano teaching en route to Ronald's studio in the couple's home. In any case, Phillips's letters make his affection for Gladys clear; one card home from Osaka addressed her as "Darling Honeybubbles."

Ronald's career in the Seattle Symphony spanned the music directorships of Karl Krueger, Basil Cameron, Nikolai Sokoloff, Sir Thomas Beecham, Carl Bricken, Eugene Linden, Manuel Rosenthal, Milton Katims, and Rainer Miedel, concluding just at the arrival of Gerard Schwarz. (As Dziekonski has observed, Phillips's fifty-six-year tenure was interrupted only by military service during World War II; his name is absent from programs in 1943–44 and part of 1945.) No wonder journalists always came to Ronald when doing a story about the "old days" at the Seattle Symphony. His memory was sharp, too, well up into his nineties. Over the years, he kept in touch with his former conductors; the archives contain such correspondence as a March 16, 1960, letter from Basil Cameron in London, in which Cameron inquires after the health of Sir Thomas Beecham, who, when Cameron last heard, had been ill with influenza.

It is clear from the archival letters that Phillips spoke and read French; he and Gladys spent six months in Paris in 1950 while he studied with Gaston Hamelin and Daniel Bonade, as well as Ulysse Delécluse and Louis Cahuzac. In turn, he later passed his knowledge on to several fine clarinet students, including Loren Kitt, Richard Shanley, Eugene Zoro, Dileep Gangolli, and Larey McDaniel.

During Phillips's long Seattle Symphony career, he also taught at the University of Washington for three decades, toured the Far East with the Los Angeles Philharmonic, and toured with the famed dancer Martha Graham and her troupe. The archives include letters home from 1956, praising the Japanese youth orchestras and decrying the Philippine cuisine's reliance on green coconuts.

Ronald also presided for many years over a chamber music series that presented a wide variety of artists and programming each Sunday at the old Seattle Art Museum (now the Seattle Asian Art Museum) in Volunteer Park. The museum series took a great deal of organizational time; Ronald not only lined up the participants (often, though not always, fellow symphony players) and the repertoire but also contacted the press every week to publicize the events. Apparently this job could be onerous. In a handwritten note correcting the total of museum concerts in a 1983 article in the *Clarinet*, Phillips wrote: "By 1989, 401 concerts, they then discontinued the concerts. What a relief!"

He was an ardent believer in the value of chamber music to symphony musicians, as well as to audiences. Ronald told me on more than one occasion, "Playing chamber music keeps you honest." He enjoyed playing in the Seattle Symphony Woodwind Quintet alongside a lineup that in the early 1970s featured four other orchestra principals: the flutist Scott Goff, the oboist Bernard Shapiro, the bassoonist Morgan Griffin, and Robert Bonnevie, French horn.

In his spare time, Phillips was an avid golfer, continuing to play until rheumatism in his hip forced him to stop only a few years prior to his death. At the age of seventy-eight, he received *Golf Magazine*'s "Age Shooter Certificate" for playing the Bellingham Golf Course in seventy-six strokes, thus better than "shooting his age." He was extremely proud of this achievement and regularly wore his "Shot His Age" lapel button.

Golf was not the only sport in which he excelled. His fellow Seattle Symphony player Bruce Bailey recalls of his old friend, "Ron liked to con the orchestra youngsters on the golf course and at the pool table. He would entice us with suggestions of a friendly game or two, then suggest sweetening it with a modest wager, then clean our clocks. At the pool table, he would casually unpack his personal pool cue, letting you know that he was a pro and intimidating you. Ron was an expert gamesman."

Debonair and disciplined, Ronald Phillips was a model to those around him, and he was highly regarded by his symphony colleagues. His fellow clarinetist and former student Larey McDaniel said at the time of Phillips's retirement that "the best musical education I ever had was playing alongside him." Ron Simon, who retired in 2011 after fifty years in the orchestra's double bass section, called him "one of a kind" in my August 7, 2004, *Seattle Times* obituary of Phillips. "He was a mainstay of the orchestra and a model for how a professional musician should behave," Simon continued. "They threw the mold away when he was made."

Bruce Bailey observed, "Sometimes the orchestra played a very late show and we were called back for an early rehearsal the next morning, at 8 or 9 a.m. Everyone straggled in, but Ron would show up impeccably dressed in a clean white shirt with a flower in his buttonhole, getting right to work by playing enormous arpeggios up and down. He showed me what a true professional was. He was one of the greatest players ever seen in Seattle."

One career milestone of which Phillips was immensely proud was his performance of the Mozart Clarinet Concerto with Sir Thomas Beecham during the second concert of that maestro's brief term (1941–43) as music director. Beecham was the conductor who coined the infamous "aesthetic dustbin" comment about Seattle, in remarks to an audience at the Washington Athletic Club on November 14, 1941. "If I were a member of this community, really I should get weary of being looked on as a sort of aesthetic dustbin." The maestro continued with an offer to help the city improve its reputation to the point where "there will be nothing superior in this country." Since his Seattle tenure lasted only two years, however, the validity of his offer is questionable.

The colorful and sometimes irascible Beecham had heard many great players and was notoriously frank about the shortcomings of his fellow musicians, which made his favorable assessment of Phillips's performance all the more meaningful. After the concerto, Beecham murmured a commendation to the clarinet soloist during the curtain calls. "What did he say?" Phillips asked another player who was standing closer to the conductor. "I never heard it [the Mozart concerto] played better," was the reply. Recalling that anecdote many years later in our interview, Phillips glowed with pride. He played that concerto about ten times in Seattle, including as his swan song on the occasion of his retirement in March 1983.

Ronald and Gladys were married for forty-two years before she died. In 1980, Phillips married Lillian Rigler, a painter and designer who had won more than one hundred awards for flower arranging. Both newlyweds, well entrenched in their respective art forms, found that while they wished to marry, neither wanted to give up their familiar home—stuffed with instruments and scores and music, or with canvases and paints and art. They kept both domiciles and lived first in one, then the other, thus keeping the best of both their worlds.

In 2003, Lillian preceded Ronald in death. The two had been a charming fixture at Seattle Symphony concerts and other cultural events in their later years—Ronald with his aristocratic profile and natty attire, and Lillian with her dramatic dress sense and eye for color. Ronald confided that after all those years heading the clarinet section, he was quite content to sit on the opposite side of the conductor and just enjoy the music.

Craig Sheppard

THE CLASSICIST OF THE IVORIES

It was Craig Sheppard's uncle, Charles Linton, who noticed him climbing up on the piano bench and trying to play the keys in 1952, when Sheppard was not yet five. He was determined to emulate his older brother, who had been taking piano lessons for the past couple of years, so Uncle Charles—for many years the accompanist of Philadelphia's venerable Orpheus Club—figured it was time to give young Craig a crack at the keyboard, too.

Within six months, Sheppard was playing everything his older brother could play, and more. And so it went, eventually on to a concert and recording career spanning several continents. A teaching career, too—first at London's venerable Guildhall School of Music and Drama in the 1980s, then, starting in 1993, at the University of Washington—has made Sheppard an important element in shaping generations of future talent; many of his former students now hold prominent positions in leading institutions around the world. But his own keyboard prowess has made him one of the most internationally prominent recitalists and recording artists in the Pacific Northwest over the past decades.

Music and Musicians magazine declared in 1986, "Sheer talent does not come much larger than Craig Sheppard's." Ten years later, *Gramophone* magazine cited Sheppard's "astounding force and charisma, playing which rides on a knife edge between abandon and control. . . . You won't easily find more exciting or, indeed, more leonine Liszt playing." And the *American Record Guide* noted, "He is almost a legend at this point, and is well known for his intelligent and moving interpretations of Beethoven and others. His Liszt is exquisitely nuanced with plenty of emotion and rubato galore."

A brilliant polymath who speaks several languages and reads widely, Sheppard conveys a personal intensity of remarkable firepower. He is a passionate and powerful pianist and has a formidable technique, but he is also a remarkable musical intellect with an encyclopedic knowledge of repertoire and cultural history. Widely traveled, he has performed and taught extensively in the Far East, Australia and New Zealand, India, the United Kingdom, and Europe; in Germany he was featured in the Berlin Philharmonic's recital series.

At the time of our interview in the summer of 2012, Sheppard was a vigorous sixty-four, about to launch a demanding tour of Australia but still looking forward to returning to his teaching responsibilities at the University of Washington. This routine—performing, touring, recording, teaching—which he took up when he assumed his academic post in 1993, seems to suit him well, and he has every intention of continuing it "well into my seventies, if they'll let me."

His life in music started in Philadelphia with piano lessons from Ellen Hindle, a gentle teacher who gave out gold stars for good progress. "She taught me the importance of memorizing my pieces, right from the start," Sheppard says. When young Craig was about eight, his parents decided it was time for a new teacher, and he began lessons with Lois Hedner, a well-known instructor in the area, who taught him for the next seven years. "Lois was a very good teacher for me. She gave me just enough rope, but also considerable discipline along with it," Sheppard remembers. "I wasn't an easy kid; I wanted to do things my way."

He played his first concert with a local community orchestra at the age of ten, with Mendelssohn's Capriccio brillante, "which I played very badly," he insists. "But it remains one of my favorite pieces." The following year, the eleven-year-old Sheppard tried out for a solo spot in a children's concert with the Philadelphia Orchestra, playing Mozart's Piano Concerto K. 467. To his mortification at the time, he lost to a nine-year-old girl (who later became a good friend). The following year, however, Sheppard played the Schumann Piano Concerto so well that he won solo opportunities in both the orchestra's winter season and its summer Robin Hood Dell series.

The Robin Hood Dell concert proved to be a turning point for Sheppard. He was playing the last movement of the Mendelssohn G-minor concerto, and, as he now remembers, "I bombed the very first two arpeggios, probably because I started too fast. My teacher, Lois, came up to me at the party and gently said, "You know, you didn't practice enough."

Sheppard, then twelve years old, was determined that he would never have that experience again. From then on he practiced more—three hours a day in the eighth grade, four hours in the ninth, five hours in the tenth. He had been in an advanced academic class from the seventh grade on, tearing through assignments at a terrific rate, and he had finished all but two subjects by his senior year. That gave him plenty of practice time to prepare for his audition for the Curtis Institute of Music, his big goal.

"I was lucky enough to get into Curtis," he remembers. "These days, they probably wouldn't let me up the front steps, with all the competition from China." At Curtis, he met his classmate and future University of Washington faculty colleague Patricia Michaelian. They both studied with Eleanor Sokoloff, a fearsome perfectionist who was ninety-eight in 2012 and still told Sheppard exactly what she thought. "I took her a DVD of [my] 2006 Bach inventions and sinfonias up in Maine," Sheppard says with a laugh, "and she put the DVD on and immediately started saying, 'Oh, I like that—but wait a minute—why did you rush there?' She was very tough on me, and I was delighted: Who else would tell a man of my age what to do?"

It wasn't so delightful back at Curtis, however. "We didn't have an easy time of it," as Sheppard remembers. "She felt that I was fighting her. She was a real detail person who heard everything. In retrospect, I realized what she gave me, and we're very good friends now."

After three years with Sokoloff, in 1968, he went to his first international competition after winning the Young Musicians Foundation competition in Los Angeles. In Montreal, he played the Prokofiev Seventh Sonata "like a tiger let out of the cage, I was so nervous." Afterward, he met the rising young pianist Garrick Ohlsson, who pointed out that Sheppard had just broken three strings on the Steinway. One of the strings was a bass string—"and those sound like a gun when they snap. I hadn't even noticed."

Hearing Ohlsson play was a revelation for Sheppard. "Garrick knew exactly what he wanted to achieve and how to achieve it, and he had such amazing control over those wonderful fingers. I decided that I wanted to have that, too, and that it was time to leave Philadelphia and go to New York. And this was probably the most important decision of my life. I remember it was the week that Bobby Kennedy died, in June 1968. I got on a train to New York and auditioned for [Sascha] Gorodnitzki and was accepted. I had taken my fate into my own hands, and I think that changed something inside of me. I wanted to be responsible for both my successes and my failures."

Sheppard went to the Busoni Competition a year later and won third prize, feeling, as he put it, that "I had redeemed myself a little." He had three years with Gorodnitzki, culminating in two degrees from Juilliard, and later, in London, he worked with Ilona Kabos, Peter Feuchtwanger, and Sir Clifford Curzon. Then he came to the attention of managers. Arthur Judson, who heard Sheppard play with the violinist Glenn Dicterow, told him, "I can make you the Gerald Moore of America," but Sheppard replied, "I would rather be the Craig Sheppard of America." (Later, Judson offered him a contract not as an accompanist, for which Moore is best known, but as a soloist.)

In January 1972, Sheppard played his New York debut at the Metropolitan Museum of Art, and then, in September, he departed for one of his major career milestones, the Leeds International Piano Competition. The famous pedagogue Nadia Boulanger was on the jury, as was Béla Siki, whom Sheppard later succeeded in Seattle. And among the competitors was Murray Perahia, already something of a legend as a soloist—and not only Perahia but also two other players who would go on to stardom, Mitsuko Uchida and Andras Schiff. "I had heard Murray play at Marlboro," Sheppard remembers. "He was in a different league from everyone else. I thought, 'Wow!'"

Nervous but well prepared, Sheppard advanced through the competition, playing the mighty Rachmaninoff Third in the third round. If you're ever going to be nervous, it's when you're playing in a major international competition before a stellar jury, competing in a field of young stars from several continents. Sheppard describes himself as "never really nonchalant onstage" but not intensely nervous if he knows the program well and is well prepared. "Sometimes the better moments [in performance] surprise me, too. You get out of the way and your instincts take over. But you always have to be aware of what you're doing."

Sheppard played brilliantly at the 1972 Leeds, and he took the silver medal to Perahia's gold, which brought him a lot of international notice. He and Perahia, who had coincidentally traveled to the competition on the same train, became good friends over the years, and eventually both relocated in London. Sheppard has nothing but good things to say about his colleague. "There's something very special about his way of looking at things. He is truly unique."

The Leeds brought Sheppard a tremendous amount of attention. "I came back with three pages of engagements; it was wonderful," he remembers. During his competition years, he also won bronze medals at the 1968 Ferruccio Busoni International and 1975 Dino Ciano Piano Competitions. In 1977, Sheppard won a bronze medal at the Arthur Rubinstein International Piano Master Competition. Rubinstein, who was ninety at the time, was so pleased by Sheppard's performance of Ravel's *Gaspard de la nuit* that he pulled a checkbook out of his pocket and wrote a one-thousand-dollar check to him as a special prize. Sheppard, who still has the check stub, remembers that afterward Rubinstein said he had a suggestion about the touch of the opening of *Gaspard*, and he "played" the opening bars on Sheppard's arm with a touch as light as a cat's paw. "I didn't wash my arm for a week," Sheppard told me.

By October 1973, Sheppard had moved to London, and he lived there for the next two decades, playing all the major European concert halls, from London's Wigmore to Milan's La Scala, as well as making frequent appearances on BBC radio and television. He performed with top orchestras around the world under such conductors as Sir Georg Solti, Sir Charles Mackerras, Yehudi Menuhin, and Aaron Copland. Not surprisingly, he developed an enormous repertoire, which includes more than sixty concertos as well as a kaleidoscopic array of great solo and chamber works from Bach to Messiaen.

"It was an amazing time," he reflects. "In June 1980, I performed thirteen times at the Wigmore [Hall], and somebody joked that I should just set up a tent and live there. I preferred the Elizabeth Hall, though, which has a wider stage, like Meany Theater." He also played a concert at the Royal Albert Hall that was attended by England's Queen Mother, and he gave a BBC television recital.

During his years in London, Sheppard also taught in a private studio, and once a week he took the train north to the University of Lancashire to teach. Other teaching included six years at the Guildhall School, ten years at the Menuhin School, and over the years a series of master classes at both Oxford and Cambridge Universities.

London had more than its share of great performers and conductors. "I found Yehudi Menuhin so inspirational," Sheppard recalls. "I played the Emperor Concerto with him and the Royal Philharmonic. People used to criticize his conducting, but I thought he was wonderful. I've rarely known anyone as sensitive to the soloist."

During the London years, Sheppard married a Danish artist whom he had known for several years. The marriage ended in 1991, but the couple have remained friends. The end of the marriage coincided with Sheppard's increasing dissatisfaction with the constant concertizing and touring. It all came to a head one evening after having played a major concert in a city where he didn't know anyone, had no visitors, and couldn't get any dinner at his hotel. Sheppard, already dejected because of the breakup of his marriage, realized that he was tired of the constant round of concerts, hotels, and travel.

He relocated to the United States in 1993, wanting something more permanent than the nomadic life of the touring virtuoso. Not long thereafter, he interviewed at the University of Washington School of Music and moved to a woodsy Seattle house where he now lives with his life partner, Gregory Wallace, a trial lawyer; the two married in 2014. In Seattle, Sheppard has found an attractive mix of teaching, performing, a little travel, and a life of the mind.

However, there's never enough reading time in his schedule. "There's so much I've never read," he says, "because I need to play. I'm dying to get to a good new novel. I remember having Sunday lunch some years back with Dame Janet Baker [the great British singer] and seeing her fantastic library. She waved her hand and said, 'When I stop singing, I'm going to sit and be able to enjoy all this.' I know how she felt!"

At present, Sheppard has no thought of curtailing a performing career that has immeasurably enriched Seattle's fans of great keyboard playing. Among the high points were a series of lecture recitals in the opening season of Seattle Symphony's then new Benaroya Hall in 1998–99; a memorable Beethoven sonata cycle that drew steadily increasing audience members over a two-season span; remarkable traversals of Bach's *Goldberg Variations* and Beethoven's *Diabelli Variations*; and regular appearances at the Seattle Chamber Music Society's summer festivals. His recitals in Meany Theater, for which his own Hamburg Steinway was always transported to the hall, have all been recorded live and won consistent international acclaim.

Sheppard loves teaching and interacting with promising young students such as the astonishingly talented twelve-year-old girl he heard on a 2011 visit to China. "I heard her play [Ravel's] *La Valse*," he explains. "She had everything. There was not one note out of place. Her rhythm was perfect, her concept of sound well developed. Her teacher told me that she had played the Prokofiev Third with the Shanghai Philharmonic when she was eleven, and she had already won international junior Chopin and Rachmaninoff competitions. One thing did strike me a bit humorous. Every time I would ask the young lady a question, she would look over at her 'tiger mother,' sitting in the corner, before answering! Yet there was obvious respect and love between the two."

"I'm convinced that these young Chinese students are our future," says Sheppard, who calls the level of talent in that country "just mind-boggling." "Sometimes I'll be working with kids, and they'll say, 'Oh, this is so difficult.' And I tell them: Do you know what's difficult? Walk through the center of Baghdad or Kabul right now. That is difficult. By comparison, we musicians have it so easy. They have no idea!"

Béla Siki, virtuoso pianist and teacher, during his Cincinnati years in the early 1980s. Photo by Sandy Underwood.

John Cerminaro, principal French horn in several major orchestras, was named to that post in the All-Star Orchestra in 2012. Photo courtesy of All-Star Orchestra.

At Home with Beethoven

Four Piano Sonatas
with Commentaries and Performances
by Randolph Hokanson

Randolph Hokanson, a University of Washington pianist whose
career has spanned nine decades, on the cover of his audio recording
*At Home with Beethoven: Four Piano Sonatas with Commentaries and
Performances* (University of Washington Press, 1989).

The inventive and colorful harpsichord virtuoso Silvia Kind in 1978, during her years on the University of Washington faculty. Photo by Cole Porter; copyright © 1978 The Seattle Times Company.

Eva Heinitz, cellist and violist da gamba, was honored in 1991 as "Grande Dame du Violoncelle." Undated family photo.

Robin McCabe, concert pianist and professor of music at the University of Washington, where she also was director of the School of Music from 1994 to 2009. Photo by Joanne De Pue, University of Washington School of Music.

A consummate professional, Ronald Phillips was a mainstay of the Seattle Symphony's clarinet section for fifty-six years. Photo by Larey McDaniel.

Craig Sheppard, international touring concert pianist and University of Washington music professor. Photo by Steve Korn.

THE COMPOSERS

COMPOSERS of classical music are an integral part of any major arts city. Unless this art form is to become a repository of history, it must be constantly renewed and redeveloped. The term "new music," however, is not always audience catnip; in fact, it can be a hard sell, partly because concert audiences are generally mistrustful of new works. New music hasn't withstood the test of time, as have the best works of previous centuries; it can be highly variable in quality, and anyone who has sat squirming through the premiere of an uninspired work may be hesitant to return and try again. But those who don't try again may also miss an acquaintance with something beautiful, profound, and entirely new.

Outside of the world of pop and commercially oriented music, the economics of composing "serious" music are dauntingly challenging. Across the country, around the world, only a handful of classical composers are able to make a living entirely from commissions, performances, and sales of their music to orchestras, opera companies, and smaller ensembles. Further, it can take a long time—months, even years—to fulfill a significant commission, and income from composing is highly sporadic. That is why most composers also hold paying positions in teaching, conducting, and residencies to supplement their compositional income.

Three composers with longtime attachments to Seattle are profiled here: a prominent native son who lives elsewhere but continues to have a substantial local impact; an international composer whose last decades were spent in Seattle, inspired by the Northwest's majestic mountains; and a respected symphonist whose long-standing association with the Seattle Symphony has included many premieres and a significant community influence as director of the orchestra's Young Composers program.

This trio is the "tip of the iceberg" of a large macrocosm of composers with local ties, many of them on the faculties of Seattle-area universities and colleges, and many of them also winners of national awards. They contribute substantially to the region's rich choral music culture, as well as to the symphonic and chamber genres, in almost every conceivable style: traditional, eclectic, electroacoustic, minimalist, folk-based, and ethnic.

For the majority of these composers—including this writer—the joy of making music and hearing a performance of one's new work more than compensates for a level of remuneration that ensures you don't quit your day job. Perhaps the world of the classical composer is one of the last bastions of disinterested idealism.

Alan Hovhaness

THE COMPOSER OF THE MOUNTAINS

The year was 1977, and Alan Hovhaness—an internationally eminent composer and a five-year resident of Seattle—had agreed to an interview for the *Seattle Times*. Excited and a little nervous, I called him to arrange a time for our talk: How about 1:30 p.m.? Or 2 p.m.?

"Could we make it a little later?" came the quiet inquiry over the phone. "I'm just waking up then."

Our 3 p.m. start time found the composer just finishing his morning coffee. He usually started writing sometime around midnight, working steadily through the night until the sun came up. Then it was time for bed.

This unusual schedule was not just the product of eccentricity. As a youngster, Hovhaness knew he wanted to be a composer, but his parents opposed his career choice. And thus began the nocturnal creative habit of a lifetime:

"My system is a bit unusual because I was a secret composer all through my teens. My family thought writing music was abnormal, so they would confiscate my music if they caught me in the act. I used to compose in the bathroom and hide the manuscripts under the bathtub. The best time for writing was at 4 a.m. or so, when everyone was certain to be asleep. Now, when I start to work, I have the feeling that this night is going to last forever. I have all the time in the world."

Hovhaness, who died in 2000, was born Alan Vaness Chakmakjian in 1911 to an Armenian father and a mother of Scottish heritage; later, the composer dropped his original surname and modified his middle name into Hovhaness, the Armenian form of "John" and the name of his paternal grandfather. (The composer's names and spellings varied over time; in 1935–36, he signed letters to the Finnish composer Jean Sibelius "Alan Scott Hovaness.") Hovhaness's parents were highly educated: his mother, Madeline Scott Chakmakjian, was a Wellesley graduate in an era in which relatively few women attended college, and his Harvard-educated father, who had emigrated from Turkey, was a chemistry professor at Tufts University. Haroutiun Hovhaness Chakmakjian introduced Alan to his Armenian heritage and taught him the Armenian language on their long walks together in Somerville and, later, Arlington, Massachusetts.

By the age of thirteen, Hovhaness had composed two operas, *Bluebeard* and *Daniel*, and both were performed at his school; his *Lotus Blossom* was performed at Arlington High School when the composer was eighteen. Because he was an accomplished pianist, he was able to get work as a soloist and chamber musician at a hotel in New Hampshire, and he won a scholarship to the New England Conservatory of Music. The lean Depression years found him struggling to make ends meet with performances, many of them as organist or pianist for Armenian and Greek Orthodox congregations.

An early devotee of Sibelius, Hovhaness and his first wife, the artist Martha Mott, visited the older composer in Finland; later, back in the United States, he gave lectures on Sibelius's music. His daughter and only child, Jean Hovhaness Nandi, born in 1935, was named for Sibelius, who was her godfather.

Favorable feedback from John Cage and Lou Harrison after a 1945 concert of Hovhaness's music helped him realize that he was on the right track. Their response, Hovhaness recalled, was "the first time that other composers understood and appreciated what I was doing." This appreciation was especially sweet after Hovhaness's unfortunate experience at Tanglewood in 1942, when he participated in Bohuslav Martinů's master class and found that his work was not well received by such peers as Aaron Copland and Leonard Bernstein. Hovhaness famously destroyed many of his early works in a bout of self-criticism (he once claimed that the number was "over a thousand"), but he recalled this period differently at different times. In 1977, he said he had burned the scores after the eminent composer Roger Sessions visited his junior high school in 1926 and urged the teenager to develop "more discipline." In our 1981 interview, however, Hovhaness said that the event happened later, after the unhappy experience at Tanglewood. Still another version of the score-destruction episode surfaced in a 1985 interview with the radio producer Bruce Duffie, whom Hovhaness told, "I just didn't have room for them [the early scores]. I finally came to a point where I found myself [as Sibelius had earlier promised he would], and I wanted to destroy everything else." Hovhaness later had a few regrets, claiming he had destroyed too much.

In 1951, after three years teaching at the Boston Conservatory, he got a short-term job as a composer with the Voice of America and moved to New York. Here, Hovhaness tried to publish his works and lost money on copying and shipping the scores and parts. Finally, he found success, first with the publisher C. F. Peters, and then with commissions from orchestras and dance companies. He won two Guggenheim Fellowships, in 1953 and 1954.

His commissions allowed Hovhaness to travel to Japan, Korea, India, and Switzerland, where he absorbed further musical influences. During his formative time as a Fulbright Research Scholar in India (1959–60), he was invited to participate in the annual Music Festival of the Academy of Music in Madras. He studied the music and instruments of the ancient Japanese *gagaku* (elegant music) tradition, which was introduced from China and became the music of the Japanese imperial court, and the Korean *ah-ak* orchestra, for which Hovhaness wrote his Symphony No. 35. In 1962, six months in Hawaii as a visiting composer at the University in Honolulu allowed him time for further *gagaku* studies.

"In an earlier incarnation I must have been an Oriental musician," he mused in a 1977 interview. He also traced his musical foundation back to the Armenian priest and composer whose name is variously transliterated as Komitas, Gomidas Vertabed, and Vardapet (1869–1935). Hovhaness considered him "the first minimalist, who created the Armenian style and was one of my greatest influences."

A major breakthrough for Hovhaness was the successful premiere of his symphonic score *Mysterious Mountain* by Leopold Stokowski and the Houston Symphony Orchestra in 1955; it was Stokowski who had urged Hovhaness to "give it a name!" Not long thereafter came the performance of his Magnificat, which also proved popular with audiences and critics. Commissions began to pour in from such stars as Jean-Pierre Rampal, Martha Graham, and Mstislav Rostropovich. Gradually, Hovhaness rose to a status enjoyed by only a handful of composers in our time: the ability to live well from the profits of his pen alone, without needing a "day job" or a teaching position to fall back on.

Success was "surprising to me, because [the] first half of my life I was known as the composer who was never performed," Hovhaness told me. "I had no luck until I was forty-one, when Stokowski decided to champion my work. I picked an opus number, 132, out of the air for *Mysterious Mountain* because people like opus numbers; then I worked backward to assign other numbers to earlier works." (An opus number is given to a single major work, such as a symphony, or a collection of smaller works.)

Hovhaness the man was a fascinating study in contradictions. Always a little otherworldly, he was quiet, shy, and rather aloof; he was married six times, which might well be a record for a classical composer. He could be modest and self-deprecating, or downright lofty, as when he declared, in a 1940 manifesto attached to a fellowship application, that he intended to "inspire all mankind with new heroism and spiritual nobility."

Strong-featured and craggy, his face was enlivened by penetrating brown eyes that often seemed to gaze at vistas unseen by others. His huge hands looked just right on the piano keyboard but almost incongruous when holding a pen, which in his grip looked the size of a matchstick. He was everyone's idea of the bemused genius, surrounded by stacks of music paper and not always watching where he was going. The prolific Hovhaness was, in fact, seriously injured when he absentmindedly tripped and fell over a huge pile of manuscripts in his basement.

The first to invite Hovhaness to Seattle, in 1966, was the farsighted conductor Vilem Sokol, who led the Seattle Youth Symphony Orchestra and taught at the University of Washington School of Music. Soon after, Milton Katims, then the music director of the Seattle Symphony, chose Hovhaness as the orchestra's composer in residence, a tenure made possible by a Rockefeller grant. Hovhaness set up permanent residence in Seattle in 1972.

Seattle proved remarkably congenial for Hovhaness, and his twenty-eight years here were extraordinarily fruitful. Inspired by a lifelong love of rugged scenery, Hovhaness found mountains aplenty in the Pacific Northwest, and he was inspired by the high drama of the 1980 eruption of Mount St. Helens—an event he commemorated in one of his most successful symphonies. He also found many champions, chief among whom was Gerard Schwarz. Schwarz's partisanship meant an entirely new level of appreciation for Hovhaness, bringing him performances, recordings, and the kind of recognition accorded to an important public figure in a city's musical circles.

Hovhaness was also lucky in choosing the Japanese-born actress and soprano Hinako Fujihara to be his sixth and last wife for a twenty-three-year-long union of extraordinary happiness and mutual support. He met Hinako at a reception following a Cornish College concert of his music. Hinako remembers, "He came in the door and saw me, and I saw his eyes somersault. When he gave me his autograph, it was very shaky. I didn't expect to see this famous composer again, but the next time I went to a concert, I looked up and he was there."

Hinako and Alan became musical partners as well as spouses. He loved her stratospherically high soprano voice, which was enhanced by her work with the noted singer and pedagogue Leon Lishner, who was then on the faculty of the University of Washington. Hovhaness wrote several works featuring his wife's voice; she was his muse. She also administered his recording company, baked delicious pies that he loved, and ran interference with outsiders so that her husband could devote himself to composition.

It was a happy and rewarding time for Hovhaness. He never went anywhere without a checkbook-sized notebook to take down the musical motifs that occurred to him wherever he might be. He sketched musical themes while waiting for his wife to emerge from a Macy's department-store dressing room; while pushing a grocery cart down the produce aisle; while waiting in line at the post office. "I get some nice ideas at the post office," he confessed in 1977. And no restaurant napkin was safe from his prolific pen.

Many famous composers were tormented by writer's block; Rachmaninoff, for instance, even sought out a psychologist. Hovhaness never knew what writer's block was. "Melodies are constantly running through my mind, even when I'm sleeping," he said. His Seattle-area houses, first in the suburb of Burien and then in Renton near the Seattle-Tacoma International Airport, filled up with boxes and stacks and piles of music; mounds of scores had to be pushed aside to accommodate visitors on a chair or a couch. Heaps of music vied with provisions for space in the kitchen and bulged out of half-closed closets.

As he aged, Hovhaness became less interested in travel and more interested in local landscapes, with their vistas of the mountains and the rugged scenery that inspired his music. During the 1980s alone, he wrote about twenty symphonies—six of them in 1986. His symphonic output officially numbers sixty-seven, though he might have composed as many as seventy-five (counting early and unnumbered works). Through 1995, his last productive year,

Hovhaness's opus numbers total a reported 434. His known surviving output includes more than four hundred works, including, in addition to the symphonies, at least nine operas, two ballets, and more than a hundred chamber pieces. Among his best-known works are those inspired by nature: *And God Created the Great Whales*, *Mysterious Mountain*, and Symphony No. 50, titled *Mount Saint Helens Symphony*.

On at least one occasion, Hovhaness had to rewrite a lost work. The manuscript of his Symphony No. 40 was stolen during a trip to his publishers in New York. Despite a public appeal on television, the manuscript (which, Hovhaness believed, had been stolen because it was in a new, handsome music case) was never recovered. He rewrote it.

Not all of Hovhaness's music has been met with rejoicing. The competitive world of classical composition is dominated by trends, cliques, and coteries. During much of Hovhaness's career, serialist and atonal works were in the forefront of the avant-garde. Critics and rivals often jeered at Hovhaness's gentler harmonies, Asian influences, and a tonality that was seen as deeply old-fashioned. (This despite the fact that the composer was also in the forefront of aleatory music and ahead of his time in anticipating the roots of what later became the minimalist movement.) That performers and audiences actually liked Hovhaness's music, in contrast to their merely enduring the less audience-friendly atonal scores of his rivals, added fuel to the heated denunciations that often marked his premieres.

In 1981, for instance, Hovhaness's *Revelations of Saint Paul*, a major choral and orchestral work, was premiered in New York, and favorably reviewed by the *New York Times*'s Donal Henahan. But the notoriously sharp-tongued critic Alan Rich, in *New York* magazine, was incensed by the performance. "The piece is garbage, 75 minutes worth," Rich declared, going on to decry "the travesties of the creative act perpetrated by the prolific Mr. Hovhaness. . . . The horror of this is, of course, the number of composers around, young and old, who could have filled those 75 minutes with interesting music, just as C-majorish (if that was the requirement) but infinitely more interesting. Shame!" Rich concluded.

Hovhaness was unruffled by the attack. "There's always been controversy," he calmly observed. "The critics may argue about the New York premiere, but the audience didn't argue. Everybody stood up, applauded, and shouted. It was lovely.

"I have to do it my way," Hovhaness went on. "I've always believed in melody, even if it isn't fashionable. I think it fills a need. We see history repeating itself: a period of complex music is always succeeded by something more simple. More and more composers are writing music [that] audiences can understand and appreciate. Music shouldn't be so intellectual. Just because something is complicated doesn't mean it's great. Great music should sound simple, even when it isn't really simple."

In the last few years before his death on June 21, 2000, Hovhaness's health began to fail, though Hinako brought him to important concerts in a wheelchair. Seattle Symphony music director Gerard Schwarz, a longtime champion of the composer whose works he had often recorded, gave him an eloquent tribute in the *Seattle Times* obituary of Hovhaness:

> I've known Alan since 1963, when I first recorded a piece of his, and I was in the [New York] Philharmonic when Andre Kostelanetz was commissioning his music. Alan was amazing; he was one of the great composers of our time. He wasn't an innovator, like Stravinsky or Schoenberg. He wasn't trying to change the world. He was trying to add beauty and sensitivity to the world. He cared deeply about goodness and about nature, and he has had a tremendous impact. Throughout it all, even in the times when his music wasn't so fashionable, he stuck to his thinking and to his distinctive style, which had a passion and also a great reserve. He stood out.

After her husband's death, Hinako Hovhaness continued to devote herself to his music and his memory, going through stacks and boxes of notes, uncatalogued works, writings of all kinds. And she wrote poetry, which she called "love letters to my husband," as a way of continuing her spiritual connection with the composer to whom she had dedicated her life.

Nature without you is a symphony without a subject
Spring without its theme.
The greens reviving from the confinement of hostile winter,
Fragrant first blossoms of spring intoxicating the air,
The glowing of magnolia buds pushing to their blossom
All this rebirth of nature, as on a stage.
Without you—no story to tell,
No pictures to take
I might as well forget my camera.
My life without you, how can I live?
In your absence I write letters to you,
I fill the empty space with my poems,
I reconstruct you, with my mind and words.
Even though your body is gone, I keep your ghost around
That's why my poem was born.

—Hinako Fujihara Hovhaness

William Bolcom

THE COMPOSITIONAL INNOVATOR

The year was 1965, and inside the University of Washington's Music Building a young, bespectacled composer was capering around at the piano in front of a fascinated audience of Music Theory 101 students. The teacher didn't look much older than the youngsters in the classroom, but Bill Bolcom was already so famous that we were somewhat in awe of his gleeful pronouncements.

"I'm going to teach you all the rules of harmony and counterpoint," he lectured, "so you can go right out and—break them all!"

Few of us in the class forgot that lesson, presented in Bolcom's only year on the University of Washington faculty: soon after, he was off to New York, and from there to the University of Michigan, where he spent the majority of his teaching career. He has been a regular presence in the Northwest, however, and a favorite source of new commissioned works for Seattle-based organizations, beginning in 1976 with a witty piano concerto in celebration of the nation's bicentennial, which was premiered by the Seattle Symphony, with Bolcom at the keyboard. In 1998, Pacific Northwest Ballet's program marking the Seattle Symphony Orchestra's departure from the Seattle Opera House to the newly built Benaroya Hall was heralded in an Opera House concert that featured the premiere of Bolcom's *Palacios Dances* (the work was revived in 2003). The opening of Seattle's Marion Oliver McCaw Hall in 2003 was celebrated with the world premiere of another Bolcom piece, the high-energy *Seattle Overture*. Bolcom and his Portland-born wife, the singer Joan Morris, return to the Northwest frequently over the years for duo performances such as a 2005 cabaret evening in Bolcom's native Everett. Pacific Northwest Ballet's codirector, Kent Stowell, chose Bolcom's duo-piano transcription of his piano rag "The Serpent's Kiss" from the piano-solo suite *The Garden of Eden* as the music for his 2004 choreography of *Dual Lish*; the work was repeated in a 2005 tribute program to Stowell and his wife, Francia Russell, upon their joint departure from Pacific Northwest Ballet (PNB).

"Break all the rules" was a lesson Bolcom himself has taken to heart, throughout an extraordinary career that has—thus far—produced important works in the symphonic, chamber, concerto, keyboard, oratorio, opera, and popular-song genres. But genres themselves have little meaning for this much-lauded maverick, who is surely Seattle's greatest native-son composer. Instead, he takes a puckish delight in tweaking the concept of musical form; the New York critic Bernard Holland has called his music "a wordless rebuttal to ideas of rank and category." For Bolcom, terms like "classical" and "pop" and "art song" and "avant-garde" have no meaning. It's all just music—and he composes in any direction his inventive muse may take him, whether it's ragtime or cabaret or full-scale opera.

"Composers like [Charles] Ives and [Scott] Joplin gave the lie to the idea that classical and popular music are separate entities," Bolcom explained in my 2012 chat with him. "This division is a relatively recent phenomenon. As for me, I just go where I'm interested. You fall into this; someone asks you to do that. I like to try all kinds of things, not just one style or genre. It's all music."

For Bolcom, the music probably started in utero; his music-loving mother, Virginia Bolcom, played classical recordings for him in the months before his birth on May 26, 1938, in the now defunct Maynard Hospital of Seattle. Virginia and her husband, Robert, a salesman who was the grandson of a Seattle lumber baron, realized that they had a full-blown, class-A child prodigy on their hands, when young Bill began playing the piano at the age of three and composing tunes not long thereafter. "Just before my fifth birthday, I began piano lessons, but developed quickly," Bolcom explains. "By age seven or so, I was playing USO evenings at Fort Lewis and similar places in the area. At age eight, I played a full program at the [University of Washington's] Henry Gallery."

In those early years, the Bolcoms moved often. Bill's father was "almost the richest kid in his college" back in the old days, as the heir to the Bolcom Canal Lumber Company in Ballard, but the crash of 1929 wreaked havoc with the family business. "My dad went to Snoqualmie, then to Bellingham, running sawmills and working on jobs the big mills wouldn't take. We moved to Everett, which was in those days a smelly mill town, and we lived on Rucker Avenue. I graduated from Everett High School—where they have the dumbest fight song ever written—in the Class of '55. I went back for the fiftieth class reunion, and it was a shock to see how many of my classmates were already dead."

Hearing Bolcom talk about his late parents, the obvious affection he feels for them is quite clear. "I loved them dearly," he says. "Dad was crazy for music; Mom played a little piano, and they played four-hands piano when they were courting. They were the world to me. I felt like an alien brought to earth, taken under the wing of these kind people who helped me find a way to relate to the natives."

Bolcom must have seemed like an alien to the kids around him, too: a musical genius who preferred the piano to baseball. His parents, to their credit (and his lasting gratitude), didn't try to cash in on their son's abilities by putting him on the stage. Instead, they contacted the music experts at the nearby University of Washington for advice on how they should help him develop his talent. They arranged for the youngster, then eleven, to board a Greyhound bus in Everett every Thursday and ride about thirty miles to the UW to take composition and piano lessons with John Verrall—"He gave me solid musical chops," says Bolcom—and also with George McKay, both of them well-known music professors and composers, and their piano colleague, Berthe Poncy Jacobson. Bolcom notes that Verrall and McKay were "more influential as teachers than as style influences"; even then, he was learning to do things his own way. His interests ranged far and wide. As a teenaged composer he wrote his String Quartet No. 2 under the influence of Roy Harris ("He was the man to beat then"), and wafts of Britten also made their way into his music.

Bolcom continued this weekly routine for seven years, until he enrolled at the UW as a full-time student. His junior high school principal was supportive, but he ran into "some trouble" in high school. But the administration had to allow him to continue the Thursday trips because the university had instituted the program. Not surprisingly, he finished his BA degree quickly, in three years. "Nowadays, the New England Conservatory Preparatory School is three times as large as the regular student body," Bolcom reflects, "but in 1949 it was unusual to have someone this young studying music at the college level."

After graduating from the UW, Bolcom studied with the renowned composer Darius Milhaud ("a very strong influence, more as a mentor than as a teacher") at Mills College and went on to earn a master's degree. In 1961, he followed Milhaud—who famously called him "a gifted monkey"—to the Paris Conservatoire, where he startled the local éminence grise, Olivier Messiaen, with his latest cabaret-style piece, "One Little Bomb and Boom!" from *Dynamite Tonight*, which Bolcom later described to the *New York Times* as "this popsy little number extolling the virtue of bombs. It was so different. It was popular theater. Messiaen was there. I'll never forget the bemused look on his face."

Bolcom returned to California to earn a doctor of musical arts degree from Stanford University, where he studied with Leland Smith. "Stanford saved me," quips Bolcom, who had nearly been drafted into the army to fight in Vietnam. "I'm not sure which was actually worse—Stanford or the army—but I would have been terrible in combat. I have flat feet and asthma." After finishing the doctorate at Stanford, it was back to the Paris Conservatoire, where he won second prize in composition in 1965. Bolcom later learned that he would have won first prize—but for his inclusion of a spiritual tune in the finale of his String Quartet No. 8. He took Messiaen's musical analysis course, and he won the first of two Guggenheim Fellowships.

By the end of that year, Bolcom was back at the University of Washington, this time as a teacher, but he didn't want to stay. "It was weird," Bolcom confesses of his return to the UW in 1965–66. "People remembered 'Little Billy,' and I was sure I was never going to live that down. And you remember what a backwater Seattle was then," he adds. "I wanted to be in New York, where there were activities and prospects, and so I spent some time there freelancing— with no [medical] insurance. It was incredibly expensive. I worked there for years, and I had a fair number of things premiered in New York, too."

In our 1976 interview, Bolcom observed, "During those years I did almost everything: orchestrations, arrangements, ghost-writing, proofreading, advisory work, and piano performances. I worked for a record company and for some theater groups. It was a wonderful experience . . . but the hours were terrible, and I had to travel all the time." More recently, in 2012, he added, "In the early years, my freelancing fees actually were losses—I made less than the expenses."

One particularly good outcome of the New York years: that's where he met his life partner and third wife, the mezzo-soprano Joan Morris, who, like him, is a West Coast native. Their musical partnership, begun in 1973, has resulted in more than two dozen highly successful albums of song, ranging from parlor ballads and cabaret tunes to Bolcom's own works. The most famous of these is possibly his "Lime Jell-O Marshmallow Cottage Cheese Surprise," a hilarious account of a fictitious dish similar to the many such concoctions Bolcom endured in his youth while playing the piano at ladies' clubs and society musicales. Morris takes on the persona of a dowager addressing her fellow club members about the culinary delights awaiting them on "culture night," and the resulting patter song invariably brings down the house. Bolcom has a great time at the piano; he was famously one of the most potent forces behind the 1970s revival of ragtime music, which he recorded and also composed; his "Graceful Ghost Rag" is a classic. His solo piano career has produced some remarkable recordings; his 1973 traversal of the complete piano works of Gershwin was named *Stereo Review*'s "Record of the Year."

During the early 1970s, Bolcom and Morris shifted their base of operations, albeit returning regularly to New York. In 1973, Bolcom, who had taught at Queens College, Yale University Drama School, and the New York University School of the Arts, found a congenial home at the University of Michigan, where he taught until retiring in 2008.

As a composer, Bolcom has been tweaking the musical establishment since his student days, and his evolving style includes a mind-boggling array of influences and directions. In more than three hundred works, he has explored and synthesized serial techniques, jazz, popular music, reggae, ethnic influences, and a huge array of genres. His magnum opus, the landmark *Songs of Innocence and Experience*, three hours in length and containing forty-six songs, required about twenty-five years of gestation before its premiere at the Stuttgart Opera in 1984. The 2004 recording, on the Naxos label, featuring the orchestras and choruses of the University of Michigan, conducted by Leonard Slatkin, won three Grammy Awards—for Best Choral Performance, Best Classical Contemporary Composition, and Best Classical Album. Bolcom first conceived the idea of setting the famous Blake poems when he was seventeen. He later told the *Financial Times* of London, "It was Blake that allowed me to advance my multifarious types of style. And it's colored everything I have done since."

In Seattle for the 1976 premiere of his Piano Concerto—commissioned by the Seattle Symphony in honor of the US bicentennial—Bolcom joked with me about the scope of the *Songs of Innocence and Experience*. "It's designed for a huge setting: full orchestra, immense chorus, and atom bomb in B-flat," he declared. Planned for a 1980 premiere, the project ended up taking four years longer. Bolcom returned to Blake again in 2008, for his forty-minute Symphony No. 8, a setting of prophetic texts of the English Romantic poet for chorus and orchestra, which was premiered with James Levine conducting the Boston Symphony and the Tanglewood Festival Chorus.

As for that bicentennial concerto, few in the house will forget the event, especially when Bolcom, at the piano, dove into the last movement, in which four themes—"Star-Spangled Banner," "Dixie," "Columbia, the Gem of the Ocean," and "Yankee Doodle"—are woven into intricate counterpoint. There also were hints of the "Oscar Mayer Wiener Song." You had to have been there: the audience didn't know whether to fall over laughing or stand up and cheer.

Not surprisingly for a composer unafraid of gigantic projects and in love with the human voice, Bolcom has excelled in the world of musical theater and opera. In the former category is his musical *Casino Paradise*, which the *New York Times* called "a compulsively hummable latter-day *Rise and Fall of the City of Mahagonny*." His three major efforts in the latter category are *McTeague* (based on Frank Norris's novel), *A View from the Bridge* (based on Arthur Miller), and *A Wedding* (after the Robert Altman movie).

Bolcom isn't ruling out another opera, either. "There's some talk of me doing an opera," he mused in 2012. "But I won't do it on spec. Over time, I've had pretty good fees: six figures for the operas." Clearly, the circumstances will have to be right to tempt him into the opera realm again.

He always has been fabled, and envied, for the speed with which he produces his compositions, but Bolcom observes that he isn't always so speedy: "I think for a long time first," he explains, "and then I write very fast. Actually, I'm in a bit of a fallow period right now." He has been working on editions of his theatrical songs, concert songs, and opera arias—"looking for engraving mistakes," as he notes, for his longtime publisher, Edward B. Marks Music. But there's always a compositional project in the hopper: in 2012, it was an improvisational work called *Games and Challenges: Something Wonderful Right Away*, which was premiered in 2013 by the ensemble Time for Three and the Indianapolis Symphony Orchestra. Next up was a solo violin suite for Gil Shaham.

When it comes to compositional methods, Bolcom is an unrepentant traditionalist. Don't look for any computer-generated scores from him, despite his enduring fascination with the new and his openness to influences from every direction. "The trouble with software," he muses, "is that it's basically confining. Even to change the time signature requires a couple of steps. And too many people let the software confine them. Composers have the need to make things a little quirky. As long as I have a copyist to make everything legible, I'm OK."

So what does Bolcom see in his crystal ball about future directions in the world of music? Not surprisingly for such an eclectic composer, he decries the wide gulf between "serious" or "classical" music and the popular music that dominates today's culture. Serious music today has been "ghettoized," he believes; both serious and pop music have become dull. What is needed, Bolcom believes, is the elimination of genre categories and more "cross-pollination" among those categories. "These days," he told me, "we're hearing the sales of personalities, not really music. But I think the cult of personality is really off track; the focus should be on the music. Joanie and I were in *People* magazine once! But we don't do anything wild. There's no soap opera about us."

One thing Bolcom finds hopeful is that there are many more singers these days who have studied acting. Thus the gulf between musical theater and opera has receded a bit, and opera casts are full of singing actors who are theatrically believable as well as vocally excellent. Conservatories and universities increasingly focus on this kind of training, and Bolcom finds that encouraging.

Few composers reach their mid-seventies without a certain amount of introspection about posterity. As a symphonist, Bolcom has not been unaware of the historical superstitions related to the so-called curse of the ninth symphony—and a composer who dies before he completes any more of them. A partial list of such composers includes Beethoven, Schubert, Dvorak, Mahler, Bruckner, and Vaughan Williams. When Bolcom finished his Symphony No. 8 and embarked on a short, fifteen-minute Ninth Symphony for Rice University in 2012, the curse did not go unnoticed. "Everybody was worried about the Grim Reaper," Bolcom jokes. "They heard the ghost whistling in the background. So far, I'm just fine! But I'm not writing any more symphonies; I'm done with that mold. It's all a matter of what you consider a symphony: my *Whitman Triptych* is probably a symphony. It's just a matter of how you name it."

For Bolcom, questions about posterity feel irrelevant. Ask him what he thinks is his best work, the music most likely to live on into the future, and he'll respond, "I'm the last person to tell you: I have no idea." He has watched with a certain amount of amusement the whim and sway of public opinion about his work over the past decades.

> The only way to deal with criticism is—you endure. The critics are like bully boys at recess who pretend to have a gun, and they shout, "Bang! Bang! You're dead!" But you don't die. Some of the people who really knocked me in the past are now praising me. It can be unsettling. Critics are doing six reviews a week and often have no idea of the big picture. Anthony Tommasini [of the *New York Times*] and Alex Ross [of the *New Yorker*] didn't know what to do with me at first. But Tommasini has called the *Songs of Innocence and Experience* one of the great pieces of the twentieth century.
>
> Years and years ago, I stopped worrying about posterity. Do you remember William Saroyan? [Saroyan, 1908–1981, the Armenian American writer and playwright who won a Pulitzer Prize for his 1939 play *The Time of Your Life*.] Joan and I got to know him years ago, and he was the hottest ticket around. Today, ask anybody under forty who Saroyan was, and they'll have no idea. Saroyan told me, "Art is what is irresistible." There is no way to know the lasting value of what you do, though. There is no way to know whether it will be irresistible—for a week, for a century.
>
> And not everything you do is going to be a big hit. Mozart bombed as much as anyone. Either what you've done is necessary or it's not, so I may as well do what I want. I'm not going to be around to know what happens to my music in posterity!

Samuel Jones

THE HARMONY SEEKER

Sometimes, if a composer is very lucky, the stars align just right and he ends up in an ideal place. A place where he can work; where there is a fine orchestra to play his music, and a good conductor who loves it—a conductor, moreover, who has the connections and energy and clout to get the music recorded and noticed.

Those were the lucky circumstances for the composer Samuel Jones, who came to the Seattle Symphony as composer in residence in 1997 and stayed for an extraordinarily fruitful period of fourteen years. In that span, he produced more than a dozen major works, all premiered by the Seattle Symphony under the baton of Gerard Schwarz, who also had a major role in arranging commissions and planting ideas. Among the commissions: lower-brass concerti for tuba, French horn, and trombone that fill a poorly served niche in the orchestral world.

"That's how it all started," says Jones of the string of new concerti. "Jerry suggested I write a tuba concerto, and it was very well received. And then the Seattle Symphony's principal horn, John Cerminaro, said, 'Me, too!' and I wrote a horn concerto. The timing and the players were just right."

The Seattle residency also proved to be a golden period for the region's young, aspiring composers. Jones's Seattle duties included the annual Merriman Family Young Composers Workshop, a yearly series of twelve-week two-hour sessions that culminate in a free concert of the students' music, performed by Seattle Symphony musicians. It's a heady experience for the youngsters, and often an inspiring one for the orchestra players and audiences.

Maybe Jones relates well to young composers because he so clearly remembers his own beginnings in Inverness, a small town in Mississippi, where he was born in 1935. Jones's musical gifts were apparent to his music-loving parents very early during his grade school years.

> The lady across the street taught piano, so I worked with her for a little while. Within the school curriculum there was a piano

teacher, so my first three years were with the piano teacher in the school, who got me going very well. The pinnacle of piano teachers in our little town was Sarah Baggett, whom we all called "Miss Sarah," and I studied with her all through my high school years.

I started writing little piano pieces in grade school. Several years later Miss Sarah told me, "I didn't have the heart to tell you, but the first piece you wrote is a dead ringer for a movement from the *Nutcracker*." Of course that is exactly what happens when you first start to compose: you start writing what you hear and what you like.

There is always that continuity. I feel it is so important to our art to remember "the continuity of music": all the great composers, consciously or subconsciously, refer back to ideas and little sparks that they expand. I like to call it "the great conversation," and it occurs between the landmark composers we all love, who go back and forth and refer to each other's works. Early Barber pieces were very similar to Brahms, for example.

I wrote my earliest compositions at the piano. But in the eighth grade I was playing baritone horn in the band, and I just loved marches. I would sit in study hall and compose a march a day—I'd write it out with just the melody but with the harmony in my mind. Some of them I orchestrated and they got played: one by the All-State Band, and I conducted it. So I was already beginning to conduct my own compositions even when I was in high school. I was bitten early by the conducting bug!

By the age of seventeen or eighteen, Jones took over the band program at Millsaps College, where he arranged and conducted music for the football band and the concert band. Excited by the idea of working with Howard Hanson, he chose the Eastman School of Music, where he found something of a mixed welcome: Jones was accepted as a theory major for the master's program, with a later, and favorable, decision on admission to the doctorate program in composition. Jones also wanted to study conducting, but Hanson's theory was that conducting somehow "bubbled up" from one's talents and experience.

Hurrying to class one day, Jones just missed the elevator and by chance found himself reading the bulletin board that posted job listings, which included the directorship of the well-regarded B'nai B'rith Chamber Orchestra. "The class be damned!" Jones exclaimed to himself then and raced to the placement director's office to apply. The director told him to take down the notice, as it had been up for a long time; Jones quickly complied.

"It all fell into place in that rich environment," remembers Jones of his experience with the chamber orchestra. "I needed string experience, and I was just eating up the repertoire. The Barber Violin Concerto! I swapped lessons with a violinist friend who needed to learn orchestration and composition. And I later took more violin lessons, but of course it was too late to become any good. I remember my teacher saying, 'Oh Sam, I wish I had had you earlier!'"

Jones felt that it was "absolutely crucial" to have a foot in both conducting and composition; each enriched his life so much. "I can't imagine life without the experience of being a conductor—or without the primal push to write my own music," he reflects.

That primal push encountered a lot of resistance in the 1960s, when atonal music—anathema to Jones, who remains committed to melody and harmony—held international sway. With consternation, Jones heard the influential Pierre Boulez's dictum that those who did not see the imperative of writing atonally were "useless." Many composers who were writing the music they loved were "literally counseled out of composition," as Jones remembers. The critical establishment loved serialism, particularly the works of Schoenberg, but Jones found his music "foreign to the way the human brain works."

Jones came of age as a composer at a particularly difficult time. He had experimented with twelve-tone music, but "it used a part of my brain that did not sing, and the urge to sing was too great." The pressure to write in accepted musical styles affected his career as a composer; Jones left graduate school determined to conduct. On Hanson's recommendation, the Utica (New York) Symphony Orchestra, which was looking for a new conductor, invited Jones to conduct two movements of the symphony he was composing as a doctoral dissertation, and he had a great success. The Utica Symphony board moved to install Jones on the podium and mount no more than a pro forma search for a permanent conductor.

"Then the richest lady in town who had kept the orchestra afloat fell in love with a South American conductor instead. I had been counting on this job. I was married, and the first child was on the way." Jones spent a long, hard summer ensued looking for a conducting position, until he finally found an opportunity at the Alma Symphony Orchestra in Michigan, a "town and gown" orchestra that is still going strong. After two years there, Jones conducted the Saginaw Symphony Orchestra for three years, and then came his big break, when he got the position of assistant conductor at the Rochester Philharmonic Orchestra. Eventually, he became full conductor there, giving eighty-five concerts a year.

Not surprisingly, Jones didn't do a lot of composing during those years, except for a piano sonata and a few other pieces; during the Saginaw period he produced *Overture for a City* and *Elegy* (composed in response to the assassination of President Kennedy). But in Rochester, except for *Let Us Now Praise Famous Men*, Jones was too busy to compose much. Here, his conducting demands were complicated by a political struggle between the board of directors and the musicians of the Rochester Philharmonic.

"I got caught up in that struggle," Jones says now, "and my position became untenable." He left Rochester in 1971, the second year of his music directorship, did some guest conducting in a range of cities, from Detroit to Prague, and in 1973—on the advice of his old mentor, Howard Hanson—decided to take the leap to Rice University, where he had been asked to start a new school of music. Hanson told him, "There is no question about it; you must go"; in retrospect, Jones is glad for that advice. What he and his colleagues achieved at Rice's Shepherd School of Music is a remarkable feat: the school, which opened in 1975, endowed by a gift from Sallie Shepherd Perkins in honor of her banker grandfather, Benjamin A. Shepherd, is today a fully fledged, well-respected music school that attracts top faculty. Their ranks have included the violinist Cho-Liang Lin, the cellist Lynn Harrell, the pianist Jon Kimura Parker, and the conductor Hans Graf.

"I had assumed I would be a professional conductor all of my life. And I was initially prejudiced against Texas because of the Kennedy assassination," confesses Jones. "I thought I'd find cactus in Houston. Instead, I found an incredibly vigorous, youthful, sophisticated city. That first year I had a total blank slate—an incredible opportunity. I wanted to blend academic and applied music at the highest possible level."

All Jones had to do was to develop a mission statement, set up the curriculum, hire faculty, develop the various degree programs, decide where on the Rice campus the new school should be housed, select the desired size of the faculty and student community, recruit said faculty and students, find additional money for scholarships, extend olive branches to the rest of the academic departments at Rice, establish strong relationships with the Houston Symphony, and make all the nascent Shepherd School's major policy decisions. That's all. It was a gargantuan undertaking for the new dean, a job that Jones likens to "composing a huge opera." Among his first hires were the composer Paul Cooper and the Houston Symphony's then concertmaster, Ronald Patterson (who later, like Jones, ended up in Seattle, where Patterson became professor of violin at the University of Washington).

Jones conducted the Houston Symphony in the official opening celebration for the Shepherd School in 1975. Six years later, there were 135 students, thirty-five faculty members, and a degree program through the master's level. Jones stayed on for a total of twenty-four years, but when he reached the age of sixty-two, he decided to take early retirement and fulfill a long-deferred promise to his second wife, Kristin, whom he had married in 1975. "I promised her that I would one day take her home," Jones says. "And I did."

"Home" was a lovely little lake southeast of Seattle, where Kristin Jones had grown up three houses north of the one the couple now occupies. (Ironically, the location is also not far from the Weyerhaeuser Company lands that almost became the site of Seattle Opera's summer Festival in the Forest home of their Wagnerian *Ring*, a long-held dream of then-director Glynn Ross that never quite came to fruition.) From Sam Jones's studio, with its well-used desk and keyboard, you can look out through the trees to the brilliant blue lake, in a setting that in many ways recalls the lake view from the "composer's hut" so beloved by Edvard Grieg near Bergen, Norway.

Not long after Jones left the Shepherd School, he met Gerard Schwarz at the Mostly Mozart Festival in New York, where Schwarz was music director; a mutual friend had sent Schwarz a bundle of Jones's scores, and the conductor expressed interest in them. Both Jones and Schwarz had had a mutual mentor in Howard Hanson. When Schwarz programmed a rare performance of Hanson's opera *Merry Mount*, Jones came to Seattle to hear it. And when Seattle's composer in residence, David Stock, completed a one-year term (during a sabbatical year) as the orchestra's composer in residence, Schwarz hired Jones for a one-year appointment—which was then renewed annually for fourteen years.

"Every year I gave him the chance to fire me, and he'd say, 'Are you kidding me?'" jokes Jones of that relationship, which became one of the longest composer-in-residence arrangements in the country. Jones relished his responsibilities teaching the Young Composers' Workshop, where about ten promising high school students (and occasionally some gifted middle schoolers) worked closely with him on projects of their choosing. He looked for "a spark, even if highly undeveloped," and then he gave the students the freedom to work in the directions they desire—occasionally nudging them into "a greater awareness of what's going on around them" in the music world.

Several of the former Young Composers are now studying at the doctoral level in institutions around the country, including the New England Conservatory of Music, Eastman School of Music, Oberlin College Conservatory of Music, and the Shepherd School of Music. "It'll take awhile before we see what they can really do as they develop," Jones says.

His own work in Seattle began with the 1999 work *Janus*, written to commemorate the inaugural season of Benaroya Hall. Several other Jones compositions followed, including *Aurum Aurorae* for organ, brass and timpani (2001), the chorale-overture for organ and orchestra *Mount Rainier Overture* (2003), *Centennial Hymn* (2003), *Benediction* (2003–10), *A Symphonic Requiem*, subtitled *Variations on a Theme of Howard Hanson* (2002). But Jones's popularity really took off with his 2006 Tuba Concerto, whose impetus came from Sandra Crowder, a member of the symphony's audience and the wife of an enthusiastic amateur tubist who had recently died. She wanted to memorialize her husband with a new piece of music, and the Seattle Symphony's tubist, Christopher Olka (who knew the Crowders), liked the way Jones wrote for the lower brass. Schwarz was pleased with the idea—and even more pleased with the results, a tuneful and charismatic concerto that was an instant hit with both the orchestra and the audiences. It was, in fact, one of the most resoundingly applauded premieres in recent Seattle history. (The concerto was later reprised in Seattle by popular demand.)

Meanwhile, the Seattle Commissioning Club was evolving, under the theory that a group of several music-loving couples could pool enough resources to underwrite a piece that none might have been able to afford individually. When the club asked Schwarz for a recommendation, he suggested a Jones horn concerto for the orchestra's principal horn John Cerminaro; the work was premiered successfully in 2008. The Seattle Symphony fans Charles and Benita Staadecker commissioned Jones's 2009 Trombone Concerto as a commemoration of their twenty-fifth wedding anniversary. For the premiere, the solo part was taken with tremendous dash by Ko-ichiro Yamamoto, the orchestra's principal trombone; the audience clearly loved it.

The Staadeckers joined another group of commissioners to fund Jones's *Reflections: Songs of Fathers and Daughters* (2011), an evocative work that drew smiles of enjoyment from the orchestra players and an enthusiastic ovation from the audience at the premiere. A Cello Concerto composed in commemoration of Schwarz's last season as Seattle Symphony music director (2010–11) featured the maestro's cellist son, Julian Schwarz, as soloist, in a performance that drew a standing ovation of unusual warmth.

Jones's influence continues in the era of Schwarz's successor on the Seattle podium, Ludovic Morlot, who asked Jones to write a short "signature song" to introduce, and conclude, all the orchestra's Discover Music concerts for children and families. He came up with the ebullient waltz-themed "Music, Hear the

Music," a favorite of Morlot's two young daughters. "Ludo and I get along very well," Jones explains, "and my relationship with the orchestra continues, even though the composer-in-residence period has ended."

He is still connected with Schwarz, as well, and he is represented in Schwarz's All-Star Orchestra recordings with the Cello Concerto (again with Julian Schwarz as soloist) and also a brand-new Violin Concerto for Anne Akiko Meyers. (Jones's music has been recorded by Naxos, CRI, Gasparo, ACA, and Centennial Records.) "I'm so excited about this project," Jones says of the All-Star Orchestra, which draws top players from all over the country. "There are those who thought they were dancing on his [Schwarz's] grave. T'ain't so!" he says, laughing. "What's been so much fun for me over the course of this period is that this is not a guy who is staying still; his musical depth is more and more impressive."

By now, Jones has been lauded by many state and national agencies, including a Ford Foundation Recording/Publication Award, grants from the Martha Baird Rockefeller Foundation and the National Endowment for the Arts, ASCAP awards, an International Angel Award, three music awards from the Mississippi Institute of Arts and Letters, and the Seattle Symphony's 2002 Artistic Recognition Award for outstanding service to the orchestra. He also received an honorary doctorate in 2000 from Millsaps College, and that same year he was inducted into the inaugural class of the Mississippi Musicians Hall of Fame.

After all these years, the process of composition is still a thrill for him. Jones holds up the score for the first movement of his latest work in progress, conducting with one hand as he hums the arching, rising lines of the opening. His eyes see the rest of the concerto, not yet committed to paper but already taking shape in his head. And on his face, there's the bemused smile of a man whose mind is racing ahead to the next phrase, the next note.

The composer Alan Hovhaness, shown here in 1994, traveled the world and was inspired by the mountains and scenery of Washington State. Photo by Michael Ter-Minasian.

The internationally celebrated composer William
Bolcom was already a University of Washington
music student at age eleven. Photo by Peter Smith.

Composer Samuel Jones's lengthy residency at the
Seattle Symphony produced several notable world
premieres. Photo courtesy of All-Star Orchestra.

THE POWER BROKERS
AND PATRONS

A N indispensable ingredient of any city's musical climate is a handful of powerful, well-connected arts advocates who do the "heavy lifting" in the classical scene. These are the people who get concert halls built; restore the health and chart the direction of orchestras; lead the "palace coups" to depose and hire conductors; advise imaginative impresarios on what is possible to achieve, and direct the progress of musical institutions. These people have power—lots of it—and they know how to use that power for the benefit of arts groups and the community as a whole. They tend to take a global view: How do the needs of a musical institution stack up against the needs of the concertgoing community? What is the best way to end an orchestra players' strike, get funding for a concert hall, and corral the support needed from public and private entities if you plan to rebuild an opera house? How do you start an opera company, or a chamber music festival? Without these power brokers and patrons even the most imaginative and brilliant dreams won't come true. Such people are an indispensable force in any classical climate. They are the agents of musical evolution.

William and Ruth Gerberding

THE COUPLE WHO MADE THINGS HAPPEN

Over the years, reports in the press have occasionally characterized William P. Gerberding with terms like "careful," "controlled," even "arrogant" and "aloof." Maybe that's how he appeared to some onlookers, when he was wearing the mortarboard of University of Washington president. But since his retirement in 1995 and until his death in 2014, Gerberding wore a very different hat: that of a mover and shaker in Seattle's classical music community. He and his wife, Ruth, have made major differences in the organizations they championed—the Seattle Symphony, Seattle Opera, and Seattle Chamber Music Society. And as a prime mover in the 1998–2003 fund-raising campaign to create the vibrant Marion Oliver McCaw Hall from the outdated bones of the former Seattle Opera House, Bill Gerberding was an indispensable force in getting Seattle Opera the hall it had long needed—and deserved.

Warm, perceptive, and funny, the Gerberdings made a great team. "Really, you should be interviewing Ruth," said Bill in an interview a year before his death. "She is the one with the musical expertise."

"Yes, I have a lifelong love of music," riposted Ruth Gerberding, "but the fact is that he was the university president, and I was his wife." Her husband demurred. "It's Ruth who is a lifelong musician; a music major in college; a player of several instruments; and an active board member of the Seattle Symphony Orchestra (SSO), Pacific Northwest Ballet, and, most important, a key member of the Seattle Chamber Music Society board. All of this affected profoundly our connection to classical music in Seattle, including our personal donations both on and off the campus. And it is, I believe, quite unusual among university presidents' spouses in this country."

It was music, the Gerberdings explain, that got them together in the first place. Ruth Albrecht had come from a musical background, starting early with piano studies and adding the clarinet in high school, where she sang in the choir and played in the band.

She and Bill met in the choir at Macalester College in St. Paul, Minnesota. "I was two years ahead of her," remembered Bill. "This was my second year of looking over the new crop of sopranos and altos, and I looked down there in the front row. And there she was." And that was it. "I had a wonderful time," Ruth recalled of those college-chorus years. "I was in a smaller group that sang Bach's Magnificat and Beethoven's Ninth with the Minneapolis Symphony under Antal Dorati."

Bill graduated in 1951; they married in 1952, and he went on to earn an MA and PhD in political science at the University of Chicago. He then taught for a year at Colgate University in New York, where Ruth joined a choir and sang such classics as the Fauré Requiem. They lit out for the "Left Coast" the following year, in 1961, where Bill's rise at UCLA was steady: first assistant and associate professor of political science, then full professor and department chair.

In 1967, the Gerberdings and their four children set out for an adventure in London when Bill took a sabbatical leave to do research on the domestic political aspects of postwar British defense policy in Asia. Living in London was a revelation; the Gerberdings heard, and in Ruth's case participated in, a rich array of concert activity by some of the best ensembles and performers in the world. They went to concerts at least once a week, often twice a week, while the kids—aged two through eight—stayed with the family's regular babysitter. The Gerberdings now look back on that time in London as an important step in their exposure to and understanding of great music.

While Bill toiled in the vineyards of British foreign policy, Ruth sang in the august London Symphony Orchestra Chorus. "Bill made me go," she quips. "John Aldous [the English choral director (1929–2010)] was there. When I auditioned, I billed myself as an alto because I hadn't sung for a while, and it must have been 'Be Kind to America Week' or something, because I got in."

After London, they returned to California—first to UCLA, then three years at Occidental College, where Bill was dean of the faculty and vice president for academic affairs. He moved back to UCLA for a two-and-a-half-year term as executive vice chancellor but was then wooed away by the University of Illinois at Urbana-Champaign, where he spent eighteen months in 1978–79—and the family felt "like fish out of water."

Only eleven months after their arrival in Illinois, Bill got a call from Seattle's Gordon Culp, who was heading the search committee for a new president at the UW. It was two degrees outside when they met at Chicago's O'Hare Airport, and the ostensible purpose of the meeting was to discuss the other candidates they had in mind, as Bill Gerberding knew all of them. "We had a long talk in early December, and in February [1979] or so, Gordon called back. He was working hand in glove with Mary Gates [the late mother of Bill Gates, and a legendary Seattle arts activist]. In effect, Mary Gates and Gordon Culp hired me."

The irrepressible Hans Lehmann, a Seattle physician who was also a UW regent and Renaissance man of wide-ranging achievements, always claimed credit for luring the Gerberdings to Seattle. He told several versions of this story, most of them hinging on Bill's appreciation of the relatively obscure Berlioz Requiem, which had recently been performed at the University of Washington. In one version of his story, Lehmann said that Gerberding's knowledge of the Requiem, and the fact that he owned a recording, settled his favorable vote, making it a unanimous 7–0 tally from the board of regents. "Hans's other version," added Gerberding, "was that the vote was 6–1: he had broken ranks and voted for Ruth."

The Gerberdings lost no time in immersing themselves in Seattle's classical music scene. Lehmann secured tickets for them to Seattle Opera's 1979 *Ring*, and they soon became season subscribers to both the opera and the symphony. A great friend of Milton Katims, the Seattle Symphony's music director, Lehmann also sought Gerberding's participation on the symphony board. But Bill volunteered Ruth instead.

She became a staunch advocate of the Seattle Symphony, remaining on the board for about twelve years, while also working on the board of Cathedral Associates, a respected presenter of concerts at Saint Mark's Cathedral. But closest to Ruth's heart was her involvement with the Seattle Chamber Music Society (originally the Seattle Chamber Music Festival), with which she has been active since shortly after its founding. "It was really hands-on in those days," Ruth remembers. "We picked the artists up at the airport and provided them with an extra car to drive. We housed several musicians who really became good friends." Among them were the violist Toby Hoffman and his cellist brother Gary, the Dutch violinist Christiaan Bor, and Mark Peskanov, a burly Russian violinist who spent a lot of time wandering around the Gerberdings' house but rarely needed to practice. These musician friends "really became a part of our lives," Ruth explains.

Equally rewarding were the close friendships formed with major figures in the Seattle arts community, among them Toby Saks, the founder of the Seattle Chamber Music Society, and the Seattle Opera general director Speight Jenkins. "Speight had been after me to join the Seattle Opera board," Bill notes. "In 1994, I told him I would join, and I've been there ever since. We have a very long and rewarding connection with Seattle Opera and with Speight."

The Gerberdings had arrived in Seattle just after the schism between the Seattle Symphony board and the community that resulted in the overthrow of the longtime music director Katims and the arrival of his German-born successor, Rainer Miedel. "I had the impression," observed Bill, "that Katims had worn out his welcome and it was time for Seattle to move up a notch." Both Gerberdings had a positive view of Miedel during his relatively short time in Seattle (1976–83) before his untimely death from cancer— "an awful tragedy," as Bill said.

The music director whom the Gerberdings have known best is, of course, Gerard Schwarz. Bill believes that Schwarz was responsible for the orchestra's steady rise in quality and reputation over the past decades. "Jerry deserves tremendous credit," Bill observed. "The orchestra is much better than it was. His contributions are immense. It's not just the hall, though getting Benaroya Hall built was a great achievement. He should be on his fourth victory lap now and feeling very good about everything."

Like many of Schwarz's admirers, the Gerberdings are puzzled by the continuing animosity toward the maestro in the New York press. "The New York critics just can't let up on him," Bill said in disgust in 2012. "This puff piece in the *New York Times* about how

Morlot had taken over the town didn't have to say a negative word about Jerry, but they did. The critics are just terrible. [In 2005] Alex Ross wrote comparing Jerry's Mostly Mozart concert to the Brezhnev bureaucracy. That was the worst thing I'd ever seen in a review."

Ruth sees a positive trajectory over time in Seattle's music institutions: "When we think back on the music scene when we arrived here, it was flourishing, but things have gotten so much better. The Seattle Chamber Music Festival was charming in the beginning, but now the quality is so much higher."

The Gerberdings have unquestionably made a mark on many aspects of Seattle's classical music scene, but the biggest contribution was Bill's decision to cochair the fund-raising campaign for Marion Oliver McCaw Hall in 1998. The other major arts groups in town had gotten their new theaters and rehearsal spaces and administrative buildings during the "arts boom" years at the close of the twentieth century, but Seattle Opera was the last to get a performance hall worthy of the work the company was producing.

Gerberding's leadership gave the project an enormous boost. His standing in the community was high, and he had attained credibility with a record-breaking financial campaign at the University of Washington. For five successful but hard-fought years, he stayed with the Opera House campaign for what became Marion Oliver McCaw Hall (named following the gift of twenty million dollars from Mrs. McCaw's four sons, Bruce, Craig, John, and Keith). "We from the opera, mostly Speight Jenkins and I, met with Pacific Northwest Ballet [PNB] leaders regularly and discussed strategy and collected names," Gerberding explained.

> Then we divided up the chores, most certainly including people
> outside that small circle. And there was a broader group that met
> more often and included staff and other board members that
> combed through lists and targeted donors below the high-end
> prospects. Some staff were well connected and smart, some less so.
>
> The most active and effective persons were from the opera,
> but PNB was important and, to a lesser extent, so was Seattle
> Center. The major action was, as nearly always, targeted at very

wealthy prospects. Don Johnson [trustee of the arts-friendly Kreielsheimer Foundation] was a major early commitment, but rumbling in the background were dreams of another and even larger donor. That turned out to be the McCaw family, five million times four, to honor their mother, a serious opera lover. Second only to that was the public-spirited Don Johnson, who agreed to step aside re the naming rights. He was more interested in getting the new hall than he was in naming it after Kreielsheimer. Good for him.

All men are created equal, but some are more equal than others. By far the major figure in pulling this off was, of course, Speight. Without him, it probably wouldn't have happened. He is a fantastic entrepreneur and a great promoter of his weird, wonderful art form.

And the greatest moment at the opening celebration was offstage and scarcely noticed: the then Seattle resident, the great Jane Eaglen, wading through the water sculpture pond outside the building in her bare feet. Seattle had come of age.

The McCaw Hall project benefited greatly from Gerberding's expertise in fund-raising and his in-depth knowledge of the region's philanthropy climate. He already knew whom to ask and how to proceed. Ruth notes that her husband became a leading practitioner of "the art of raising incredible amounts of money." He had done so in the UW's Campaign for Washington, a game changer launched by Bill's 1989 announcement of an unprecedented effort to raise two hundred million dollars from the private sector, a goal that was exceeded by thirty-four million dollars and put the UW in the top five public universities with private contributions. Bill claims that he had "just arrived here at the right time" and had a great staff, headed by Marilyn Dunn; he also noted that Boeing Company's generous contribution could be attributed to the fact that the Boeing chairman emeritus, "T." Wilson (1921–1999), liked Ruth.

Despite Gerberding's successes, the UW post was not easy. There were budget cuts, Pac-10 football sanctions against the Huskies for alleged violations of regulations, and a media fracas over Gerberding's decision to replace the worn carpet in the UW president's house (which hosted as many as eighty public functions annually) with an expensive, built-to-last carpet. Gerberding called the resulting kerfuffle in the press "petty and silly."

Almost as soon as he had brushed the quad's cherry tree blossoms off his suit, Gerberding became immersed in financial and administrative intrigue at Seattle Opera. "I don't know that I had any particular eagerness to raise money or become involved in the governance of music organizations, or a sense of obligation . . . well, I suppose I had all of those. We were just typical faculty members who had wandered into administrative positions, but not people who spent a lot of time with governors and captains of industry," Bill observed. "By the time we got here and were perceived as important people, the arts community was starved for people in our positions. I think I was more flattered than anything else. Ninety percent of the money we give away is self-serving—it's for the symphony and the Chamber Music Society and the opera. We want our toys to be better toys!"

Associating with, and helping out, some of the greats of Seattle's arts scene—among them Schwarz and Jenkins—was also a reward in itself. So was getting to know people whose contributions to these art forms had made so much possible. "I was amazed to discover," Bill said, "that there were really high-powered, wealthy patrons of the arts in this community and I didn't know them at all. Jerry Hanauer [Gerard Hanauer, 1927–2007, an entrepreneur who gave fifteen million dollars to Seattle Opera] and I became very good friends, and Jerry and Ruth and I would go to dinner in his last couple of years. He was one of the most delightful, intelligent people I've ever met."

What spurred Gerberding into his postretirement arts-activist career?

"I didn't become involved as heavily as I did in the arts community because I was some sort of civic-minded saint," he replied. "I'm none of those things. I never made money like university presidents make today, but I never felt underpaid. Now that we have a little, our decision to invest in the arts is really a self-serving choice—we just love the arts and particularly our music."

And what could be more fun, both Gerberdings say, than getting to know someone like Speight Jenkins really well? Ruth observes, "We sat about three rows in front of him at the opera, and he always jumped out as we exited and said, 'What did you think?' One time, I said, 'It's not my cup of tea.' He's always interested in what you think—and why."

The couple sees bright days ahead for Seattle's music scene. Bill commented on a recent trip to hear Seattle Symphony music director Ludovic Morlot conduct a rehearsal of the University of Washington Symphony Orchestra. "They did the [Beethoven] *Coriolanus Overture*, and for forty-five minutes he taught them how it should be played, and it was just beautiful."

Not all "top dogs," whether they're university presidents or artistic directors, know when it's time to step down. Bill Gerberding did. After sixteen years at the UW, he observed, "I got out at the right time. I didn't overstay. Ruth and I have found the years since I left the university to be incredibly rewarding, because of our involvement in the music community. We feel very good about what has been achieved here, and we feel very positive about the future."

William Bain, Jr.

THE ARCHITECT OF THE BOARDROOM

The German poet Johann Wolfgang von Goethe called architecture "frozen music," and that concept has long resonated in the life of the Seattle architect and arts advocate William Bain, Jr. Both architecture and music have enthralled Bain since his youngest years. And though he made his professional career with the first of those two disciplines, Bain has proved a vital force in the Seattle music scene as well—as a board leader, strategist, donor, and administrator.

When Bain studied architecture at Cornell University in the 1950s, the department of music was situated next to the school of architecture, and Bain was drawn to both disciplines. He decided he wanted to be an architect who could also play jazz, so he headed to the music department on a mission. "Fine!" was the reply. "You need to begin with the piano. We'll give you something to start out with."

They gave him some Bach, which the instructors called "the best way to learn jazz." No instruction; just the piano score. "Well, it was overwhelming, let's just say that," Bain said with a laugh in an interview at his home in the spacious downtown Seattle condo he had designed and developed with his wife, Nancy, and another couple. However fine a pianist he may have turned out to become, few would doubt that Bain made the right decision when he turned into the architecture building instead of the music department. Bain's choice of profession and his lifelong love of music have led him in a direction that has been most fortunate for Seattle lovers of music, since he became an ardent supporter and an intelligent administrator of this art form.

Wiry and fit, Bain, born in 1930, has a young man's enthusiasm for the world around him, and an eye for detail that may border on the obsessive. There is not a line, a corner, an alcove, or a vista in the Bain home that has not been deeply considered. A conservatory-cum-dining room, an elegant glass box, gives Nancy Bain, who is a national horticulture judge, the scope she needs for her gardening. If their home were a piece of music, it would be a twentieth-century symphony: contemporary but harmonious. "When people talk about architecture and urban design," Bain observes, "they often make references that could apply to both music and design. Thus a building or a space has cadence, rhythm, progression, compression, and expansion—descriptors that all apply to music as well as design."

Bain loves listening to every kind of music, from chamber music and opera to twelve-tone music, and, of course, jazz. But architecture is definitely in his blood. Born in Seattle in 1930, he is the son of the architect William J. Bain, Sr. (1896–1985), and Mildred "Billee" Clark Bain (1904–1991); he and his siblings had "an idyllic childhood" surrounded by their father's work: a succession of Seattle-area homes designed by Bill, Sr.

After studying at Cornell under such architecture luminaries as Philip Johnson, Buckminster Fuller, Paul Rudolph, and Romaldo

Giurgola, and wielding the saber on the fencing team, Bain graduated in 1953 with several academic prizes for design. At the conclusion of his army commitment, instead of following his classmates by working in the offices of well-known New York architects, Bain joined his father's architectural firm. The two Bains always worked on separate projects, which allowed young Bill to establish independence.

One of his first big jobs with Naramore, Bain, Brady, and Johanson (NBBJ) was as partner in charge of the concert hall at Whitman College. Cordiner Hall is an exquisite little gem of acoustical warmth and elegantly simple design. The hall and its surroundings are full of happy memories for Bain, who says, "It was my personal job. I just loved it. We were back there last summer, and I stopped in to see the hall. What's most rewarding is that the students have taken good care of it—there are no graffiti or anything. Every interior surface of the hall is a convex curve, except for the rise of the orchestra floor. The balcony is essentially a bridge, and thus the audience is enveloped by the orchestral sound. The project team was wonderful to work with." Bain's later success in arts administration probably owes a great deal to the collaborative spirit at NBBJ, where he and his colleagues set aside egos as they considered everyone's ideas and options.

Bain's list of significant architectural projects since the 1960s is imposing, ranging from educational facilities to huge commercial projects and major hotels. A recurring theme in his work is a connection to the arts and culture: Bain's fingerprints are all over the design of the Bagley Wright Theatre (built in 1983 and home of the Seattle Repertory Theatre), the Everett Community Theatre (1993), and Seattle's Paramount Theatre renovation (1994), as well as Cordiner Hall.

Public service and philanthropy have been bywords in the Bain family. "I think it comes from my parents. They used to go to Pioneer Square and serve food [to the homeless and needy] every Thanksgiving," Bain remembers. "It wasn't an onerous obligation, just something that was the right thing to do. And it's amazing how quickly you get drawn in to public service: the great thing is how rewarding it is because of the wonderful people you meet."

Bain had a major influence on Seattle's classical music community during his thirteen years as member and, eventually, president of the Seattle Symphony board. He realized early on that board meetings "needed to be more energized and more interesting," and since the organization was all about music, he brought in symphony musicians to play and explain the works they loved. Among the high points: a visit from the fabled cellist Mstislav Rostropovich, who played for the directors.

In the late 1970s, when Bain became active on the board, not all sixty-five members were "very participatory," as he remembers. "We told them that lending their name wasn't enough; they either had to work or contribute money." The orchestra had just undergone a substantial upheaval when Bain was asked to become board president—and it was about to undergo another tumultuous period, one of the most trying eras in recent history. The board of directors had engineered the ouster of the music director Milton Katims after twenty-two years of service and a bitter fight, and in 1976 Katims's replacement, the German-born conductor Rainer Miedel, had just arrived. The community was divided between fans of both maestros.

Bain liked Miedel: "We had a fine relationship. He would occasionally borrow one of my records, to hear a different interpretation of a piece. I think over time there was some opposition to him in the board, but I didn't pay attention to it. I think that Rainer was good both technically and artistically." But the new maestro didn't have an easy time in Seattle. "The first few years of Rainer's tenure were terrible from a political standpoint, with the divisive situation between the pro- and anti-Katims camps," Bain recalls. "It was very unfortunate, and didn't go away quickly."

Worse, labor negotiations with the musicians were deteriorating to the point that terms like "work stoppage" began to surface. An ambitious tour of Europe had been planned for 1980, but it seemed increasingly clear that a strike might derail the tour and imperil the orchestra's financial future. A further complication was that the symphony musicians also played for Seattle Opera and Pacific Northwest Ballet. As Bain recalls:

I could see the strike situation evolving. At that time I was still fairly new in that role [as board president]. I had never been involved with any strike before. I was horrified at the idea, and at the way some of the musicians were dealing with the strike. There were really some bad things happening; people were keying cars, which is a nasty and cowardly thing to do.

My job as president was to run the symphony working with the board and with Lanham Deal, the general manager, who was excellent. I looked into the long history of the board and decided that two years was an appropriate length of term for a president. Additionally, I saw the need for another person, a chairman, someone more interested in fund-raising.

Bain says he looked for a "major figure who commanded respect in the fund-raising community. Someone like Walter Straley." He knew that Straley, the founding president of Pacific Northwest Bell, had just retired from the telephone company, "right about the time I had decided to change the board leadership from just the president to this new model: president and chairman. The chairman would focus on the fund-raising, and the president would focus on running the symphony."

Straley accepted the chairmanship, and he met with Bain over breakfast once every month or so to discuss symphony issues. Straley had a lot of experience with strikes in his years with the telephone company. Even after the orchestra strike was settled, and the European tour was able to go forward, Bain and Straley and the board had a great deal of work still to do. Community support for the orchestra had fallen off, and because no fund-raising had been done in advance of the tour, the debts had piled up. The shock of Miedel's early death in 1983 meant more unexpected change.

"By now, I had been president for two years and already had Walter on board, so I thought it might be a good time to make the transition," Bain recalls. "Also, I had gradually developed a feeling that there ought to be term limits for board positions. I still feel that way. I think you can stay too long and get stale, and there is an unhealthy dependence on you. At the time, the symphony presidency was ostensibly a two-year term; however, board presidents who were successful were often beseeched by the board and staff to stay on. Once you have been in a role for so long, a lot of people say, 'Oh, we can't let you go.' It can be beguiling, but it's absolutely wrong. I wrote a clear letter to the board describing the past history of the presidency and my reasons for letting someone else take a turn."

Board presidency at the Seattle Symphony has sometimes carried with it a social, even political, role that extends beyond the boardroom. In 1965, a time of social unrest and the rise of racial equality, three African American women arrived at the then-annual fancy-dress Symphoneve gala, which African Americans had not previously attended. The Congress of Racial Equality (CORE) had notified the police that the women were likely to be turned away. No police were necessary, however, because Paul Ashley, then the symphony board president, and his wife seated the women at their own head table, made them welcome, and cordially introduced them to all the leading citizens at the event. What might have been an awkward confrontation in less enlightened hands became an enjoyable evening for all.

Over time, the structure of board leadership shifted. The role of chairman, which Bain had added, increased in importance. By about 2010, the chairman, at that time Leslie Chihuly, became the acknowledged leader and spokesman for the board.

Bain, who has long since traded his symphony boardroom seat for a seat in the concert hall, says he still works "night and day" at NBBJ, where he enjoys the give-and-take with the bright, young, enthusiastic people at the firm. Three mornings a week, he goes running in the nearby Olympic Sculpture Park. Bain and his wife are regulars at Seattle Opera and Pacific Northwest Ballet, and they are also fans of the Seattle Repertory Theatre and Town Hall Seattle, where Bain was a board member. Everywhere the Bains go, people want to talk to them about culture. "My eye doctor is a huge fan of the opera, and when I go in there for my regular checkup, we end up talking about the opera. We talk about *Attila*; we talk about *Don Quixote*. And then we get around to the eye chart."

Hans Lehmann

THE RENAISSANCE MAN

The extraordinary life of J. Hans Lehmann sounds like the plot
for a most improbable adventure film. A German-Jewish escapee
from the Nazis, he brought about the exodus to the United States
of more than twenty family members, trained as a doctor in three
countries and three languages, joined the US Army and returned
to liberate his home village in northern Germany, rose to success and prominence in the Seattle medical community, founded
a major hospital, served as president of the University of Washington board of regents, and was, until his death in 1996, a prime
mover in Seattle's arts community, as well as one of the founders
of Seattle Opera, Pacific Northwest Ballet, and Seattle Chamber
Music Society.

The term "Renaissance man" might have been coined to
describe Dr. Lehmann, who, in addition to all his other activities,
also collected East African art and Asian snuffboxes and wrote
two remarkable books. His moving memoir, *A Time Out of Joint*,
was followed by *Out of the Cultural Dustbin*, an engaging history
of Seattle's cultural scene that he wrote together with his wife,
the artist Thelma Gerstman Lehmann. Brilliant, opinionated, big-
hearted, and witty, Hans combined a brash self-assurance with an
endearing, though less prevailing, modesty. On social occasions,
he could often be seen zeroing in on women and showering them
with the kinds of gallantry rooted in an older and less politically
correct era. He was endlessly enthusiastic about the musicians he
admired, but Hans was never a mere cheerleader; he had a very
good ear, and a keen eye for a second-rater or a poseur.

Dr. Lehmann's remarkable odyssey began in 1911 in the little
town of Barsinghausen (population 6,000), near Hannover in
northern Germany. His father owned several businesses, and the
family, which was Jewish, was well assimilated into local society.
Only seven years after young Hans's birth came World War I, and
his father and uncles went off to fight. They returned to a world in
which, as Lehmann later wrote, "the Kaiser had gone, the fiber of the
nation was gone, every man's savings were gone." The ruined "new

Germany" printed reams of marks, creating inflation so steep that at its height one American dollar was worth four trillion marks—a figure that, as Lehmann helpfully points out in his memoirs, "has twelve zeros." Always at the top of his class in school, Hans was certain that his destiny lay in medicine and not commerce.

As Lehmann pursued his medical studies in Heidelberg, and later in Freiburg and Munich, he watched with increasing horror the rise of Hitler and his brown-shirted thugs; he attended a Nazi rally himself to experience the "sea of chauvinistic ecstasy" surrounding the Führer. Upon entering the auditorium for his course in clinical surgery, Lehmann was stopped in his tracks by a sign declaring that "Jewish students are only allowed to occupy the last two rows of seats in this auditorium."

"Was I going to let an uneducated Austrian ex-housepainter and political brigand dictate to me, a German with at least three hundred years of proven ancestry in Germany, that I am a second-rate citizen and a pariah?" Lehmann fulminated in his memoir. He refused to cross the threshold, choosing instead to complete his medical training at the Università per Stranieri (University for Foreigners) in Perugia, Italy, where the fascist government had not yet adopted Hitler's anti-Semitism. Lehmann traveled to Rome and Naples to hear opera and became friends with the then-unknown pianist Rudolf Serkin.

Relocating to America in March 1936 was not without its difficulties for Lehmann, who was determined to emigrate with as many family members as possible. There was a last-minute drama: denounced by his best friend and "blood brother" from childhood, who had become an enthusiastic Nazi (and later, on the infamous "Kristallnacht," demolished the Lehmann business premises), Lehmann had to bribe his way onto a ship in Hamburg. By dint of hard work and a little luck, this now penniless immigrant learned English and passed his medical qualifying exam a mere ten weeks after stepping off the ship in New York. He worked in hospitals, secured a spot at Seattle's Columbus Hospital, completed his internship, and passed his final medical exam in 1937. Soon after, he set up a clinic in Ballard, where his practice began to flourish. Now he could start earning money to pull his relatives—some of them already in concentration camps—out of Hitler's grasp.

Hans was able to free more than twenty of his relatives, including his mother and two sisters. To his deep sorrow, his beloved Uncle Siegfried, who had been grievously wounded fighting for Germany in World War I, was not among them. Because Siegfried could not bring himself to break Jewish law and travel during the High Holidays, he missed his opportunity to escape, and he and his family of seven perished in the death camps.

This terrible episode has a happier coda. More than thirty-five years later, in 1980, the city council of Barsinghausen renamed the street in front of both Siegfried's and Hans's family homes Siegfried Lehmann Straße. Lehmann, his wife, Thelma, and twenty other family members returned to Barsinghausen to celebrate the unveiling of the street sign; a twin to the sign accompanied the Lehmanns back to Seattle, where they proudly displayed it at their own house.

Perhaps it is typical of Hans Lehmann's impetuosity that upon seeing Thelma Gerstman for the first time at a party, he walked across the room to her, kissed her, and declared, "I am going to marry you." He launched an all-out campaign to win her—even answering her home phone pretending to be her father and announcing to hopeful suitors that she was forbidden to date. Thelma was a gifted artist who so impressed Seattle Art Museum's founder, Dr. Richard Fuller, that he chose her to present a solo show in 1939. Later, she became part of a Seattle artists' circle that included such famous Northwest artists as Kenneth Callahan, Guy Anderson, Mark Tobey, and Morris Graves. Seattle concertgoers regularly get to see one of Thelma Lehmann's paintings at the balcony level of Meany Theater.

Hans was slightly underwhelmed by Seattle's cultural scene. His initial impression ("gray cultural boredom and self-satisfied acceptance of intellectual mediocrity") was leavened somewhat by his discovery of the Seattle Symphony Orchestra, which Lehmann, in *Out of the Cultural Dustbin*, called "one of the bright lights that pierced the drabness." He purchased fifteen-dollar season tickets—the first, and assuredly the cheapest, of more than fifty later subscriptions.

On the podium that first season was Basil Cameron, whom Lehmann remembered as "an accomplished British conductor," and the guest artists included some real legends, including the pianist and composer George Gershwin, the violinist Josef Szigeti, and the tenor Lauritz Melchior. The seventeen-year-old Isaac Stern, then a virtual unknown, also made his Seattle debut that season; Stern was to become a close friend of the Lehmanns.

Hans and Thelma were present on the occasion when Sir Thomas Beecham, the flamboyant English conductor who was Seattle Symphony's music director from 1941 to 1943, uttered both his famous "aesthetic dustbin" remark about Seattle and his promise to raise the city's profile. Yet Beecham proved a poor fit for Seattle. Lehmann cites Beecham's curt ejection of a press photographer at one concert as the beginning of a retaliatory feud with the newspaper's music critic; he mentions Beecham's pursuit of his future wife, the attractive pianist Betty Humby, while Lady Beecham languished on the other side of the Atlantic, as another factor in the conductor's short tenure in Seattle.

But before Beecham left, Lehmann was on his way to army service in Europe, another "stranger than fiction" period whose details would do credit to the most imaginative movie screenwriter. Eleven years after he had left Germany for Italy and then the United States, Lehmann came back to his homeland as a US Army medical officer, arriving first in England along with fourteen thousand other soldiers on the *Queen Mary*, where every stateroom was crammed with up to twenty inhabitants. After D-Day in June 1944, he traveled with his unit to Utah Beach and finally arrived in his hometown of Barsinghausen. He knocked at the door of his own house, discovering to his delight an uncle, aunt, and three cousins. They were the only family members to have survived in Germany, as Lehmann's aunt had married an Aryan and their children were half Aryan. The end of the war hadn't come a moment too soon: as Lehmann recounts, the aunt had been consigned to the next cattle train bound for Auschwitz. Lehmann observed the concentration camps firsthand when he arrived at the slave labor camp of Nordhausen, where he saw "thousands of corpses loaded on freight trains. I attended to the hundreds of prisoners, near dead from starvation, inhabiting the barracks six layers high."

After these horrific experiences, Lehmann returned to Seattle determined to make the most of peacetime cultural opportunities. He returned to his medical practice, expanding it into the Ballard Community Hospital, and joined the faculty of the University of Washington School of Medicine as a cardiologist. Lehmann also returned to Seattle's concert halls, where he found mixed rewards. Filling Beecham's shoes at the Seattle Symphony had proved difficult. His successor on the podium, Carl Bricken, did not earn Lehmann's admiration; in his opinion, the players were "unimpressive" and the music was "boring."

And so Lehmann entered for the first time—but assuredly not the last!—the process of steering the fortunes of the Seattle Symphony, on whose board he served for forty years. Lehmann and his friends were agreed that Eugene Linden's conducting of the Tacoma Philharmonic Orchestra was inspiring, and they joined a group of supporters that included the grande dame of Northwest impresarios, Cecilia Schultz. Linden lost the Seattle podium, however, to the French maestro Manuel Rosenthal. Undeterred, Linden's supporters, including Lehmann, evolved a project to launch an opera company in Seattle with their favorite as the conductor. Schultz named the new company Pacific Northwest Grand Opera Company; the organizers were full of dreams and plans but had little knowledge of the hard realities of budgets and fund-raising.

Meanwhile, at the Seattle Symphony, Rosenthal was ousted in 1951 after it was discovered that Claudine Verneuil, whom he had presented to Seattle as his wife, was in fact his mistress. Once again, the Seattle Symphony board had to mount a conductor search, and Lehmann joined in with gusto. He and the manager, Ruth McCreery, appointed as guest conductors a string of eminent composers: Heitor Villa-Lobos, Carlos Chávez, Howard Hanson, Aaron Copland, and the charismatic Leopold Stokowski, while a local favorite, the UW's Dr. Stanley Chapple, served as a de facto resident conductor. Though he had many fans, Chapple didn't get the nod as the permanent music director. Among other reasons,

Lehmann and others thought that the SSO should not have to share its conductor's services with the university.

Lehmann came into his own as kingmaker after he met Milton Katims on a trip to New York in the winter of 1951. A Katims fan from the time of the NBC Symphony concert broadcasts, Lehmann wanted Katims to be the next Seattle Symphony conductor—even though Katims facetiously asked him, "Where is Seattle?" The search committee was won over by Lehmann's ardor and Katims's charisma, and the twenty-two years of the Katims era began, complete with intimate chamber music evenings, glamorous social events, musical innovations, and a steady parade of intriguing guest artists, all involving the Katims's close friends Hans and Thelma. Katims, an adroit politician, also addressed countless civic groups to enlist them in an important cause: a bond measure to expand and upgrade Seattle's Civic Center. This led to the acquisition of the seventy-four-acre site that became the home of the 1962 Seattle World's Fair.

As the old Civic Center metamorphosed into the Seattle Opera House for the World's Fair, Lehmann joined a group planning an opera production to herald the fair's grand opening. The only opera the planners deemed grand enough for this occasion was Verdi's *Aida*, and they hired the New York stage director Harry Horner, who chose singers from the Met, the Joffrey Ballet for the opera's dance scenes, and spectacular new sets and costumes. Five sold-out nights of exciting drama were the result. Another result created a less satisfactory drama: a thirty-five-thousand-dollar deficit, almost insurmountable in those days. Paul Friedlander, the scion of a prominent family of jewelers, and other culture buffs at that point created the Patrons of Northwest Civic, Cultural, and Charitable Organizations (PONCHO), whose auction Lehmann called "a night-long fund-raising bash of food, fun, and booze" to cover the deficit and create seed money for the founding of Seattle Opera.

Now that Seattle had an Opera House, two companies emerged as presenters of productions there: the Seattle Symphony, with Katims conducting such favorites as *La Traviata* and *Carmen*, and a new Western Opera Company, led by the German conductor Herbert Weisskopf. The latter group had been formed in 1962 by the local arts activist Helen Jensen and the artistic director Richard Valente, under whom the company presented *Hansel and Gretel* (in December 1962), *Madama Butterfly* with the soprano Lucine Amara (in March 1963), and *Die Fledermaus* (in May 1963).

As Lehmann notes in his memoir, there wasn't room on the Seattle landscape for two opera companies: one alone would be difficult enough to fund. So the Western Opera Company backers and the Seattle Symphony representatives got together to "smoke a peace pipe," as Lehmann put it. He narrowly avoided being nominated as the first president of the newly formed Seattle Opera Company—"*Gott im Himmel*, not me!" Lehmann was later proud of his efforts to fend off attempts by the San Francisco Opera and its general director, Kurt Herbert Adler, to import their productions for a Seattle season (an importation also opposed by the arts activist Sam Rubinstein). Instead, Seattle Opera was to have its own independent charter, and its general director would be Glynn Ross, of whom the Lehmanns heartily approved.

In his memoir, Lehmann reprints a letter from Ross written on the brand-new Seattle Opera stationery: "Dear Hans and Thelma: December 1, 1963, I went on salary for your newly formed opera company in Seattle. December 17th we arrived, all of us. Thank you for choosing me. Faithfully, Glynn."

"As a member of the Opera board, I often disagreed with Glynn, unwilling to follow his flight of ideas," Lehmann later wrote. "Red-faced, I must now admit that Glynn was mostly right and I was wrong." When Ross asked him for advice about presenting the first Seattle Wagnerian *Ring*, Lehmann told him, "I imbibed the towering tunes of Wagner's *Ring* with my mother's milk, and I am bored with them and find them dated and so does every opera buff in Germany." Luckily, Ross was undeterred, and Lehmann, admitting himself to have been seriously mistaken, eventually declared himself "brainwashed enough that I would accept almost any cockeyed scheme conceived and concocted by the infallible Imperator Ross." When, twenty years after his arrival in Seattle, Ross began to face growing opposition, Lehmann describes with clarity and empathy the grace with which Glynn and his wife eventually accepted the inevitable.

Ironically, Lehmann had been the Seattle Symphony's board emissary to the man—Katims—whom he had championed earlier, in 1973, when the majority of the board had voted to remove him as music director and give him an "artistic advisor" title instead. The maestro's decision to fight led to a painful battle in which Lehmann found himself squarely in the middle. He liked Katims's successor and sympathized in retrospect over Rainer Miedel's "tragic, Werther-like role" at the Seattle Symphony, where he had to fire players who no longer made the grade. He also had to struggle through a musicians' strike and fiscal difficulties before dying far too young.

Lehmann was entranced by the charisma and musicality of the young Gerard Schwarz, and he devoted his efforts to persuading Schwarz to succeed Miedel as Seattle Symphony's music director. Having by that time stepped down from the Seattle Opera board, Lehmann did not participate in choosing Glynn Ross's successor, but he became an enthusiastic fan of Speight Jenkins, applauding his "impeccable taste, good looks, charm, and the courage to try unconventional interpretations of old warhorses."

Lehmann discovered that, as a University of Washington regent, he could enroll in courses for free, and he did so with gusto, particularly enjoying music history classes. He was also an enthusiastic amateur clarinetist and studied with the great Ronald Phillips, the Seattle Symphony's longtime principal clarinet, but always admitted that he didn't have the discipline to work on rudimentary exercises: he wanted to get straight to the Mozart, Weber, and Brahms masterworks for that instrument.

His connection with the University of Washington first brought the Lehmanns in contact with the new faculty cellist Toby Saks, who had arrived from the New York Philharmonic and was eager to bring her favorite musical genre, chamber music, to Seattle audiences. The Lehmanns joined forces with other music lovers, including George and Arlene Wade, in the heady experience of creating the new Seattle Chamber Music Festival.

A tireless warrior for music, Lehmann somehow found time to serve for fourteen years on the Seattle Arts Commission and nine years on the Seattle Center Commission, and he campaigned almost obsessively to establish Seattle and Perugia as sister cities, in fond memory of his years studying in Italy. (For this achievement he was named a Cavalier Officer of the Order of Merit, Italy's equivalent of the French *Légion d'honneur.*) "He was a man of immense breadth and depth," said his friend, the former UW president William Gerberding, who worked closely with Lehmann both at the UW and on the arts boards. "He was brilliant."

Six years before Hans's death, he and Thelma were awarded the Governor's Award for the Arts in 1990, the same year in which Hans finished his *A Time Out of Joint* autobiography and began writing the second memoir, *Out of the Cultural Dustbin*, together with Thelma. Hans Lehmann lives on in his remarkable legacy of Seattle's music and opera institutions, shaped forever by his and Thelma's philanthropy, imaginative vision, and sheer hard work.

Samuel N. Stroum

THE MOVER AND SHAKER

It isn't easy to categorize Sam Stroum's contributions to Seattle's classical music world.

Was he a donor? Absolutely. Stroum was a megadonor not only to music but also to an estimated three hundred arts and social service causes. He gave away a reported two million dollars annually in the last two decades of his life. The Grand Lobby of Benaroya Hall is named for him and his wife, Althea, as testament to their generosity.

Was he an administrator? Certainly. Stroum's leadership of the Seattle Symphony board of directors is credited with saving the financially troubled orchestra in the early 1990s, when he threw his clout behind the orchestra and partnered with the bank executive Richard P. Cooley to wipe out the symphony's deficit.

Was he a power broker? No one who knew him can doubt that. Charles F. Osborn, the first trustee (through 1992) of the Kreielsheimer Foundation, once told me, "When Sam Stroum calls you up and asks if he can come by your office at 9 a.m. the next day, you don't say no." When Sam talked, people listened—and acted.

It was impossible to be in the same room with him and not sense his enormous vitality. He led the way in supporting the arts, and his example, and his persuasive powers, brought other donors in his wake.

Arts groups revered Stroum for his investment acumen, his long-range planning ability, his organizational skills, and, most of all, his clout in the community. Certainly his generous checks were also hotly desired. But more even than financial generosity, the arts need the kind of leadership only a few at the top can provide, and Stroum was the man who could make a capital campaign suddenly spring into viability.

Stroum always told others that he didn't want to wait to dispense his assets until after death, because it was far too much fun giving money away. He did this while running his own personal investment firm and chairing two committees on the University of Washington Board of Regents, where his views on strategic planning and finance were eagerly sought.

Stroum reveled in his ability to give—and to motivate others. "Fortunately, I don't need a lot of sleep," he told me in 1997, four years before his death from pancreatic cancer at the age of seventy-nine. "In Seattle, there are so many good organizations it's not just a matter of turning down the bad ones. My strategy is to give while I'm alive; it's hard to get any pleasure out of it when you're gone. You can write a check and watch it do so much good. The young people with drive and talent and great ideas know how to squeeze every dollar in that check and get great results with it."

He was always farsighted. In 1997, when Stroum was winding up the campaign to rebuild the Henry Art Gallery at the UW and simultaneously wrestling donors into place for Benaroya Hall, he explained, "Look at the Henry Gallery. I headed the capital campaign, and it's now built; it'll knock your socks off. But I look at what it still needs: an endowment. Extending the capital campaign from twenty-four million up to thirty million would put six million more into an endowment to sustain that organization in the long term, and now—when there's all the excitement about the new building—is when that has to happen. To lose that opportunity would be short-sighted."

Even while pushing the Henry Gallery's campaign forward, he forged ahead with funding for Benaroya Hall. "We've given a significant gift to the symphony's new hall," he said in 1998. "But they want me for a crucial job: soliciting the large gifts. That has always been a task reserved for a small core group of people who command respect for their level of wealth and what is done with it." To get the "naming grant" in place for the smaller recital hall inside Benaroya Hall, Stroum threw in three million dollars, to bring the seven and a half million dollars from the Illsley Ball Nordstrom Charitable Foundation up to the ten and a half million dollar mark and ensure that the recital hall would bear the Nordstrom name.

Giving to musical causes came naturally to Stroum and his wife, Althea, who were both lifelong devotees of the arts. Althea traced her love for music back to her youth, when her uncle was a close friend of Leonard Bernstein. Sam, born in Boston during the Depression and one of seven children raised by Russian-born Jewish parents, saw his father's furniture business collapse, which made the youngster all the more determined to succeed. When he graduated from high school in 1939, the family finances made college impossible, so Stroum joined the Army Air Corps. A quirk of fate—his short-term leave from army training to attend his sister's wedding in September 1941—saved him from the Bataan Death March. His squad had shipped out to the Philippines while he was away.

Stroum became a crew chief and flight engineer and was assigned to ferry new Boeing B-17 bombers off the camouflaged assembly lines south of Seattle to wartime departure points around the country. At a Jewish United Service Organization (USO) center near Seattle's Sorrento Hotel, where he lived with his fellow aviators, Stroum "went looking for corned-beef sandwiches and found my wife instead," he later said. He and Althea Diesenhaus were married in 1942.

After his military service ended in 1945, Stroum, by now a father, hoped to attend college. But the family had no money, and his second daughter was on the way. He got a job in sales, then started companies of his own; in the 1950s, he founded an electronics distribution company, ALMAC Stroum Electronics. ("ALMAC" combined the names of Althea and his daughters, Marsha and

Cynthia). He also acquired Schuck's Auto Supply; these and other business ventures became the source of the wealth that allowed the Stroums to become philanthropists through their five foundations. Close friends and neighbors—not only in Seattle but also in Rancho Mirage, California—with Jack and Becky Benaroya, they must have had some lively conversations about arts and philanthropy over the years.

No one could have found more contentment in giving away money to good causes than Stroum. When he died in 2001, obituary writers called him "the godfather of giving" and cited his ability to inspire other philanthropists. "I've walked this earth long," Sam had mused when I spoke to him at their desert home in 1997, "and I've been blessed with good health and good energy. I have no complaints."

Deborah (Card) Rutter

THE POWER BEHIND THE PODIUM

The summer of 1992 in Seattle was so chilly and rainy that Deborah Rutter was ready to turn right around and head back down the coast to California. "It was just a miserable summer in Seattle," Rutter recalled in 2012. "I remembered thinking, 'What have I done?'"

Raised in the San Fernando Valley and having worked in Los Angeles, the incoming executive director of the Seattle Symphony Orchestra was accustomed to summers in which the sun actually shone. But there was more than weather on her mind when Rutter came north to take up the reins of the orchestra's top administrative post. The Seattle Symphony finances were in a perilous state; the orchestra was crammed into the Seattle Opera House, along with the Seattle Opera and Pacific Northwest Ballet, all three vying for performance dates in a facility with only six open dates in a given year. "I remember sleepless nights every two weeks before making payroll, wondering if we were going to run out of money," Rutter recalls. The symphony finances were essentially hand to mouth. Rutter was indeed "sleepless in Seattle."

Eleven years later, when Rutter went on to the Chicago Symphony Orchestra, she left behind a Seattle Symphony that was transformed in almost every way. The orchestra's financial problems had not disappeared: that's never going to happen, in a financial model in which even sold-out ticket sales can provide only about half an orchestra's income. But the era of daily crises was over; the orchestra was on a sounder financial footing, and it was performing in a new home that is the envy of orchestras around the world.

At the beginning of Rutter's tenure in Seattle, the orchestra had seventeen thousand subscribers, a contributed income of three million dollars, and a ninety-five-concert annual season. When she left, the Seattle Symphony had nearly forty thousand subscribers and annual contributions greater than seven million dollars, and it presented more than 220 annual concerts. Rutter was one of the most important leaders in the 159-million-dollar campaign to build Benaroya Hall, which opened in 1998.

And then? She went on to become the president of the Chicago Symphony Association in 2003, a time when even the most optimistic and ambitious executive might have faltered. The Chicago Symphony Orchestra (CSO), one of the country's largest and most respected orchestras, operates on a considerably grander scale than does Seattle, and it has an international presence in the world's great music festivals and tours regularly. But the CSO was drowning in red ink, burdened with a six-million-dollar deficit, at that time one of the most troubling in the symphonic community.

"I will bring a new perspective to them," Rutter said, and she certainly did. But where did she find the optimism to leave a comfortable throne in Seattle and undertake the six-million-dollar challenge? "I'm lucky enough to have survived in this field long enough to develop some thinking about this," Rutter said of the fraught subject of fund-raising and deficits. "My confidence comes from my belief that this art form speaks to all people, all races, all backgrounds and experiences. If you believe that, it is your mission to figure out how to sustain the orchestra. We exist because the community wants us to exist; they value and want great music. That's the motivation to stay at it, from one week or one season to the next. And yes, there are sleepless nights worrying about finances. But there are rewards."

"After thirty-four years in this business," Rutter added, "I can't tell you how many times I balanced a budget. But I can tell you about the great musical highlights I have heard, and the experiences where what we do has changed people's lives. Money is the means to the end of making sure we have an orchestra."

In Seattle, Rutter ensured that future by taking the Seattle Symphony off life support with challenge grants, aided by help from great donors like the Benaroya family, foundations—notably the Kreielsheimer Foundation—and companies such as Boeing. Those successes ensured that the orchestra qualified for support from the National Arts Stabilization Fund, whose work in Seattle transformed the finances of several of the major arts groups. "We hadn't been pushing all the levers," reflects Rutter. "The Seattle Symphony felt like a very young organization, less mature. In Seattle, we had so much opportunity. We were very audience focused. In Chicago, the biggest challenge was that the attitude had been, 'We're going to present this and that, and you all are lucky to be able to come to the concerts.'"

How did Rutter get up the nerve to pull up stakes, uproot her young daughter, and go to Chicago to shovel away a six-million-dollar deficit? "Sometimes," she reflected in 2012, "I look back on my changes, from Los Angeles to Seattle to Chicago, and I think I was already waiting for this moment, both for myself and the orchestra. The time was just right; the opportunity was there." In Chicago, Rutter has had to move a huge and mighty institution along a path toward becoming more nimble and able to change and respond to audiences. As she points out, "You need the confidence that you're going to succeed."

When you ask about the source of all that confidence, Rutter points first to her parents, who never used the phrase "You can't." She describes her father as "one of the first feminists" and her mother as "a self-created individual." Rutter grew up in the San Fernando Valley during the 1970s, when she learned to play the violin, and she continued her studies at Stanford University, where she was also librarian and stage manager for the university orchestra. There was a formative junior year abroad in culture-drenched Vienna. During the summers, she was already working for the Hollywood Bowl, the summer home of the LA Philharmonic. Rutter worked her way up from there and soon became the orchestra manager of the LA Phil.

"It's not part of my DNA," she claims, "to think I can't do something. And, of course, it helps that I had an impossible first boss." That first boss was the late and feared Ernest Fleischmann (1924–2010), the German-born impresario who, beginning in 1969, ran the Los Angeles Philharmonic with an iron fist. He feuded with conductors (especially André Previn, who called him "an untrustworthy, scheming bastard") and critics (notably Martin Bernheimer, who termed him "ruthless, a manipulator, and very smart and very progressive"). "Ernest was impossible," remembers Rutter. "But he did teach me, in a nasty way, about investing in the right places and about critical values—how to do things in the best possible way with the best possible people. There were some pretty amazing conductors at the Philharmonic: Carlo Maria Giulini, Michael Tilson Thomas, Simon Rattle. I learned some salutary lessons from Ernest: How can I be better? He brought me to tears once. I had written the contract for the orchestra's European tour, and I wrote, 'Paris, France.' Ernest was shouting, 'Why in the world would you write France?' Another time, he told me I was handing out the musicians' boarding passes wrong."

By the time she came to Seattle, Rutter had also become managing director of the Los Angeles Chamber Orchestra, where she worked from 1986 through 1992. There, she met the trumpeter-turned-conductor Gerard Schwarz, who had just added the Seattle Symphony music directorship to his hefty résumé. Rutter had learned toughness and effectiveness from Fleischmann, but she had also learned how not to act, unless you want to make the people around you crazy. Her experience with Los Angeles venues, in that era before the building of Disney Hall, also gave her a good sense of what worked in concert hall design and what did not. In Seattle, Rutter immediately saw the advantages of moving the proposed site for the Seattle Symphony's new home from the much-researched Seattle Center site to the downtown spot where it was eventually built. The results outpaced her expectations—except in two small particulars. "I think the hall is great," Rutter says, "but there were only two things that disappointed me. We had to take the toilets out of a couple of dressing rooms. And we were never able to build the big conference room I had hoped for."

What Benaroya Hall gave the Seattle Symphony was considerably more than a performance venue that is now the envy of many of the world's great orchestras. The hall gave the symphony the opportunity to be creative about how the orchestra's services could be used, as well as when and how the programming could be presented. Before September 1998, when Benaroya Hall opened, the subscription concerts were held on Mondays and Tuesdays, not days when audiences most wished to attend concerts. Now, however, the orchestra was free to play when audiences wanted to come; no more sharing the old Opera House with the Seattle Opera and Pacific Northwest Ballet.

"It was really exciting to have the opportunity to diversify the programming," Rutter explains. "Some concepts worked better than others. The Light Classics were not as well received as we had hoped. Some of the popular crossover programs were successful, and some were not. But I was very pleased with the way we were able to use the orchestra. Playing in so many different ways—the baroque series, the Mozart series, new music—keeps them fresh. It was especially gratifying to be able to expand the education programs through Soundbridge [the hall's learning center]."

Asked for her peak moments in Seattle, Rutter pauses to consider. "Working with the Watjens [Craig and Joan Watjen, the donors of the Watjen Concert Organ in Benaroya Hall] and with Patricia Kim [the education director]; the opening of the Garden of Remembrance [a memorial to fallen soldiers, the gift of Priscilla Bullitt Collins]—those were very important and special for me. I also remember being in the hall during an earthquake, and we made a mad dash for the auditorium. Inside the auditorium you couldn't feel a thing; it was insulated from its surroundings, and realizing that was a moment of great pride. Then reality kicked in, and I said, 'Oh my God, where's my daughter?'" (Safe in her preschool, as it turned out.)

Also among Rutter's great Seattle moments was hearing Stravinsky's *Firebird* in the hall during the first rehearsal. "Most of all," she adds, "you get to know very special people who are passionate about music and their community and who give so much. It's a privilege to know them." And she doesn't forget them. Rutter returned to Seattle in May 2012 to attend the memorial for the late Jack Benaroya, who with his wife, Becky, had given more than fifteen million dollars to build the hall bearing their name.

In her field, Rutter is famous for knowing what she wants and figuring out how to get it. As she puts it, there's no reason that Seattle should have been able to build Benaroya Hall, but enough people believed in it and didn't give up. "If there's something you really want to happen," she notes, "why should you give up on it? If it doesn't happen the way you want, you try another route."

After her 2003 arrival in Chicago, it was apparent that the CSO needed a new conductor to replace the departing Daniel Barenboim. The number of maestros of sufficient stature for that stellar job is small and select, and they are in such high demand that they're hard to land. Rutter says she had to visit many conductors who could conceivably be candidates for the music directorship, to test their interest. In December 2004, Rutter had her eye on Muti, and she sent him flowers to celebrate the reopening of La Scala Opera, where he held the post of music director. She met him in January 2005.

"I saw him conduct in Paris," Rutter remembers, "and I thought, oh my gosh, I do believe that I am witnessing an individual who works in the way the Chicago Symphony makes their music. I was absolutely convinced he needed to work with the CSO. And I liked him as a person." Later, in 2010, Muti told the *Chicago Tribune*, "Deborah kept coming and visiting me here and there, so I realized that when she [said she] wanted me there, she really meant that she wanted me. I felt that she was a woman of great personality and [at] the same time could be strong, and after one second could be charming. And could be deep, and at the same time to have a great sense of humor that is very important in life. [At] a certain point, I felt if this lady is the face of the orchestra, why not?"

It would be hard to find a better endorsement of Rutter's effectiveness in Chicago. "All the things we do are interconnected," she explains. "We need to build an audience, to present programs of a certain sort. And then, from conversations with a foundation or an individual, we discover that they have an interest in that subject. I'm constantly flipping through lenses—the way you do at the eye doctor—to see where I get the greatest clarity. What are all these people going to think of this program or that development? Our donors are civic leaders and passionate music lovers. If you're not thinking about your donors, you can overlook opportunities or make terrible mistakes. You have to be crystal clear about your project, what it costs, what can happen as a result. And you will be surprised at what can happen."

One Seattle example involves the Watjens, the donors of Benaroya Hall's concert organ. They accepted an invitation to come to an event; Rutter got to know the couple, whom she calls "fascinating, interesting people" with strong musical backgrounds, and they made a connection. They had not previously made a gift to the Seattle Symphony approaching the level of their grant of more than one million dollars to build the organ, but Rutter showed them the possibilities of what a gift of that kind could mean. Hearing that mighty pipe organ in concert with friends and fellow music lovers later gave Craig and Joan Watjen enormous pleasure.

"If you pay attention to the people around you, there will be many rewards in getting to know them," Rutter says. "It's not all about Deborah Rutter. It's about getting to know the needs and interests of generous people, and doing this with absolute integrity. You do research; you come prepared, and you have a community of interest in this great orchestra."

You have to be unafraid, and you have to be bold. She hates the often-stated claim of the fund-raiser who says, "Give this once, and I'll never ask you again." Instead, Rutter favors saying, "Give once and I will show you why you will want to give again." And they do. One Chicago donor gave a six-figure gift once, a five-figure gift twice, and then a multimillion-dollar gift over a span of a few years. "The worst thing that can happen is that they will say no," Rutter states. And the more the requester is respected, the likelier it is that the answer will be yes. That's why arts groups always line up their heavy-hitter donors to persuade their peers to join them in philanthropy: it's very hard to say no when someone who is powerful and convincing makes the request.

Rutter's career trajectory continues to rise: In December 2013, after presiding over the Chicago Symphony's most successful year yet in both ticket sales and fund-raising, she announced her move to the Kennedy Center for the Performing Arts in Washington, DC, where she is now president. The *Washington Post* hailed her as "one of those rare individuals everyone likes."

Was she universally liked in Seattle? When Rutter left Seattle for Chicago, some observers cited perceived friction during Gerard Schwarz's lengthy tenure as the Seattle Symphony's music director as a reason for her departure. Rutter demurs. "People making music live a difficult life," she believes.

> There are always music critics picking nits, and people second-guessing what conductors do. It's a really hard job, standing up there and leading the orchestra and interpreting the music. Jerry and I had a fantastic working experience for a long time. We were hand in glove throughout the building of Benaroya Hall, and I am a great advocate for what he has done in Seattle. But it is the job of the chief executive to ask hard questions along the way, and it is not fun to have a person saying, "How long is the right amount of time for a music director to stay in that post?"
>
> And not just the music director. I was there eleven years [as executive director in Seattle]. Candidly, people shouldn't be in those roles too long. I look back and think about how many years we worked so successfully together and figured out important issues like the tour to Carnegie Hall [for the orchestra's centennial in 2004]. I don't think our relationship was contentious or strained, but asking—and getting—the tough questions isn't easy for anyone. It was my responsibility to raise those questions.
>
> But look at what we did for Seattle! I think our impact on Seattle was immeasurable. That's the reason we do this job: to make a difference in this wonderful art form that we love.

Sam and Gladys Rubinstein

THE KEY ADVISORS

If it weren't for the Rubinsteins, Seattle's musical landscape might look quite different—and a lot less interesting. It was Sam Rubinstein who counseled a young and inexperienced Toby Saks on the formation, structure, and funding of what would become the Seattle Chamber Music Festival, the region's leading classical music festival. Years earlier, it was Sam who assessed and countered an early coup d'état at the fledgling Seattle Opera that would have edged the founding general director Glynn Ross out of a job before he had had a chance to begin—and might have turned the company into yet another failed attempt to launch a professional opera company in this region. That there was a Seattle Opera in the first place is also due in large part to Sam Rubinstein's determination to thwart efforts to make Seattle merely one of the "run-out" sites for visiting productions from San Francisco Opera.

And it was both Rubinsteins who threw their considerable clout behind the young incoming Seattle Symphony music director Gerard Schwarz when he first came to Seattle in an interim conducting position. They welcomed Schwarz and his new wife, Jody, so warmly that they later chose the Rubinsteins as godparents to their two children, Gabriella and Julian.

The Rubinsteins' taste and judgment were celebrated in other arts circles as well; they were important collectors of early twentieth-century European art, which the Seattle Art Museum exhibited in 2004–5, and they were key movers in the establishment of the museum's outdoor Olympic Sculpture Park. The Rubinsteins also played a crucial role in the founding of the Pilchuck Glass School. Their interest in Seattle Opera's fortunes, both advisory and financial, continued on after Sam's death in 2007 for Gladys, who lived until 2014 and took on the role of "season presenter" in honor of her operaphile husband.

The Rubinsteins' love affair with music started early. He played the violin; she learned the piano. Those early musical experiences may have proved formative in their long lives together as arts philanthropists. They were particularly involved in the Seattle Symphony, Seattle Opera, and Seattle Chamber Music Society, but they also gave generously to a wide span of other arts, culture, education and human-services causes.

The former Gladys Seidenverg grew up in Alaska, where her father had moved after the Gold Rush. When it was time for college, Gladys went south to Seattle to attend the University of Washington, where she met young Sam Rubinstein at a sorority open house. He was only nineteen but had already graduated from the UW in engineering. Sam's career path was stalled, according to Gladys, because of anti-Semitism, so he went to work in his father's seafood finance and brokerage company. During World War II, he became a second lieutenant in the Army Air Corps. "He didn't have to go into the service, because he was in the food business. But he told me he had to go; he wouldn't feel right otherwise. Sam was sent to Yale to learn to operate the Norden bombsight; he could take it completely apart and put it together," Gladys recalled. "His group left for India, and we wrote long letters to each other. While Sam was gone, our son Mark was born." Upon Sam's safe return from military service, Gladys's only regret was that "I had to start cooking again. I was a terrible cook! Sam put up with it for a while, and finally he said, 'I can find somebody to do this better.' I was very relieved! And so was Sam."

Not long after the war, in 1947, Sam's father died and Sam took over; the young businessman soon began building the company, which eventually included nine seafood canneries in Alaska and Washington, as well as a substantial fleet of fishing boats. Following the sale of his Whitney-Fidalgo Seafoods, he bought two retail businesses: the discount chain Bonanza Stores and the G. O. Guy drugstores. Other business interests extended from shopping centers and fast-food stores to American Passage Marketing (Seattle FilmWorks). He was a founding director of Pacific Northwest Bank, now integrated into Wells Fargo, and served on the board of Starbucks during its formative years.

As the business successes mounted, the Rubinsteins found themselves able to engage in arts philanthropy. Both of them were passionate about music. "Sam loved the opera and opera singers," Gladys recalled, "and I loved symphonic music. When we got married, he had all these recordings of old opera singers he loved, and I learned to love them, too." The Rubinsteins became involved with the Seattle Symphony partly through the offices of their friends and fellow orchestra enthusiasts Hans and Thelma Lehmann. "Hans was the one who really got us interested in the symphony and got Sam to be on the board," Gladys remembers. "As things went on and we became more able to give to the symphony and other arts groups, we started doing more."

Prior to the 1963 founding of Seattle Opera, a movement sprang up to bring the San Francisco Opera to Seattle for regular residencies, as Gladys recalled. Sam took action. "Sam said 'Absolutely not! We are going to have our own opera company in Seattle.' We were always involved, right from the beginning with Glynn Ross. And then Speight [Jenkins] came along, and who could refuse him? Not us! Sam and I made our decisions together about giving. Each of us had ideas about what to support, and we always talked them over. We didn't have disagreements; we learned to appreciate each other's favorite arts. As time went on, we were more able to help out, and we saw how much need there was for giving."

Sam Rubinstein's judgment in business and the arts was highly regarded. After Sam's death, his old friend, the attorney Irwin Treiger, said, "Everyone turned to him for advice. He had a reputation for being tough, but he was extremely fair. He was very successful in all his endeavors and worked hard in the first part of his life so that he could give the money away in the latter part."

The Rubinsteins were in Rancho Mirage when the cellist Toby Saks called to ask Sam's advice about starting a summer chamber music festival. He offered both valuable advice and support, the latter in the form of a challenge grant that was contingent upon matching funds raised elsewhere; the Rubinstein imprimatur gave the fledgling project instant legitimacy. The festival led to one of the Rubinsteins' more unusual gifts. "One season, there was a heat wave," said Gladys of the festival, which then played in the attractive but airless St. Nicholas Hall at north Seattle's Lakeside School (incidentally, the alma mater of Bill Gates). "It was terribly hot inside the theater. Sam said, 'Nobody's going to sit there in this heat. We need air-conditioning right now!'" And they got it, which was enormously appreciated by performers and audiences.

The Rubinsteins were in the forefront of many Northwest arts institutions, but they never looked for recognition. The Seattle Symphony made many requests before Sam and Gladys assented to receiving the Seattle Symphony Arts Award. They were also honored by ArtsFund, Seattle's united corporate fund for the arts, with its Lifetime Dedication to the Arts Award.

The Rubinsteins have been major benefactors of the Seattle Public Library, University of Washington Press, Virginia Mason Hospital, Northwest Kidney Center, and the Seattle chapters of the American Jewish Committee and Jewish Federation. At the time of Sam's death, Mimi Gates, then the director of the Seattle Art Museum, called him "a compassionate human being with a wry sense of humor. He cared deeply about his city and its cultural life. All the arts institutions benefited greatly from his advice, courage, and tough questions." Over the years, the Rubinsteins were particularly generous to the Seattle Symphony Orchestra, in large part because of their appreciation of and close relationship with Gerard Schwarz. "Sam and I thought the symphony improved a great deal during Jerry's years there," Gladys said. "He did a tremendous job for the orchestra and the community. We were very glad to be a part of that success."

The Rubinstein family had more than its share of tribulations. Two of their newborn children did not survive. After the second death, Gladys went away for a rest to a golf resort near Los Angeles. "I never touched my clubs. I just sat there, doing nothing. I had to get over what had happened," she remembered in 2013. Their surviving son, Mark, who has two children now, became a professor of economics at the University of California at Berkeley. He is a music lover but "is not as involved as we have been."

Sam's health struggles were a frequent counterpoint to the successes of his last decades. In 1970, he lost his larynx to cancer; later, he developed kidney problems and spent the last eight years of his life on kidney dialysis. In 2007, after a series of health crises, he made the decision to refuse further dialysis. "He wanted to do things his way," said Mark, "even when it came to his death."

Sam loved the Northwest, but he and Gladys frequently escaped from the Seattle drizzle by heading south to the Palm Springs area. They had bought a small house at auction and were sitting there one Saturday afternoon at about 4 p.m. when Sam suddenly said, "I think I'm going to build a house," as Gladys recalled. "He called a leading architect, Bill [William] Cody, and said, 'I want to build a house, but I don't have the property.' Bill said, 'When would you like to see me?' Sam said, 'How about now?' Sam was a very fast decision maker! He never looked back."

Not surprisingly, the Rubinsteins got involved with the arts scene in Palm Springs and its environs. Sam was a president of the Friends of the Philharmonic at the McCallum Theatre of Palm Desert, which presents some of the world's great orchestras and performers. Both Rubinsteins were also very active in the Palm Springs Art Museum, where Sam was a board member and president. His advice was instrumental in the museum's decision in 2012 to establish a branch of the Palm Springs Art Museum in Palm Desert.

At the time of Sam's death, Mark Rubinstein gave an appreciative statement to the *Seattle Times* that showed the lighter side of his father: "Sam possessed a unique sense of humor. He once owned an inboard speedboat, which mysteriously kept sinking while tied to the dock. He renamed the boat *Happy Bottom*, his favorite translation of Gladys's name."

After her husband's death, Gladys continued the philanthropic interests of the family by donating to arts, health, social services, and other causes. She was a founder of Gerard Schwarz's All-Star Orchestra, which gathers top orchestral musicians from around the country to record and broadcast performances of great repertoire. Before her death in January 2014, Gladys also continued to make important contributions to Seattle Opera as a tribute to her opera-loving spouse. "I ask myself, what would Sam do? What would he like to happen?" Gladys reflected of her continuing philanthropy, shortly before her death in January of 2014. "Then it is easy to decide."

THE PATRONS

Perhaps it is poetic justice that I have saved this category for the last section of this narrative, because patrons truly are the "bottom line" for classical music and other performing arts. No matter how brilliant the musicians, no matter how gifted the composers and conductors or how innovative the impresarios, without an enlightened donor community there can be no symphony or opera. The crucial equation in the nonprofit performing arts is approximately fifty-fifty: even if all the tickets to a performance are sold and the house is full, the ticket income can make up only about half of the expenses of presenting the performance. Knowledgeable patrons are vital partners in the making of great music, in Seattle as elsewhere.

Anyone who imagines Seattle's great music philanthropists as a group of dull moneybags or check writers, however, is seriously mistaken. These people are brilliant, imaginative, dedicated, and quirky; how they amassed their wealth and why classical music is important enough to them to devote their assets to its support make for enticing reading.

What kind of a person gives twenty million dollars to an opera company? What would make someone wish to give nearly sixteen million dollars to an orchestra for a concert hall, with no desire that it would be named after him? Why would a multimillion-dollar donor roll up his sleeves and spend his afternoon painting the door of a theater? Each of these people has a different story.

In what follows, we will meet a "First Citizens" family who guided Seattle's arts and educational institutions for fifty years; a family whose fortune came from feathers but whose passion was for Wagner's *Ring*; a couple so trusted by both the Seattle Opera and the Seattle Symphony that they engineered the search for successors to Gerard Schwarz and Speight Jenkins; a billionaire computer genius who sees his arts philanthropy as a "partnership with Uncle Sam"; and the couple who changed the course of Seattle's music with a concert hall that truly is for everyone.

Buster and Nancy Alvord

THE PRACTICAL DONORS

Most arts philanthropists have a handful of favorite causes. The Alvord family has dozens of them, spread over three generations of generosity that has made their name a touchstone among activists who make a difference in Seattle.

The Alvords—most prominently, the late Dr. Ellsworth C. "Buster" Alvord, Jr., and his wife, Nancy Delaney Alvord—have supported many Seattle cultural institutions, among them the Seattle Symphony, University of Washington, Seattle Repertory Theatre, Seattle Art Museum, ACT Theatre, the Henry Art Gallery, KUOW Radio, Northwest Women's Law Center, the C. G. Jung Society and its library, the Church Divinity School of the Pacific in Berkeley, and University of Puget Sound in Tacoma. Their commitment amounts to much more than their names on a check and a donor list. They've chaired the committees, jump-started the organizations, brought in new talent, and been the brooms that swept several organizations into greater cleanliness.

Neither Buster nor Nancy played a musical instrument, studied acting, or painted pictures, but that didn't stop them from becoming the "Medicis of Seattle," as the former University of Washington president William P. Gerberding once put it. The breadth and depth of their activities and their largesse are especially impressive considering that Buster was also head of neuropathology at the University of Washington's School of Medicine, the author of several books and articles, and a board member of three major professional organizations. Somehow, he and Nancy also managed to raise four children and help steer more than half a dozen Seattle arts institutions toward artistic excellence and financial stability.

The Alvords first turned their enthusiasm and energy toward the institutions that blossomed in the years following the 1962 Seattle World's Fair, giving one thousand dollars each to the Seattle Repertory Theatre and the Seattle Symphony. Then they rolled up their sleeves and went to work for the arts—for five decades.

Still sharp and lively at ninety-one, Nancy Alvord recalled, "I remember the ACT Theatre in its first place in Queen Anne, in that old building where they needed to redo the plumbing. Buster went off to a meeting one Sunday, and when he came home, I asked him, 'How was the meeting?' And he said, 'Well, I painted the front door.' The whole board was there, painting the place. We moved here at a great time, right at the beginning of everything. So many groups were starting up. It was a busy time for Seattle."

Nancy became deeply involved with the Seattle Repertory Theatre, where she became the first woman board president during the crucial four years when the company's new theater, named in honor of Bagley Wright, was being planned and researched. "Buster was most interested in the symphony; Lanham Deal [the general manager] was one of his very closest friends, so they worked together. And with all of the personalities involved with the Seattle Symphony, going around shooting each other down, that was a difficult time."

The Alvords became the Seattle Symphony's first million-dollar donors, and they stayed with the orchestra through some of its toughest fiscal times. They also helped bail out the fledgling Seattle Repertory Theatre in the early 1960s when the company couldn't pay its bills. Buster and Nancy also rallied to the cause and with other contributors helped to pay off the debt for Pacific Northwest Ballet (then Pacific Northwest Dance) when it ran out of money.

The Alvords never tooted their own horn. Sara Hoppin, a fellow ACT Theatre board member, said in 1991 that they were noted for "quietly working behind the scenes and pitching in." Nancy Alvord remembers: "Everything was new—all these groups—and I had no background for this. Most of the boards in town made a few mistakes in that early period that they wouldn't make now. There were strikes, and there were big problems with personalities, and then there was the time when the conductor didn't get along with some of the board"—this was in reference to the Seattle Symphony situation in the mid-1970s, when Buster, then board president, was the kingpin in the board's decision to replace the long-running music director Milton Katims.

At home, *l'affaire Katims* was a major topic of conversation during that period. "We talked about Milton Katims probably thirty-six hours a day," remembers Nancy. "Buster was completely done up in the politics, and I was not. But I listened." Both Alvords said that the controversial departure was worth their effort: "Lanham said of Rainer Miedel [Katims's successor] that he moved the orchestra up a whole level. He wasn't here very long, but he changed things."

Despite their later immersion in the Seattle Symphony's progress, the Alvords had not been eager musicians in childhood. Nancy's early piano lessons didn't "take." Neither did Buster's. In 1999, he said, "My mother tried, but my teacher might well have said what my son's piano teacher later remarked as she left our house: 'There must be an easier way to make a living.'" The piano lessons may not have been a success, but the Alvords and their four children were closely knit. Their daughter, Kathy Alvord Gerlich, remembers, "Doctors keep odd hours. But we'd all have dinner together almost every night. We'd wait for him."

Nancy says that Buster provided the impetus for the couple's decision to give to the arts. He often said, "Keep a third, give a third to Uncle Sam, and give a third away." Following his father's lead (the senior Ellsworth Alvord had established the Alvord Foundation for Education in Washington, DC, in 1937), Buster and Nancy Alvord, together with their children and grandchildren, have endowed seven chairs and a Brain Tumor Center at the UW School of Medicine.

In 1991, Buster confessed what the highlight of his career had been: "conducting the Seattle Symphony." Then he and Nancy burst out laughing. He had led the orchestra in the "Star-Spangled Banner" at a concert in the mid-1970s. He took this role extremely seriously, calling it "the challenge of a lifetime" and even indulging in a little professional coaching. "He gave 'artist photos' to all his children and signed them 'the Maestro,'" Nancy chuckles.

Buster may have summed up the family's philosophy best in 1999, when he said, "Seattle has been so good to us that paying back just seemed natural. We have received far more than we have given."

Jerry and Lenore Hanauer

THE IMAGINATIVE OPERAPHILES

They "met cute" in New York, when they were both young bohemians and she was working in a coffee shop providentially named Rienzi—the title of an early Wagnerian opera. The marriage of the aspiring actress and the future feather magnate didn't last a lifetime, but Lenore and the late Gerald (Jerry) Hanauer stayed friends, and both became philanthropists, giving with a generosity that made many things possible for Seattle Opera and other causes.

To say that the Hanauers have been successful is like saying Mozart wrote a few little ditties. Hard work, imagination, foresight, and yes, a little luck have been elements in the family's rise to riches. Their son, Nick Hanauer, a self-described "plutocrat," is a multimillionaire venture capitalist and writer of books; his brother, Adrian, is an owner of the Seattle Sounders major-league soccer franchise and the team's general manager.

This kind of future success was not even a remote possibility in the mind of the young Philadelphia girl Lenore Ettelson when she was going to the symphony and opera with her music-loving family. Lenore and her sister, Meryl, took piano lessons; Meryl was the one who "actually liked to practice and got really good," as her sister remembers. (Meryl Ettelson, who debuted with the Philadelphia Orchestra at the age of thirteen, performs with her Houston-based White Oak Trio.)

"Our lives were always filled with music," Lenore Hanauer remembers of her early years. Hoping to become an actress, she went to the school run by Philadelphia's Hedgerow Repertory Theatre, then on to New York. "I studied dance and acting; I tried to study singing, but that was a disaster," she remembers. "And then I met Jerry in New York. We were just kids, and we lived in the Village when there really were bohemians. I worked in the first coffee shop on MacDougall Street. They played jazz and drank espressos at Rienzi." She also waited tables at the iconic Bitter End pub in Greenwich Village, where she "saw all those stars before they were stars. Woody Allen did his first stand-up comedy there; he was so nervous that he used to run offstage and throw up in the bathroom. Bill Cosby, Joan Rivers, Jimi Hendrix, Marshall Brickman, and Judy Collins all played there."

At home, Lenore Hanauer liked to listen to her collection of long-playing opera records. Opera was new turf for Jerry Hanauer, who liked symphonic music, literature, and dance but was not yet an operaphile. "*Götterdämmerung* was always my favorite," she explains. "I had a friend named Hilda, and she called, and Nick answered the phone—he was just a toddler—and he said, 'Who's this?' She answered, 'Hilda,' and he said, 'How's Siegfried?'"

The family's budget didn't allow for expensive opera tickets, so the Hanauers listened to the Metropolitan Opera broadcasts on the radio, as well as to Lenore's records. Jerry's career as a stockbroker waxed and then waned: "We were very poor," Lenore remembers. "The feather factory was here in Seattle, and his father wanted him to come. There were a lot of riots going on in New York, and I didn't want my kids to grow up in that environment."

The "feather factory" was Pacific Coast Feather, the privately owned market leader in the down and feather industry. Established in 1924, it was not thriving in 1965, when Jerry Hanauer and his family left New York for Seattle. During Jerry's three decades running Pacific Coast Feather, however, sales rose from about $850,000 annually to about $250 million. Along the way, the two older Hanauer sons, Nick and Joff, joined the firm and made it even more successful, much to their father's joy. (Joff, who intended to succeed his father at the helm of the company, was tragically killed in an automobile accident in 1998, a profound loss on every level to the family and the business. In 2007, Jerry established the Joff Hanauer Endowment for Excellence in Western Civilization at the University of Washington, in memory of his son.)

"I made Nick and Adrian take piano lessons, and they were both quite talented, but they preferred playing soccer," Lenore Hanauer recalls. Gradually, the Hanauers became involved with the Seattle Opera and Seattle Symphony, attending opera productions with Jerry Hanauer's mother, whom Lenore remembers as "quite a cultured lady." The increasing success of the family's business made it possible to attend more concerts, and Lenore, who still keeps a weather eye on the firm, got involved with Seattle Opera, volunteering to sell tickets.

Lenore started doing previews for the opera, alongside the late Perry Lorenzo, a charismatic and brilliant speaker whose passion for opera was the stuff of legend. "Perry did the previews, and I cooked," Lenore says, laughing. "I did dinners at previews [for the Seattle Opera Guild] for twelve years. I like to cook, and it started off being thirty, then forty, then fifty people. If it was a German opera, I would make sauerbraten and sauerkraut; one time for the *Ring* I did wursts and salads. For *Lakme*, I made Indian food. For *Porgy and Bess*, it was Cajun food. It was a huge undertaking, and then Perry would come on, and he would bring singers, and, oh my God, it was so much fun." Finally, Lenore finally ran out of recipes. She's now thinking of putting together a cookbook with a friend who is a graphic artist.

In 1984, Lenore and Jerry divorced, but they remained friendly, putting family values first and celebrating holidays and birthdays together. Her later arts philanthropy was made possible through a family connection—and because of Lenore's own kind heart. "I was one of the first investors in Amazon, and that was through my son, Nick. Nick had a friend who had a friend in New York, and she said, 'Jeff Bezos is coming to Seattle to see if he wants to live there, so could you show him around?' They were going to start this Amazon, and they could do it anywhere. Because he didn't know anyone else in Seattle, he and his wife Mackenzie came to our house, for Thanksgiving or Christmas. I really liked them. Then when it was time for Amazon to get started and they needed some money, Nick came to my office, and said, 'Mom, do you want to give some money to Jeff for his business?' I said, 'Oh sure, honey, they're so nice.' So I gave them twenty thousand dollars, and before you know it, it was sixty million! And I had just thought, 'Oh, they're so sweet.'"

Flabbergasted by her change in circumstances, Lenore assessed the situation and realized that she now was in a position to be a donor who could make a difference. "My growth into philanthropy was sort of slow; it had never occurred to me that I could have enough money to do that. My first gifts were to the opera, but also to agencies like the United Way." When Seattle Opera's general director, Speight Jenkins, invited her to lunch to discuss the finances for an upcoming *Ring*, this connoisseur of Siegfried and Brünnhilde had already written a check before she arrived at the lunch—"a pretty big check, too. He was shocked."

More possibilities arose when Nick's company, Avenue A Media (later aQuantive), was acquired by Microsoft for 6.4 billion dollars in 2007. This success later made possible Jerry's gift of twenty million dollars to the opera's endowment fund. "I have two foundations," Lenore explains. "One is my Lenore Hanauer Foundation with my friends on the board, and I do my social issues giving out of my own foundation. I give to the arts out of the Seattle Foundation. I also am a donor to the Seattle Symphony; I think the new maestro, [Ludovic] Morlot, is really fun, and I like his programming. I always thought Gerard Schwarz was wonderful, but in the arts you also need change. I really enjoy getting rid of the money. What am I going to spend it on? My intention is to do something worthwhile. I have everything I need, and I travel a lot." (Lenore experiences wildlife and local culture in far-reaching destinations, from Antarctica to Kyrgyzstan).

Lenore Hanauer believes that philanthropists—particularly in America—have taken over from rulers and governments that subsidized the European origins of classical art forms. As donors, the Hanauers set an example to their sons, who are following suit by giving to education, history, and the arts, among other causes. As Lenore puts it, "It runs in the family."

"I really think it's important for a city to have an opera and a symphony and a ballet and an art museum," Lenore explains. "Jerry did, too—he just epitomized caring about culture. For him, the opera was a real passion. I'm way more critical than he was; it's not very often that I think something is just perfect. But he just loved the opera, no matter what. Jerry was a unique person. He always listened to new ideas with an open mind, and he was very, very generous."

Others certainly concur. At Jerry Hanauer's death in 2007 at the age of eighty, his obituaries and tributes from public figures, friends, and family overflowed with recollections of his generosity and intellectual brilliance. It was impossible to read the tributes from people like William Gerberding and Speight Jenkins without wishing that you had had the opportunity to know Jerry Hanauer personally.

"He was an intellectual in the best sense of the word," Gerberding said of his fellow philosophy major when he was notified of Hanauer's passing. "He was an extremely thoughtful, interesting man." Jenkins remembered him for his "many interests, but a real passion for the arts—and through art, the preservation of Western civilization."

John and Laurel Nesholm

THE ACTIVISTS FOR THE ARTS

You know you're talking to music lovers when they tell you they haven't missed a Seattle Opera production or a *Ring* cycle since they attended the company's *Der Rosenkavalier* in 1969, when they were dating. Ever since their marriage a few months later, John and Laurel Nesholm have planned their travel and other activities around the Seattle Opera and Seattle Symphony schedules. They've served on two of the most crucial music search committees of the early twenty-first century, finding the successors to Seattle Symphony's music director Gerard Schwarz and Seattle Opera's general director Speight Jenkins. And through their Nesholm Family Foundation, the Nesholms have become a team, augmented by their daughters, Kirsten and Erika, that not only funds the opera (with gifts totaling well over ten million dollars) and other performing arts but also makes generous contributions to health and human services and public school education in Seattle.

The Nesholms' deep roots in this region and their passionate advocacy of the arts have made them among the most valued donor activists in the Northwest. They're smart, quick, keen assessors of talent and need, and they have the kind of overview that makes their perspectives and their advice eagerly sought.

His family wouldn't have guessed that John Nesholm was born to be a music lover. He didn't play an instrument; he didn't sing; he hated music appreciation classes. But the recordings he bought for his new hi-fi system gradually taught him "the language of music—it's a language like any other, and you can learn it by hearing it again and again," he later said. From Mozart to Varèse, Nesholm got hooked on classical music. "My first live concert was a Beethoven Nine in Lewisohn Stadium in New York, and it was just amazing. I started going to concerts. I remember Leonard Bernstein conducting the Shostakovich Five very, very fast. The next time I heard it anywhere near that excitingly was with Ludovic Morlot in Cincinnati."

Nesholm attended the Boston Symphony during his college years at the Massachusetts Institute of Technology (MIT), where he graduated in 1965. His first live opera was Wagner's *Götterdämmerung*; he was also present at one of the formative performances of Seattle Opera history: the gala production of Verdi's *Aida* celebrating the 1962 World's Fair. In 1968, John finished his tour of duty in the navy in Seattle and started attending Seattle Symphony concerts, as well as Seattle Opera productions that he "liked better each time." That was also the year when he met his future wife on a blind date. In January 1969, they attended *Der Rosenkavalier*, and they both loved *Tosca* when they saw that together.

Laurel Nesholm had grown up in the tiny hamlet of Acme, Washington (population 250, then and now), located to the north of Seattle in Whatcom County. There were no live performances of operas or symphonies to attend. But the family made its own music: everybody sang, and a coveted birthday gift for Laurel's pianist father was sheet music for the keyboard. Later, she took up the recorder and played quartets by Palestrina and Bach. In 1972, Laurel began her forty-year career as a volunteer for Seattle Opera, first in the ticket office, later on the board of directors.

In 1987, the family's serious philanthropy began with the Nesholm Family Foundation, created in his will by John's father. A senior executive with United Parcel Service, who began by driving a UPS truck as a high schooler in Seattle, Elmer John Nesholm had always been committed to Seattle, his hometown. "He was a problem solver," John explains, "and wanted to work for the community. When he was setting up the foundation, he asked us: 'Are you OK with it? Will you run it?'"

They were, and would. It was a steep learning curve. With the help of three nonfamily board members and, more recently, with that of their daughters, the Nesholm Family Foundation has directed change-making grants to carefully chosen causes, including many arts organizations. About 40 percent of their philanthropy goes to the arts, including more than ten million dollars over time to Seattle Opera and more than three million to McCaw Hall.

For the Nesholms, the arts begin at home. They may be the only family who once headed to downtown Seattle to buy a washing machine and ended up bringing home a piano. "Those were the days when you could buy major appliances at the downtown department stores," Laurel remembers. "On our way to the store, we passed Sherman Clay [a Seattle piano dealer]. We went in to look at the pianos. We bought one. It was one of our more spontaneous moments."

The Nesholms wanted their young children to have musical opportunities. The girls could elect to hear a recording of *Appalachian Spring* or the "Ride of the Valkyries" while lying on the couch, instead of taking a more conventional nap. Sunday dinners were always served with classical music in the background. Later, when one of the girls came across some often-heard music in a music appreciation class in college, "I could almost taste the roast beef when I heard that Mozart concerto." Not surprisingly, both daughters are opera devotees.

All of the Nesholms take the responsibility of the foundation very seriously. "We think it is important to help build the cultural infrastructure of the city: the arts make Seattle what it is, nationally and internationally," John says. "Grant making is a rigorous process, involving site visits, getting to know the organizations, getting feedback. It gives us an appreciation of what is going on in the community." Besides the opera and symphony, the Nesholms support a variety of groups, ranging from the Seattle Repertory Theatre and ACT Theatre to the Early Music Guild and the Meany World Series. Because the family has ties to nearby Bainbridge Island, they're active there as well.

Laurel Nesholm is proud of her role on the search committee that brought Morlot to the Seattle Symphony. She was appointed at the suggestion of Speight Jenkins to serve as the Seattle Opera's representative on the search committee, as the musicians of the Seattle Symphony are jointly employed by the symphony and the opera. Laurel told me, "I went to rehearsals of all the visiting conductors, and I had a sense within ten to thirty minutes what the relationship would be between the musicians and the conductor—whether he or she could get the musicians to play differently and to shape the piece." John added, "It was obvious right away that Morlot was something special."

For John Nesholm, there is an extra measure of satisfaction in the long association of the region's arts community with his firm, LMN Architects, formerly Loschky, Marquardt, and Nesholm, of which he is a founding partner. LMN has designed the city's two most important musical venues, Benaroya Hall and McCaw Hall, and collaborated with other architects in such projects as the Henry Art Gallery, Experience Music Project, Seattle Public Library, and Seattle Art Museum. Nesholm says that it has been "an amazing experience to hear the first music in a hall that we worked for and that is so important to all of us."

A long-term opera trustee, he says, "Seattle Opera is where everything comes together for me: our love of the art form, our firm's design of McCaw Hall, our family's involvement in the company, and our foundation's ability to support both the hall and the work that goes on within it." His greatest Seattle Opera responsibility was chairing the 2012–13 international search for Speight Jenkins's successor (the English-born Aidan Lang), for which he headed a twelve-member committee with a consultant and the stakeholders in Seattle Opera: the five union groups, including musicians and stagehands, the executive director Kelly Tweeddale, and an artistic advisory committee. That the search took place during a well-publicized downturn in Seattle Opera's finances, which required the cancellation of key productions and the sidelining of the highly regarded Young Artists' program, surely added to the stresses of planning the opera's future.

It's probably a greater challenge to find a great opera artistic director than a great symphony artistic director. For one thing, the opera candidate doesn't come in and conduct the orchestra; his or her efficacy must be tested in other, less obvious, ways. As a director, Speight Jenkins is sui generis; nobody else in the profession operates in quite such a hands-on manner. One thing seems clear: Seattle Opera's mission will go forward, and an important part of that is its dedication to the works of Richard Wagner, particularly his epic *Ring*. "We're not known around the world for our *Traviata*. We're known around the world because we do the *Ring* so well," Nesholm explains.

Both the Nesholms regard the current funding climate in the United States with concern. Laurel notes that the philanthropic community has changed its focus in recent years from "greater good" grants for major institutions to "trying to solve smaller and more specific problems." "It's tomorrow that counts," says John Nesholm. "Yesterday's grants are all gone. It's what we do today and tomorrow that matters. It's an amazing gift to learn so much about our community, how it works, and what it needs. And how we can help."

Charles Simonyi

THE GENIUS PHILANTHROPIST

When Charles Simonyi was a child in Hungary, his family and friends gathered around the gramophone to hear Bach's *Saint John Passion* played on old 78s, discs that had to be changed every few minutes because of their short recording capacity. Thick stainless-steel needles carved their way through the grooves in which young Charles could see the undulations that miraculously made music. His own daughter, Lilian, born in 2011, listens to classical music on her iPad, tapping on colors and images that play different music clips, depending on the color: a Mozart symphony, a little Bach, some Tchaikovsky.

How times have changed, thanks to innovations in electronics! Simonyi himself has been one of the most important and successful innovators of our time as the chief architect for Microsoft Word and Excel, and his early fascination with music has developed into a lifetime of appreciation. So profound is the significance of music in Simonyi's life that he has, through his Charles and Lisa Simonyi Fund for Arts and Sciences, devoted ten million dollars to the Seattle Symphony Orchestra, in addition to substantial grants to other arts and educational and research institutions.

"It goes without saying: a world-class city needs arts," Simonyi explained in a 2013 interview at his Intentional Software offices in Bellevue. "I want the arts to be right next door. I can go to Bayreuth any time I want to; not all my neighbors can. I want to meet them in the concert hall and at the art museum. Music has a socially uplifting function. If you think of the arts as beneficial drugs, music is the most potent, the fastest acting—it's the penicillin, the aspirin. Musical memory is something we can recall more vividly at any time than the visual arts or theater performances. After your sense of smell, music is the next deep memory that you retain from childhood. And it's one of the first things you learn."

It's lucky for fans of the Seattle Symphony and other music organizations that Simonyi is also a music lover and philanthropist. When the billionaire software genius and two-time space traveler established what was then called the Charles Simonyi Fund for the Arts and Sciences, the 2003 kickoff grant was a remarkable gift to the Seattle Symphony at a point when the orchestra needed to match a five-million-dollar gift from Jack and Becky Benaroya. The Simonyi grant presented the five-million-dollar matching money and an additional five million dollars for the orchestra's endowment fund. It also catapulted Simonyi to new prominence in Seattle's arts community; as of this writing, he is the all-time second-largest donor to the Seattle Symphony, right behind the Benaroyas.

The Charles Simonyi Fund was renamed the Charles and Lisa Simonyi Fund for Arts and Sciences after Charles's 2008 marriage to Lisa Persdotter, a beautiful Swedish woman who became the mother of his two daughters in 2011 and 2012. Over its ten-year history, the fund also made generous gifts to education, as well as to a wide spectrum of arts organizations here and elsewhere, including Gerard Schwarz's All-Star Orchestra, the Russian National Orchestra, the Metropolitan Opera international radio broadcasts, and the Salzburg Festival. In 2013, the fund closed as planned, after having dispensed more than one hundred million dollars to the arts and sciences. Simonyi continues with private philanthropy and has said that he might consider establishing a new fund "within five years."

Interviewing Charles Simonyi is like observing a popcorn popper: ideas pop in all directions. He may seem rather quiet spoken, but you're always conscious of the mercurial mental energy across the table from you. The conversation might veer from linguistic details of Danish and Swedish to the trivium and quadrivium, the Egyptians' ability to calculate the volume of a pyramid, and how the Beatles' "She Loves You" sounded in Communist Hungary when the radio signal was jammed by censors. At the end of the interview, you know you've seen only a tiny smidgen of this remarkable man whom the *New York Times* has called "arguably the most successful programmer in the world."

Simonyi is a man whose focus is "a mile deep," according to Susan Hutchison, a former Seattle TV news presenter who headed the Simonyi Fund and has known him for over two decades. "He wants to focus on the composers he really likes," Hutchison noted. "Bach is one of them. Charles definitely knows Mozart and Beethoven, and he loves Bartók." Simonyi is proud of being the narrator in the Seattle Symphony's landmark 2007 production of a performance of Bartók's *Bluebeard's Castle*, with spectacular sets by the glass artist Dale Chihuly and Simonyi reading the prologue in the original Hungarian. He calls it "maybe the best production ever."

Seattle Symphony's music director laureate Gerard Schwarz once observed, "Charles will come backstage after Seattle Symphony concerts, and he not only really knows the pieces, but he can sing them to you. He is a real music lover. He's extremely knowledgeable about music." During our interview, Simonyi illustrated some points about opera in translation by singing snippets of *Carmen* and *The Marriage of Figaro*, both in the Hungarian version he heard in his childhood. "Toreador, kill the bull," he translates after doing the opening lines of the Toreador aria. "It's pretty basic."

Simonyi led the Microsoft teams that developed both Excel and Word, the program in which I have written all of these chapters. It is the Microsoft phase of his career that built the wealth underlying his current philanthropy. But Simonyi is considerably more than a computer visionary. The son of the brilliant theoretical engineer Karoly Simonyi, who died in 2001, Charles has always taken his father's advice: "Do always the best job that you can, work much harder than you are expected, and the money will be thrown after you."

In the Simonyi household, there was a lot of music, including informal concerts when Simonyi's pianist mother played Beethoven's Kreutzer Sonata with violin-playing friends. Young Charles, however, didn't share his mother's performance genes. "I was supposed to learn to play the piano, and I had no talent whatsoever. I have a good ear, but no musical talent, and also I didn't have time. But I remember going to the piano teacher; she had magazines, and I saw a picture of Wieland Wagner's minimalist productions [at Bayreuth], and I couldn't believe there was such a thing." As a youngster, he heard *La Traviata* and *Der Rosenkavalier* at the opera. "I wasn't exposed to Wagner at all; my parents thought he was too heavy for me," Simonyi remembers. But Wagner later became one of his favorites: "Later I could travel and went to Bayreuth about four or five times, which enlarged my experiences quite a bit."

As a secondary school student in Hungary, the sixteen-year-old Simonyi got a part-time job in a computer lab as a night watchman, overseeing a big Soviet Ural mainframe already obsolete in the West. One of the laboratory engineers taught him to program. "Even my late childhood misery I consider a great advantage, because I learned all the generations of computers in a way that literally no one in my age group has done," Simonyi explains. At the age of seventeen, he was invited to work at Regnecentralen in Copenhagen, where one of the first Algol compilers was developed. He thus departed the Iron Curtain legally; what was illegal was the pivotal moment of his life: his decision not to return to Hungary, but instead to defect at the age of eighteen to the United States.

"The most important thing in my life was being able to live free," he said. "I was extremely lucky in traveling first to Denmark and then to Berkeley and teaming up with the most outstanding people, weaving my way through those connections to Xerox Palo Alto, and then to Microsoft. When I went to Berkeley, the first thing I did was get a small hi-fi and buy LP records, and I took some courses in music appreciation there," Simonyi recalled. "Music was certainly the funnest thing I did at Berkeley. I wasn't into drugs or rioting and there wasn't much else. I remember going over to San Francisco because André Watts—he's half Hungarian, you know—was playing Brahms's First Piano Concerto. What a wonderful performance!"

His new freedom in America didn't mean that life was easy: he had to learn English, and the threat of deportation was always there, until he was finally granted American citizenship in 1982. Meanwhile, he was busy earning degrees at Berkeley and Stanford University (finishing with a PhD in 1977). Simonyi's work career blossomed after his fateful 1980 meeting with Bill Gates ("a transformational experience"), which led to a two-decade-long Microsoft career that became the stuff of technolegend.

Simonyi describes his tenure at Microsoft in musical terms: "The early years of Microsoft were very exciting times—a crescendo that came to a tutti, if you will, in 1995." He left Microsoft in 2001, to found his own company, Intentional Software Corporation, together with Gregor Kiczales of Xerox PARC. "Your life changes all the time," Simonyi has said of his decision to make that career change. "I had this particular dream of knowledge processing and knowledge acquisition, and I wanted to pursue that dream, and it was probably best done on my own." He envisages that the removal of conventional programming languages from the construction of the human–computer interface has the potential to lead to a new economics of computer software development.

It's possible that the future successes of Intentional Software may lead Simonyi to restart his fund. Simonyi sees such philanthropic organizations as an important part of the American model for maintaining the arts. "In Europe, the arts are greatly supported by public financing, which is good, but it has its downside. The downside is that you get the idea of 'official art.' The good news is that the classics are almost always part of the official art, because they are free—no royalties—and by and large noncontroversial."

Because there's next to no state funding in this country, private sources, including businesses, foundations, and philanthropists, provide the 50 percent of operating costs that earned income cannot cover. "Frankly, I can't think of a better model," Simonyi admits. "The problem with state financing is that if you don't win, you are out of luck and you have no recourse at all. Whereas here, if Carnegie turns you down, you can try Ford. And I think the variety of interests and foci is so much greater with private funding."

One frequently cited reason for giving to the arts is that such gifts are tax deductible. Is that one of Simonyi's reasons for giving? "Some people are confused about deductibility: the donor is still out the money. Yes, you can write it off against the losses, but you don't get the money back. But the people who receive the money get more. Uncle Sam says if you're a 501c3 nonprofit group, we're going to add perhaps 20 percent to your donation. From the recipient point of view, that's fantastic. From the donor's viewpoint, I feel it's an honor for me to be together with Uncle Sam as a partner in supporting the arts."

Simonyi radiates a kind of practical optimism when he looks back at his forebears and forward to the future of his young family. "What's important for us," he observes, when asked about future music lessons for his children, "is for the girls to thrive with the talents they have. We have both had experiences where maybe we were encouraged by our parents to do things that backfired. In Lisa's case, she had some bad experiences with some very nice activities. I had bad experiences in my childhood with fish, and I don't eat fish. I certainly will expose our girls to great music in many ways. We sit at the computer together, and I have a big classical library and always play some nice music. Lately I have been playing Beethoven's Sixth Symphony; I love that for the girls. They will certainly have the chance of playing music if they want to do it."

And Simonyi plans to be around to hear it. "I certainly expect to live until a hundred. I'm just starting. Better late than never!"

Jack and Becky Benaroya

THE ULTIMATE BENEFACTORS

Of all music lovers, Jack Benaroya would be the last to toot his own horn. Gerard Schwarz had to twist his arm to get him to agree to put the family name on the new concert hall after Jack and Becky's family foundation made what was in 1993 the largest-ever gift to a nonprofit organization in western Washington: nearly sixteen million dollars to launch the building campaign.

At that time and many others, Jack Benaroya made himself available for press interviews because what he did was news, and he was unfailingly gracious about it. But it was easy to tell that he neither sought nor enjoyed media attention. He was a positive, optimistic man who enjoyed the act of sharing his immense wealth with causes that meant a lot to him. If he could have given every gift anonymously, however, he probably would have done so. The concert hall gift was to have been anonymous, but as he remarked in 1998, there was "so much pressure in the community to identify the donors that we finally agreed."

The arts, particularly classical music, were highly important to Benaroya, but he and Becky also gave generously to education and medical research, particularly in the field of juvenile type 1 diabetes, which afflicts their youngest grandson. Their gift to the Virginia Mason Medical Center (VM) was the catalyst for the construction of VM's Benaroya Research Institute. The Benaroyas have also been staunch supporters of the Jewish community. Their heritage is Sephardic Jewish, and they are descendants of Jews who were expelled and escaped from Spain in 1492.

Jack's family came from Beirut (then in Syria, now in Lebanon) in 1921, and they settled in Montgomery, Alabama. Jack was born only twenty minutes after their arrival; one of his biographies prepared by the Benaroya Company notes that he was "always the impatient type." Later, the family moved across the country to Vallejo, California, where they ran a grocery store and delicatessen. After Jack's older brother, Ralph, moved to Seattle and founded the beer-distributing firm Consolidated Beverages, the rest of the family followed him to Puget Sound. Jack graduated from Seattle's Garfield High School in 1939 and then entered the family business full time.

During World War II, Jack served in the US Navy, first at Pasco (Washington State) and then in the Pacific theater. In 1942, he married Rebecca Benoun, and they lived to celebrate their seventieth wedding anniversary together. Their son, Larry, joined his father in their business; in 1984, he took over the reins of the Benaroya Company.

After the war, Jack rejoined the family's Consolidated Beverages, where he invented and patented a pallet-loading truck for the beverage-distributing business that became the industry standard. In 1951, he began a truck-body business whose success allowed Benaroya to enter another field at which he proved a wizard: real estate. He evolved the concept of business parks: quality warehouse structures leased to small business. He was almost immediately successful. Before long, the company had 750 tenants.

"I never really liked the beer business," he said before his 1995 induction into the Puget Sound Business Hall of Fame. "Trucks go out in the morning with a load of beer and they come back at night with a load of empties. There's not much creativity involved. So I wanted to get out, and real estate was my exit." The Jack A. Benaroya Company soon employed seventy-five people, including architects, project managers, CPAs, and in-house attorneys. In 1984, Jack sold his six business parks for a reported $318 million, but he kept busy with investing and philanthropy. Among his more successful investments: buying into a small start-up company called Starbucks in 1986 and staying with it as it grew.

On March 6, 1993, Jack phoned his good friend Gerard Schwarz to invite him and his wife, Jody, to lunch the following day at Seattle's august Rainier Club. He had "a situation he wanted to discuss," as Schwarz recalls. About six or seven weeks earlier, he had been reading one of my articles in the *Seattle Times*, in which I wrote about the need for a new home for the Seattle Symphony and the Kreielsheimer Foundation's contribution of land and site studies. "It was the second or third time I had read about this. It just seemed to me that they [the Kreielsheimer trustees] were being very generous and gracious," Jack said in 1993, "and I thought, somebody needs to give this a little impetus."

That "little impetus" certainly floored Schwarz when, at the luncheon, Jack told him he thought the symphony should proceed with the project—and would a gift of ten or fifteen million dollars get it started? Schwarz recovered quickly enough from his astonishment to pick the larger figure. Within a few days, the Benaroyas made the fifteen-million-dollar commitment through the family foundation; additional funding attached to the gift helped stabilize the symphony's finances. At the time the gift was announced, Jack shared one of his favorite quotes: "Public service is the rent you pay for the space you occupy on this earth." Another favorite of his was Winston Churchill's famous remark: "You make a living by what you get. You make a life by what you give."

Beyond the initial gift to the concert hall, the Benaroyas volunteered and paid for several costly upgrades. The hall's north wall, for instance, was originally specified to be precast concrete, but that material didn't seem right. "I didn't feel that was nice enough, facing the city," Benaroya said prior to the 1998 opening of the hall. "I felt it wasn't of the same quality as the balance of the building. So I requested Kasota stone, quarried in Minnesota; it looks like limestone, but you usually think of that as coming from Italy, and this is American. I wanted to embellish the wall, and Jerry [Schwarz] selected a quotation by Aaron Copland that I think is very appropriate."

The quotation reads:

SO LONG AS THE HUMAN SPIRIT
THRIVES ON THIS PLANET,
MUSIC IN SOME LIVING FORM
WILL ACCOMPANY AND SUSTAIN IT
AND GIVE IT EXPRESSIVE MEANING.

To make the long entrance gallery even more impressive, Jack commissioned the glass master Dale Chihuly to create two mammoth, intricate glass chandelier sculptures to hang at the north and south ends of the gallery. The immense, convoluted shapes in clear glass and gold leaf arrest the concertgoer's eye with each visit to the hall. "Dale is a very dear friend," Jack said at that time, "and I've known him for many years. His chandeliers are going to give everyone who enters the hall a lot of pleasure for a long time to come."

Almost every detail of Benaroya Hall drew his attention. He suggested the noted fabric designer Jack Lenor Larsen, a former Seattleite who had attended the University of Washington and was a personal friend of the Benaroyas, to design the carpet. "I think it's gorgeous," Benaroya said just before the opening. "I also asked [designer] Terry Hunziger to consult on the interiors."

As the crucial opening night approached, when the new Benaroya Hall would be experienced for the first time with the full orchestra, Jack's anxiety grew. Would the veteran acoustician Cyril Harris have gotten it right, or would Seattle have to deal with an Avery Fisher Hall of their own? That New York concert hall has been through several modifications in the hope of improving what are widely considered unfortunate acoustics, and with mixed results. Yes, Benaroya Hall had been built on time and on budget, but when the orchestra started up—would the music sing, or be stifled?

When an instrumental ensemble tested out the acoustics, just before the opening, Jack and Becky heard the hall's sound for the first time. As she tells it, Jack's relief was so great that tears came to his eyes. "It's even nicer than I expected," he said then of the sound of the hall. "Some have said it's world class; I hope it is." That hope has been borne out over the years in concert after concert, and visiting orchestras almost invariably say, "We want to take this hall home with us."

As the years went by, Jack grew a little frailer, mainly from the effects of Parkinson's disease. He continued to attend Seattle Symphony concerts and functions whenever he could, always with his beloved Becky by his side. When he died in 2012 at the age of ninety, his public memorial service took place at Benaroya Hall, with Gerard Schwarz and the Seattle Symphony performing, ten speakers, and a grateful audience that had frequent recourse to the Kleenex. Afterward, the crowd was served two favorite dishes of

Jack's: chocolate ice cream and the combination of iced tea and lemonade known as "Arnold Palmers." His tastes weren't fancy, but he knew what was good.

Jack and Becky's son, Alan, who is also a music lover, once said of his parents, "When you make a gift, it is an investment in a person. Their gifts to the Seattle Symphony were their investment and belief in Jerry Schwarz." That connection has immeasurably enriched both the givers and the fortunate recipients: all those who enter the Hall That Jack Built.

William P. Gerberding's landmark University of Washington presidency was succeeded by decades of remarkable arts leadership with his wife, Ruth. University of Washington Photography.

Architect William Bain, Jr., proved an equally savvy architect of the Seattle Symphony's development during the 1970s and 1980s. Photograph by Gudmundur Ibsen.

Doctor, donor, author, and arts activist Hans Lehmann, shown here with his artist wife Thelma, was
a key figure in the development of both the Seattle
Symphony and Seattle Opera. Photo from Lehmann
and Lehmann, *Out of the Cultural Dustbin* (Seattle:
Crowley Associates, 1992).

An extraordinarily generous donor to the arts and civic causes, Samuel N. Stroum also revitalized the leadership of the Seattle Symphony in the 1980s. Photo courtesy of the Stroum family.

Deborah Rutter, a virtuoso arts manager, in 2015, shortly after she was named president of the John F. Kennedy Center for the Arts. Photo by Todd Rosenberg.

Sam and Gladys Rubinstein, donors and arts leaders who helped steer the fortunes of the Seattle Opera, Symphony, and Chamber Music Society, in an undated photo. Courtesy of the Rubinstein Family.

To Melinda,
the other side of a study
in grace under pressure!
Best wishes,
Buster
"The Maestro"

Buster Alvord's "artist photo" commemorating one of his happiest Seattle Symphony moments, on the podium in the mid-1970s. Photo from the author's collection.

Gerald Hanauer, one
of Seattle Opera's
most generous donors
and a visionary
trustee, in 2007. Photo
by Rozarii Lynch.

Lenore Hanauer,
opera activist and
donor whose founda-
tion supports civic
causes as well as the
arts, 2007. Photo by
Bill Mohn.

John and Laurel Nesholm, opera lovers and prime movers in the selection of new Opera and Symphony directors, in front of the Kreielsheimer Promenade at Marion Oliver McCaw Hall, 2006. Photo by Rozarii Lynch.

Charles Simonyi, a software billionaire whose 2007 space flight was the first of two such voyages, created a foundation for the arts and sciences that made him one of the all-time top Seattle Symphony benefactors. Photo by Greg Gilbert; copyright © 2006, The Seattle Times Company.

Jack and Becky Benaroya during the construction
of the hall that opened in 1998 and bears their name.
Seattle Symphony Collection.

CONCLUSION

THE book you have just read is a snapshot in time: a view of a field and its figures that are constantly in flux and moving in new directions. This is the nature of a classical music community, indeed, of any community made up of gifted and remarkable people who are innovators. People profiled here will change destinations; they will die, as have a few already, during the writing and editing process of this book; they will go on to new things. More of them will arrive and rise to prominence. The community in which they operate is a living organism in continual movement.

Not all that movement is positive. The classical music world of Seattle is not a story of unalloyed success and a steady path upward in achievement. Over time, groups have risen and fallen. As we have seen, the Northwest Chamber Orchestra filled a unique niche in the early 1970s, only to falter and disappear three decades later when it changed a winning formula in the face of greater competition. Similarly, the Seattle International Music Festival, launched triumphantly from a host group presenting annual visits of the Santa Fe Chamber Music Festival, lost its focus, changed its venues and title, and failed to survive as competition arose from the Seattle

Chamber Music Society. One of the most venerable of all Seattle's classical institutions, the Ladies' Musical Club, composed of musically talented women who auditioned for membership, evolved over the years from the region's leading presenter of international touring artists to a more modest organization that supports education, young artists' career development, and member performances.

As we look outside Seattle, there are disturbing and worrying examples of trouble, even extinction, in musical institutions once considered unassailable: curtains or setbacks for the New York City Opera, San Diego Opera, Honolulu Symphony Orchestra (later the Hawaii Symphony Orchestra), New Mexico Symphony Orchestra (later the New Mexico Philharmonic), and Syracuse Symphony, among others. The much-publicized woes of the admired Minnesota Symphony Orchestra sent shivers up the spines of symphony communities across the country. Even the venerable Philadelphia Orchestra and the Louisville Orchestra went into Chapter 11 bankruptcies in 2011 and 2010, respectively. Keeping classical music relevant to today's audiences is an ongoing challenge.

At this writing, Seattle's major musical groups have been smart and lucky. Over the years, they have weathered serious economic downturns by retrenchments, all of them difficult—and, music lovers hope, temporary. Recent measures have included salary concessions by the musicians of the Seattle Symphony and belt tightening at Seattle Opera.

Despite economic vagaries, Seattle's music scene has helped to put the region on the international cultural map during the past several decades. Arts watchers around the world know this city not only for its sports teams and tech companies but also for the flying horses and airborne mermaids of Seattle Opera's Wagner *Ring* and Seattle Symphony's imposing and widely recognized discography. Fans of chamber music know and respect Seattle Chamber Music Society's festivals, which feature talented performers from several countries; venturesome performances of new works by groups like the Seattle Chamber Players; and the region's thriving early-music community.

The current musical environment and, to a great degree, that of the future have been shaped by the remarkable innovators who came before. It's impossible to understand the current climate of classical music in Seattle without knowing what, and who, preceded the present. In these pages, you have met some of the most colorful and influential figures of the past half century.

Not even the most brilliant prognosticator could have stood on the site of the Seattle World's Fair in 1962 and imagined the cultural landscape of today. We can only guess what the process of musical evolution will bring to Seattle five decades from now. That there *will* be great music, in some familiar or unfamiliar form, seems inevitable to the music lover. As Aaron Copland wrote, "To stop the flow of music would be like the stopping of time itself, incredible and inconceivable."

ACKNOWLEDGMENTS

All the subjects of these chapters—living and dead—consented at one time or another to sit for extensive interviews, telling me about their fascinating lives and experiences. For this I'm eternally grateful; without their help and their candor there would be no book. What a privilege to talk to this colorful collection of performing artists, composers, educators, philanthropists, impresarios, captains of industry, and various brilliant individuals who have contributed so much enrichment to Seattle's music community.

This is in many respects a personal memoir, based in large part on discussions with music professionals and those who knew them over many years, rather than a research tome, and the Sources section is consequently dominated by interviews.

I'm indebted to the many people who contributed time and effort to securing photos (and permission to use them) to accompany the written portraits, from the University of Washington Libraries Special Collections to the UW School of Music, the individual musicians themselves, their heirs, and the photographers who once upon a time took their pictures. A warm thank-you to Melanie Ross, Jonathan Dean, and Monte Jacobson at Seattle Opera, and to Joanne De Pue at the University of Washington, for their help. The online historical archives of the *Seattle Times*, my former employer for thirty-one years, have been indispensable.

A round of thanks to the people at the University of Washington Press, particularly to editors Lorri Hagman, Jacqueline Volin, and Juliane Brand, and to photo editor Tim Zimmermann.

To my husband, family, and friends who listened patiently and gave support during this lengthy process, my enduring thanks: Howie Bargreen, Dr. Owen Bargreen, Maren Bargreen Mullin, Dr. Candace Young, and Bonnie Blanchard chief among them.

And my grateful love to my sweet grandmother, the late Leonora Anderson Moxness, who bought our family a piano when I was four years old and started my life in music.

The author at age four.

SOURCES

This section is divided by chapter and section. In each section, I list first all direct interaction with the subjects of this book and other individuals—the personal interviews I conducted and correspondence I received—as well as interviews conducted by others; then, in alphabetical order, I list the most important printed and audio-visual sources I consulted for background material. Most of the quotations in the book are from my interviews, but for quotations taken from a secondary source, I append, when appropriate, a parenthetical snippet of the opening words. —M. Bargreen

INTRODUCTION

AUTHOR INTERVIEWS
Peter Donnelly, December 7, 2004.
Michael Miropolsky, September 23, 2013.

SECONDARY SOURCES
Melinda Bargreen, "Oberhauseners Step off a Foot-stomping Ovation for the Symphony," *Seattle Times*, April 17, 1980 ("even the double bass is bowed by the tender hand").
Melinda Bargreen, "The Russians Are Here," *Seattle Times*, December 22, 2002

(Gennady Filimonov, "I think that we [Russians] are very passionate about what we do").

Randolph Hokanson, *With Head to the Music Bent: A Musician's Story* (privately published [Lake Forest Park, WA: Third Place Press], 2011).

Megan Lyden, "The Soni Ventorum Wind Quintet," DMA diss., University of Washington, 2000.

Tom Robbins, "Viva Variety: Katims Stirs Rare Mixture of Many Moods," *Seattle Times*, January 13, 1963 ("It was a night of passion").

Alex Ross, "Women, Gays, and Classical Music," *New Yorker*, October 23, 2013 (Yuri Termirkanov, "The essence of the conductor's profession").

Harold C. Schonberg, "Seattle's New Cultural Role," *Seattle Post-Intelligencer*, June 10, 1962 ("flat-floored, unpleasant Civic Auditorium").

Eric Scigliano, "Fifty Years Ago, Seattle Center Gave Birth to a Hub of Creativity," *Puget Sound Business Journal*, May 4–10, 2012 (David Brewster, "Seattle got too big too fast").

MAESTROS

Milton Katims: The Toscanini Protégé

AUTHOR INTERVIEWS

Bruce and Mariel Bailey, January 30, 2012.

Randolph and Janet Baunton, March 27, 2012.

Randolph Hokanson, March 27, 2012.

Milton Katims, June 22, 1990; April 11, 1992; January 21, 1995; April 1, 1996; June 19, 1998; June 24, 2002; June 19, 2004.

Pamela Katims Steele, January 4, 2012.

Heidi Lehwalder, April 12, 2012.

JoAnn Ridley and Mary Randlett interview, October 26, 1993.

Milton Katims, October 26, 1993 ("when the orchestra was making decisions I should be making").

SECONDARY SOURCES

Albert Goldberg, *Los Angeles Times*, June 17, 1962 ("an Oriental fantasy out of the Arabian Nights").

Wayne Johnson, "Katims on the Go," *Musical America*, May 1972 ("Culture Hero No. 1").

Wayne Johnson, "Milton Katims: He Led Cultural Renaissance," *Seattle Times Magazine*, August 8, 1976.

Milton Katims, "Symphonic Diversions," *Musical America*, May 1989 ("there was no need to be concerned").

Milton Katims and Virginia P. Katims, *The Pleasure Was Ours: Personal Encounters with the Greats, the Near Greats and the Ingrates* (Mill Valley, CA: Vision Books International, 2004).

Milton Katims Memorial Celebration, Meany Hall, University of Washington, program, March 12, 2006.

J. Hans Lehmann and Thelma Lehmann, *Out of the Cultural Dustbin: Sentimental Musings on the Arts and Music in Seattle from 1936 to 1992* (Seattle: Crowley Associates, 1992) ("like an airplane pilot who had been grounded").

Leroy Ostransky, "A Composer Is Happy Milton Stayed," *Tacoma News Tribune*, July 14, 1974.

"Rosenthal's Wife in Paris Claims Never Divorced from Conductor," *Seattle Post-Intelligencer*, headline, October 16, 1951.

Rainer Miedel and Cordelia Wikarski Miedel: The Maestro and the Maestra

AUTHOR INTERVIEWS

Rainer Miedel, October 5, 1976, and January 11, 1977 (for *Everett Herald*); January 27, 1980; April 20, 1980; November 16, 1980 (for *Seattle Times's Pacific Magazine*); June 23, 1981.

Cordelia Wikarski Miedel, April 13, 1977 (in German; subsequent interviews in English); June 13, 1991; April 11, 2012; April 17, 2012.

SECONDARY SOURCES

Melinda Bargreen, "Miedel: No Myths, Just Music," *Seattle Times's Pacific Magazine*, December 16, 1980 ("The church choir wanted me to be its conductor").

Tim Janof, "Conversations with Cordelia Wikarski-Miedel," Internet Cello Society, 1995, www.cello.org/Newsletter/Articles/cmiedel.html, accessed January 4, 2015.

Gerard Schwarz: The Consummate Music Director

AUTHOR INTERVIEWS

Bruce and Mariel Bailey, January 30, 2012.

Randolph and Janet Fisher Baunton, March 27, 2012.

Scott Goff (telephone conversation), April 24, 2012 ("one of the great conductors of the world").

Gerard Schwarz, September 7, 1986; June 8, 1991; May 5, 1993; September 8, 1993; November 30, 1993; December 1, 1993; July 6, 1994; September 11, 1994; September 9, 1995; September 7, 1996; September 13, 1997; November 2, 1997; April 30, 1998; July 31, 1999; October 25, 1999; September 13, 2001; June 14, 2003; September 7, 2003; February 2, 2004; May 18, 2004; May 31, 2004; August 8, 2004; September 4, 2004; March 20, 2005; May 1, 2005; July 7, 2006; September 3, 2006; February 23, 2007; May 25, 2007; August 17, 2007; December 12, 2007; September 6, 2009; June 26, 2010; October 7, 2010; May 3, 2011; June 8, 2011; June 12, 2011; January 2, 2012; September 5, 2012.

Anthony Tommasini (telephone interview), August 18, 2004.

SECONDARY SOURCES

Melinda Bargreen, "Diamond's Sparkling Career Stands Test of Time," *Seattle Times*, July 19, 2001 ("I get so many letters").

Melinda Bargreen, "A Musical Vision," *Seattle Times*'s *Pacific Magazine*, September 7, 1986 ("not always to my greatest joy"; "He didn't ask us what to do").

Martin Bernheimer, "Confessions of a Talented Workaholic," *Los Angeles Times*, Calendar section, November 26, 1989.

Martin Bernheimer, review of concert, April 1, 2004, Carnegie Hall, London *Financial Times*, April 7, 2004 ("splendid ensemble").

R. M. Campbell, "Symphony Musicians Warned on Improper Behavior," *Seattle Post-Intelligencer*, October 14, 2006 ("an expression of rebellion").

Peter Davis, "Amadeus Ex Machina," *New York*, August 18, 1997.

Jeremy Eichler, review of concert, April 1, 2004, Carnegie Hall, *New York Times* online, April 6, 2004 ("the musicians play for Mr. Schwarz").

Peter Hellman, "Gerard Schwarz's Magic Wand," *New York*, June 23, 1986.

Joseph Horowitz, "A Trumpeter Turned Conductor," *New York Times*, March 9, 1980.

Allan Kozinn, "From Brass to Baton with Gerard Schwarz," *Symphony*, February–March 1981.

Allan Kozinn, "A Mostly Mozartean So Far: Mostly a Success?" *New York Times*, July 25, 1999 ("below the highest rung"; "You look at someone like me").

Herbert Kupferberg, "Conductor Gerard Schwarz: Consolidating on Both Coasts," *Ovation*, July 1986 (Martin Segal, "He is going to be one of the greatest conductors").

Herbert Kupferberg, "Gerard Schwarz, Musician of the Month," *Musical America*, December 1982.

Norman Lebrecht, "The Lebrecht Report," August 20, 2004, www.scena.org/columns/lebrecht/040818-NL-Two%20Classes%20of%20Orchestra.html, accessed January 4, 2015 ("Schwarz recruited new section leaders").

Joe Riley, "Review: Russian Burst of Electricity," *Liverpool Echo*, January 13, 2005 ("10—Electrifying").

Royal Liverpool Philharmonic Orchestra news release, April 16, 2004.

Harold C. Schonberg, review of New York concert by the Los Angeles Chamber Orchestra, *New York Times*, 1980 ("there is no place for him but up"); quoted in Allan Kozinn, "A Mostly Mozartean So Far."

Nancy Shear, "The Rapid Ascent of Gerard Schwarz," *Music Magazine* (Toronto), July–August 1981.

Holly Sheridan, "Concluding Commissions: Seattle Celebrates Gerard Schwarz's Commitment to New Music," *New Music Box*, May 31, 2011 ("Those who know me well").

Anthony Tommasini, "An Orchestra Revitalized by Leadership," *New York Times*, August 5, 2004 ("just wrong for the job").

Daniel Wakin, "Pickup Orchestra of Stars, Made for TV," *New York Times*, August 31, 2012.

Daniel J. Wakin and James R. Oestreich, "In Seattle, A Fugue for Orchestra and Rancor," *New York Times*, December 16, 2007.

Heidi Waleson, "The Rise of a Young Conductor," *New York Times Magazine*, February 23, 1986.

Ludovic Morlot: The Symphonic Innovator

AUTHOR INTERVIEWS

Ludovic Morlot, June 28, 2010; July 9, 2010; June 30, 2011; July 13, 2012.

SECONDARY SOURCES

Richard S. Ginell, "Morlot, Ax and the Philharmonic Take a Direct Route," *Los Angeles Times*, January 25, 2013.

David Mermelstein, "Seattle Symphony's French Revolution," *Wall Street Journal*, September 22, 2011.

John von Rhein, "Morlot Still in the 'Promising Category' but Chen's Tchaikovsky Is the Real Deal," *Chicago Tribune*, May 7, 2010 ("not great, but admirable").

Daniel Wakin, "Seattle Gets a Maestro of Skill and Luck," *New York Times*, June 29, 2010.

Zachary Woolfe, "A Symphony's Leader Takes Seattle by Storm," *New York Times*, January 28, 2012.

Peter Erős: The Old-School Maestro

AUTHOR INTERVIEWS

Peter Erős, December 1, 1991; July 31, 1994; December 6, 1998; April 10, 2012.

Erős's student Jonathan Pasternack, April 20, 2012.

SECONDARY SOURCE

C. Alice Goodkind, "In Rehearsal with Peter Erős," in *Musicians of the San Diego Symphony* (privately published, 1980).

Vilem Sokol: The Patron Saint of the Podium

AUTHOR INTERVIEWS

Vilem Sokol, May 21, 1995; May 14, 1996; March 30, 1997; October 8, 1998; September 13, 2003.

SECONDARY SOURCE

Vilem Sokol, "Memories of My Boyhood" memoir (privately published, August 2000).

Stephen Stubbs: The Early-Music Innovator

AUTHOR INTERVIEW

Stephen Stubbs, December 27, 2012.

SECONDARY SOURCE

Miranda Loud, "A Conduit for Something Magical," video, http://vimeo
.com/42679420, accessed April 13, 2013.

George Shangrow: The People's Maestro

AUTHOR INTERVIEWS

Bonnie Blanchard, February 5, 2013.

Daisy Shangrow, February 20, 2013.

George Shangrow, February 1, 1985; December 5, 1990; January 13, 1990;
August 28, 1994; December 17, 1997; December 20, 1997; June 9, 1999;
December 15, 1999; February 12, 2003; December 12, 2003; February 27,
2004; July 28, 2004; March 17, 2006.

Dennis Van Zandt, January 19, 2013.

SECONDARY SOURCE

Don Duncan, "Music Makes His World Go 'Round," *Seattle Times*, February 18,
1969 ("you'd swear must be at least 50").

Resident Conductors: The Vital Links in the Music Community

AUTHOR INTERVIEWS

Robert Anderson, April 19, 1991; October 23, 1991; April 14, 1992; July 20, 2000;
October 23, 2002; September 8, 2007.

George Fiore, October 14, 1999; September 27, 2004; June 17, 2007.

Asher Fisch, July 15, 2004; July 10, 2010; July 25, 2012.

Stewart Kershaw, January 4, 2007.

Stephen Rogers Radcliffe, October 19, 2006.

James Savage, January 10, 2013 ("Peter made my job"; "really sings, just like a
choir").

R. Joseph Scott, September 19, 1991; February 28, 1997.

Adam Stern, January 8, 1990; October 12, 1992; December 14, 1992; September 15,
1993; March 2, 2000; March 15, 2006.

Dean Williamson, November 17, 1998; July 1, 2002; August 22, 2007; January 7,
2008.

Hans Wolf, November 20, 1978; March 9, 1990; November 19, 1991; December 12,
1995; April 18, 1997; October 19, 2000; March 20, 2001; April 10, 2002;
March 21, 2003.

SECONDARY SOURCES

Melinda Bargreen, "For 41-Year-Old Cascade Symphony, It's Time to Play On—
with New Maestro," *Seattle Times*, October 27, 2002 (Robert Anderson, "I
don't know any other orchestra").

Melinda Bargreen, "How Do You Get to 90? Practice, Practice, Practice," *Seattle
Times*, September 18, 2007 (Robert Anderson, "I always told my students").

IMPRESARIOS

Glynn Ross: The Bantam of the Opera

AUTHOR INTERVIEWS

Glynn Ross, June 29, 1978; August 11, 1978; December 30, 1979; November 23, 1980; March 1, 1981; August 2, 1981; December 20, 1981; February 6, 1983; April 17, 1983; August 25, 1983; July 27, 1984; October 13, 1990; October 6, 1997.

LETTERS TO THE AUTHOR

Glynn Ross, July 2, 1996 (calling the Arizona *Ring* "the event of a lifetime. Better than Bayreuth! Honest!").

Hans Lehmann, June 2, 1992 ("As soon as I can find").

SECONDARY SOURCES

Melinda Bargreen, "Glynn Ross, 90, Turned Seattle into Opera Destination," *Seattle Times*, July 21, 2005.

David DiChiera [president of OPERA America], "A Tribute to Glynn Ross," speech presented at Opera America's 14th Annual Conference, December 12, 1983.

Emil Franzi, "Verdi Valley," *Phoenix*, October 1991 ("Ross arrived in Tucson").

John Graham Architectural Firm, "Pacific Northwest Festival in the Forest," flyer (ca. 1975).

James Grant, "Twilight Time," *Opera News*, June 1998.

Sarah Moore Hall, "The Seattle Opera's Glynn Ross May Not Be Rudolf Bing, but His *Ring* Makes the Box Office Zing," *People*, 1979 ("I may pull some cheap tricks").

Helen Jensen, "Great Ages of Music: Unearthing Seattle's Musical Past," memoir (privately published, 2002) (called the merger "great news").

Kenneth LaFave, "Ringing Out a Career," *Arizona Republic*, March 22, 1998.

J. Hans Lehmann and Thelma Lehmann, *Out of the Cultural Dustbin: Sentimental Musings on the Arts and Music in Seattle from 1936 to 1992* (Seattle: Crowley Associates, 1992) ("inadequate scenery and shabby costumes"; "At this juncture").

Glynn Ross, "The Book," unpublished autobiography, 2 vols., courtesy of the Ross family ("Remember, in three thousand years"; "leaned back in his chair"; "I 'took the current when it served'"; "An idea fell into my lap"; "One of his Arizona backers reported driving by a bus transit bench with a big 'Don't Lose Your Seat!—at the Opera!'").

Glynn Ross, farewell speech, annual meeting of the Seattle Opera Association, Rainier Club, June 21, 1983 ("not taken into account").

F. B. St. Clair, "Wizard of the West," *Opera News*, September 1983.

Mahmoud Salem, *Organizational Survival in the Performing Arts: The Making of the Seattle Opera* (New York: Praeger Publishers, 1976) ("that of a charismatic benevolent autocrat").

Winthrop Sargeant, "The Ring's the Thing," profile of Glynn Ross, *New Yorker*, June 26, 1978 ("They called me Maestro"; "a lot of fat people standing around"; "a wonderful time sitting in the audience").

Harold C. Schonberg, "In Seattle, Wagner's *Ring* as He Conceived It," *New York Times*, August 7, 1977 ("Wagner's *Ring* as he conceived it").

Lon Tuck, "Seattle's Ring: The Victory of Regional Opera," *Washington Post*, August 2, 1981.

Bill Zakariasen, "Stagecoach to Valhalla," *Opera News*, June 1996.

Speight Jenkins: The Ring *Master*

AUTHOR INTERVIEWS

Speight Jenkins, March 17, 1983; July 13, 1983; August 21, 1983; April 24, 1988; July 1, 1990; July 1, 1990; July 1, 1990; August 15, 2003; September 11, 2012.

Charles McKay (telephone interview), February 28, 2011 ("Speight may be unique").

Evans Mirageas McKay (telephone interview), February 25, 2011 ("You can't complain").

LETTER TO THE AUTHOR

Lawrence Brownlee, February 15, 2013 ("I look at my career").

OTHER INTERVIEW

Speight Jenkins, conversation with Nina Totenberg at NEA Opera Honors award ceremony, October 27, 2011 ("My job is to welcome singers").

SECONDARY SOURCES

Melinda Bargreen, "Enigma of the Opera," *Seattle Times*, August 21, 1983 ("Either Jenkins will have to learn very fast").

Melinda Bargreen, "Shaping a World of Wagnerian Proportions," *Seattle Times's Pacific Magazine*, September 20, 1998.

Stephanie Blythe, speech, National Endowment for the Arts Opera Honors Awards, November 3, 2011 ("Speight sits in the room with you").

"The 150 most influential people in the 150-year history of Seattle and King County," *Seattle Times*, October 14, 2001.

Marc Shulgold, "Jenkins to Direct the Seattle Opera," *Los Angeles Times*, January 2, 1983 ("Dallas-born opera dilettante").

"Speight Jenkins: 2011 NEA Opera Honoree," National Endowment for the Arts Opera Honors Awards, YouTube video, 7:20, from the ceremony webcast live on November 3, 2011, https://www.youtube.com/watch?v=nTqzPf1IiDE.

"Speight Jenkins's acceptance speech at the National Endowment for the Arts Opera Honors," Washington, DC, November 3, 2011, www.seattleoperablog.com/2011/11/speight-jenkins-acceptance-speech-at.html, accessed April 12, 2013.

"The 25 Most Powerful Names in U.S. Opera," Opera News, www.operanews.

com/operanews/issue/article.aspx?id=1730&issueID=78, accessed March 27, 2015.

Stephen Wadsworth, speech, National Endowment for the Arts Opera Honors Awards, November 3, 2011 ("a cross between the best professor"; "visits his lead singers before").

Toby Saks: The Impresaria

AUTHOR INTERVIEWS

Toby Saks, November 2, 1978; May 20, 1979; January 2, 1988; April 16, 1990; April 2, 1991; May 2, 1993; March 24, 1997; January 6, 1999; July 3, 1999; July 1, 2001; July 2, 2005; July 1, 2006; July 3, 2010; July 1, 2011; October 9, 2012.

SECONDARY SOURCE

Melinda Bargreen, "Acclaimed Musician Toby Saks Dies," *Seattle Times*, August 1, 2013.

Louis Richmond: The Chamber Orchestra Pathfinder

AUTHOR INTERVIEWS

Dorothea (Deede) Cook, October 4, 2012.

Louis Richmond, October 3, 2012.

SECONDARY SOURCES

Melinda Bargreen, "British 'Thinking' Octet Will Open Rendezvous," *Seattle Times*, October 15, 1981.

Melinda Bargreen, "Northwest Chamber Orchestra Bows Out, Bankrupt," *Seattle Times*, March 17, 2006.

Melinda Bargreen, "N.W.C.O. Draws Droves," *Seattle Times*, December 26, 1977.

Melinda Bargreen, "Richmond Will Relinquish Post as N.W.C.O. Conductor," *Seattle Times*, July 10, 1979.

Hugo Kugiya, "A Once-professional Cellist Returns to His Love, and Helps Others along the Way," Crosscut.com, February 25, 2011, http://crosscut .com/2011/02/25/arts/20595/A-onceprofessional-cellist-returns-his-love-helps, accessed April 13, 2013.

"Louis B. Richmond: Senior Advisor," biography, Richmond Public Relations website, www.richmondpublicrelations.com/who_founders.html, accessed April 13, 2013.

VIRTUOSI

Béla Siki: The Elegant Stylist

AUTHOR INTERVIEWS

Béla Siki, January 27, 2012.

Robin McCabe, March 27, 2012 ("We had a hot class full of big talents).

LETTER TO THE AUTHOR
Anton Nel, March 20, 2012 ("My classmates and I were very much in awe").

SECONDARY SOURCES
Melinda Bargreen, "It Was a Special Night for Fans of Béla Siki," *Seattle Times*,
    April 30, 1993.
Frank Dawes, "Béla Síki," in *The New Grove Dictionary of Music and Musicians*,
    ed. Stanley Sadie (London: Macmillan, 1980).
Milton Katims and Virginia P. Katims, *The Pleasure Was Ours: Personal Encoun-
    ters with the Greats, the Near Greats and the Ingrates* (Mill Valley, CA: Vision
    Books International, 2004) ("One reading of any work").
Béla Siki, *Piano Repertoire: A Guide to Interpretation and Performance* (New
    York: Shirmer Books, 1981).

John Cerminaro: The Man with the Golden Horn

AUTHOR INTERVIEW
John Cerminaro, November 9, 2012.

SECONDARY SOURCES
R. M. Campbell, "Symphony Musicians Warned on Improper Behavior," http://
    seattlepi.nwsource.com/classical/288655_ss014.html ("He came here with
    undoubtedly").
Khan Academy (All-Star Orchestra), "French Horn: Interview and Dem-
    onstration with Principal John Cerminaro," www.khanacademy.org/
    partner-content/all-star-orchestra/instruments-of-the-orchestra/brass/v/
    french-horn-interview-demo#!, accessed December 11, 2014.
"Meet John Cerminaro: Principal Horn," *The Score*, http://blog.seattlesymphony.
    org/?p=1562, accessed March 20, 2013.

Randolph Hokanson: The Old Master

AUTHOR INTERVIEWS
Randolph Hokanson, April 23, 1991; February 21, 2004; October 4, 2005;
    March 28, 2012.

SECONDARY SOURCES
Melinda Bargreen, "Piano Man Emeritus Lends Hands for Benefit," *Seattle
    Times*, October 7, 2005.
Randolph Hokanson, *With Head to the Music Bent: A Musician's Story* (privately
    published [Lake Forest Park, WA: Third Place Press], 2011) ("How is the
    musical space"; "I was very much a student"; "What a wonderful break this
    was for me!").

Silvia Kind: The Free Spirit of the Harpsichord

AUTHOR INTERVIEWS
Ueli Dubs, March 27, 2006.
Silvia Kind, April 18, 1978; May 21, 1978; October 10, 1984.
George Shangrow, March 16, 2006.
Eileen Swanson, May 19, 1978.

LETTERS TO THE AUTHOR
Silvia Kind, 1978–2004.

SECONDARY SOURCES
Silvia Kind, "Barocke Cembalo-Musik," *Neue Zeitschrift für Musik*," vol. 128 (1967).
Silvia Kind, *Monologe*, ed. Ueli Dubbs, Internet memoir (in German), www .silviakind.ch/Monologe.htm, accessed April 11, 2013; all English-language translations are mine.
Kent Stevenson, "Silvia Kind, a Rare Treasure," *University of Washington Daily*, April 5, 1974.

Eva Heinitz: The Greatest Gambist

AUTHOR INTERVIEWS
Eva Heinitz, January 5, 1986; December 1, 1991; February 2, 1997.

LETTER TO THE AUTHOR
Catherine Schatzel, January 21, 2015.

SECONDARY SOURCES
Melinda Bargreen, "Music Sustained Heinitz through 90 Years," *Seattle Times*, February 2, 1997 (Otto Klemperer, "the best viola da gamba player he had ever known").
Tim Janof, "Conversation with Eva Heinitz," Internet Cello Society, December 20, 1997, www.cello.org/Newsletter/Articles/heinitz.htm, accessed April 11, 2013.
Pamela Roberts, "Eva Heinitz: Cellist, Gambist and Musician Extraordinaire," http://evaheinitz.blogspot.com, accessed January 7, 2015.

Robin McCabe: The Keyboard Diplomat

AUTHOR INTERVIEWS
Robin McCabe, April 17, 1991; April 16, 1994; February 11, 1995; May 13, 1995; July 1, 1995; March 23, 2002; February 21, 2004; January 22, 2005; May 2, 2006; January 19, 2007; February 26, 2012.

SECONDARY SOURCES
Raymond Ericson, "Music in Review: Piano Skill Shown by Robin McCabe,"

New York Times, April 6, 1975 ("a talented and independent-minded young pianist").

Allen Hughes, "Pianist: Robin McCabe," review of concert at Alice Tully Hall, December 8, 1981, *New York Times*, December 10, 1981.

Nedra Floyd Pautler, "The Real McCabe," *Columns*, June 1995 (Joseph Bloch, "an ideal student").

Helen Drees Ruttencutter, *A Pianist's Progress* (Crowell: New York, 1979).

Ronald Phillips: The Consummate Clarinetist

AUTHOR INTERVIEWS

Ronald Phillips, March 3, 1983 (for the *Seattle Times*) (Gershwin, "boot it out").

Bruce Bailey, February 19, 2013 ("Ron liked to con the orchestra youngsters").

LETTER TO THE AUTHOR

Greg Dziekonski, March 14, 2013 ("He joined the orchestra as second clarinet").

SECONDARY SOURCES

Melinda Bargreen, "Phillips Plays a Beautiful Farewell," *Seattle Times*, March 8, 1983 ("He was a mainstay of the orchestra").

Mary Kantor, "Ronald Phillips: Living Legend," *Clarinet*, September 2003.

J. Hans Lehmann and Thelma Lehmann, *Out of the Cultural Dustbin: Sentimental Musings on the Arts and Music in Seattle from 1936 to 1992* (Seattle: Crowley Associates, 1992).

[title unavailable], *Seattle Star*, November 15, 1941 (Sir Thomas Beecham, "If I were a member of this community").

The author also consulted letters, notes, articles, and other memorabilia in the Ronald Phillips Archive, University of Washington Music Library.

Craig Sheppard: The Classicist of the Ivories

AUTHOR INTERVIEW

Craig Sheppard, August 20, 2012.

SECONDARY SOURCES

Melinda Bargreen, "An Enthralling Musical Journey with Pianist Craig Sheppard at the Wheel," *Seattle Times*, April 25, 2008.

Melinda Bargreen, "Pianist Makes Impressive Debut at UW," *Seattle Times*, February 28, 1994.

Melinda Bargreen, "Tidbits Add Intrigue to Performance," *Seattle Times*, January 20, 1999.

Rob Barnett, "Craig Sheppard Interview," MW—Classical Music Web, August 30, 2002, www.craigsheppard.net/interview.htm, accessed December 1, 2014.

Alan Becker, review of recording by Craig Sheppard of Liszt's *Années de Pèlerinage*, books 1 and 2, *American Record Guide*, July–August 2012 ("He is almost a legend").

[Attribution unavailable], review of concert, July 1986, Queen Elizabeth Hall, London, *Music and Musicians* magazine, 1986 ("Sheer talent does not come much larger").

[Attribution unavailable], review of EMI reissue of Liszt recordings, *Gramophone*, February 1996 ("astounding force and charisma").

For more information on Craig Sheppard, see www.craigsheppard.net.

COMPOSERS

Alan Hovhaness: The Composer of the Mountains

AUTHOR INTERVIEWS

Alan Hovhaness and Hinako Fujihara Hovhaness, December 20, 1977; August 1, 1979; March 1, 1981; June 2, 1981; July 20, 1997.

LETTERS TO THE AUTHOR

Alan Hovhaness and Hinako Fujihara Hovhaness, 1977–2014.

SECONDARY SOURCES

Melinda Bargreen, "Composer Hovhaness Dies at Age 89," *Seattle Times*, June 22, 2000.

Donal Henahan, review of performance of *Revelations of Saint Paul* by Musica Sacra, *New York Times*, January 30, 1981.

Wayne Johnson, "Famous Composer Alan Hovhaness in Town," *Seattle Times*, February 11, 1966.

Theodore W. Libbey, Jr., "Hovhaness at 36: Symphonies, that Is," *Washington Star*, January 19, 1979.

Alan Rich, review of performance of *Revelations of Saint Paul*, by Musica Sacra, *New York Magazine*, February 16, 1981 ("The piece is garbage").

William Bolcom: The Compositional Innovator

AUTHOR INTERVIEWS

William Bolcom, March 6, 1976 (for the *Everett Herald*); May 3, 1994 (for the *Seattle Times*); May 15, 2012.

SECONDARY SOURCES

Anne Feeney, "Artist Biography [William Bolcom]," AllMusic, www.allmusic .com/artist/william-bolcom-mn0000167256/biography, accessed March 29, 2015 ("His solo piano career has produced").

Matthew Gurewitsch, "William Bolcom: A Big Year for a Full-service Composer," *New York Times*, February 24, 2008 ("this popsy little number"; "a compulsively hummable latter-day *Rise and Fall of the City of Mahagonny*).

John Marmor, "From Rags to Riches," *Columns*, June 2003 ("Bernard Holland has called his music 'a wordless rebuttal to ideas of rank and category'").

Kristin Palm, "William Bolcom Biography," MusicianGuide.com, www

.musicianguide.com/biographies/1608004489/William-Bolcom.html, accessed March 29, 2015 ("It was Blake that").

Christopher M. Wright, "The Unrepentant Eclectic," 2005, http://williambolcom .com/index.php?contentID=1038, accessed January 6, 2013.

Samuel Jones: The Harmony Seeker

AUTHOR INTERVIEW
Samuel Jones, July 11, 2012.

SECONDARY SOURCES
Jack Fishman, "Sam Jones Retires," in the blog "David Filner on Classical Music," http://blog.mysanantonio.com/davidfilner/2011/05/sam-jones-retires/, accessed April 13, 2013.

Bernard Jacobson, "Seattle Symphony Brass Concerto Celebrates a Silver Wedding," *Seattle Times*, April 3, 2009 ("It was certainly enormously enjoyable").

"Mississippi Writers and Musicians: Samuel Jones," http://mswritersand musicians.com/musicians/samuel-jones.html, accessed April 13, 2013.

POWER BROKERS AND PATRONS

William and Ruth Gerberding: The Couple Who Made Things Happen

AUTHOR INTERVIEW
William and Ruth Gerberding, March 8, 2012.

SECONDARY SOURCES
Lily Eng and Susan Gilmore, "Gerberding Builds a Reputation as a Survivor," *Seattle Times*, October 3, 1993.

Sally Macdonald, "UW is $ucce$$ful—70,000 Times—Gerberding's Style Helped University Raise $252 Million in Its Endowment Drive," *Seattle Times*, November 24, 1991.

Alex Ross, "A Little Late-Night Music," *New Yorker*, August 29, 2005.

Zachary Woolfe, "A Symphony's Leader Takes Seattle by Storm," *New York Times*, January 28, 2012.

William Bain, Jr.: The Architect of the Boardroom

AUTHOR INTERVIEW
William Bain, March 7, 2012.

SECONDARY SOURCES
Melinda Bargreen, "Symphony Faces Crucial 6 Weeks," and "Symphony Shows Larger Contributions in 1978–79," *Seattle Times*, July 26, 1979.

Kay Calhoun [daughter of the Seattle Symphony's board president Paul Ashley], April 19, 2012.

Marga Rose Hancock, "Bain, William James, Jr. (born 1930), Architect," *HistoryLink* essay 9234, December 30, 2009, www.historylink.org/index .cfm?DisplayPage=output.cfm&file_id=9234, accessed April 14, 2013.

Hans Lehmann: The Renaissance Man

AUTHOR INTERVIEWS
Hans Lehmann, September 6, 1991; December 13, 1992.

LETTER TO THE AUTHOR
Hans Lehmann, August 1985.

SECONDARY SOURCE
J. Hans Lehmann and Thelma Lehmann, *Out of the Cultural Dustbin: Sentimental Musings on Art and Music in Seattle from 1936 to 1992* (Seattle: Crowley Associates, 1992).

Samuel N. Stroum: The Mover and Shaker

AUTHOR INTERVIEWS
Samuel N. Stroum, March 27, 1988; August 12, 1998; January 16, 1990; July 19, 1990; July 7, 1991; May 5, 1993; April 27, 1997; September 7, 2003.

SECONDARY SOURCE
James E. Lalonde, "Seattle's Dean of Philanthropy—Samuel Stroum Bucks Tradition and Puts His Philanthropic Ways on Center Stage," *Seattle Times*, September 30, 1990.

Deborah (Card) Rutter: The Power Behind the Podium

AUTHOR INTERVIEWS
Deborah Rutter, September 9, 1992; April 29, 1997; April 9, 2003; July 26, 2012.

SECONDARY SOURCES
Bob Cook, "Orchestrating Change," *Stanford University Alumni Magazine*, July–August 2005.
"Deborah F. Rutter Named President of the Kennedy Center for the Performing Arts," December 10, 2013, www.kennedycenter.org/about/admin/ PressRelease-Rutter.pdf, accessed March 29, 2014.
Anne Midgette, "New President Deborah Rutter Is Kennedy Center's Breath of Fresh Air from Windy City," *Washington Post*, August 29, 2014.

Sam and Gladys Rubinstein: The Key Advisors

AUTHOR INTERVIEW
Gladys Rubinstein, February 20, 2013.

SECONDARY SOURCES

Melinda Bargreen, "Gladys Rubinstein, Benefactor of Arts, Dies at 92," *Seattle Times*, January 27, 2014, http://seattletimes.com/html/thearts/2022770580_rubinsteinobitxml.html, accessed January 7, 2015.

Melinda Bargreen, "Sam Rubinstein, Savvy Businessman, Gave Back to Seattle, Dies at Age 89," *Seattle Times*, February 2, 2013, http://seattletimes.com/html/localnews/2003552460_rubinsteino2m.html, accessed January 3, 2013 (Irwin Treiger, "Everyone turned to him for advice").

R. M. Campbell, "Sam Rubinstein, 1917–2007: He Shaped and Supported City's Arts," SeattlePI.com, February 1, 2007, www.seattlepi.com/news/article/Sam-Rubinstein-1917-2007-He-shaped-and-1227101.php, accessed January 3, 2013 (Mimi Gates, "a compassionate human being with a wry sense of humor).

Buster and Nancy Alvord: The Practical Donors

AUTHOR INTERVIEWS

Buster and Nancy Alvord, May 14, 1991.
Nancy Alvord, January 17, 2013.

SECONDARY SOURCES

Melinda Bargreen, "The Alvords: Modest, Unassuming, Honored," *Seattle Times*, May 14, 1991 ("quietly working behind the scenes").

Jean Godden, "Was that Black Tie or Bad Tie?" *Seattle Times*, May 5, 2003.

Cassandra Tate, "Alvord, Ellsworth C., Jr. (1923–2010), and Nancy Alvord (b. 1922)," HistoryLink.org Essay 7304, May 17, 2005, www.historylink.org/index.cfm?DisplayPage=output.cfm&file_id=7304, accessed January 8, 2013.

"Three Generations Donate $3 Million to Honor Two UW Physicians" and "UW Recognition Award," *Columns*, June 1999.

Jerry and Lenore Hanauer: The Imaginative Operaphiles

AUTHOR INTERVIEWS

Adrian Hanauer, December 5, 2007.
Lenore Hanauer, December 3, 2012.

SECONDARY SOURCES

MacFadden Communications Group, "Birds of a Feather," history of Pacific Coast Feather, www.thefreelibrary.com/Bird+of+a+different+feather%3A+as+it+celebrates+its+125th+anniversary,...-a0206851816, accessed February 18, 2012.

Seattle Opera, "Seattle Opera Announces Major Gifts Totaling $21.5 Million," press release, July 11, 2007, www.seattleopera.org/_downloads/press/releases/Annual0709.pdf, accessed March 18, 2013.

John and Laurel Nesholm: The Activists for the Arts

AUTHOR INTERVIEW

John and Laurel Nesholm, January 7, 2013.

SECONDARY SOURCE

Seattle Opera, "Seattle Opera Announces Major Gifts Totaling $21.5 Million," press release, July 11, 2007, www.seattleopera.org/_downloads/press/releases/Annual0709.pdf, accessed March 18, 2013.

Charles Simonyi: The Genius Philanthropist

AUTHOR INTERVIEWS

Susan Hutchison, November 5, 2012.

Charles Simonyi, March 20, 2006; January 10, 2013.

OTHER INTERVIEWS

Charles Simonyi, interview with Charlie Rose, May 14, 2012 (www.charlierose.com/view/content/12360); July 9, 2012 (www.charlierose.com/view/clip/12448); both accessed April 11, 2013.

SECONDARY SOURCES

Brier Dudley, "From Hungary to the Galaxy, Simonyi's Goals Always High," *Seattle Times*, October 27, 2006.

Keller Group, "Mission Accomplished: Simonyi Fund Fulfills 10-year, $100M Plan," press release, March 1, 2013.

Jason Pontin, "Awaiting the Day when Everyone Writes Software," *New York Times*, January 28, 2007 ("arguably the most successful programmer in the world").

Jack and Becky Benaroya: The Ultimate Benefactors

AUTHOR INTERVIEWS

Jack and Becky Benaroya, May 5, 1993; June 1994; July 29, 1998; August 31, 1998.

SECONDARY SOURCES

"Jack A. Benaroya: He Redefined Commercial Warehouse Space, Creating the Concept of Industrial Parks and Spreading Benaroya Business Parks across the Region," biography, Puget Sound Business Hall of Fame program, 1995.

"Jack Benaroya," biography, courtesy of the Benaroya Company, July 2011.

Steven Lowe, "Who Is Jack Benaroya?" Seattle Symphony opening gala program, September 1998.

Patti Payne, "A Community Pauses and Pays Tribute," *Puget Sound Business Journal*, May 18–13, 2012.

CONCLUSION

Aaron Copland, "The Pleasures of Music," *Saturday Evening Post*, July 4, 1959 ("To stop the flow of music would be like the stopping of time itself").

INDEX

Ross, Glynn, 7, 115, 130–40
Ross, Melanie, 331
Rostropovich, Mstislav, 53, 54, 205, 235
Royal Concertgebouw Orchestra, 15, 85, 90
Royal Liverpool Philharmonic Orchestra (U.K.), 72, 76
Royal Philharmonic Orchestra (U.K.), 91
Rozgonyi, Agnes, 86
Rubinstein, Arthur, 7, 92, 132, 187, 222–23
Rubinstein, Sam and Gladys, 69, 155, 279, 292–96, 323
Russell, Francia, 241
Russell, Margaret, 109
Russian musicians in Seattle, 17–22
Ruttencutter, Helen Drees, 207

S

Sachs, Curt (musicologist), 195
Saint Paul Chamber Orchestra, 166
Saint Petersburg (formerly Leningrad) Philharmonic, 20, 54
Salem, Mahmoud, 140
Salonen, Esa-Pekka, 29
Sams, Carol, 13, 109
Samuel, Harold, 186, 187
Sanders, Murl Allen, 109
Sands, Linda, 144
San Francisco Symphony, 91
Santa Fe Chamber Music Festival, 154, 155, 162, 327
Sargeant, Winthrop, 133, 138
Savage, Greg, 165
Savage, James (conductor), 105, 121–23
Schatzel, Catherine, 205–6
Schenkman, Byron, 23
Scherchen, Hermann (conductor), 195
Schiff, Andras (pianist), 222
Schnabel, Arthur, 8, 202
Schneider, Alexander ("Sasha"), 34
Schonberg, Harold C. (*New York Times*), 6, 73
Schreker, Franz, 201
Schultz, Cecilia, 134, 277
Schuman, William, 58, 69
Schumann-Heink, Ernestine, 8

Schwarz, Alysandra, 66
Schwarz, Daniel, 66
Schwarz, Gabriella, 64, 292
Schwarz, Gerard, 21, 28, 59, 61–76, 82, 133, 167, 179, 181, 183, 184, 215, 236, 239, 249, 254, 255, 256, 263, 266, 280, 287, 291, 292, 295, 296, 304, 305, 310, 311, 315, 316–17, 318, 319
Schwarz, Jody, 65, 66, 68, 292, 316
Schwarz, (Dr.) John, 66
Schwarz, Julian, 64, 255, 292
Scott, R. Joseph, 22, 119
Scottish National Orchestra, 91
Seattle: expansion of arts facilities and concert halls, 24–25 (*see also* Benaroya Hall; Marion Oliver McCaw Hall; Meany Hall); socioeconomic changes in, 9–13, 17–22
Seattle Arts Commission, 164
Seattle Baroque Orchestra, 23
Seattle Center, 6, 65, 165, 264, 280, 287
Seattle Chamber Music Society (formerly Seattle Chamber Music Festival), 154–60, 262, 264, 280
Seattle Chamber Singers, 101, 109, 110, 111
Seattle Choral Company, 114
Seattle Civic Symphony, 11, 214
Seattle International Chamber Music Festival, 161–62
Seattle Men's Chorus, 114–15
Seattle Opera, 4, 6, 7, 8, 11, 12, 21, 30, 111, 112, 115, 116, 117, 121, 129, 130, 131, 134–40, 141, 144–53, 171, 253, 260, 262, 263, 266, 270, 272, 273, 278, 279, 280, 288, 292, 293, 294, 296, 297, 301, 302–9, 321, 323, 324, 328
Seattle Opera House (later Marion Oliver McCaw Hall), 7, 28, 29, 35, 59, 64, 141, 161, 241, 260, 264, 278, 284, 288
Seattle Pro Musica, 13, 114
Seattle Sounders, 301
Seattle Symphony Orchestra, 4, 6, 7, 8, 10, 11, 14, 16, 18, 19, 20, 21, 27, 28, 29, 30, 32, 34, 35, 38–44, 47–48, 54, 56–59, 64, 69–76, 79, 83–85, 91, 96, 101, 106, 109, 112, 114–17, 119–22,